SLURP SENDS!

On Becoming a Green Beret
Book 1

*Reflections and Experiences of a Vietnam War
Green Beret A-Team Member*

CONTENTS

PREFACE

To begin with, I want to give a big shout-out to Faith Meyer Yeung (daughter of John "Tilt" Meyer of MACV-SOG fame, and a distinguished writer of Vietnam War history) for editing my manuscript, and Jacquie Cook for her wonderful work at preparing my manuscript for publication. In addition, I want to thank all my friends and Facebook friends and followers for their help and encouragement in my endeavor. Also, thanks a ton to my wife, Linda (aka "The War Department"), for putting up with my years of researching and writing my story, as well as the numerous messes I made with research print-outs strewn all over the house. (By the way, she loves that nickname.)

This book began as an effort to put down in print an autobiography for my children and grandchildren to read, so they would have an idea of who their father/grandfather was and did before they were born. As the reader can see, the project took on legs, and expanded greatly in scope. It's still for my children (now expanded to great grandchildren), but has turned into a labor of love, and much research, as well as a book to share with the masses.

I enlisted before Vietnam really got off the ground (Feb 1962), although our first Special Forces Southeast Asia War loss was in 1957. When I enlisted, I didn't know much about Vietnam; at least not since the French had left with their tails between their legs. I went there in February 1966; about the same time SF began its escalation. Before that time, some of my teammates had already been in South Vietnam.

I saw several teammates go over the pond after we returned from Ethiopia, including married teammates from that mission. We had even discussed that possibility while in Ethiopia. I was fortunate enough, for some reason, to have constantly been assigned to some sort of special assignment; keeping me busy and, thankfully, out of the post details that seemed so prevalent in SF at the time. Many men volunteered to go to South Vietnam just to get out of the constant base details.

It wasn't until I heard about Harold Bennett's execution that I decided I needed to go over there. I had seen too many of my friends, married and single, going to Nam, while I was happily busy Stateside. Many of those friends didn't return. There were also times that friends returned after I heard they had been KIA. It was a shock to the system when that happened.

I felt left out of the action, and powerless to help my friends; plus I had a burning desire to get even for my friend's execution. That was when I called Mrs. Alexander and asked to be placed on orders for South Vietnam, ASAP. Given the amount of time that had passed, I think I would have felt empty without having been there had I not gone to Nam when I did.

I was fortunate that my mother told me to write regularly, and not to leave anything out of the letters. That, and the hundreds of photographs I took with my little Kodak Instamatic camera gave me the help I needed to remember almost everything that happened in Ethiopia and South Vietnam.

Much of this publication has been garnered from memory, backed by letters written to my parents. My mother saved almost every letter I wrote home, including all of them from when I was in Special Forces. While I was in Vietnam I also wrote regularly to a good friend, Stewart Stephenson, a medic from the 6th Special Forces Group during my time with the 6th. He saved all my letters, and sent copies of them to me, while I was working on this book. The letters were especially useful given the fact that we were not permitted to keep diaries when on overseas missions. The photos and letters are what drove me to write the book.

Through it all, I have done a wealth of research, in many cases learning things that I had forgotten about, and in other cases, that I had no idea happened, or existed. The research has entailed a lot of reading on my part, as well as searching out official historical documents and military publications.

I attempted to gather information from as many venues as possible, to reduce the chance of the information I have presented being incorrect, or questionable. I have attempted in every way possible, to substantiate what I offer as facts. In many cases you will see descriptions of history and battles, which I was not a part of. I include most of them in order of occurrence, rather than when I first learned about them. In many of those cases, I did not learn the circumstances until I read about them, while researching this book.

Through the last few years of this project I have come up with new ideas for a couple new projects, including a possible history of Special Forces ("Green Berets"). The Special Forces history project will probably forever be a "work in progress," as that history will continue through the future. It will probably be published in volumes, as I complete various eras. It will also, hopefully, be handed off to someone willing to continue the project, as I'm already an old geezer.

I was asked, a couple years ago, to be the historian for two of the camps I was in, Cai Cai and Vinh Gia. That is my next project. The Special Forces Museum also expressed interest in publishing some of the 500+ photographs I took during my time in Special Forces. During the last few years I have shared numerous excerpts online with my many SF Brothers (a "secret" vetted-only group of thousands of former and present Green Berets) and other Facebook "friends." Through those friends I learned even more, and made some edits in my manuscript, to alter information I learned was false, or misleading. The response to my story has been undeniably overwhelming, with people wanting me to get this book in print. So, here it is.

You'll notice I treat what many of you consider to be serious subject matter with humor. In combat situations one must treat many instances with humor. Without humor, a soldier can be driven crazy. In Special Forces, although we were extremely serious men, we laughed a lot. It was a way of coping with the life-threatening events of war. Many considered much of our humor to be "dark" humor, with subjects having no boundaries. Anything went!

I have tried to describe, as best as possible, what it was like being in South Vietnam, and being involved in a firefight, with bullets aimed at me. It's difficult to describe precisely how one feels in those situations. The truth is, you must have been there to really understand the feelings and thoughts involved in the process.

Sometimes, average, ordinary, usually unexceptional men, will rise above the average, and become exceptional men, unselfish heroes, given the right circumstances. I saw that a lot while I was in Vietnam. I truly believe that almost every Special Forces soldier I served with and fought next to was capable, at any time, of becoming a hero. All it took was the right moment and circumstances. That is why there remains such a strong bond within the Special Forces and former Special Forces community. It has been said, and I believe whole heartedly to be true, "once Special Forces, always Special Forces." The training and experiences never go away, becoming a part of our lives and thought processes.

If you ask a person what he did in Vietnam, and he says, "I can't tell you what I did in Vietnam, because it was Top Secret," you can generally interpret that to mean the person was never in combat, and quite possibly not even in Vietnam, or the military service. During the war there were a lot of highly classified jobs and missions, but they have all been declassified. There was, in fact, what many called a "secret war" being conducted during the Vietnam War. The men participating in the secret war were generally men of elite units in Vietnam. All the classified information about that "secret war" has also been declassified.

I agonized for quite a few years, about what to title this book. Finally, a friend on Facebook suggested "Slurp Sends." The long story, made short, is that due to my propensity to eat very quickly at my first camp in Vietnam, I was nicknamed "Slurp." I describe it in the chapter titled "Cai Cai." The nickname stuck, following me throughout my experiences in Vietnam. I became so well known as "Slurp," that I proceeded to sign off radio communications messages with "Slurp Sends!" That also has become my Facebook persona, ending all my posts with, "SLURP SENDS!"

De Oppresso Liber

SLURP SENDS!

SLURP SENDS!

On Becoming a Green Beret
Book 1

Dick James

CHAPTER 1

BEFORE THE ARMY

Much of this publication has been garnered from memory, backed by letters written to my parents. While I was in Vietnam I also wrote regularly to a good friend, Stewart Stephenson, a medic from the 6th Special Forces Group during my time with the 6th. He saved all my letters, and sent copies of them to me while I was working on this book. The letters were especially useful given the fact that we were not permitted to keep diaries when on overseas missions.

New York & Pennsylvania

I was born in Flushing, on Long Island, in Queens County, New York on 7 October 1942, ten months after the Japanese attack on Pearl Harbor. I was apparently conceived on 31 December 1941, New Year's Eve. I must assume that the dirty deed was done after a celebration of the end of a sad year for America and the beginning of a new year, and hopefully, better times ahead. I never questioned my parents about it, but using my ever-present thought processes, I'm wondering if perhaps my father was told he was going to be sent overseas, and mom and dad decided to have a child before it was too late.

Since I have no brothers or sisters, I figure they either decided they had come up with the perfect human child, and needed no more; or, they decided I was such a problem child that they didn't want to take a chance on another one. It's too late to ask them now, and I haven't found any information to substantiate either hypothesis, so I will have to live with the question being unanswerable. Of course, my assumption is that I was (and am) the perfect child/human being, although most of my friends would probably disagree.

Having only lived in Flushing for the first year of my life, I don't really feel I can claim it as a home that had anything to do with the shaping of my life, or a home that I can even remember. I only know that we lived in a large apartment complex. Somewhat like living life as a military brat, constantly moving from place to place, I became an airline brat.

Mom worked after graduating from high school, but once I was born, she remained a stay-at-home wife and mom for the remainder of her life. Maybe that's proof that I was, in fact, a problem monster child. In the month of my first birthday, my dad was sent overseas to Belem, Brazil (and later Africa) to work on seaplane bases for his employer, American Export Airlines (AEA). He was on loan to the U.S. Navy Reserves. Mom and I moved into my grandmother's rooming house in downtown Bedford, Pennsylvania.

To date myself, when using the phone in Bedford, we simply lifted the receiver off the hook, depressed and released the hook several times, quickly, to get a live operator on the line, then gave the four-digit phone number or the name of the person we wanted to call to the operator, or asked for the long distance operator for long distance calls. There were, of course, no cell phones. There weren't even answering machines (unbelievable). The phone was either answered, gave a busy signal (yeah, no call waiting either), or rang, and rang, and rang....

One of the things I enjoyed about that era was that almost all breakfast cereal boxes had a toy of some kind in it to lure the children. The breakfast cereal I ate depended upon which toy I wanted at the time, not which tasted the best, or even was best for me.

The first time I was in any way introduced to warfare was early in

14

my life, at grandma's rooming house during World War II. The house was located on Pitt Street (the Lincoln Highway) in town. The Lincoln Highway was, at that time, a major cross-country highway that was a very busy thoroughfare. The Lincoln Highway, at that time, ran from the east coast to the west coast. I spent a lot of time sitting in grandma's sunroom porch, facing the street, watching, with much interest, as the many civilian trucks and long military convoys passed through town.

Ireland

In October of 1946 we moved to Limerick, Ireland. Dad worked for America Overseas Airlines (AOA, name changed from AEA in 1945), and had been transferred to their facility at Shannon Airport, in Ireland.

Because we were dependents of an employee, we rode on airline passes, which meant we didn't have to purchase a ticket. The only headache was the fact that we could only ride "space available." That meant that we could only get seats if seats were available at the time of the flight. There were occasions during which we basically lived in the airport, sleeping on airport benches, awaiting a flight that had at least two seats available.

We were the last to board, having to wait until the last minute to make sure nobody purchased a ticket at the last minute. When we were finally cleared to board, we walked out the terminal exit door, onto the tarmac, then to the rollaway stairway that was used in those days for passengers to load onto aircraft. We boarded an American Overseas Airlines DC-4. It was a four-engine propeller-driven aircraft, with a cruise speed of about 227 mph, and a range of 4,250 miles.

The pilot started the aircraft's four engines one at a time. As each engine roared to life, the pilot would trigger the next engine's starter, bringing another engine roaring to life. The engines shook, and shuddered, as they came to life. It took a while, but he finally got them running smoothly, and warmed up. The pilot then taxied us out to the active taxiway, for takeoff. We twisted and turned going around some other planes, and across runways. We kept going further away from the airport terminal, and closer to the water. When it looked like we had finally reached about the limits of the airport, we pulled into a hardstand.

There, the pilot seemed to put the aircraft to the test. All four engines roared to life, screaming, and blowing dirt all over the place. Finally, seemingly happy with the functioning if the engines and safety of the aircraft, the engines were slowed down to a dull roar, and I could almost hear again.

The pilot taxied out onto the centerline of the runway. He pulled forward, to line up perfectly with the centerline, and slowly added full power. We slowly began to accelerate down the runway, clumsily picking up speed, as we bounced down the strip. It seemed like forever, but partway down the landing strip, the nose of the lumbering giant began lifting off the runway, and we slowly left the runway, climbing ever so slowly.

After takeoff, we headed northeast towards Gander, Newfoundland, for our first refueling stop. After close to a four-hour flight, we began a slow descent into Gander. After landing, we taxied to the airport terminal. There, all the passengers exited the aircraft, and entered the terminal, while the aircraft was refueled.

Newfoundland was, and is, weird when it comes to worldwide time zones. Unlike the remainder of the world, it had its own little time zone that was half an hour different than the time zones to its west and east, and always working on the half hour as the remainder of the world worked on the hour.

Because we had a long flight ahead of us, the plane had to be totally filled with fuel, so we had an hour wait until the aircraft was ready to go again. We re-boarded after the refueling. The next leg of the trip was going to be a real doozy.

It was dark as we departed Gander. After takeoff, we headed east for our final leg of the journey to Ireland. Almost all the remainder of the trip was during darkness. There was nothing to see, but the black of night, out the aircraft windows. I was tired, bored, and airsick.

Just as it was turning daylight outside, we began a slow descent, still over water. We had lost three and a half hours due to time zone changes and had been in the air for about nine hours since Gander. Finally, we arrived over land, and not long afterwards landed at the

Shannon Airport in Ireland. My first flight on an aircraft lasted about thirteen hours, an experience I did not enjoy. I was tired, and still sick to my stomach.

Dad was waiting for us at the airport. After retrieving our luggage, we loaded into his newly purchased enclosed Jeep. Our destination wasn't far away. He had rented a room in a rooming house for us in Limerick. We lived there the entire 20 months we were in Ireland.

I don't remember much about our time in Ireland. One thing that sticks in my mind about Ireland was the lush green countryside and the rain (rain, rain, and more rain). It was no wonder everything was a lush green. My mother related to me a funny story about Ireland that involved me shortly after arriving there. We had just walked out the door for a walk in the neighborhood, when I asked her if they had painted the sidewalk. She laughed, telling me the pavement looked different because it was dry rather than the normal wet.

During the summer of 1947 we all took a vacation. We flew back to the U.S. to visit with both grandmas and Grandpa James (Grandpa Blymyer, mom's dad, had passed away) in Bedford PA. It was another l-o-o-o-n-g round trip, on American Overseas Airlines Douglas DC-4s, riding standby on airline passes. I became sick to my stomach on both flights, spending way too much time in the toilet.

In September of 1947, I began school at Leprechaun School (honest, that was the name) in Limerick, Ireland. I went to first grade there. We wore little brown caps with yellow stripes and a leprechaun quilted above the short front visor (I still have it). In addition to other things, I learned a little bit of Gaelic (Ireland's historical language) there.

It took a while for dad to get used to driving on the left side of the road, but he managed to not get in any accidents (that I know of). Mom and dad loved traveling throughout Ireland, taking in the beautiful sights and numerous castles. I was taken along, but I was too young to really understand the significance and history of what I was seeing.

Sweden

In June of 1948, we moved to Stockholm. While living in Sweden, we

17

flew round trip across the Atlantic Ocean at least yearly to visit mom and dad's parents in Bedford. We still flew using airline passes. Many were the times we spent hours, and sometimes days, in the airports waiting for an available seat, sleeping on benches and airport floors.

The flights were always lengthy affairs, flying on propeller driven Douglas DC-4s, Lockheed L049 Constellations, or Boeing "Stratocruiser" (double-decker) aircraft. The route included fueling stops (and sometimes lengthy layovers due to bad weather in Reykjavik, Iceland and Gander Field, Newfoundland.) Reykjavik and Newfoundland were some especially bad locations. My early years of riding in airplanes should have soured me against all flying. I doubt that there was a single trans-Atlantic trip on which I didn't throw up.

One trip across the Atlantic was particularly lousy. We were heading to Reykjavik, Iceland. We had been in the air for close to nine hours, the last part of it in stormy conditions. The stormy conditions bounced the aircraft around, quite a bit, causing me to be scared, and my stomach to become upset.

The sky was lit by lightning exploding everywhere. I truly believed that the aircraft skin was way too thin for safety. I kept expecting to see a lightning bolt pierce right through it. Our entire approach to Reykjavik, and the landing, was during a driving rainstorm. I was very happy when we finally came to a stop and were able to unload. Hard ground had never felt so wonderful.

Because the storm was predicted to last through the night, we were transported in a crew van to a Quonset hut on the airport, while the paying customers were transported to a hotel in town, to remain overnight, and return the following morning for the flight continuation. We "slept" on cots. It was a very fitful sleep, what with the rain pounding down on the metal Quonset hut.

If you have not endured a raging thunderstorm in a Quonset hut, you have not endured the worst noises a thunderstorm can throw at you. It is mean. It can scare the living crap out if a youngster. By morning, the storm had subsided, and we once again loaded onto our aircraft, for our final leg to Stockholm.

The first place we lived in was a large apartment building in the

Stockholm suburb of Gardemoen. We only lived there for three months. During the 2½ years we were in Sweden, we lived in four different homes and I went to three different schools for kindergarten through 2nd grade. The longest we lived in any one place in the Stockholm suburbs was one year in Bromma. It was there that I made friends with a Swedish boy, with whom I remained a pen pal for several years after returning to the United States. When we lived in our first home, the apartment building, mom often took me to a nearby fairly large, shallow lake. I had a sailboat that I loved to play with in that lake.

"Most sorts of diversion in men, children and other animals, are in imitation of fighting." — *Jonathan Swift*

One Christmas I received a present that I had especially wished for: It was a very large toy castle with knights and other figures to go with it. I was overjoyed when I saw it under the tree. Sweden was also where I took my first photograph. I borrowed mom and dad's Kodak Brownie camera and photographed (in black and white) an advertising flier on a power pole just down the street from our house.

The castle and knights began my fascination for warfare, which later included lots of toy soldiers and model ships and airplanes, with the war arena being the backyard in Castro Valley, CA. My favorite reading material was always books describing warfare, mostly dealing with the individual fighter pilots, soldiers and small, specialized military units.

On 31 January 1950 U.S. President Harry Truman announced that he had ordered the development of the hydrogen bomb. It most likely did not make the news in Sweden but would affect my future life in the United States, in a very direct way. For some, in the United States especially, it would make for a different mental and sometimes physical lifestyle, causing fear in the minds of most.

One of my proudest moments was on 9 November 1950: being part of the enormous crowd that lined a wide boulevard for the burial procession of the recently deceased King Gustav V of Sweden, who had passed away on 29 October at the ripe old age of 92. He had no real political power, having voluntarily ceded his power decades prior.

A school holiday had been declared for his funeral procession, and mom and I had managed to get a place to stand in the front row along the route. I was extremely proud because, at the young age of 8, I felt like this made me close to Swedish royalty. I felt more Swedish than American at the time. I say that not because I wasn't proud to be American, but because I was proud to feel such a connection to the country in which I was residing at the time.

Snow fell steadily as we watched the procession within yelling distance of such European royalty as the new King Gustav VI, as well as King Haakon of Norway, King Frederick of Denmark, and numerous other luminaries. I was taking part in world history. Little did I know at that time that later I would shake the hand of a country's ruler, twice, and march in front of a newly empowered president of the United States.

Because I was enrolled in Swedish schools, all my instruction was in the Swedish language. Thankfully, children pick up languages quickly, especially if they have no other children to play with who speak their native language. I picked up Swedish very quickly (including the dialect); so well that the Swedes thought my parents had come to Sweden and adopted me. Lending to that false impression was the fact that I had blondish hair and blue eyes, like so many Swedes. When my parents went shopping, they always took me along to interpret for them. The only time my parents didn't take me along was when they went on vacations throughout Europe. I was always left at home with our Norwegian maid.

It always interested me that our maid was in Sweden. She mentioned many times how much she and many other Norwegians disliked Swedes. The reason for this almost hatred of Swedes was the fact that Sweden remained firmly neutral throughout World War II. That neutrality was used by the German Navy to harbor its warships in Swedish ports and waters. The Nazis used Swedish waters as an away-from-home base for its many naval attacks on Norwegian soil. The Norwegians fought hard against the Germans but were usually outnumbered.

I learned quickly during Swedish winters that I was never going to amount to anything on skis. I constantly tried skiing down the street in front of our house, only to end up face down in the snow. It was a lost cause! It still is! Put me on a pair of skis and within seconds an indentation the size of my body will appear in the snow.

Pan American Airways (PAA) acquired AOA on 25 September 1950, which led to dad having to find a new job, and us returning to the U.S. in January 1951.

Pennsylvania & California

Dad didn't have any job leads yet, so we once again moved into grandma Blymyer's rooming house in Bedford, PA. I was placed in the second grade but was immediately accelerated to the third grade because my education was so far advanced for my class.

Things were so different than in the European schools I had been attending. Football to me was soccer. I understood nothing about American football. The same was true with baseball and basketball. In addition, I understood absolutely no American slang words. I made very few friends in Bedford. Most of the other students saw me as a foreigner, despite the fact I spoke perfect English and had been born in New York.

I enjoyed walking down to the river (about a hundred yards behind the house) and watching all the Pennsylvania Railroad steam locomotives pulling heavy freights through town on the other side of the river. I loved the sights and sounds of those old steam trains.

Behind the rooming house was a large intercontinental trucking company, with a maintenance garage and many tractor-trailers. Grandma owned the property, leasing it to the trucking company. Semi-trucks were constantly coming and going. I was occasionally permitted to sit in a truck cab in the lot, which was a special treat.

Mom and grandma worried about me a lot, what with a large tree I loved to climb in the back yard, the trucks coming and going behind the house, the fact that the street we lived on (Pitt Street) was the "Lincoln Highway" (a very busy federal highway that went all the way to San Francisco, on the Pacific Coast), and the river only a block away behind the house.

One time I came very close to a bad occurrence. A friend of mine and I loved to play at the river. We decided to build a secret wharf and raft. We got on the raft and began propelling it with a long pole (a la Huckleberry Finn). Our trouble came when we got too far out in the river for the pole to reach bottom. Suddenly we were at the mercy of the river's current, and it was moving swiftly.

Thankfully we had built our raft sturdily. The river became wider and shallower a bit downstream, allowing us to pole over to the riverbank. We never did that again! One of my other favorite things was to go to nearby Bedford Springs and fish, although I NEVER caught a single fish.

In June 1951, dad got a new job. He was hired as a dispatcher for California Eastern Airways, a charter airline out of Oakland, CA. As dispatcher, he was responsible for the operational safety of all of CEA's aircraft. That entailed determining air routes to be taken, as well as where and when the aircraft were to be fueled. It was then up to dad to brief the air crew as to what to expect along the route in the way of weather conditions.

We moved west, to Castro Valley, CA, driving the entire distance from Bedford to the San Francisco Bay Area. During that trip I must have driven my parents wacky. It was a very long trip. No Interstate highways, or even freeways existed at the time. We also didn't take a direct route. We were sightseeing while moving.

We went as far north as Pierre, South Dakota, then continued west to Yellowstone National Park, where we spent a few days. Every time I saw a tourist trap shop I yelled out to stop. To keep me happy on the trip, mom and dad probably stopped at every tourist trap I spotted on the highway, especially if it was in the shape of a teepee, and there were quite a few.

When we went through Nevada it was hot. Back in that day there were no air conditioners. Inside the car, it was not very comfortable while going through the desert, as well as being a very boring scenic segment. The car was "cooled" by a fan contraption, known as a "car cooler" (aka swamp cooler) that attached to the front passenger window. It was a cylindrical tube that looked like a canister-style vacuum cleaner, and "cooled" water that was in the fan, utilizing water evaporation. Ours was a ram-air powered unit that only cooled when the vehicle was in motion. The lower the humidity, the better the cooling by evaporation worked. By the time we reached California on U.S. Route 50, I think I had decals for every town and state we went through.

Because our house wasn't completed when we arrived, we had to live for a few months in the Mission Bell Motel on East 14th Street in East Oakland. That was extremely boring. Thankfully it was only for a short while. Before I began school, in September, we moved into our new home. A school had just begun to be built, for our neighborhood. In the meantime, I had to walk a mile to, and a mile from, school each day.

Life in the Castro Valley area was nothing like I had ever imagined. There seemed to be a constant fear of possible nuclear attack from the Soviet Union. We were constantly shown short movie clips about the danger of, and the suggested means of avoiding the dangers of, a nuclear attack.

We were walked through the "duck-and-cover" exercise on a regular basis. When the warning horn sounded, we immediately jumped underneath our school desks, and covered ourselves with our arms. We knew not to take the warnings lightly, because there were so many important military bases in the San Francisco Bay Area. We also knew that there were Nike defensive missile bases right in our own town of Castro Valley.

Dad didn't work at California Eastern for a very long time, as the company went out of business. Thankfully, he was quickly able to find a job, first selling Electrolux vacuum cleaners, door-to-door, then selling General tires.

I began working early in my life, not taking much time away from work from then on. The month I turned twelve years old, while still in 6th grade, I got a full time job as a newspaper boy for the Oakland Tribune. It meant running my own business, and having to do it to everyone's, including my own customers', satisfaction.

My paper route was the furthest out of all the routes in Castro Valley, in the northern hills of town. I got to do a lot of bike pedaling with a heavily laden bicycle that had three gears. I attained advancing carrier recognition levels within the newspaper very quickly, mostly due to my salesmanship and work ethic.

A lot of new homes were being built in the East Bay during that time, especially in Castro Valley, Hayward, San Leandro and San Lorenzo. Housing developments were sprouting up almost anywhere there was a large enough vacant area. On weekends that dad had off, he would drive me to those new developments, drop me off, and I would spend hours going door-to-door, signing up new Oakland Tribune customers, right and left.

Dad, in the meantime, would drive off to shopping center parking lots, checking the tires on every car and writing down the license numbers of the cars that had badly worn tires, then pick me up later in the day at a designated place and time. In that era, dad was able to obtain the mailing addresses of the license plates he had noted. We would spend evenings addressing postcards to those people with the worn tires, so dad could mail them the following day.

I continually won free trips (Livermore Rodeo, Salinas Rodeo, California State Fair, Santa Cruz Beach Boardwalk, etc.) due to new subscription contests the paper would run regularly. It was very rare that I wouldn't qualify. I kept moving up the ladder as a carrier, winning higher and higher awards.

I was constantly invited (with my dad and Tribune Area Manager, Mr. Agee, as escorts) to award dinners in Oakland. Mr. Agee was very happy with my output. It made him look good also. I have quite a few certificates from the newspaper. At my parents' insistence, most of what I made went toward my future college education.

As soon as I got out of school on weekdays, I rode my 3-speed bicycle about a mile from school to downtown Castro Valley, on Castro Valley Boulevard. There, I would roll and wrap each of my sixty-some newspapers with a rubber band and place them in my newspaper saddlebag. Twice a week, I also had to stuff the inserts in the newspapers before rolling and wrapping them. That was usually twice a week, Sundays and Thursdays. Upon completion of that I would begin my two-mile uphill pedaling climb to the beginning of my route. I did that seven days a week.

As a newspaper boy, I was a very hard worker. I had about sixty customers on my route, which was far-flung in a farming area. It was a daily newspaper, so I worked seven days a week. The homes were not close to together, so the route was very spread out. I guaranteed that every daily newspaper was porched. If it was raining, I also made sure the newspaper was safely wrapped and covered, to keep it dry. That included placing the porch mat over the newspaper, to protect it.

I never ever got a complaint from my route. This was no easy task to accomplish, as much of my route was comprised of individual farms. It meant I rode my bicycle all the way to each house, even if it was in the "back forty." It made for a lengthier route, but also guaranteed each of my customers receiving the very best possible service.

I didn't spend much of my own money. I would occasionally spend 25¢ to watch the Saturday serial movie at the local theater (Chabot Theater) in downtown Castro Valley. I usually watched Flash Gordon or Red Ryder. I also played an occasional game of miniature golf at the course next to where I picked up the newspapers downtown. The only time I did that was when the newspapers had not been delivered to our pickup point on time.

Upon finishing my route, I would almost always stop on the way home, at the Seven Hills Market, pick a dill pickle out of the pickle barrel for 10¢, and play a couple rounds of baseball on the store pinball machine at 5¢ a game, while munching on my pickle. To round out "all my free time" I was also a Cub Scout and later, Boy Scout, and Explorer Scout.

Attempting to earn a swimming merit badge, my mother took me to the Hayward Plunge (a LARGE indoor swimming pool) weekly, for swimming lessons. What a lost cause. I never came even close to the requirements.

I participated in several Boy Scout week-long campouts, and once participated in a jamboree at what was then Parks Air Force Base near Livermore, CA. The scoutmaster couldn't find any jamboree activity I was competitive at, so he entered me in the fly-casting competition. I was NEVER an ardent fisherman (nor would I ever become one), and I only had a day to practice, but I WON the event. Total shock to me and my Scoutmaster!

Because of our constant moving and lack of long-time friends caused by it, I became a master at entertaining myself. I played a lot of games, including ones I would invent, that required only one player. These were usually sports games, where I would play one team against another, keeping statistics and records. I became quite good at mathematics because of that.

I managed to prove my accident-prone nature in Castro Valley. I seemed to be an accident waiting to happen. There was a large field behind our house that was perfect for sports games and playing war, or cowboys and Indians (which I played a lot).

One time I decided we needed a backstop for our small game of baseball. There was a wooden construction truck ramp, made of extremely heavy timbers, in the field. It was the type that heavy equipment operators used to drive bulldozers onto flatbeds. At my urging we managed (barely) to drag it to our makeshift ball field, where we manhandled it to an upright position and steadied it with a couple pieces of wood. You might know, the person it decided to fall onto was me. After a visit to the doctor's office, I came home with a cast on my leg.

Another time I was shooting target practice with my archery set. One of my arrows broke in half. I proceeded to fix it by wrapping it tightly with a rubber band. Knowing it would not fly straight and true and was therefore worthless for target shooting, I decided to see how far I could shoot it. I drew the bow back the maximum distance and let fly. The arrow didn't go very far. In fact, it seemed to shake and flounder in the air, which had me perplexed.

As my friend and I were walking back home he told me to look at my left hand. Imagine my shock to notice a lot of blood and about 6 inches of wooden shaft stuck through my index finger knuckle. I hadn't even felt it. When I got home my mother was in a panic. To the ER we went, post haste. Let me tell you: getting the 6"-long, large splinter out of a knuckle (with it sticking out both ends) is much more painful than putting it in the knuckle was. The doctor didn't use any painkiller, and was manhandling that sucker, trying to get it out. My mother was almost in shock, and I was in a ton of pain.

Another ER visit came when I was delivering newspapers. One of the houses on my route had a German shepherd dog. He constantly barked at me but was always in the garage. This one time the garage door was open, but I did notice the dog was attached to a rope. I rode my bike partway up the driveway and cocked my arm to throw the newspaper onto the porch.

The rope the dog was attached to was MUCH longer than I thought. He tore at me, jumping towards my throat as I threw the paper. I reacted by throwing my left arm up in front of my throat. The dog bit down and immediately had much of my forearm in his mouth. He wouldn't let go. I was finally able to get to the end of the rope, at which time I tore my arm out of his mouth, leaving much of it still in his mouth, a bloody mess.

I don't know how many stitches were required to put the arm back together, but it was a lot. I still have about a 6" scar across my arm from it. The doctor in the ER said that if the bite had been just a fraction of an inch deeper, I would have lost the use of my arm. I learned later that the dog had been a military attack dog, trained to go for the throat if attacked. He apparently considered my arm being in a throwing position to be a threatening attack. What bothered me most about the occurrence was the fact that the dog owners were forced to have the dog put down.

I learned first-hand about ambulance-chasing lawyers from that incident. The lawyers came out of the woodwork trying to get my parents to sue. They wouldn't hear of it! Nobody in our family has ever attempted to make our lives richer at the expense of others. It was a stance that would stick in my mind throughout my life, and I'm proud of it.

I was constantly afflicted with head colds that would quickly spread to ear infections. My parents had their medical benefits through Kaiser Foundation Hospital, an HMO. Kaiser decided to test me for allergies. Twice a week I had to go to the Oakland Kaiser to get stuck with a needle about 24 times each visit. The nurse would draw special liquids from different vials with a syringe, and then inject each one into a marked area of my forearm.

After about 12 injections per arm, I sat and waited for a specified time, I think about thirty minutes. At the end of that time, they checked my arms. Those injection locations that turned red and were slightly swollen were noted and written down. Each one represented an allergy. We went twice a week for a month or so. Boy did my arms light up. I had a lot of allergies, including all animal hairs (we had two cats who I loved, and every once in a while new kittens from mama), feathers (I slept on a feather pillow), chocolate (need I say, I loved chocolate), house dust (next to impossible to keep up with, but mom tried her best), etc., etc.

Like I mentioned earlier, I loved to play cowboys and Indians with my neighbor friends (all three or four of us). I also enjoyed playing war. There were no sophisticated looking pistols or rifles in that era. I did have a cap pistol but used a bat as a rifle. Our location was perfect for it. Nearby were fields and small stands of eucalyptus trees, which were perfect for hiding behind.

When I couldn't find enough friends to play cowboys and Indians or war, I played by myself, in our back yard, entertaining myself. I enjoyed putting together plastic models, especially of ships. I also had lots of small plastic soldiers. The back lawn was the ocean, upon which the ships would travel. The flower gardens surrounding the lawn were the jungle islands, where the ships would offload attacking soldiers.

The best times were when I could obtain firecrackers. I should have known then that I loved explosives so much I would eventually become an explosives expert. On occasion I was able to obtain firecrackers, I put them to good use, blowing up my plastic ships. I was in seventh heaven watching one of my ships being blasted apart.

Because of the time spent working my paper route, I couldn't participate in many sporting activities. I did, however, participate in the local area summer baseball league, similar to Little League. I have never been able to figure out how, but one year I was selected for the All-Star team. I was proud but had no idea how I made it. Maybe they felt sorry for me, or maybe everyone who played my position (which, I think, was right field) was worse than me that year.

Because of my short and skinny stature, I was picked on quite a bit while attending junior high school. That probably contributed to the fact that I was an extremely shy individual at that time. One of my homeroom teachers even picked on me a lot. My parents chewed her out on a few occasions. I despised that teacher, the only one I have ever hated. My grades suffered that year because of it.

High School

In 1956 I began high school at the newly opened Castro Valley High School. I continued working my paper route during my high school years at Castro Valley. Nothing significant happened to me during my 1½ years at Castro Valley H.S., except almost totaling the school's Driver's Education car during driver's training in my sophomore year. I was being taught parallel parking, with two other students in the back seat and the instructor in the right seat, when I accidentally mistook the accelerator pedal for the brake pedal. We proceeded over the shallow planted embankment, out of control. Our driving instructor was not a happy camper. The school gardener probably wasn't either.

When we had wrestling in physical education, I was the continual loser. Unknown to me at the time, the year 1957 would have quite an impact on my future life. It was during that year that U.S. Army Special Forces began its involvement in South Vietnam, sending a team from the 1st Special Forces Group (Airborne) on Okinawa. The team was sent there to begin training Army of the Republic of Vietnam soldiers at the Commando Training Center in Nha Trang. Those trainees later formed the nucleus of the Vietnamese Special Forces.

In January of 1958 dad was hired by Southwest Airways (the old one, not the present Southwest), promoted to station manager for the airline and transferred to Monterey Peninsula Airport, in Monterey County, CA. Southwest became Pacific Air Lines on 6 March of that same year. Dad found a rental house in Carmel-by-the-Sea, and we moved in. We lived there during our entire stay in Carmel.

I immediately began attending school at Carmel High School midway through my sophomore year, again knowing absolutely nobody. I was treated as an outsider. I managed to make a few friends, one of which was a former German citizen whose father was the head chef of the posh Carmel Highlands Hotel Restaurant. Another friend was an exchange student from Kuwait (of Russian parents). My third friend was an actual American, in fact a native Carmelite.

On 31 January 1958 the U.S. successfully launched Explorer I, its first satellite, into orbit, thus officially entering the Space Age. It also marked the beginning of a further fear of possible nuclear war from the skies and spying from outer space. The American-Russian space race was in full gear.

With the fact that dad's career field was in aviation, I quickly became interested in becoming a military fighter pilot and eventually landing a job as an airline pilot. But that didn't stop me from also being interested in ground warfare.

Although not really associated with warfare, two of my high school friends (Gerhard—German, and Boris—Russian) and I spent a lot of time after school planning a road trip south through Central America to South America. Most of the planning included weapons we would carry (for protection) and rations and other supplies we would pack along. It was a very ambitious undertaking that never ever came anywhere close to fruition.

If you didn't have a sense of humor when moving to Carmel-by-the-Sea, you probably got one during your life there. Carmel was not your everyday typical American town. It was (and still is) a resort town (with TONS of tourists running around, especially in the summer), with a large artist community.

During my U.S. Government course, we were required to attend Carmel-by-the-Sea city council meetings. These meetings were very entertaining at times, comparing favorably to comedy club shows. What made Carmel city council meetings even funnier was the fact that the participants were trying their best to be serious.

During one meeting the subject of overcrowding due to tourism was discussed. People came up with ways to alleviate the problem. One suggestion was to build a wall around the town and charge admission to all non-citizens of Carmel. It was then brought up that Del Monte Properties (aka Pebble Beach and 17-Mile Drive) did that, and it didn't help. Scratch that idea!

Then it was suggested that parking meters be placed downtown, but because they would look ugly, it was determined that it would be a bad idea. One enterprising soul (an artist, no doubt) suggested that the base of the parking meter could be a fake tree stump, with a fake squirrel sitting on the fake stump. The person parking could put their money into the squirrel's mouth. Because of the absurdity of the cost of such an undertaking, the idea was scrapped. There are still no parking meters in Carmel, and the parking situation is even worse to this day.

I took two years of German while at Carmel High. We had an American teacher. One of my fellow students was my German friend, Gerhard. I have no idea why he was taking the course, other than maybe thinking it would be a cinch A grade. Well, that was hardly the case. There are many different dialects of German, and Gerhard spoke a dialect other than what Mrs. Hill was teaching. He was constantly trying to correct her, which infuriated her. He was lucky to even get a passing grade.

In English class, I had a teacher named Mrs. Bell. She was a jewel. A great teacher. However, she would embarrass me to almost tears when she'd call on me to recite anything. That's how bad my shyness was.

In my senior year, I took a history course. My teacher was Mr. Stumbo. Poor guy. A couple of us constantly referred to him as Mr. "Dumbo." He caught me doing that a couple times and sent me to the principal's office. The only times I ever got into trouble in high school. One thing I despised about history was having to learn specific dates. That part of the curriculum always seemed like a waste of time.

One of the students at the high school had a World War II halftrack, with rubber tank treads and the roller in front that was used during the war to knock things down. He made side money by downing trees with his halftrack. Talk about creativity.

Some other students (especially those from Pebble Beach) owned not one, but two cars (the students, not their parents). I couldn't even get permission from my father to drive his car, much less have one of my own. When I graduated from Carmel High School my graduation present was being able to drive my parents' car once in a great while.

During my junior year at Carmel High School I tried out for

offensive end on the junior varsity football team. At the time I was one of the shyest, shortest and skinniest kids in the senior class. I quit after just a couple weeks. I couldn't take it! My father had purchased football shoes for me and told me he would never again purchase any sports equipment for me. That really hurt! In fact, it impacted my life forever. Since that day I have searched for things to challenge me, making a point to succeed in each challenge, to prove to my dad (who has since passed away) and myself, that I can take it, and I'm not a quitter (any more).

Later in my junior year I played catcher (second string) on the Carmel junior varsity team and did well at the position, although I was the world's worst hitter. I think my batting average was .000. I don't recall getting so much as one hit during the season (in fact, I was usually happy just to make contact with the ball).

I was an especially bad batter when facing a curve-ball pitcher. To this day I can vividly remember an opposing pitcher who had a real roundhouse curve. He would pitch the ball, it would initially come toward my body, I would hit the dirt, and I would hear (very loudly) STEE-RIKE! That happened numerous times during the game, resulting in me walking or striking out every time I faced him. I got very dirty and spent a lot of time brushing dirt off my uniform. In my senior year I tried out for the varsity team but was cut (at least I didn't quit).

I wanted something to do, so I decided to try out for the track team (my German friend, Gerhard, ran the mile on the track team and talked me into trying out). The season had already begun, but I had to prove to myself (and dad) that I could make it. The coach tested me at every event and finally decided I might be best suited for the 880-yard run.

The 880 was a rather difficult event but suited me fine. It was that day's equivalent of the present-day 800-meter run. It was not a "dash" like the 100, 220 or 440. Nor was it a long-distance run like the mile. It was a mix of dash and run, relying a lot on strategy and the runner determining when to begin the final dash to the finish line. It was also a very physically draining run.

Carmel High School was a perfect location for training for distance and endurance runs. Three times a week we would run from the school (on State Route 1, the Pacific Coast Highway) down the long (a few miles) steep hill on Ocean Avenue through Carmel-by-the-Sea to Carmel Beach. There we would run the length of the beach twice (on the dry, very soft sand, NOT the firm damp sand), to be followed by running back UP the LONG STEEP hill to the school.

I began as the number three 880 runner on the team, but by season's end, I was the number two. I missed going to the state finals by less than a second. We had an excellent track team, beating many larger schools. I can still remember us taking 1-2-3 in the 880 against Monterey High School (a much larger school).

Three of my favorite locations in the Carmel area were the beach (especially Carmel River Beach on the south side of town close to the mission), Point Lobos State Reserve south of town on State Route 1 (the Coast Highway) and Big Sur (further south on Route 1). During the summer I especially enjoyed Carmel River Beach when the river was dammed by sand that had formed a barrier, thus forming a small lake behind the dune.

The water in the Pacific Ocean was always VERY cold. Comparatively speaking, the lake water was warm. My favorite thing to do was jump into the ocean, then run across the sand dune and dive into the lake. It was like entering a bathtub with warm water in it.

Point Lobos was awesome because of the many trails and the wildlife. The seashore trails were some of the most scenic I had ever seen. At that time, the state wasn't as strict about staying on the trails as they are now. I spent many weekends at Point Lobos climbing the trees and rocks, many times enjoying geysers formed by the rock formation and watch the water fly over my head. Had my parents known the places I would go in Point Lobos they would never have permitted me to go without their supervision.

At Big Sur I went crawdadding on the Big Sur River. Those suckers were there for the catching. My friend Ron and I would each take a bucket, string, and raw bacon to the river. We'd tie the bacon to the string, drop it into the river along the edge (especially in front of underwater tree roots) and pull it out when a crawdad would clamp down on the bacon. The crawdads were so gung-ho about being caught and eaten, they would hold onto the bacon until they were in the bucket, at which time they would conveniently release the bacon. Talk about cooperative! Many were the weekends when I would enjoy a supper of crawdads.

I hated swimming in high school. However, it was mandatory to pass the swimming test in Carmel High School. My swimming skills "sucked." I usually swallowed a goodly amount of the chlorinated water in the pool and spent a lot of time throwing up in the locker room after swim sessions. I was especially bad at treading water. Thankfully my PE (Physical Education) teacher, Mr. Mosolf, persisted with me, and I passed. If he had not, I would probably have flunked the swimming test (fully clothed, boots and all) required for Special Forces. I always credit Mr. Mosolf with helping me attain a can-do attitude.

Also, during my senior year, I applied for and was accepted to attend a night course at Monterey Peninsula College in Monterey. The course I took was the basic private pilot course. I enjoyed the course immensely and did well and made a good grade. That cemented my wish to become a pilot. At that time, I had no idea how special it was that I was accepted to take a college course while in high school. I found out later that it was highly unusual to be accepted; in fact Carmel High School prided itself in its students taking college courses while in school, as well as the percentage of students that went on to college.

Ron and I belonged to the Monterey Peninsula Archery Club that met monthly in Monterey. The club had its own indoor archery range, which made it possible to practice archery throughout the year. One of the things that surprised me was the number of archers in the club who hunted wild boar in Carmel Valley with A BOW & ARROW. My thought was "you've got to be kidding me!" If I was to ever hunt wild boar with a bow and arrow, I would be sure to have a machine gun as backup. Those suckers have a mean disposition and will charge humans at the drop of a hat, but especially when wounded, as I was reminded when I was in Ethiopia years later.

San Jose State College

During my first year at San Jose State I finally went on my FIRST EVER DATE. I had never gone on a date in high school. In fact, I didn't even go to the Senior Prom. I met and seemed to hit it off with a girl at the San Jose State freshman indoctrination session at Asilomar (Pacific Grove, on the Monterey Peninsula), and began dating her. That only lasted a few weeks. I was very shy and did not know the first thing about dating. I was a definite amateur at the game.

Shortly afterwards I met a girl through the two new male friends I made in the neighborhood, Terry and Hal, both fellow San Jose State students. My friends and I did a lot together, including double and triple dating.

Because my grade point average in high school was mediocre at best, the only reason I was accepted into San Jose State was my extremely good college entrance exam results. Being as interested as I was in the aviation field, I decided to major in Aeronautical Operations, and joined the college U.S. Air Force Reserve Officer Training Course (R.O.T.C.) and Alpha Eta Rho aviation fraternity.

Being in R.O.T.C. brought in a few extra coins monthly, since the government pays R.O.T.C. cadets. In the beginning I wasn't very good in close-order drill (marching, etc.) in R.O.T.C. Because the course was supposed to train us to become officers, we had to learn how to lead and give orders to people.

One time I was leading close-order drill. I was marching backward, giving marching orders. I gave the order "column right, march!" and the column immediately began marching to the right. The only problem was, they marched directly into a fence. I had wanted them to march to the right as I was looking at them, not realizing that right to me was left to them (since I was facing them, not facing the direction they were facing). I got totally flustered and didn't know what order to give. I should have said "squad, halt," but instead stood there like a bump on a log. I was a member of the San Jose State U.S. Air Force R.O.T.C. unit for a year and a half.

I didn't do well in typing class while at Carmel High School (in fact I dropped out of it because I thought it would be too difficult) but decided to type all my class notes while at San Jose State. It was a lot easier to read my notes, and it required that I go over my notes again, while typing, thus assuring that I go over all material at least a second time. It was a good learning aid. It also resulted in my becoming an excellent typist. Fast enough, in fact, to give any professional secretary a run for her money.

During the summer between high school and college my height spurted up. I suddenly went from being one of the shortest kids in my age group, to one of the taller. This, I felt, was reason enough to try out for the San Jose State freshman basketball team. The freshman team was the step before the varsity team.

Although I had never previously played organized basketball in school, I managed to make the team, as a last string guard. We had an excellent team, playing such teams as Stanford, California and U.S.F. (University of San Francisco, alma mater of then famous basketball pro Bill Russell), as well as several central California Junior College varsity teams.

We won most of our games and I managed to play about five minutes all season. After the season ended, my coach (Danny Glines) told me that the only reason I made the team and was kept on the roster was because of my drive and never-give-up attitude.

I later found out that Coach Glines had been a U.S. Army Green Beret before becoming a coach. It didn't surprise me to learn that. He drove us hard, physically. On top of that, he always did everything we did, setting an example. He was shorter than every one of us, but in phenomenal shape.

One of my college friends had a very "cool" old Ford. He had painted it (with house paint) a flat pink. Boy, did it stand out! He had also put a speaker in the front grill and had a microphone (to talk to girls through the car grill) and a 45rpm record player under the car dash. We spent a few nights a week cruising 1st and 2nd streets in downtown San Jose with rock and roll music playing loudly through the car grill. We managed to get a lot of attention and meet a few girls. It was a cheap form of entertainment.

I missed part of the basketball season due to an extremely bad accident. One evening, my college friend, Terry, and I decided to drive over Route 17 to Santa Cruz and cruise around the beach for a while. We ended up finishing the trip over the hill in an ambulance, at the hospital in Santa Cruz.

At the time, Route 17 was a wide highway with no protective center dividers, and considered to be somewhat dangerous, with a history of bad accidents. On the Santa Cruz side of the hill a station wagon, being driven from Santa Cruz, began drifting toward our side of the highway (it was 4 lanes at that location). My friend honked his horn and began moving our car to the right to avoid.

We were straddling the edge of the roadway on our side when the cars hit head-on, both vehicles moving at approximately 55 mph. I had just expended life number one of my nine lives. My friend's chest was very bloody, and he was very woozy. I smashed the front windshield to smithereens and had some blood, and plenty of glass, in my hair. The man in the station wagon had a minor cut on his lip. Both cars were a mangled mess, ready for the junkyard.

When the CHP officer arrived, he said he had expected everyone to be deceased. The man driving the station wagon apparently fell asleep at the wheel. He was treated for his cut and released on the spot. My friend and I were transported to the nearest hospital, where my friend was found to have suffered only a badly bruised chest, with superficial cuts. The emergency room staff cleaned the blood and glass off my head and pronounced me good to go.

A couple weeks later at my birthday party at home, my new girlfriend, Phyllis, playfully hit my forehead with a tennis shoe. WOW! The pain was immediate and excruciating! I was taken immediately to an emergency room, where it was found that I had suffered a very bad head concussion in the accident. I was ordered to 2 weeks' bed rest with care not to bang my head in the least way, for fear of major damage, or worse, death. Surprisingly, apparently nobody had checked me for a concussion when I was in the Santa Cruz emergency room. I have suffered numerous concussions since then.

Harry Edwards gave me my first education in racial prejudice. He was a Negro. He had been given a full scholarship to San Jose State

(SJS) because of his track and field ability. At that time San Jose State had one of the top track-and-field teams in the nation. In fact, our track and field coach, Bud Winters, was the United States Olympic Team Track & Field Coach. My Carmel High School coach had wanted me to try out for the SJS Track & Field team because of my good showing as an 880-yard runner at CHS, but I felt I would have been way over-classed.

Edwards was a multi-sport athlete. He became the starting center on our San Jose State Freshman basketball team. For some strange reason, I always seemed to be assigned the job of guarding him during our practice scrimmages. Maybe our coach didn't want my other team members, who were much better players than I ever was, to get hurt. Edwards was a very physical player.

I left every practice with bumps, bruises, aches, and pains, courtesy of Edwards. He was such a physical player; in fact, that he fouled out of every game we played in that season. He was so "physical," in fact (some people considered him to be outright dirty), that many fights were the results of his "fouls."

Harry was from a poor family. During the Christmas break, he could not afford to go home to celebrate Christmas with his family. After receiving mom and dad's okay, I invited him to spend Christmas Day with us. He refused. In later years he became an activist in the black movement against racial prejudice, claiming all the whites at San Jose State had shunned him.

I know from personal experience that what he said was a lie. He had an attitude against whites, and a chip on his shoulder, and it showed, especially after he graduated. He became a well-known black activist in the San Francisco Bay Area, constantly being seen or quoted in newscasts, railing against the white community.

In January 1961, Soviet Premier Nikita Khrushchev announced the Soviet Union's support of "wars of national liberation." It thus became clear, that the Soviet Union was declaring a strategy to undermine already weak emerging nations of the third world.

On 20 January, John F. Kennedy was sworn in as the President of the United States. In his inaugural address, Kennedy stated that the United States would "pay any price, bear any burden, meet any hardship, support any friend, oppose any foe, to assure the survival and success of liberty," thus making it clear that the Soviet Union would not have free reign in their attempt to gain allies through liberation.

Kennedy would become a big part in the history of the United States Army Special Forces later that year. He had campaigned against the defensive strategy of the United States during that era. Ten days after his inauguration, he announced his intention to make changes in our country's defensive strategy, as well as to modernize our limited war and non-nuclear war capabilities.

Kennedy urged that our military be flexible enough to be able to withstand a nuclear attack, as well as be prepared to engage in small unit and guerrilla warfare. He noted that most wars since 1945 had been non-nuclear in nature, mostly conflicts involving a guerrilla warfare scenario.

Kennedy's first test came in August 1961, when the Soviet Union began constructing a high wall surrounding the Western sectors of Berlin, supposedly to block East German defectors. The wall became known as the Berlin Wall. Kennedy's reaction was to order an increase in U.S. armed forces and to call up many reservists and reserve units. He also sent additional units to Germany, and reinforced the units assigned to West Berlin. Within two months, the Army's regular troop strength was tripled, to 120,000 troops, including two National Guard divisions activated to duty.

One of my college friends (Hal) had a Volkswagen bug. He was interested in car rallies. I became his navigator. We did very well, placing high in every rally we participated in. It was a lot of fun and kept my math skills in practice. It also helped me learn map reading and land navigation.

I was able to borrow dad's Chevy Biscayne occasionally, to take downtown (with the excuse that I had to go to the San Jose State Library for a project). I found out right off the bat that dad was keeping track of miles driven and I wasn't going to be able to drive it much. However, Terry mentioned that we could unhook the odometer during our jaunts.

Then I found that dad always kept track of gas mileage also, so I learned, quickly that I had to put 25-50¢ worth of gas in the car after each run. Dad kept surprising me though. Numerous times I would come home, and he would chew me out for accelerating the car too quickly. Terry and I scoured that car for anything that would indicate fast acceleration, such as maybe some sort of an accelerometer (if any such thing existed). We found nothing! I had noticed that the windshield washer would squirt a little bit of water onto the window at times during quick accelerations, and cleaned that after every use, but he still knew.

In later years (many years, in fact) I finally found out that he had a bag of tools in the trunk of the car. Those were his indicators of my driving. When he told me that, I told him I had been driving 1st and 2nd streets those nights and had unhooked the odometer. We both had a good laugh at getting something over on each other. It wasn't often I managed to win.

I worked the summer between my freshman and sophomore years as a garbage man for Ron's father. He owned the contracted garbage service (Adams & Sellards) for Pebble Beach (17 Mile Drive area of the Monterey Peninsula). It was very hard work (harder than most garbage route jobs), as well as long hours, but it certainly put me in shape. The garbage had to be thrown up and over the truck sides.

The garbage route was not curbside pickup (remember this is Pebble Beach, home to some of the richest people in the United States). We had to go into the backyard, pick up the garbage can, and carry it on our shoulders to the truck on the street. We also picked up any trash they had set out for pickup.

It was amazing what they would throw out. If a stereo system had a tube go out, rather than purchase a new tube to place in the system, the system was ditched, and a new system purchased in its place. Also, any furniture that got a nick in it was thrown out. A lot of very worthwhile and expensive objects were thrown out. We had a section of the truck designated just for these items. The owner of the service had his home pretty much furnished with these items.

The pay was decent given my age, giving me a pretty good bankroll of spending money for college. I also used muscles I never knew existed. It put me in excellent shape for what was to unexpectedly come in my near future.

While working in Carmel that summer, I went shopping at the old Mediterranean Market downtown. I purchased some boxes of chocolate-covered insects at the store. If I remember correctly, the chocolate covered insects included crickets, grasshoppers, bees and ants.

While cruising through San Jose during the school year we would always end the night stopping at a drive-in for a burger and soda. After finishing our meals, when the carhop came to pick up our window trays, I would offer her a piece of chocolate candy. Right after they bit down I would tell them what they were eating. Almost all the carhops seemed to be bad sports. I learned to be ready to get out of there fast after telling the girls.

In December of my sophomore year I got a job as an "interviewer" with "Great Books of the Western World." I worked weeknights and weekends, not leaving much spare time. My job consisted of canvassing an appointed area. My spiel was basically that I was not selling, only interviewing for the target's opinion.

The interview included showing and describing the "Great Books of the Western World" set and annual encyclopedia of events, basically selling them on the product, although I could not write up a contract even if the customer wanted to buy. After the session was over I would write up a review of the session. If I gave a positive spin on the interview the "manager" would follow up with a "sales call."

My manager, Mr. Brown, had such a large percentage of sales on the positive spin follow-ups, that he began following up on every place that I got my foot into. He said he had never had such a large percentage of sales on follow-ups.

I found out that the ribald stories that are spread about door-to-door salesmen are apparently more true than false. In the short time I was in the business, I had numerous "romantic" opportunities presented to me, but I was too shy and lacked the knowledge of how to follow up on my opportunities. Boy, was I naïve!

In my Fall Sophomore semester, my girlfriend, Phyllis, broke up with me and began dating another man. I was devastated. I thought I was head over heels in love with her. She was my life. Without her I was lost. My grades took a nosedive and my attitude went downhill. I couldn't concentrate on my studies at all.

"It may be laid down as a primary position, and the basis of our system, that every Citizen who enjoys the protection of a Free Government, owes not only a proportion of his property, but even of his personal services to the defense of it." — George Washington

I decided to make my girlfriend feel sorry for me, by enlisting in the U.S. Army. The reason I chose the Army was because I had been told by an optician that I had less than 20-20 vision. That meant no flying in the Air Force. I found out later that I had 20-20 vision and the optician had made a mistake. Oh, well!

I enlisted for U.S. Army Airborne (paratrooper), Unassigned. At least the Army was only a three-year enlistment, compared to the four years for the other services. I wanted to be in the toughest outfit, despite being afraid of heights. In high school I feared diving off the regular diving board at our swimming pool and never dove off the high diving board. I told the recruiter that I wanted to be inducted on February 14th (St. Valentine's Day) to get even with my girlfriend. Boy was that an intelligent decision on my part (said facetiously)!

"Ask not what your country can do for you—ask what you can do for your country." — John F. Kennedy

CHAPTER 2

BASIC COMBAT TRAINING

"The highest obligation and privilege of citizenship is that of bearing arms for one's country." — *George S. Patton, Jr.*

Induction Center

I woke up very early, on Wednesday, 14 February 1962. My life was about to change, drastically. My dad drove me to the San Jose bus depot. I had been given a bus ticket by the U.S. Army, for a free one-way trip to Oakland CA. I boarded a Peerless Stages bus in San Jose, riding it to the Oakland Bus terminal. There, I was met by a military bus, which transported me, free of charge again, to the Oakland Induction Center.

Several of us were met by a government employee, who led us to the section of the center that was responsible for giving induction physicals. I had no trouble passing the Army physical. After passing it, we were led to another section of the building, in which we took the oath, and signed on the dotted line.

I, along with the rest of the inductees (mostly draftees), repeated the Oath of Allegiance. We all raised our right hands and repeated, "I, Richard Harry James, do solemnly swear that I will support and defend

43

the Constitution of the United States of America against all enemies, foreign and domestic; that I will bear true faith and allegiance to the same; and that I will obey the orders of the President of the United States and the orders of the officers appointed over me, according to regulations and the Uniform Code of Military Justice, so help me God." At that point in time, my family became the United States Army.

Vietnam was one of the furthest things from my mind. As far as I can remember, I didn't even know that there were some (very few, actually) American troops in South Vietnam, involved in a war. Processing at the Induction Center took up most of the day. The processing included a physical.

I was deemed physically fit, at 6'1" tall, and weighing 151. Yeah, I was tall, and skinny. While there, we received our individual service numbers, different for each of us, to identify us throughout our military service. Our serial number was to our military life what our Social Security number was to our civilian life.

My service number began with the capital letters RA, denoting that I was an enlisted soldier, in for 3 years. Those who had been drafted had a serial number beginning with US. Reservists and national guardsmen had their own distinctive letters.

Late in the afternoon all of us boarded a chartered Peerless Stages bus for the three-hour trip to Fort Ord (a few miles northeast of Monterey, CA) for Basic Combat Training (BCT). I was very familiar with the route down to Fort Ord since I had been on the same roads not more than a few years earlier. At San Jose we took U.S. 101 South, and rode through numerous orchards and farm fields, passing through the towns of Morgan Hill and Gilroy.

We eventually turned right, onto State Route 152, heading towards the Pacific coast, and Monterey. Farm fields greeted us almost all the way. Not far north of Monterey, large sand dunes appeared on the right (west) side of the bus. From having lived there a couple years before, I knew that on the other side of those dunes was Monterey Bay, and then the Pacific Ocean.

Just south of Marina, we turned left, and came upon a guard shack and wire fencing, the main entrance to Fort Ord. The bus driver stopped the bus, handing what looked like a set of orders to the Military Policeman (MP) at the gate. The MP motioned the bus driver to continue, at which time he put the bus in gear, and entered the base. As far as the eye could see ahead of us were single and double-story plain wooden buildings.

If we had any doubt before, we now knew we were all embarking on a new life, in a strange new world, that of the U.S. military. We belonged to the Army, period! Our freedom and family security had vanished.

The bus ride from the Induction Center to Fort Ord had seemed longer than it actually was, made longer by the fact that those who had been drafted didn't really want to be on the bus, especially since it was going to an Army base. They, and those of us who were first-time enlistees, knew absolutely nothing about what would be facing us, when we arrived at our destination.

The men onboard who were prior service (served prior as enlistees or draftees) knew what lay ahead but weren't talking much. The trip took much longer than present-day trips there, because there were no multi-lane freeways or Interstate highways in those days. We came up to a large wooden sign that read "U.S. Army Reception Center, Fort Ord, California." We had arrived!

"The reason the American Army does so well in wartime, is that war is chaos, and the American Army practices it on a daily basis." — From a post-war debriefing of a German General

Reception Center

Civilian "reception centers" offer free coffee and treats, a purposely feel-good experience. We learned to forget that in the Army Reception Center. Sure, you'll get free coffee…at mealtime, in a regimented mess hall.

As soon as the bus pulled into the Reception Center and stopped, we were herded off the bus and told to "Fall In!" Of course, almost all the recruits had no idea what he was talking about, so the cadre had to explain that "Fall In" meant to form as a group, in formation. He showed us how to form up, in a formation. With the help of other

NCOs, he gave us instructions on how to line up and determine correct distances apart from each other, using outstretched arms, and lining up directly behind the man in front of us, for those who weren't in the front row.

The words "meatball," "screw-ups," "bozos," and quite possibly "shitheads" were probably bandied about, to describe us, out loud, and quite often during the process. One of the men was seen with one of his hands in his pocket. That's how we learned that we were NEVER to be seen with hands in pockets. If caught, the question was almost always, "Recruit, what is your right (or left) hand playing with?" Another possible remark was, "Recruit! Stop playing with yourself, IMMEDIATELY!"

The NCO (Noncommissioned Officer) in charge explained, very authoritatively, that he was going to read off our names, alphabetically, and that we were to respond by yelling, "HERE SERGEANT." He reiterated that he was not to be called "SIR," because he was a sergeant, therefore having to work for a living, unlike officers, who were to be referred to as "sir." The ranking cadre NCO then read off our names in alphabetical order, by last name. When my name was called, "JAMES, RICHARD HARRY," I responded loudly with "HERE SERGEANT," as we were instructed.

Upon completion of the roll call, the NCO then read off the rules and regulations that we were to abide by, including the fact that we were NOT to leave the Reception Center area under threat of being considered AWOL (Away Without Leave), which would be dealt with harshly. That included making phone calls. Remember that in the early 1960s the main ways of communicating were by landline telephone or written letters.

The only phones available for personal use were banks of pay phones located in strategic areas about the barracks area. We were immediately warned that using those phones was not permissible until later in our training cycle. Even later in our training cycle, using the pay phones was an effort in frustration. There weren't enough available phones for the quantity of trainees present.

If one wanted to use a telephone, he had to stand in line for long periods of time, hoping that the people in front would keep their conversations short and sweet. Long conversations occasionally resulted in fights, begun by frustrated trainees waiting in line. Even when we were finally permitted to use the pay phones, it was a rare occasion that I called home, usually when I needed money. I relied on writing letters for private, easy communications.

I could already tell that this was going to be a psychological adjustment for me. There was no doubt it was an unfamiliar way of life, and we were all going to have to adjust to it. We were going to become soldiers, whether we wanted to, or not. It would become imperative that my fellow recruits and I learn self-discipline.

It was ironic that, although we were there to learn how to fight for the defense of freedom for our fellow countrymen, we had to relinquish our freedom. On the other hand, we were the personification of the term "equal rights." Each of us, no matter the civilian background, financial worth, or race, was treated just as badly as the other. The Reception Center's mission was to turn civilians into soldiers. It was a tune-up for recruits, prior to entering the official U.S. Army Basic Combat Training (BCT), aka Basic Training.

Our group was billeted at the Ft. Ord Reception Center for processing during our first five days in the Army. We were each paid a "flying $20." That was Army terminology for advanced pay, to be used for purchased required toiletries, etc. We were given a list of the items we would be required to have, then "marched" down to the local PX (Post Exchange, military version of a small general store).

One of the nice things about the PX was that there was no tax charged on your purchase. Also, you were charged the cheapest possible price. The PX was a military establishment operated for the convenience of military personnel, not an attempt to make a profit. As an example, the price for a carton (ten packs of twenty cigarettes each) of cigarettes was $2.

The items listed included toiletries, a can of "Brasso" (for shining brass items), a can of shoe polish, a small shoe polish applicator brush, a large shoe brush, a comb (whether needed, or not), etc. Each was part of what would be a required display in the top drawer of our footlocker, which was also to be displayed a certain way.

We were given a sheet of paper showing EXACTLY how the items in the footlocker, wall locker, etc., were to look, with each item with its own designated place. We were then "marched" to the unit supply room, to receive what I was to learn over time was the standard U.S. Army bedding issue: mattress cover, two sheets, two olive drab blankets, and a pillowcase. We were then "marched" to our barracks.

When we went somewhere, we always did so as a group, either marched in formation or double-timed (running at a jogging pace) in formation, something akin to an orderly herd of animals on the move, kept in order by the shepherd, an NCO. When I say "marched," I refer to our group's ragged attempt at walking in step with each other, following the cadre sergeant's "left, right, left, right," etc.

We were supposed to lead off on our left foot, when ordered to march. Not doing so was normally what began the problems some men had with marching in unison. Some of the men seemingly had problems differentiating left from right, resulting in the soon-to-be often heard loud comment from a cadre. "Your other left, recruit," or something in the same vein.

According to the Fort Bragg Training Center *Yearbook, January 1969*, "When a basic combat trainee is learning to become a soldier he no longer walks—he marches. He marches over every type of terrain imaginable…. The objectives of this type of training are to teach the individual soldier the principles of march discipline, march hygiene, preparation and adjustment of packs, and to provide a series of practical exercise in cross-country marches…. Trainees test their training by experience and learn a final lesson to cherish a most precious piece of equipment—their feet."

Almost all soldiers smoked cigarettes. In fact, a ten-minute smoke break was authorized every hour. The NCOs weren't going to keep us from that break, because they were craving a cigarette also. The NCO in charge explained how we were to dispose of those cigarettes, aka "coffin nails," upon completion of smoking them. There were two accepted methods. The first was to dispose of the cigarette in a "butt can." Butt cans were everywhere on a military post. They were empty

#10 food cans with a layer of water (or sand) in the bottom of the can.

Butt cans were hung on nails in all barracks bays, on almost every wooden post, and at the entrance to almost all post buildings. They were usually painted red. The second method of disposal was to field strip the cigarette. In the military, the term "field strip" meant to tear a piece of equipment down completely.

When referring to a cigarette, "field strip" meant to tear the cigarette paper lengthwise, dumping the ashes on the ground, and stepping on them to assure they were out. The paper was then rolled into a very small ball, and placed into a pocket, as well as the filter if smoking a filtered cigarette. Throwing a cigarette butt on the ground (not disposing of it in a correct manner) was a punishable offense if caught.

The next order of business was a very basic lesson on how to make a bed, "Army style." We were shown, in detail, how we were to make our beds the Army way. The sergeant in charge spent a lot of time on that subject. It was obvious that our drill instructors were going to be sticklers, when it came to detail.

In the Army, all beds had to be made with hospital corners, and they had to be made with perfect 45° angle hospital corners. In addition, all blankets had to be perfectly smooth, and tight enough that a quarter could be bounced off the blanket. All our color coordinated olive drab blankets had a large "U.S." stamped onto them. When the bed was made, the U.S. had to show, on the bottom section of the bed.

After making our beds, we were "marched" to the mess hall for our first military meal. We formed a line, grabbed the top lightweight large steel tray, with sunken separations for different foods, and walked the "chow line," sliding our trays along shiny metal tubing while the servers along the line placed their idea of a serving upon our trays. There was no choice. We were to eat what we had been served. The Army had their idea of what was good for us.

Supposedly, the military had tested different foods and meal selections, and came up with the "perfect" meals to keep us nourished and in shape for our mission. This was a wake-up call. It was my first taste of Army food. Yuck! I will, however, admit that there was one

Army meal, a breakfast, that I thoroughly enjoyed, and I don't think ANY mess sergeant could screw it up. "Shit on a Shingle," aka SOS, known by civilians as chipped beef on toast. I loved it, and still do.

That first night in the barracks was an eye opener, and an extremely rude awakening. Where were the toilet stalls? I needed to poop in the privacy of a stall. Privacy? You don't need no privacy in the Army, recruit! You're in the Army now! You get to live, or die, all in a very public setting. Army latrines (the Army word for bathrooms) were totally open. That included the urinals, the toilets, and the showers. During my first year, or so, uncomfortable, or not, I pretty much learned to hold it, until everyone was asleep. Then I could usually poop in privacy.

The following morning, we were "marched" to the Reception Center Barber Shop. The first order of business (of course) was a haircut. By the time the barbers (three or four of them) were done scalping us (which had to have taken less than a minute per recruit), the floor of the barbershop had a thick layer of hair on it. And, to think, we even had to pay for the "head shave," more commonly known as a "buzz cut." After the haircuts, none of our civilian friends would have recognized us. In fact, when I got up from the chair and looked at myself in the mirror, I didn't recognize me.

We were "In the Army Now!" The haircut begged the question, "Why did they require us to have a comb in our footlocker?" Hell, there was no way it was functional, given the fact that the Army had just made sure we had no hair, to speak of. I thought it was rather stupid to have to buy a comb, and then display it in the footlocker. None of us had enough hair remaining to comb, and even if we did, wouldn't the best place for a comb be in your pocket?

"Excuse me, but is green the only color this comes in?"—Goldie Hawn in "Private Benjamin"

Immediately following our special hair styling at the "salon," we were "marched" to the Reception Center supply shed and issued our clothing and equipment, including a duffel bag in which to carry our new issue. That was known as our "initial issue." What a laugher! If a clothing store ever sized its customers the way the Army did, the store would never get any return customers. The nice thing about it was the fact that we didn't have to labor over what color or style we wanted to wear on any given day.

Our fashion choice was simple: olive drab and Army style. No need to debate what color-coordinated items to choose. Olive drab (OD) was the style of the day. No salesman needed. Some of the clothing did fit, somewhat. The first thing we were issued was the duffel bag.

As we went from station to station, each supply man would give us the once over, go over to a rack, grab however many of the items we were to receive, and then shove them at us, marking it off on the list each man carried. If we complained that it wasn't going to fit, the pat answer was, "You'll grow into them." We immediately stuffed them into our duffel bag and went to the next station. The item that took the longest to fit was the boots. As much time as soldiers spent on their feet, the boots had to be a good fit. Nobody wanted a soldier with foot problems.

The clothing was our permanent issue, which we would have to carry with us from assignment to assignment. It included bag, duffel; belt, cotton, web (1 each); boot, combat, leather (2 pair); buckle, web, brass; cap, garrison, wool, Army Green 44; cap, service, Army Green 44; cap utility, poly OG 106; coat, wool, Army Green 44; drawers, cotton, white, thigh length (6 each, aka boxer shorts); jacket, field, OG 107; glove inserts, wool knitted (2 pair); glove shells, leather, black; insignia, Branch of Service, EP; insignia, service cap, bronze, EM; insignia, U.S., EP (2 each); necktie, wool, black (2 each); raincoat, nylon, taupe; shirt, cotton, twill, 8.2 oz., khaki, Shade 1, short sleeve (4 each); shirt, cotton, poplin, 4 oz., khaki, Shade 46 (3 each); shirt, utility, cotton, OG 107 (4 each, fatigue shirts); shoe, dress, oxford, plain toe, leather, black; socks, cotton, black (3 pair); socks, cushion-sole, black (5 pair); towel, cotton, white, bath (2 each); trousers, cotton, sateen, OG 107 (4 each, fatigue pants); trousers, cotton, twill, 8.2 oz., khaki (4 each); trousers, wool, Army Green 44 (2 each); and undershirt, cotton, white, quarter length sleeves (6 each).

All the clothing we were issued, through careful packing, would fit in the duffel bag. That issue, plus our required toiletries, were all we were authorized, and all that was expected to be seen during inspection of our quarters. Some personal items, such as writing equipment, were also permitted. We were also issued two metal identification tags, embossed with our name, service number, blood type and religion. Those were more commonly known as "dog tags," to be worn, on a chain around our necks, always.

As soon as we returned to our barracks, we were told how to mark certain items of clothing and equipment, in the prescribed manner and location, with our names and service numbers. That included all footgear, headgear, helmet liner, belt and duffel bag. We were told to do so that evening. We had to use indelible, waterproof, permanent marking ink, white for dark items, and black for light items. Then we had to place all our civilian clothing and belongings that were not permitted to be in the barracks, in a bag, to be returned to us upon graduation, or to be sent home.

Following the issue of our uniforms, we were marched to a large building, and seated at desks. Our DI announced that we were there to take the Motor Vehicle Driver Selection Battery I (MDB-I) written tests. The test supervisor proceeded to explain how the test would be administered, how we were to progress on the test, and how long we would have to complete the test. In later years I found that I had scored well on the test.

Following the testing, we were marched to another building, where we received our many inoculations, to protect us from disease. I don't remember how many shots we received, or what they were for, but it was too many. I don't even think we were told what each shot was for, just that the Army required us to receive all the inoculations.

We rolled up both of our sleeves and formed a line. That line moved slowly between two lines of white-coated medics. Each medic gave a specific inoculation, armed with what looked like a Buck Rogers style large ray gun. The gun was a pneumatic device that was supposed to inject just the right amount of inoculation serum into each man's body.

Each shot felt like a punch in the arm. There were instances in which we received shots in both arms at the same time. A couple men passed out. I had received so many shots as a child (mostly because of my many allergies) that they didn't faze me one iota. It was, however, disconcerting to see grown men pass out from a mere inoculation. How in the world were they going to react when they were being shot at with bullets, or saw a mangled body?

While there, we were advised that sick call was available to any, and all, of us during the morning formation. At that time, we could notify the noncommissioned officer (NCO) in charge of us that we wished to be seen by a medical specialist about an illness or ailment. The NCO would fill out an "individual sick slip," hand it to the requesting individual, and grant permission for that individual to report to the dispensary to be looked at by a doctor.

Upon arrival at the dispensary, the doctor was responsible for deciding whether the individual was fit for duty or should be admitted to a hospital or confined to quarters for his ailment. That doctor was authorized to give medical advice and treat minor illnesses and injuries.

After diagnosis and/or treatment, the sick slip was returned to the unit headquarters. Just the mere thought of all the work involved in requesting to go on sick call was enough to keep many of us from going on sick call. The second reason we didn't want to go on sick call was the thought of having to be re-cycled to another training unit, having to repeat some of the training, if the doctor considered us sick enough to not be able to immediately return to duty.

On the 16th we went through a barrage of aptitude tests, to determine each of our strengths, as an aid to determine what Military Occupational Specialties (MOS, aka jobs) we would be most adept at. I didn't know it at the time, but I scored very high in all but a couple fields. Those test scores would follow me around for the remainder of my time in the Army, entered on my Army DA Form 20, Enlisted Qualification Record.

The testing was followed by orientation lectures, during which we learned about Army life, and how we were expected to act. Basically, they told us that a soldier was to go where he was told to go and do what he was told to do. Of course, that meant that telling somebody of higher rank "where to go" if you disagreed or disapproved of an order, was not considered to be acceptable conduct, and would result in punishment.

We were given very fundamental instructions on the basic positions we would most likely be told to assume. That included sitting, standing, marching, double-timing (running), formations, etc. YES, the Army had a wrong way, and an Army way, of when, and how, to sit.

We had already been somewhat versed in the very basic orders, such as "attention," "parade rest," "at ease," "left face," "right face," "about face," "forward march," "column left march," "column right march," etc. At that early stage, we were not expected to be perfect, but mistakes were immediately corrected, and if the mistake was obvious, the comment from the cadre usually included a disparaging remark, or cuss word.

One of the favorite remarks of cadre was on the order of, "Your other left (or right), recruit!" when a soldier turned the wrong direction. Some of the basics included standing ramrod stiff upright, with arms straight down, and fingers slightly cupped along the outside seam of the trousers, feet forming a 45-degree angle with heels touching, when at "attention." We were also to keep our heads erect, facing forward, with the chin drawn in.

There wasn't much difference between the positions of "at ease" and "parade rest." In both positions the feet were set apart about eight inches and the hands were clasped behind the back. The difference was the relaxation factor. While at "parade rest" the knees were almost locked, the hands interlaced in the open position and motionless in the small of the back. The body was rigid, and the head was facing straight ahead, motionless. When standing "at ease," the body was relaxed, and the head could move about. Marching ALWAYS began by stepping out with your left foot first, followed by the right, left, etc.

Administrative details were covered while in the Reception Center. This included the recording of information for inclusion in our personal military files. The paperwork that caused me the most concern was the will. I guess I had never really thought of myself as anything but invincible. The possibility of death at that young age was an eye-opener, and nothing I was comfortable to think of and, much less, to discuss with a stranger.

Pay procedures were covered, including the fact that we would be paid on the first of each month. We learned that we would be entitled to 2½ days of leave, with pay and allowances, per month of active duty. Unlike civilian jobs, in which leave time usually increased with seniority, it was a rock-solid regulation, no matter what rank one held.

Personnel traveling as individuals to and from overseas assignments were authorized 30 days leave upon request. That leave was not subtracted from leave accumulated on the individual's records.

"In no other profession are the penalties for employing untrained personnel so appalling and so irrevocable as in the military." — General Douglas MacArthur

Headquarters Company, 1st Battle Group, 1st Brigade

On Monday, 19 February, we were assigned to our Basic Training unit. I was assigned to Headquarters & Headquarters Company, 1st Battle Group, 1st Brigade (aka H-1-1, or Head-1-1). There were about 200 of us, and we were transported to our new barracks, which were fairly modern looking three-story high brick cement buildings, built in the early 1950s. Each building housed all the company office space required, and a company mess hall on the bottom floor of one end of the building.

It was there that we learned the truth of the popular saying about there being a "Right Way," a "Wrong Way," and the "Army Way." Truer words have never been spoken. In civilian life, if a job was assigned to you, it was usually considered to be up to the assigned individual, as to how best to accomplish the job, just so long as it was accomplished. In the Army, it was not only imperative that the job was completed, but that it was done one way, and only one way: the Army way. We quite quickly realized that logic went out the window, as soon as we entered the Army.

Another term we learned the meaning of, rather quickly, was "shithouse rumor." To us low-ranking enlisted men, the Army seemed to run on rumor. The lower your rank, the better the chances were that you heard a lot of "shithouse rumors." "Shithouse rumor" was any information that had little or no basis of fact or validity, and had a

Me wearing soft cap and brand new fatigue jacket. I have that not yet trained, or dangerous, hired killer look of someone who knows not what he is doing.
(my photo)

strong chance of being totally false. During training cycles "shithouse rumors" abounded. The first rumor to be spread was that the Army covertly included saltpeter (potassium nitrate) in our food, supposedly to reduce our sexual drive.

To begin with, saltpeter was not an anti-aphrodisiac. In fact, it was used in explosives. Hell, the Army didn't need no stinking chemical to reduce our libido. The training and long hours were tiring enough to do the job. Basic Training was like no other scenario that a civilian would ever, or will ever, see in his or her lifetime. That was where the civilian became a warrior, and, in many cases, an adult. The eight weeks spent in Basic Training would, for many, shape a lifetime.

"Discipline is the soul of an army."—*George Washington*

Upon arrival to our assigned unit, a corporal in spit-shined combat boots, highly starched, form-fitting fatigues, a light blue dickey, and a very shiny black helmet liner, greeted us, instructing us to get in formation (of course, having to help us). The corporal announced that he was to be our drill instructor. He was going to be our master, and we were to be his slaves. He was the all-powerful, having absolute power over all of us, twenty-four hours a day, seven days a week.

Behind him stood a young second lieutenant, in spit-shined combat boots, highly starched, form-fitting fatigues with a light blue dickey, a Ranger patch above his 6th Army shoulder patch on his left shoulder, and paratrooper wings above his U.S. Army patch, which was above his left chest pocket on his uniform. He was also sporting an extremely shiny black helmet liner.

The corporal called us to attention and took roll call, announcing each last name, followed by first name and middle initial. The last names were always called out in alphabetical order, so one would know when their turn to answer was near.

Upon completion of taking roll, the corporal made a perfect military about-face and, facing the second lieutenant, smartly snapped his right arm and hand to a perfect military salute, announcing loudly, "SIR, ALL PRESENT AND ACCOUNTED FOR." The lieutenant, just as sharply, returned his salute, saying "THANK YOU CORPORAL."

Me wearing U.S. Army Class-A uniform. I'm sporting the unusually happy look of a trainee who knows not what is ahead. (my photo)

Both men then returned to the position of attention.

The second lieutenant gave the order "PARADE REST," at which time the corporal and all of us peons assumed the position of "parade rest." Parade rest was assumed by smartly placing both arms behind the back, the back of one hand against the palm of the other, while at the same time smartly placing both feet about shoulder width apart, and standing rigid, as in the position of attention.

The lieutenant proceeded to explain what was to be expected of us while under his command. Following his speech, the corporal immediately performed another perfect military about-face, called us to attention again, performed another perfect military about-face, snapped another perfect salute to the second lieutenant, which was again returned by a similar perfect demonstration of a military salute by the lieutenant, stating that he was turning the formation over to the command of the corporal. The second lieutenant then made a smart military right face and proceeded to march out of the area.

The corporal commanded us to "STAND AT EASE." The corporal then proceeded to tell us what HE expected from us. He warned us that we were never to stand, or walk, with our hands in our pockets. That was extremely un-military. If seen with hands in the pockets, the expectation and comment would be that the soldier was playing "pocket pool" (playing with himself).

We were then questioned about our military experience and assigned to platoons and squads. Our group was broken down into five "platoons" of about 40 men each, forming our company. We had some prior service personnel who were assigned as temporary platoon leaders and given armbands with sergeant stripes to wear.

Because of my R.O.T.C. experience I was assigned as a temporary squad leader and given an armband with corporal stripes. I was extremely proud. Although I was temporarily promoted because of my R.O.T.C. experience, Basic Training was NOTHING like college R.O.T.C. In R.O.T.C. you were pretty much among your peers, whether it be level of financial worth or intelligence. In Army Basic Training that was far from the truth. The differences between the trainees were like night and day in all ways.

The Army decided to test what I heard was a new idea. Those of us who had volunteered for Airborne (paratroopers) were assigned to a special platoon. The little spit-shined lieutenant took it as his personal task to whip us into shape, in preparation for what we would be expected to do during Jump School. We did a lot of double-timing (running).

Thus began what seemed like forever going through Army training (more than 14 months, to be exact), and being screamed at by our instructors and cadre. It also began the enlargement of my vocabulary, not only because of the ever-present military terminology and acronyms, but also because of the enormous list of cuss words heard and thus, spoken, within the ranks of the military. It didn't take me long to learn and utilize four letter words in their supposedly correct context.

The corporal then trooped our platoon upstairs to our new quarters, which were large, dormitory-style rooms housing each platoon. That corporal would be our platoon NCO for the remainder of our Basic Training cycle. One of his favorite sayings when one of us screwed up or couldn't understand his instructions was, "What's your major malfunction, Private?"

All our beds were double bunks, which lined each side of the open bay. The heads of each bunk were on the outside of the bay. Against the wall were our wall lockers, one per person, located behind our bunks. At the foot of the bunks, lining the bay corridor, were our footlockers, also one per person. There were no chairs in the barracks, the footlockers being deemed by the Army as acceptable seating for soldiers.

Rather than mess up our neatly made bunks, we all opted to sit on the footlockers until later in the evening, when we knew our bunks wouldn't be inspected for neatness. Our little corporal advised us that any imperfection in the way our bed was made would result in the tearing apart of our bedding, and having it thrown on the barracks floor, to be made again; next time perfectly. I still make my bed with hospital corners, knowing no other way to do it.

We were advised that Quartermaster (military) laundry service was available on a voluntary basis on all Army bases. We were also advised (highly recommended) to use this service while in Basic Training, because of the lack of free time to do our own required laundry services, which included lightly starched fatigues. Laundry day was once a week. We, of course, had to pay a small monthly flat fee for this service. The Army constantly found ways for us to spend what little pay we received.

We were then shown how to polish our shoes and boots, again up to Army standards. The corporal explained how to clean our shoes and boots first, brushing and cleaning them with a brush and soft cloth, then using a toothbrush (not the same one you brushed your teeth with) to remove any dried mud from between the sole and upper section of the footwear.

Then he used the toothbrush again, this time to apply polish to hard-to-get areas of the boots. He then took a can of black shoe polish, removed the lid, and poured a little water into the lid. Grabbing a tattered T-shirt remnant, he dipped the rag into the polish and proceeded to rub the polish into the boot leather, occasionally dipping the rag into the water and continuing to polish. He did this until the entire boot had been "spit-shined." He also showed us how a cotton ball or old handkerchief could be used to obtain the same shine.

Next the corporal demonstrated how to polish our brass (belt buckle, saucer cap insignia, and Class A uniform lapel insignias), all with "Brasso" and a cotton ball or handkerchief. He even showed us how to take apart our belt buckles and thoroughly clean the inside of them. Talk about overboard cleanliness.

A couple of the words I heard constantly, and used occasionally myself, were "Mickey Mouse" and "chicken shit." Those were terms used to describe the soldier's feeling of something or someone being overly nit-picky. That happened a lot in the Army, especially in training, and resulted in those two words being uttered on a regular basis. Spit-shined boots and extreme shines on our brass were good examples of these comments.

Our little corporal then showed us how to run the floor buffer. It was an electric machine, weighing about forty pounds and having about a forty-foot long power cord, that looked easy to operate, but took a little bit of training to "master." If you didn't operate it correctly it could get out of hand on you and go wild. The machine had a round rotating brush pad underneath it that buffed the waxed floor. The high speed of the buffer pad was what shined the floor.

The floors were to be cleaned spotless and buffed every morning. Pulling the "On" lever that was on the right side of the two-handed handle started the buffer. Machine navigational control came from tilting it in the correct direction. Tilting the machine handle slightly and slowly up resulted in the buffer traveling to the right. A down tilt would send it left. The easy way to remember was, "raise right, lower left." It was imperative that the tilting motions be minimal, or the resulting movement of the buffer could go out of control.

The machine did a great job of polishing the floor, and a person who was able to control the buffer well, could make some very professional looking buffing designs on the floor. There were some recruits who just could not get the hang of operating that machine. They were always assigned to other duties. We always worked the buffer in a rearward direction, to not have to walk on the newly buffered floor, thus spoiling the pattern on the shiny floor. There were times that we made a game of running the buffer.

We were not permitted to have any civilian clothing, so everything in the wall and footlockers were military issue or required toiletries, all placed in an assigned manner (as demonstrated by the corporal). Clothes were hung in the wall locker in a specific order, with caps placed on the shelf near the top in specific locations, and shoes and boots placed on the bottom floor of the locker, also in specific locations.

The footlocker had a tray placed in the top portion of the locker. Toiletries, and socks and underwear (all folded or rolled to exact specifications), were placed in the footlocker and tray. They, like the items in the wall locker, were placed in a specific location and order. It was requirements like that which were deservedly called "Mickey Mouse," devoid of logical reason, but standard Army procedure. The wall and footlockers were apt to be inspected at any time, without notice.

On 20 February Lieutenant Colonel John Glenn took off for a little trip into outer space. He became the first American citizen to orbit planet Earth. The space race with Russia continued. On Friday,

23 February, our group learned the term "GI Party."

It wasn't truly a party, in the fun sense. It was, instead, a work party. Every Friday night in U.S. Army Training facility barracks nationwide, was time for a GI work party. The barracks denizens were, at that time, expected to clean their place of residence, perfectly, passable for a white glove inspection Saturday morning.

"Discipline strengthens the mind so that it becomes impervious to the corroding influence of fear." — Field Marshal Bernard Montgomery.

We seemed to never be able to please that little short shit corporal, and he delighted in letting us know so. He always wanted things done quickly and perfectly. It seemed, at times, that perfection was never reachable, at least in his mind. That sorry shit kept on our asses day and night, always trying to correct our "incorrect" ways. We described his antics as "chicken shit."

On 26 February, the Monday following our arrival at H-1-1, we began our eight weeks of Basic Training. We began a daily schedule that was filled with concentrated, intense, non-stop instruction. The topics for the first two weeks were very diverse, familiarizing us with elementary dismounted drill and ceremonies, among other things. The main reason for such instruction was to impart discipline and military tradition into our previously civilian heads.

The dismounted drill was a method of teaching us to work together, and be able to respond instantly and correctly, to commands. It was supposed to turn us into reliable parts of a cohesive Army unit and prepare us for more advanced instruction.

Our daily schedule was basically as shown below:

0430 hours (4:30 a.m.) Reveille—dress, shave and wash up, make bed to Army standards, and quickly clean designated barracks area.

0500 (5 a.m.) formation—daily information disseminated by drill instructor, and march to mess hall for breakfast. At this time recruits could go on sick call (dispensary to see a doctor).

0600 (6 a.m.) police call and PT (Physical Training).

0700 (7 a.m.) formation—movement to training area.

1130 (11:30 a.m.) marched or transported to mess hall for lunch.

1230 (12:30 p.m.) formation—movement to training area.

1630 (4:30 p.m.) formation—march to mess hall for dinner.

1730 (5:30 p.m.) drill instructor briefing and mail call, the most important event for mental stability.

1800 (6 p.m.) personal time—shine boots, polish brass, general cleanup, relax, read a book, write letters until:

2100 (9 p.m.) lights out (bedtime) for the barracks.

Bugle calls, broadcast over loudspeaker systems throughout the main part of military posts, announced most of the important "military times." "First Call" was the initial bugle call one might hear daily. It was the same call as could be heard at a horseracing track when it was "Post Time." It was designed to wake people up.

"Reveille" was played at the time the flags were raised on post. "Retreat" was played when flags were lowered. When "Reveille" or "Retreat" was played, everyone on post was supposed to stop what they were doing, stand at attention (stop the vehicle, exit, and stand at attention if in a vehicle), and salute the nearest flag. Taps was played at the official end of the day, and at funerals.

Reveille was followed by an NCO (known as a CQ, Charge of Quarters) coming through the barracks screaming at the top of his lungs or banging garbage can lids like cymbals to wake us from our deep, weary, sleep. We all began getting ready for the day as quickly as possible, and thoroughly cleaning our living quarters, sweeping and mopping the floors and making the latrines look pristine. There were no morning doldrums permitted.

Activity began immediately. We learned very quickly that no morning laziness was permitted. Morning formation was the initial formation and roll call, followed by marching to the mess hall for breakfast. Following breakfast was another formation, followed by Police Call, then close to an hour of physical training (PT).

When we marched or ran, we usually chanted cadence, led by the NCO or lieutenant in charge of the event. The initial cadence called by the cadre leading us was either "Left, Right, Left, Right," etc., and "One, Two, Three, Four, One, Two, Three, Four," etc. When running, the numbers would only be chanted as the left foot struck the ground. Cadence chants aided recruits keeping in step.

Later chants we used would now be deemed extremely politically incorrect. Chants included references to one's genitals, sex acts, nationalities, etc. One of the later marching chants we learned was "You're in the Army now, you're not behind a plow; you'll never get rich, by digging a ditch; you're in the Army now."

Some other favorite chants were:

- Got a gal, lives on a hill; she won't do it, but her sister will.
- I want to be an Airborne Ranger; I want to live a life of danger.
- Don't know, but I've been told, Army wings are made of gold; I don't know, I've heard it said, Navy wings are made of lead.
- Ain't no use in looking down, there ain't no discharge on the ground.
- Cadre: You had a good home, but you left.
- Troops: You're right!
- Cadre: You had a good home, but you left.
- Troops: You're right!Cadre: Sound off.
- Troops: Sound off!
- Cadre: Sound off.
- Troops: Sound off!
- Cadre: 1-2-3-4 Sound off.
- Troops: Sound off!
- See the girl from Kansas City? She serves whiskey from her titties. See the lady wearing black? She makes her living on her back.

Jody was a favorite fictitious civilian target of military chants. He was despised by all military men. Jody was everything bad, when it came to civilians. He was a backstabbing, home wrecking, thieving, draft dodging son-of-a-bitch. Some samples of his work were included in these chants:

- Ain't no use in going home, Jody's got your girl and gone.
- Ain't no use in feeling blue, Jody's got your sister too.
- Ain't no sense in looking back, Jody's got your Cadillac.
- Your baby was lonely as can be, 'til Jody provided some company.

The Army was fanatic about neatness. In fact, the Army preached cleanliness. I have never seen anybody or any organization that was so fanatical about cleanliness as the Army, except hospitals.

A favorite joke was telling about the sergeant who walked into his barracks screaming, "Why is there trash in my trash can?" I can still remember a drill instructor yelling at us because he found cigarette butts in the barracks butt cans.

Police Call was nothing more than a formation to clean the exterior company area of ALL items that were not part of the landscaping, and sometimes those things that were naturally there, like pine cones. Believe it or not, there was an Army way to pick up trash also. The NCO lined us up, side by side, an arm's length between each of us. He would then order us to move out.

A favorite directive was that the sergeant wanted to see nothing but asses and elbows, picking up everything that didn't belong on the ground in front of each of us. The Army hated cigarette butts. Even though we were taught how to field strip a cigarette, many soldiers seemed to delight in disobeying that order. The fact that cigarette filters existed made field-stripping even more difficult.

Inspections were the norm during Army life. During training we were subjected to inspection several times a day. Once a week we had major inspections, where the cadre would come through the barracks looking through everything, including our personal items. The truth is, if an inspector wanted to fail you, they could and would.

There was nothing you could do if an inspector wanted you to fail. There were just too many ways to fail an inspection. I went through one instance where, as hard as I looked, I could not find the flaw that an inspector pointed out to me. He saw a speck of dust that I couldn't see, even with my 20-20 vision. He didn't want me to get a weekend pass, so I didn't.

When you saw the inspector put on a white glove for inspection, you knew you were screwed. There was no way to perfectly clean a barracks. No matter how hard you tried, that asshole could get dust on his white glove. There were even weekly inspections after being assigned to a unit. The penalty for failing an inspection in a unit was the revocation of the weekend pass. That really sucked.

The Army even had an annual inspection, called the IG (Inspector General) Inspection, during which ALL unit items were inspected and accounted for with a fine-tooth comb. There were Army men who specialized in inspecting units. The IG was the most hated inspection of all.

PT was a mix of exercises that included push-ups, sit-ups, eight-count push-ups (also known as burpees), squat jumps, jumping jacks, etc., followed by a run (double-time in formation, and in step). PT would be on my schedule every morning for more than a year of the training lying ahead for me. It would become a part of daily life.

On occasion, it would be our turn on the duty roster to be the company Fireguard. Fireguards became an important nightly duty during the days of wooden barracks, heated by wood or coal fired heating units. Each barracks had to have one man on fireguard from the time of "lights out' until reveille.

Besides watching for fires, it was the duty of the Fireguard to be an area security guard and to report any recruit attempting to go AWOL. The Fireguard duty shift lasted two hours per recruit. At the end of his two hours, the recruit on duty would awaken the next recruit scheduled to relieve him. Another nightly duty was CQ Runner. The CQ Runner was detailed to perform various jobs for the CQ.

Every Friday night was GI Party time. That meant that the entire unit was required to clean the barracks, scrubbing all noticeable, as well as non-noticeable, objects, not missing a thing. The barracks, the unit area, and the troops, had to be ready for a white glove inspection the following morning. Inspections included every individual's wall and footlockers. Nothing was private. It was all out there, and unlocked, for everyone to see.

The second day we were issued our M-1 Garand rifles. As future combat soldiers, our weapons would become our most important pieces of equipment. We were immediately told that the weapon would ALWAYS be referred to as a rifle, NEVER a gun.

Punishment for referring to our rifle as a gun would result in public humiliation, in the form of standing in front of the unit, rifle in hand. The miscreant would have to raise his rifle, stating, "This is my rifle," followed by grabbing his crotch and stating, "This is my gun," raising his rifle again, stating, "This is for killing," and grabbing his crotch again, stating, "This is for fun." We were shown how to march with our rifles, and marched back to our barracks, where we placed our rifles in a locked rack, in a locked arms room.

"But that was war. Just about all he could find in its favor was that it paid well and liberated children from the pernicious influence of their parents." — Joseph Heller, Catch-22

There was very little free time, which bothered many of the recruits very much. It was a very difficult lifestyle change for most of them. It wasn't that difficult for me. Even though I had been going to college, I lived with my parents and had to account to my parents for every minute. That made it a lot easier for me to adapt to the Army. Also, as a child we had moved a lot, so I didn't rely a lot on friends, and was used to adapting to new situations.

"Mail Call" was the most popular time of the day. It was a daily ritual (except Sundays), usually toward the end of the day. A mail clerk (or cadre) would call out the name on each piece of mail, and the soldier it was addressed to would answer, "Here!" (or, "Here, Sergeant") and go forward to be given the letter (or package). Receiving mail was always a great feeling. Having no mail (especially if it happened too many days in a row) was dejecting. Of course, "Dear John" letters were worse than nothing, and quite a few of those were delivered to service members.

Unbelievably, the Army even had a special way to seat oneself. Just when I thought we had already covered all the strange nuances of Army life, we were instructed in the Army method of sitting, being further reminded that there is the right way, the wrong way, and the Army way of doing almost everything. We were marched into the classroom and ordered to remain standing in front of our seats. The drill instructor then explained the art of seating oneself.

Of course, as in almost all Army movement commands, there was a preparatory command prior to sitting. We were told that when being seated, all the trainees had to sit in unison. The preparatory command was, "TAKE," at which time all men would prepare their bodies to sit. That was followed by the command, "SEATS!" at which time all men would immediately sit, in perfect unison. We had to practice that "simple" movement numerous times, before we finally did it "correctly."

Among the first things we learned were the Army structure, ranks, the official chain of command (all the way up to the President of the United States, who was the Commander-in-Chief [CIC]), who and what we were required to salute, and how we were to do so.

There was only one way to salute, the U.S. Army way, of course. The salute was to be rendered very smartly, with the right hand. The hand was brought up to the front tip of whatever hat was being worn (or forehead, if a hat was not worn), with the thumb and fingers rigidly extended and held together, palm facing downward. The tips of the longest fingers were to touch the front of the cap (or forehead), the outside edge tilted very slightly downward.

There were three basic combat arms branches within the Army: Infantry, Armor and Artillery. Those were the branches that most often engaged directly in combat. The Infantry was the basic arm, primarily utilized to close with the enemy. Armor was the mobile arm, generally considered to be the speedy method of bringing violence upon the enemy. Artillery provided long-range fire support for the Infantry and Armor.

The Army also had numerous service and special branches attached to it. The Service Arms included the Corps of Engineers (construction and destruction), Signal Corps (communications and surveillance), Military Police Corps (law & order and security), Adjutant General's Corps (personnel administrative services), Quartermaster Corps

2nd Lt. Joseph L. Rheney
Mess and Executive Officer

2nd Lt. Jack R. Musselman
Platoon Leader

E-8 Robert D. Gossard
First Sergeant

E-7 Billy R. Burris
SDI

M/Sgt. A. Agpalasin

SFC Wm. R. Akers
Supply Sergeant

SFC J. Montgomery

Sgt. Carmona

Sgt. Tyler

Sgt. Walton

Cpl. McDonald
Company Armorer

Cpl. Smith

PFC Case

Pvt. E-2 Faucett
General Clerk

The cadre that was assigned to my Basic Training unit. (graduation book photo) (supplies and equipment), Finance Corps (all financial matters), Ordnance Corps (weapons, ammunition, etc.), Transportation Corps (land transportation), Chemical Corps (chemical, biological, and radiological [CBR] warfare), Women's Army Corps (clerical, administrative, and technical duties), and Intelligence & Security (self-explanatory).

Among the Special Branches were Judge Advocate General's Corps (legal branch), Chaplains (morality and religion), Army Medical Service (all matters of health), Inspectors General (confidential agents and unit inspectors), and Army Aviation (not considered to be a separate combat arms or corps at the time).

The Army rank structure was as follows (E numbers denoted enlisted pay grades; specialists being paid the same as NCOs in the same pay grade, but were not considered to be in leadership positions), from the bottom to the top:

Enlisted Grades
    Private E-1 (no stripe on sleeve)
    Private E-2 (no stripe)
    Private First Class E-3 (one chevron stripe)

Non-Commissiond Officers *(Except the Specialist Grades)*
    Corporal E-4 (two chevrons)
    Specialist 4th Class E-4 (eagle on sleeve)
    Sergeant E-5 (three chevrons)
    Specialist 5th Class E-5 (upside-down rocker over eagle)
    Staff Sergeant E-6 (3 chevrons & 1 rocker)
    Specialist 6th Class E-6 (2 upside-down rockers/eagle)
    Sergeant First Class E-7 (3 chevrons/2 rockers)
    Specialist 7th Class E-7 (3 upside-down rockers/eagle)
    Master Sergeant E-8 (3 chevrons/3 rockers)
    Specialist 8th Class E-8 (4 upside-down rockers/eagle)
    First Sergeant E-8 (3 chevrons/3 rockers/diamond in middle)
    Sergeant Major E-9 (3 chevrons/3 rockers/star in middle)
    Command Sergeant Major E-9 (3 chevrons/3 rockers/eagle in middle)

Warrant Officer Grades *(Not normally considered to be leadership positions)*
  Warrant Officer 1 W-1
  Chief Warrant Officer 2 W-2
  Chief Warrant Officer 3 W-3
  Chief Warrant Officer 4 W-4
  Chief Warrant Officer 5 W-5

Commissioned Officer Ranks
  Second Lieutenant O-1 (gold bar)
  First Lieutenant O-2 (silver bar)
  Captain O-3 (2 silver bars)
  Major O-4 (gold oak leaf)
  Lieutenant Colonel O-5 (silver oak leaf)
  Colonel O-6 (silver eagle)
  Brigadier General O-7 (one gold star)
  Major General O-8 (two gold stars)
  Lieutenant General O-9 (three gold stars)
  General O-10 (four gold stars)

We were warned that first sergeants and sergeants major were to be considered as next things to God by us. If they asked us to jump, our only question should be "How high, first sergeant," or "How high, sergeant major." We were also advised that first sergeants were sometimes called "Top," "Top Sergeant," "First Soldier, "First Shirt," and "First Pig" (which had better be said with reverence).

I had already learned who, what, and how to salute in college Air Force R.O.T.C., so our lesson on that subject was a review for me with not much new to learn. Saluting began in ancient times, to indicate that the individual doing the saluting meant no harm and was not carrying a weapon in his hand. During the era of knights, the knight would raise the visor of his helmet, thus revealing his face, to show he meant no harm.

In more modern times, the gesture was changed to removing one's hat, as in tipping a hat to a lady. That was altered to moving the hand to the hat, after headgear became strapped on, and difficult to remove. The hand to the hat, or forehead if hatless, became ritualistic, done with a snappy gesture, in modern times.

When and who to salute was generally determined by the major local or area commander. In general, persons entitled to a salute included all U.S. military commissioned and warrant officers, as well as commissioned officers of nations friendly to the U.S.

When outdoors, all military members were also required to salute any general officer in a vehicle, provided the vehicle bore the general officer's star on the license plate. When outdoors in a group that was not in formation, if an officer approached, the first man to notice the officer was required to call the group to attention, followed by the entire group saluting the officer.

When reporting to an officer, enlisted men were required to stand at attention and salute the officer upon reporting, as well as just prior to departing. Enlisted men were also required to salute an officer after a conversation with him, as either of you were prepared to leave. All military were required to salute the National Colors or Standards (flag) when out of doors and when the National Anthem or To the Color was playing, again when out of doors.

When the National Anthem or To the Color was played, even moving vehicles had to be brought to a halt. Persons in the vehicle or on motorcycles were then required to dismount (exit the vehicle), stand at attention facing the music or flag, and smartly render a salute until the last note had sounded. It was also stressed that the flag of the United States of America represented the living country and was therefore considered to be a living thing.

A favorite phrase, if we were in doubt as to who and when to salute, was "If it moves, salute it." You couldn't get into trouble for saluting a person or thing that was not deemed worthy of a salute, but heaven help you if you missed saluting a person or thing that was worthy of a salute.

Next, we learned how to determine military time (which is based on a 24-hour clock, rather than the civilian 12-hour clock). It was a much better method of stating time, as there was less chance for error. If, for instance, a commander was to schedule a meeting for 6 o'clock, the meeting time could be at 6 a.m., or 6 p.m. Stating the meeting time being at 0600 hours (6 a.m.) or 1800 hours (6 p.m.) erased all doubt.

Any time that was in the morning (a.m.) was the same as civilian (omitting the colon [:]), whereas afternoon and evening hours were determined by adding 12 to the civilian time (again omitting the colon [:]). As an example, 6:30 a.m. civilian time was described as 0630 hours (zero-six-thirty, or oh-six-thirty) in the military, and 4:00 p.m. was 1600 hours (sixteen hundred, or one six hundred). From the beginning, all our schedules were given to us in military time. Some of the poor recruits had to use their fingers to determine afternoon military times, but the 24-hour clock became second nature after a few months. I still use it.

On the 28th we all received our first paycheck. The Army paid once a month, on the final working day of the month, in cash. We were lined up in front of the Paymaster for our pay. "Sir, Private James reporting for pay!" followed by a snappy salute, since the Paymaster was always an officer. WOW! I received a whopping $78. That was where I learned of the "philanthropic" nature of the U.S. Army.

All of us were HIGHLY urged to donate a certain minimum amount to United Way. It was a little more than a hint. I later learned that one thing commanding officers were rated on was their ability to entice their men into donating monthly to causes endorsed by the Army.

If you truly considered our profession to be a 24-hour-a-day job, then we were being paid about 11 cents per hour. Even if you considered our job an 8-hour-a-day, 5-days-a-week job (didn't I wish!), we were only being paid 44 cents per hour.

There was a lot of classroom training in basic, including a course on 2 March, in which we were taught the UCMJ (Uniform Code of Military Justice), which covered behavior while in the military, and the punishment that could be meted out if that code of behavior was not adhered to. We were especially warned of the punishment for going AWOL (Absent Without Leave).

There was a vast array of Army regulations to become familiar with, some seeming very petty. There were also numerous rules and codes to memorize word-by-word, including the Code of Conduct and General

Orders. Following the UCMJ class was the Code of Conduct class, in which we learned the Code of Conduct and General Orders. I was to learn later, that memorization of the Code of Conduct and General Orders would become very beneficial, especially when detailed to guard duty.

The Code of Conduct

(1) I am an American fighting man. I serve in the forces which guard my country and our way of life. I am prepared to give my life in their defense.

(2) I will never surrender of my own free will. If in command I will never surrender my men while they still have the means to resist.

(3) If I am captured I will continue to resist by all means available. I will make every effort to escape and aid others to escape. I will accept neither parole nor special favors from the enemy.

(4) If I become a prisoner of war, I will keep faith with my fellow prisoners. I will give no information or take part in any action which might be harmful to my comrades. If I am senior, I will take command. If not, I will obey the lawful orders of those appointed over me and will back them up in any way.

(5) When questioned, should I become a prisoner of war, I am bound to give only name, rank, service number, and date of birth. I will evade answering further questions to the utmost of my ability. I will make no oral or written statements disloyal to my country and its allies or harmful to their cause.

(6) I will never forget that I am an American Fighting Man, responsible for my actions, and dedicated to the principles which made my country free. I will trust in my God and in the United States of America.

General Orders

(1) To take charge of this post and all Government property in view.

(2) To walk my post in a military manner, keeping always on the alert and observing everything that takes place within sight or hearing.

(3) To report all violations of orders I am instructed to enforce.

(4) To repeat all calls from posts more distant from the guardhouse

than my own.

(5) To quit my post only when properly relieved.

(6) To receive, obey, and pass on to the sentinel who relieves me all orders from the commanding officer, officer of the day, and officers and noncommissioned officers of the guard only.

(7) To talk to no one except in the line of duty.

(8) To give the alarm in case of fire or disorder.

(9) To call the commander of the relief in any case not covered by instructions.

(10) To salute all officers, and all colors and standards not cased.

(11) To be especially watchful at night and, during the time for challenging, to challenge all persons on or near my post and to allow no one to pass without proper authority.

In the same vein was our class on the rules of warfare. It sounds counter-productive, but there actually were rules about how a war was to be fought. I had always felt that the best way to win a fight was, basically, to cheat. I mean, what the hell; if you're trying to win a fight (who in the hell wants to lose it) you should use every trick in the book, fair or not, to do so. Here we were being told that we had to kill, or be killed, fairly. Wow! What a strange concept.

The rules of modern warfare (at the time) had been initiated at the Geneva Conventions, and were officially called "International Humanitarian Law." The most recent rules had been formulated in 1949, after World War II, to address the many atrocities that so many people had been subjected to during that war. The initial Geneva Convention had been held in 1864, at the behest of the "International Committee for Relief to the Wounded," later known as the "International Red Cross." International Humanitarian Law did not forbid war, but defined how wars were to be fought humanitarianly, if that was possible.

To begin with, it was stipulated that any hostilities not be initiated until such time a "declaration of war" was announced, or at the very least, that an ultimatum be announced, with a conditional declaration of war. Some obviously excellent rules were that it was illegal to (1) misuse a white flag (the symbol of surrender — in other words, you could not wave the white flag, then attack the enemy as it approached),

(2) kill or injure anyone who has surrendered, (3) attack anyone who is defenseless, or (4) attack any structure or location that is being used as a hospital. In fact, injured or debilitated troops, medical personnel, and chaplains were given protection, and the wounded or sick had to be given medical treatment, friend or foe, and treated humanely.

Prisoners of war were also protected by the Geneva Conventions, limiting what could or could not be done with them. POWs could be asked basic questions, only to identify them, such as determining their rank for purposes of treating them to the respect they deserved for their rank and status. Beyond that, POWs could not legally be forced to answer other questions, and were, in fact, not required to answer any questions.

Torture was strictly forbidden, as was the threat of punishment. It was also stipulated that no armed force could use the enemy's flag or uniform/insignia, or the Red Cross symbol, for their own purpose. The use of chemical and/or biological weapons was strictly forbidden, as was the use of any weapon or ammunition whose purpose was to inflict maximum pain or suffering.

One of the classes we attended was the venereal disease class. Of all classes, it was the UGLIEST! We saw a slide show, during which we were "privileged" to see, what were probably the ugliest cases of venereal diseases to have been seen, in the history of the U.S. Army. Those photos were just plain gross. I don't know how many other men were affected by the class, but it sure as hell scared the crap out of me. It almost made me want to remain a virgin.

Those images have remained in my mind ever since I viewed them. They affected my thoughts about sex, until the first time I saw a good-looking woman, while I was drunk. My next meal was difficult to eat, after seeing all those rotted penises. Leave it to the Army to ruin my mental stability and my appetite.

Some of the classes were so boring that, especially with the lack of sleep, it was very difficult to remain awake. Because of the varying degree of intelligence and education of the recruits, instruction had to be geared for the lowest level of intelligence and education. That made it very difficult for many of us to maintain our interest. That was especially true on a warm day, soon after eating a big breakfast, and enduring physical training, which had made us tired.

We were told to be on the alert for Communist spies in and around our base, who might want information about activities on the base. We were warned not to discuss military matters with any stranger, especially if they had a foreign accent.

The company headquarters (orderly room) kept a duty roster. All eligible troops were on the duty roster. The duty roster was used to make sure all company details (KP, guard duty, CQ runner, etc.) were assigned equitably. It was a requirement that all men in the company check the duty roster on a regular basis to check for possible detail assignments. Missing a detail assignment was inexcusable.

I quickly learned to dislike (in addition to Army food) the petty details that were thought up to keep us busier than we needed to be. Not long after being assigned to the training company, and despite my new temporary rank of corporal, I had to stand fireguard. Fireguard began at the time of "lights out" in the barracks. There was one Fireguard per floor in the barracks. It required that the person on watch be vigilant for fire in the barracks. In case of fire, he was to shout "Fire," pull the fire alarm, and wake every person on his designated floor. Fire watch was a two-hour detail. I usually wrote letters during fire watch but was unhappy at the thought of losing two hours sleep when I had the detail.

Another boring overnight detail was that of CQ runner. The CQ was the "Charge of Quarters." He was usually an NCO who was in temporary command of the company area during the overnight hours. He stayed in the orderly room. As CQ runner, I had to stay awake to answer phones and deliver messages to the barracks, while the CQ slept in the orderly room.

Equally stupid, to me, was the ritual of removing hard wax from the floor of the barracks floor, utilizing a dull mess kit knife, followed by immediately re-waxing the floor. I guess it made sense to the Army, in some unknown way, but the sense of it flew right over my head, never to be understood. It certainly wasn't easy work.

The most hated duty roster detail a soldier could be assigned to was KP (Kitchen Police, aka kitchen patrol or keep peeling). It began extremely early in the morning (sometimes 0300 hours—3am), and was a very dirty, sweaty job, unless you were fortunate enough to be assigned to the only semi-clean job in the mess hall, dining room orderly, and didn't end until the mess hall was spic and span, sometime after the final meal of the day. Favored troops, and/or the first to arrive at the mess hall on their duty day, usually were able to get the cushy or easier jobs.

I felt the worst KP job by far was cleaning the grease trap, pots, and pans, especially on already warm days. The poor individual working that job was known as the "pots & pans man." The grease trap was a large box that collected all the grease from each meal's preparation. It had to be cleaned three times a day, well enough to pass a white glove inspection. It is impossible to accurately describe the horrors of having to deal with that terrible piece of equipment. Cusswords would be the only accurate description, with "repulsive" being included in the mix.

Whereas silverware and meal trays could be placed in a dishwashing machine, such was not the case for pots and pans. Those had to be scrubbed and rinsed, and scrubbed and rinsed again, until spic and span, utilizing scalding hot water. After completion of the job, the trainee was uncomfortably soaked, clear through, from water and sweat.

Many men complained about peeling potatoes, but it was, in actuality, a very clean job, although tedious. It meant making sure hundreds of potatoes were entirely peel-less. Some mess halls made the job easier, by have an automatic potato peeler. It consisted of a large tumbler that had a sandpaper-like interior. You dumped the spuds inside, turned on the machine, and let the rotating tumbler do the work. Of course, the machine didn't remove all the skin, so each potato would have to be inspected and the remaining skin removed by hand.

As civilians, when we cook we try to limit the amount of pots, pans, and utensils we dirty, knowing that we need to clean them ourselves. Such was not the case in the Army. The cooks had their KPs to wash their soiled wares, so there was no need, nor attempt, to think about the work they were creating as they prepared the meal.

I learned the meaning of, and need for, "midnight requisitioning," aka "scrounging" while in Basic. Equipment needed for a job at hand was not always available to the unit. In that case borrowing, without permission, also known as "midnight requisitioning," was the ultimate operation for mission accomplishment. It sometimes became a lifesaving proposition in Vietnam.

We came to realize, very rapidly, that if one of our group screwed up, all of us would pay. This was true in Basic Training, Advanced Individual Training, and Jump School. It became very easy to hate a constant screw-up. When you threw a bunch of young men from different backgrounds and races into a new, difficult, stressful situation, tempers had a way of flaring. I witnessed a couple fistfights in the barracks during training.

Trainees had a way of punishing those who were constant troublemakers or screw-ups. This special punishment was termed a "blanket party." It was an effective, although brutal, way to mete out punishment for wrongdoing. While the target was sleeping, a blanket was thrown over him (so that he could not identify the perpetrators, and to reduce his chances of struggling). The subject was then beat, painfully, but not badly enough to require hospitalization.

I never saw or participated in a blanket party but did witness recruits being threatened with one. Just the threat of a blanket party was enough for the perpetrator to mend his ways. Blanket parties were against regulations in the Army, but the act was well known and, on extreme occasions, used.

Some of the hardest things for new recruits to learn in Basic Training was the "manual at arms" and movement while in formation, also known as dismounted drill. This came easy to me because of my experience in college Air Force R.O.T.C. First, we learned dismounted drill, when not carrying our rifles. The initial lessons comprised of "TEN-HUT" (the position of attention), "AT EASE", "PARADE REST," "LEFT FACE," "RIGHT FACE," and "ABOUT FACE," as well as how and under what circumstances to salute.

There was only one right way to accomplish a left face, right face, or about face. The most difficult of them was the "about face" movement. It was comical watching some of the trainees as they attempted to do a correct "about face." They just couldn't get their foot movements down correctly, tripping over their own feet as they tried.

Unbelievably, some poor souls didn't even seem to know the difference between left and right. Occasionally the drill instructor would order "LEFT FACE," and some idiot would execute a right face. To that, the favorite reaction of the drill instructor was to scream, of course loud enough for everyone within a 100-yard radius to hear, "YOUR OTHER LEFT, DUMBASS!"

When at the position of attention, we were to stand ramrod straight, with both arms straight down, thumbs and forefingers touching pants seams, heels together, toes slightly out, knees locked in place, shoulders straight, stomach in, chest out, chin tucked in, eyes looking straight ahead. No movement was permitted while at attention.

When a group formed for inspection, or any official movement or announcements, the designated leader first called it to the position of attention. To do that, the leader assumed the position of attention, then announced loudly, "GROUP (or other unit designation), TEN-HUT." "Ten-hut" was short for "stand at attention." After that order, numerous movement and/or position orders could be given.

After learning the rudiments of the individual movements, the instructors tried to teach our group of malcontents (most of them had been drafted) the unit marching movements. When learning group movements, we began with the most basic lessons, namely marching, and doing it in step. That was a boondoggle. Even with the help of the cadre, "FORWARD . . . MARCH . . . LEFT . . . RIGHT . . . LEFT . . . RIGHT," etc., it was a group that looked as if it would never learn to march anywhere near correctly. Surprisingly, the group seemed to learn, slowly but surely. Of course, this led to the cadre graduating from the "LEFT, RIGHT," to the normal military marching cadence count, "HUT . . . TWO . . . THREE . . . FOUR . . . HUT . . . TWO," etc.

The Army manual stated that the speed at which all soldiers would march was 76 steps per minute. Some of the trainees had to be taken aside and given individual instruction, but they eventually got it. We then moved on to the more difficult column and large formation marching.

Next was learning how to do all the former movements while toting our rifles. By the end of our eight-week training cycle, some of us looked decent. I had done the marching, facing movements, etc., in R.O.T.C., but never with a rifle. That was a learning situation for me.

The Army had this thing about memory aids. Their favorite was using words to help remember learning points. Some of their favorites were:

Reporting Information (SALUTE)
S ize
A ctivity
L ocation
U nit
T ime
E quipment

Terrain Analysis (COCOA)
C ritical features
O bservation
C over and concealment
O bstacles
A venues of approach and withdrawal

Prisoners of War (SSSSS)
S earch
S eparate
S ilence
S peed
S afeguarding

There seemed to be an acronym for just about everything, including keeping things simple. The favorite acronym for that was KISS:

K eep
I t
S simple
S tupid

Although the Air Force has always considered 15 November 1961 to be the official start of America's advisory war in Vietnam, the Army and Navy claim the beginning date to be 15 March 1962, while I was going through Basic Training. 15 March officially began what would be known as the first of seventeen campaigns in the Vietnam War, that of the "Advisory Campaign." This, even though Military Assistance Advisory Group (MAAG) personnel had been officially authorized to accompany South Vietnamese units into combat on 20 January, and the 1st Special Forces Group began sending Green Berets to South Vietnam on 24 June 1957, well before the official beginning date for the Army. In fact, the first advisors were a 35-man MAAG team that had arrived in country on 2 August 1950.

On 21 September 1961, President John F. Kennedy had announced that the United States would provide additional military and economic aid to South Vietnam. In January 1962, there were 746 U.S. advisors in the field in Vietnam. That number would jump to more than 3,400 by June.

On 2 February 1962, three U.S. Air Force personnel were killed (KIA) onboard a C-123 when it was shot down during a defoliant training mission in South Vietnam. Only nine days later (11 February) six airmen and two MAAG soldiers were KIA when their SC-47 Air Commando aircraft was shot down during a leaflet-drop mission.

Finally, on the day I enlisted (14 February), American soldiers were officially authorized to fire on the enemy IF the enemy had fired at them first. The first Special Forces soldiers were KIA on 7 and 8 April. At that time, I had no idea what Special Forces was. Two members of Detachment A-335, Company C, 1st Special Forces Group were captured, THEN EXECUTED, after a firefight. Two other Green Berets were captured during that same encounter, and later released. Less than two years later, I would be serving with, and later going overseas with, one of those released Green Berets. And so it began!

The first aid training we received was very basic, but still something brand new for most of us. Medics were brought in to teach us how and when to use the equipment in a basic first aid kit. The skills used in making and using an improvised splint for an arm or leg were demonstrated, followed by each of us constructing a splint. We received the same training for tourniquets, being warned never to leave a tourniquet in place for long periods of time, but to loosen it occasionally.

Because soldiers carried weapons and worked in a situation where bullet wounds and wounds caused by explosive devices were common, classes were presented on how to treat and dress a gunshot or burn wound. We were also taught how to determine whether a snake was poisonous or not, and how to treat a poisonous snake bite, as well as being shown, and subsequently required to demonstrate, artificial respiration.

The gas chamber was probably the most disliked part of training. It was hard to get used to the fact that the Army was going to put its own troops (me included) through a gas chamber and fill the air with chemicals that were normally reserved for the enemy, as a last-ditch resort. We received classroom training on chemical warfare. Warning signs and recommended actions to take were covered, as was information about each known chemical.

Training included the use of the Army issue gas mask. We learned the accepted methods of donning the mask, speed being one of the essential tasks. We were then taken to the gas chamber. We were led into the chamber in small groups (about a dozen each), with gas masks already on our heads, and ordered to stand against the outside walls of the small shed, backs against the walls. Instructors stood in the middle, facing the recruits. CS gas, 2-chlorobenzalmalononitrile (also called o-chlorobenzylidene malononitrile), was released.

As the gas spread inside the structure, the instructors ordered us to take off our gas masks, keeping an eye on each of us, looking for signs of panic or inability to follow orders. The symptoms came almost immediately, including eyes burning, tearing, burning in the nose, runny nose, burning in the throat, coughing, rising blood pressure, very hard to breathe, and in some cases, nausea and vomiting. We were then individually asked questions, including our names and serial numbers. That's when all of us wished our serial numbers were a lot shorter.

It was difficult remaining calm, which was what was expected of us. After everyone completed answering the questions, one at a time, we were ordered to put our gas mask back on. We did so, quickly, but correctly. Any mistake required starting all over. We certainly learned quickly, that it was a lot easier donning the mask correctly in class than with the real thing.

I was happy to exit the building upon completion of the training session. The outside fresh air never felt so good, and we began to feel better very quickly. During later field training, we had gas masks as part of our equipment. At unannounced times one of the cadre threw a smoke grenade, used to simulate a gas attack. We were to react as if it was a gas attack, donning our gas masks as instructed.

Can you say "M-O-O-O-O?" We were transported almost everywhere on "cattle trucks." They were long flatbed semi-trailers that had about three or four-foot-high wood sides. I felt like saying, "MOO" every time we rode on one of those trailers. When we were ready to depart, the rear gate of the trailer was lowered, portable steps were hung on the rear, and we climbed them to get onboard, like cattle loading via special chutes. Wood benches went the length of the trailers, from front to rear, in the middle and on the sides. We sat on the benches, facing outward and inward, with no seatbelts. The trailers were long enough, so that more men could fit in them than in a bus.

As one could imagine, the ride wasn't anywhere close to the "comfort" of a bus. Sometimes I swore the truck driver missed gears on purpose, just to make our ride as uncomfortable as possible. They were also experts at hitting potholes.

On rare occasions we got to ride on our version of a limousine,: a rattletrap bus, the driver of which always seemed to have troubles shifting gears smoothly. I don't know what it was about military drivers, driving manual transmission (stick-shift) vehicles, but almost all of them had trouble shifting gears. It was not unusual at all to hear the grinding of metal against metal, and the resulting jerk caused by a missed gear.

"If a country is worth living in, it is worth fighting for." — Manning Coles

The rifle used by the Army in 1962 was the M-1 Garand, a World

War II era relic (originally going into production in 1936): single-shot, shoulder fired, air cooled, eight-cartridge capacity clip, .30-caliber, 11¼ pound, semi-automatic rifle.[1] The Garand was heavy and cumbersome. The M-1 Garand was the Special Forces issued rifle until the mid-1960s.

We were given two weeks of training on the M-1, which mostly included marksmanship. We learned all the specifications of the weapon. It had a maximum range of 3,450 yards, and a maximum effective range of 500 yards. Maximum range was the greatest distance at which the rifle was expected to fire, inflicting casualties or damage. Maximum effective range was the greatest distance at which the rifle was expected to fire accurately.

The M-1 was known to cause a very painful "M-1 thumb" if the correct procedure was not followed when loading the ammunition clip into the rifle. First, the operating rod handle was firmly pulled back, as far as possible. Then it was permitted to gently move forward, until stopped by a latch, making sure the bolt and operating rod handle were securely locked.

The right thumb was used to press the clip into place from the top. The clip was loaded into the chamber from above, pressing down with the thumb, keeping your hand extended down the right side of the rifle, just forward of the operating rod handle, making sure the clip was seated and locked in place. Then, the thumb was withdrawn VERY quickly, while pulling the hand up from the weapon receiver. Slowpokes learn the lesson the hard way, the result being a very red, sore, thumb that hurt for quite a while, reminding the soldier that he screwed up. I learned that the difficult way, by error. Many were the "M-1 thumb" I suffered through.

We were taught how to field strip the rifle — in other words, how to take the weapon apart, to fix it if it was malfunctioning, or to clean it. That, of course, meant that you had to remember where each part belonged, to put it back together again, functioning.

The instructors first showed us, step by step, how to disassemble, and then assemble, the M-1. They reminded us that we might have to break down our weapon at night, reminding us also how important doing it correctly would be, while in a combat situation.

There were contests to see who could disassemble and reassemble his rifle the fastest, including while wearing a blindfold, to simulate field stripping the weapon at night. It was best to know how to do this blindfolded, in case it was required while in a combat situation in the dark. We were then shown how to perform maintenance on the rifle, including cleaning the inside of the barrel.

We were also given a very short orientation on the Army-issue Colt 1911A1 .45-caliber pistol. This weapon had been a mainstay of the Army since World War I. Its design was based on John Browning's original 1898 patent for a recoil-operated autoloader mechanism. It had been an official U.S. armed forces sidearm longer than any other continuous-use military weapon in any nation's history. Its simple user-friendly design couldn't be beat for reliability, endurance, and effectiveness.

The 1911A1 was an air-cooled, semi-automatic, recoil-operated, magazine fed (7 bullets) hand weapon. When a person was hit by the big, slow moving (825 feet per second) bullet, they knew it. It had great stopping power and made the pistol a good personal weapon. Its downside was its range and accuracy. It had a maximum range of 1,500 meters, but a maximum effective range of only 50 meters, making it best suited for close-in combat and self-protection. We were taught how to disassemble and assemble the weapon for cleaning, as well as some of the idiosyncrasies of the weapon.

It wasn't until a few days into our weapons training that we were finally issued ammunition and were able to fire our rifles. The Army wanted to make sure we could understand and follow directions, before permitting us to handle a loaded weapon. We were transported to the firing range on one of Fort Ord's infamous cattle trucks. It was a short ride to the firing ranges on the dunes next to Monterey Bay. The dunes were used as the backdrop for the firing ranges. A large area on the other side of the dunes, on Monterey Bay, was off limits due to the possibility of rounds going over the dunes, and into the bay.

We filed off the bed of the semi-trailer and gathered in the stands behind the range. There we were given last minute instructions, as well as the extremely important safety lecture. We were given a lot of very important rules to follow while at the range. When the lecture was completed, we were lined up behind the firing stations, weapons unloaded, and pointing up. We were given some last-minute instructions before each number one man on the firing line took his position.

Because each weapon had its own idiosyncrasies and sight discrepancies, each man had to zero his weapon at a 200-yard range first. That was required to make the weapon as reliable as possible, aim wise. As I mentioned before, the Army (as well as the other services) had a major love affair with acronyms. We learned our first weapons-related one on the firing range. It was a memory aid, to be used when firing our weapons — as if anybody in his right mind is going to remember the memory aid when under attack from an enemy. That first word memory aid we learned was "BASS." BASS was associated with rifle marksmanship. BASS was interpreted as Breathe, Aim, Slack, and Squeeze, in that order.

"LOCK AND LOAD," the Range master called out loudly, when it was time to finally fire our weapons. The troops made sure the safety was on and proceeded to load a clip in the rifle. I heard a couple of loud "SHIT!" complaints on the line, as a few men didn't load their clips correctly, suffering the ubiquitous "M-1 thumb."

"READY ON THE RIGHT?" yelled the Range master. The man in charge of the firing line on the right yelled back, "READY ON THE RIGHT!" "READY ON THE LEFT?" the Range master continued. The NCO in charge of the left line yelled back, "READY ON THE LEFT!" The Range master responded with "READY ON THE FIRING LINE!" Rifle safeties were switched to the "off" position.

"WATCH YOUR TARGETS! FIRE!" Suddenly a volley of noisy shots rang out. I was firing a weapon (other than a bow and arrow) for the first time in my life and, truthfully, learning how to kill. It was exhilarating. After zeroing our weapons, we began firing on the range with the shorter-range targets, gradually moving to targets that were situated further from us. That was a good way to get us comfortable with a deadly weapon. That was also one of the more dangerous things we did during Basic.

During "train fire" we learned the proper method to fire the rifle when standing, kneeling, prone (lying down), and with the rifle resting on a solid object. Holding still while pulling the trigger was my main problem. I was nervous and pumped at the same time. We had to learn to always squeeze the trigger very slowly and carefully when shooting at a target. Pulling the trigger quickly (jerking) would result in the rifle being pulled offline.

I wasn't the best shot in the class (by a long shot) but I held my own. Since I had never handled or fired a bullet-firing weapon, I felt that was to be expected. When the last bullet was expended, it became obvious to the rifleman, and anyone nearby. The metal clip flew noisily in the air with a ping, and hit the ground, making another noise if it hit cement, rock, or metal. If the enemy was listening for you to run out of ammo in your weapon, the M-1 would respond quite nicely with the "loud" ping. I managed to qualify as a "sharpshooter" on the M-1, and "marksman" on the .45-cal. pistol. The best qualification was "expert." That authorized me to wear my first Army-issued badges on my uniform, that of the Marksman Badge, Pistol, and Sharpshooter Badge, M-1 Rifle.

Our Basic Training unit commanding officer decided he wanted the unit to have a basketball team to participate in the base basketball league. Because of my basketball experience at San Jose State I was selected to be the player/coach of our unit basketball team. I didn't mind it at all, especially since it got me out of a lot of boring useless military crap, like details.

Details included cleaning everything spic-and-span, doing KP, nighttime fireguard for the barracks, etc. The Army, especially during training cycles, tried to keep everybody busy, no matter how ridiculous or worthless the project was. Our team didn't play spectacularly, but we held our own, especially with the fact that we hadn't been together very long and didn't have a lot of time to practice.

After learning how to fire the rifle, our weapons training included some minimal firing time with .30-caliber machine guns, just enough for familiarization. We were also taught how to use the rifleman's heavy artillery; hand grenades. Another dangerous activity, an entire day was set aside for learning all about the hand grenade, and how to throw it. Our instructors went over how to pull the pin and throw the grenade, by the numbers, over, and over, and over, and over... well, you get the idea. An Army favorite is teaching "by the numbers." This was especially true during our hand grenade training.

We were first taught how to arm the grenade (feet about shoulder width, both arms horizontal, even with the shoulder, one hand on the hand grenade, the other on the pin, with the index finger in the circular pin pull ring, pull the pin, maintain pressure with the thumb on the metal lever ("spoon") to keep it from releasing, thus beginning the time fuse operation), then throw it. Despite what you see in movies, the pin cannot be pulled out of a hand grenade with the teeth, unless you wish to break your teeth. This fact was immediately emphasized by the instructors.

The constant warnings about the dangerous nature of the hand grenade made for a healthy nervousness while handling the deadly object. Remembering that during my short career as a catcher on the Carmel High School baseball team, my most difficult action to master was that of throwing the ball accurately to second base, from behind the plate, I figured I was going to need a lot of practice throwing hand grenades.

The act of throwing the grenade released the safety spoon, thus arming the grenade. Most hand grenades had a 4-6 second delay prior to detonating. Believe it or not, there was an Army accepted way of throwing the grenade, which I don't think I ever used in real life. The Army's concept of a throwing motion just seemed awkward to me.

Our initial training was with dummy grenades (no explosive component), followed by training grenades (which at least "popped" when detonating), then the real thing. The real thing didn't happen until afternoon, after the instructors had determined that we knew enough about grenades that we weren't going to accidentally kill each other. Individual bunkers had been erected for each trainee to use for throwing hand grenades. That way, if someone made a mistake, the explosive blast damage would be limited to inside the bunker. It also protected the thrower from being injured by shrapnel if the grenade wasn't thrown far enough.

We were trained to throw the grenades from the standing, kneeling, and alternate prone positions. After throwing the grenade we immediately hit the ground. While throwing the real grenade, we had an instructor with us. All in all, the concept of throwing a hand grenade really was very simple: pull the arming pin, throw the grenade at the target, and duck.

After learning the use of hand grenades, we learned how to fire rifle grenades, using an adapter for our M-1 Garand rifles, the rifle butt placed against the knee (while kneeling), and the rifle at an upward angle. It increased the range of the grenade significantly, but accuracy was difficult.

While on the subject of explosive materials, we were introduced to land mines, both anti-personnel and anti-vehicle varieties, American and Communist. We learned the standard minefield marking signs, as well as the danger signs to look for in case of unmarked minefields.

The most common mines, with detonators and explosives removed, were shown to use for identification purposes. We learned the nomenclature of each, and then were taken outdoors for a lesson on how to probe for mines. We were instructed to take our bayonets out of their scabbards, kneel on the ground, and gently push the blade into the ground at an angle. Upon feeling solid resistance, we were instructed on how to mark the location of the object and report it. Our mine training was of very short duration.

"Courage is fear holding on a minute longer." — *General George S. Patton*

The training that bothered me somewhat was bayonet training. What bothered me was the fact that it was predicated on the fact that we might, at some time, get involved in a situation where we would be required to fight face-to-face with the enemy, bayonet-to-bayonet.

We were taught that the order "FIX BAYONETS" meant that we were to remove our bayonet from its scabbard on our belt, and snap it onto the end of our rifles. We were taught this maneuver by the numbers and shown, in slow motion, the moves that we would be expected to make when involved in bayonet combat.

We were marched to a combat bayonet course. It consisted of fake soldiers, which we "stabbed" with our rifle-affixed bayonets. We never really practiced in real time against each other, just in slow motion, with the bayonet covered by the scabbard, for safety purposes.

We were also instructed how to use a lensatic compass to not get lost while out and about. As we entered the classroom, we were each handed a lensatic compass. The first thing we saw when we entered the room was a gigantic, clear plastic and wooden compass placed on an easel. Talk about a training aid! No matter where you sat in the room, you could make out every part of that compass. One of the things the Army was very good at was making oversized training aids.

The instructor stressed that our compass could save our life, or at the very least, keep us from getting lost. We were reminded that when we were assigned to a military unit (other than training unit), each of us would be issued a lensatic compass, among other items of equipment. During the first hour the instructor went over the nomenclature of the compass, and some basic pointers on how it was used.

It was amazing how many trainees seemed to know nothing about a compass, much less how to use it. I had been fortunate in that I had been a Cub Scout and a Boy Scout, having been thoroughly trained in the use of the compass. I'll have to admit that using the compass wasn't the easiest thing on earth. Some of those poor city slickers were, however, totally lost.

The instructor told us to take our compasses out of their cases and follow along as he named each part, explained the reasons for each part, and how it was used. He explained that each tick mark around the edge of the circular dial denoted one degree, and there were 360 degrees in a full circle. He also told us that magnetic north was at 0/360 degrees, magnetic east was 90 degrees, magnetic south was 180 degrees, and magnetic west was 270 degrees. The degrees about a compass were known as magnetic azimuths.

Notice in the above descriptions I have specified magnetic directions. The first thing we had to know was that the true North Pole and magnetic "North Pole" were not in the same location on Earth. In fact, they were more than 500 miles apart. Navigation was dependent upon the navigator's knowledge of that fact, and the direction of north. Maps were drawn utilizing true north. Compasses were used to determine magnetic north. The needle in the compass would always point to magnetic north, or a nearby strong magnetic field, if any existed.

Depending upon where on Earth we were located, that would determine the difference between magnetic and true north. It was known as the deviation and had to be known to determine a true azimuth, as differentiated from a magnetic azimuth. Deviation was a very difficult subject for most of the recruits to grasp.

Variation (aka declination) was the difference between true and magnetic north. Basically, the deviation is westerly if you're on the east coast, and easterly if on the west coast. Most maps used for navigation showed the magnetic declination for various locations on the map, also known as an Isogonic Line. A declination of 0° indicated that, at that location, true and magnetic north were in line from that given point, known as the Agonic Line.

When attempting to determine a magnetic heading from a true heading, one had to add west variation, or subtract east variation. If, on the other hand, one knew the magnetic heading, but wanted to determine the true heading, the reverse would be true, subtracting west variation, or adding east variation. Because the magnetic north pole changes annually, it was always advised to utilize current maps, especially when using them for navigational purposes.

When sighting a compass, the sighting line was pointed toward the target. The degree reading shown under that line was the magnetic azimuth to the target. When told to move in a certain magnetic direction, the compass was rotated until the given azimuth appeared at the sighting line. That line was then followed, to move in the specified direction.

Rather than constantly holding the compass up, to follow the line, it was a lot easier to pick a point in the distance that was on that line. Then the individual could just go to that location. That minimized possible errors. We were warned to keep away from all magnetic fields when using a compass. That included anything metallic. The worst offending magnetic field was normally derived from high-tension power lines. We had to be at least 60 yards away from power lines to obtain accurate readings. Even a rifle or steel helmet created inaccuracies. One had to remain at least a yard from these objects that soldiers carried on a regular basis in combat.

After a couple hours of classroom training, we were all taken to the field to practice what we had learned on a compass course. That included learning our normal pace length on level ground. Knowing one's pace length made it possible to accurately measure distance while striding in a set direction.

There were some variables, including: 1) pace lengthened on a downslope and shortened on an upgrade; 2) a head wind shortened the pace and a tail wind increased it; 3) sand, gravel, mud, snow, and similar surface materials tended to shorten the pace; 4) falling snow, rain, or ice caused the pace to be reduced in length; and 5) poor visibility, such as in fog, rain, or darkness, generally shortened your pace. Knowing that, an instructor could tell us to go in a given direction for a certain distance, and we should have been able to find the target location simply.

The compass course was our final test as to our understanding of the use of the compass. We were given the magnetic heading and distance to three separate locations. We were instructed to follow those headings and distances to find each objective. Our mission was to find each objective before continuing to the next objective.

After learning how to use the magnetic compass, we were given some basic instruction in map reading. Once again, that was a subject that I already had a working knowledge of also, having learned map reading in Cub and Boy Scouts, and in my college Private Pilot course.

Once again there was a very large training aid, a simulated military map, placed on an easel. Each of us was also given a map to follow. A map was basically nothing more than a view of the ground as could be seen from above, if in an airborne craft—the only difference being that buildings, roads, railroad tracks, mountains, etc., were depicted by special marks, icons, or shapes.

I couldn't understand why, but the trainees had a lot of trouble with basic map reading, especially when it came to determining the grid coordinate for a point on a military map. And, that was supposed to be just the very basics of map reading and land navigation.

Besides learning the various objects marked on a map, we were shown how to interpret elevation lines, determining elevations, as well as determining the difference between hills and valleys. The distance between elevation lines determined the steepness of a hillside: The closer the elevation lines to each other, the steeper the slope. The opposite was true if the lines were far apart. That signified a very shallow slope.

Determining one's grid coordinate location on a map was of primary importance for letting other people/units know exactly where one was located. It also kept a soldier from getting lost. On military maps, grid squares were placed on the map, designating a portion of the Earth. Each horizontal line and vertical line had a numerical designator. The squares formed by these lines were 1000 meters by 1000 meters in size, on military maps. To find a grid smaller than 1,000 meters square, one had to interpolate. The numbers increased from left to right, and from bottom to top, of the map. Within those lines, one could pinpoint his location, or that of the target, by interpolation.

Our lessons began by learning simple four-numbered grid coordinates (1,000 x 1,000-meter squares), followed by slightly more complex six-numbered coordinates (100 x 100 meter-squares), and followed lastly by even more complex eight-numbered coordinates (10 x 10 meters).

When giving a grid coordinate, the lowest number of the vertical line was always given first, followed by the lowest number of the horizontal line. Therefore, a grid coordinate given as 1181, would designate a 1,000 x 1,000-meter square between vertical lines 11 and 12, and horizontal lines 81 and 82. The location within that square could be broken down even further, by interpolating even more, usually only as exacting as a 10 x 10-meter square. As an example, grid coordinate 1126 8114 would designate a grid square of only 10 x 10 meters large.

In early April Special Forces suffered its first "official" casualties of the Vietnam conflict. On 8 April a Republican Youth unit advised by four U.S. Special Forces was overrun, all four Special Forces men being captured during the action. SP5 James Gabriel, Jr. and SSG Wayne E. Marchand had been badly wounded. Unhappy about the fact that the wounded Americans were slowing their withdrawal, a Republican Youth militiaman who had deserted to the Viet Cong was told to execute the wounded Americans. He did so with a bullet to each man's head.

The remaining prisoners of war, SFC Francis Quinn and SGT George E. Groom, were forced to stay with the withdrawing Viet Cong, but were able to slow the movement, causing confusion among the Viet Cong when helicopters were heard overhead, above the low-lying heavy clouds. For unknown reasons Quinn and Groom were released on 1 May, a mere ten miles from the location of their capture.

I first met George Groom a little more than a year later, when we were preparing for a mission to Ethiopia with the 6th Special Forces Group. You would never have known that he had gone through such a harrowing experience. In fact, I didn't learn of his experience until I began collecting information for this book.

Sometime during the latter part of Basic, we were notified that we would be inspected on the following Friday. We were also told that those who passed inspection would be the recipients of weekend passes. On the appointed Friday afternoon, we were inspected.

It was amazing how expert Army training personnel were in the art of finding flaws during an inspection. We were gigged for flaws that we couldn't even see with our naked eyes. Not a single person passed. If I remember correctly, I was gigged for a speck of dirt inside my helmet liner, attached to the hidden part of the headband.

The sergeant promised to re-inspect us that evening. There was a flurry of activity. Men were working their tails off to fix flaws and search for more possible gigs. That evening came and went. Finally, just before time for lights out, we were told that we were to be re-inspected the following morning, Saturday.

"Bring them together by treating them humanely and keep them together with strict military discipline. This will assure their allegiance."
— *Sun Tzu*

By noon, there had been no re-inspection. Almost to a man, there was anger and frustration at the treatment we had received. About three-fourths of us (yes, me included) dressed in our class A uniforms and snuck off post to spend a weekend pass that had not been granted. I hitchhiked up to San Jose to visit my parents for the weekend.

Lo-and-behold, either because our actions were expected, or because somebody noticed a lack of personnel in the company area, it was decided to have a Sunday morning formation. All of us who were not in formation (a very large part of the company), were reported as AWOL (absent without leave).

Monday morning those of us who had been reported as AWOL Sunday morning were called out of formation and ordered to report immediately to the First Sergeant's office. The line was LONG. I think there were about thirty, or more, of us in the line. The line extended from the First Sergeant's doorway, down the hall, around the corner, and out the front door of the company building.

As luck would have it, a passing chaplain saw the line, inquired as to the reason for the line, and upon learning the reason, as well as the resulting troop morale, immediately spoke to the company commander. Before my part of the line reached the First Sergeant's door, those of us still in line were ordered to disperse and join the unit for the day's training.

I never heard any further about the incident. I'm sure, however, that it was included in my service record as a black mark, because it wasn't until more than a year past my three-year enlistment was up that I finally received a Good Conduct Medal. A member of the U.S. Army was authorized the Good Conduct Medal after three successive years of acceptable conduct.

The unofficial bible for Army noncommissioned officers, *The NoNCOm's Guide, 19th Edition* by The Stackpole Company (©1966), says, in part, "When a man goes AWOL he puts a black mark on your record as a leader.... Failure to get leave or passes is the most common cause [for normal men to go AWOL.] Do all you can to insure a fair allotment of leaves to your men.... **Unfair treatment** by their leaders is another reason why men go AWOL. In a study, men emphasized such instances of bad leadership as **broken promises**, partiality in granting leaves and passes, and a lack of interest in the soldier's problems. Men do not leave a command where they are... **fairly treated**." Bold emphasis in the prior quote is that of the author's.

During the latter part of Basic we spent most of three days in the field for daylight and nighttime tactical training. We did a tactical march out to our bivouac (camp) area, in two lines (one on each side of the road), carrying all the equipment (which was dictated to us) that we would need for the training exercise. During the march fake attacks on us were initiated, and it was our responsibility to react to the intrusions correctly. That was, after all, our final practical exam.

All of us were assigned partners, with whom we would be tent-mates. Army soldiers carried somewhat heavy canvas tent halves when going to the field. They were carried rolled, on top of the backpack. As described, a tent half is only half of a tent. Two tent halves had to be snapped together to form a whole pup tent. The other tent half belonged to a fellow soldier. Each soldier also carried a small section of rope, a three-piece tent pole, and half of the tent pegs required to erect a pup tent, about five.

The pegs were pounded into the ground and pulled out, using our Army-issue entrenching tool. It was a portable, foldable shovel carried by each soldier, attached to his backpack. The entrenching tool could be used as a pick device by opening it to the 90-degree position, and as a shovel by opening it fully to 180 degrees.

Upon reaching the location at which we were to encamp, our first job was to select the "perfect" spot for a tent. Ideal would be level ground. Upon selecting the site, the two shelter halves were snapped together on the long seams, and the tent was laid out perpendicular to the prevailing wind direction. That was followed by inserting the two assembled poles into the grommet at each end of the snapped tent seams, placing the other end of the pole on the ground, and then running guy ropes to tent pegs in the front and rear of the tent. Following that, the sides of the tent were staked to the ground.

The final step in the erection process was one of the most important, especially if there was any chance of rain. The entrenching tool was used to dig a shallow ditch around the outside of the tent, with a drainage outlet leading to the lowest elevation of the ground. This was done to channel any rainwater away from the interior of the tent, keeping the inside dry, and as comfortable as could be expected.

It was during the field training exercise (FTX) that I learned about MCIs. Prior to that we had been fed hot meals that had been transported from the mess hall, out to the location of our field training. Meal, Combat, Individual (MCI), commonly mistakenly called C-rations, were an Army in-the-field staple. The MCI replaced the old C-rations.

When we went to the field for our field exercise, we were fed MCIs, which we ate from our mess kits. Our mess kits consisted of two deep oval aluminum dishes, plus a knife, fork, and spoon. A drinking cup was included as part of our canteen. The drinking cup was also aluminum, carried in the bottom of the canvas canteen holder, the bottom of the canteen fitting perfectly inside the cup.

Some of the rations were good, while some were so horrible, and hated, they couldn't even be traded for other rations, notably the Ham & Lima Beans rations. They were sickly, ugly, smelly, and a dirty gray color. They sure didn't look like any ham or lima beans I had ever seen. Ham & Lima Beans were also called "Ham & Slimas," "Ham & Muthas," "Ham and Mother F***ers," "Ham & Shit," etc. The list of names for Ham & Lima Beans was endless, and gross.

I learned later that some men carried hot sauce with them to the field, for use with some of the uglier tasting rations. In fact, The McIlhinney Company, manufacturers of Tabasco Sauce, printed and disseminated a very popular booklet of recipes for the C-rations. I still couldn't fathom Ham & Lima Beans; hot sauce, or ketchup, or any other taste changer being added.

An MCI breakfast usually included eggs and/or meat in a can, hardtack biscuits (or cookies or crackers) in a can, peanut butter or jelly in a can, powdered hot chocolate in a packet, coffee in a packet, sugar in a packet and a 4-pack of cigarettes.

Lunches and dinners usually included a meat and vegetable meal in a can, coffee in a packet, sugar in a packet, a fruit in a can, and a dessert in a can (the usual favorite was Pound Cake, followed by Cinnamon

Nut Roll, and last, the usually thrown away Fruit Cake). Also included was an accessory packet that contained a book of matches, a small packet of toilet paper, packs of instant coffee, Chiclets gum, powdered creamer, sugar, salt and pepper, as well as a small 4-pack of cigarettes.

The older MCIs included Camel, Lucky Strike, Chesterfield, and Pall Mall packs, with Winston filter cigarettes being added later. My favorite MCI meals were Spaghetti w/Beef Chunks in Sauce, Beans w/Meatballs in Tomato Sauce, and Beans w/Frankfurter Chunks in Tomato Sauce. Each complete meal was supposed to provide about 1,200 calories.

You rarely knew how old the "C-rations" were. That is unless your packet of cigarettes was a green-label Lucky Strike pack. I ran across green-label Lucky Strike packs occasionally. Green-label Lucky Strike packs were ONLY produced prior to 1942. You could tell that the rations were new if they contained filter cigarettes, which I also ran across on occasion.

Later in my Army life, I managed to learn how to improve on some of the dinners (except the Ham & Lima Beans). Usually the improvement came out of a hot sauce bottle. To open the canned products, the MCI carton contained the greatest military invention of all time; the handy-dandy ½" x 1" opener, can, P-38, hand operated. A GI became so familiar and expert at utilizing the P-38 that he could open a can just as quickly with it as with an automatic can opener. I still carry one on my keychain, as do many former GIs.

I didn't mind the peanut butter, but some soldiers considered it to taste bad and threw it out. If, however, you had dysentery, the peanut butter did a great job of stopping "the runs." As oily as the peanut butter was, it could also be used to make smoke candles, or to boil water for coffee. The downside of using it to boil the water was that it left a greasy black stain on the bottom of the canteen cup.

The field training included live fire training (aka Night Infiltration Course), escape and evasion, land navigation and night firing of our weapons. The live fire training and escape and evasion were the two subjects most feared by most of the recruits. Before our escape and evasion training, rumors were rampant that anyone caught could expect to be tortured through beatings. That made us try all that much harder not to get caught. I managed to be one of the lucky recruits to evade capture.

Live fire training consisted of crawling (utilizing the previously taught low crawl) on the ground about a hundred yards, while cradling your rifle, in a ditch, under barbed wire stretched across the courses, toward machine guns firing live bullets over our heads. It was the nearest thing to actual combat fear that the Army could test us for. It was a nerve-wracking experience for the uninitiated, but instilled confidence in most of us, which was its objective.

The machine guns were set in place so that the bullets would pass three feet above our heads, while pre-set explosive rounds went off all around us, simulating incoming artillery rounds. As a safety feature, steel bars were secured horizontally, under the machine gun barrels, to guarantee that they could not fire any lower.

The machine guns fired tracer rounds (rounds that you could see in the dark), making them even more ominous. Recruits were safe unless they panicked and jumped up in the air. I didn't have any problem with the bullets flying over my head, but I certainly didn't leave any wasted space between my body and the ground while crawling toward the machine gun.

It was during this part of my training that I received the dreaded "Dear John" letter, not from my ex-girlfriend Phyllis, but from none other than her new fiancée. I had found my Jody! How sweet of him! He wrote, "All is fair in love and war, and since you decided to prepare for war, we decided to fall in love." He was EXTREMELY lucky he wasn't within my reach when I read the letter. Mad would be a polite word to use for my feelings for him at that time.

My girlfriend knew nothing about the letter and chewed him out royally when I told her about it years later. They got married shortly after I received the letter! When our field training was done we tactically marched back to our unit barracks.

Basic Training had been exactly what the name implied, basic. We learned the very basics of military life, to prepare us for our future years in the Army. Those of us who went through Basic Training will never forget the experience. Those who haven't, can't even imagine what it was, or is, like. Our Basic Training schedule had included eight weeks of 10-14 hours a day, Monday through Friday, with Saturdays usually reserved for inspections and administrative duties.

Sundays were our only days off, but even at that we were usually restricted to the company area, even on Sundays except, of course, for those individuals who wished to attend a church service of their own choosing, on base. The training to fine-tune what we had already learned and to prepare us for our new career would come after Basic, and was known as Advanced Individual Training (AIT).

My AIT was scheduled to be in the field of heavy, crew-served infantry weapons. Even AIT wouldn't fully prepare us for combat. That preparation had to come from the unit level, after graduation from AIT. The ultimate preparation for combat would be combat itself.

A couple days before graduation we were given our final PT Test to make sure we were physically prepared to move on to AIT. The test consisted of a mile run, the low crawl, the horizontal ladder, the dodge, run and jump, and the grenade throw.

Finally, Friday, 20 April, was our final day of training, and we had our Basic Training graduation ceremony on the unit parade field the following day. I was very proud to be selected for the class graduation ceremony drill team, doing a precision close-order drill routine during the ceremony.

I did a lot better than I had done in Air Force R.O.T.C. I looked very sharp in my highly starched and pressed long-sleeve khaki uniform, pants bloused inside my spit-shined boots, colored dickey on my neck, highly polished brass insignia attached to my lapels, web gear belt around my waist, and highly polished, silver-plated helmet on my head.

My mother and father and my new "girlfriend" June, our family neighbor from across the street, attended the ceremony. I had finally completed Basic Training, and my first step toward a totally new way of life. I had entered the service with basically no focus on what I wanted to do in later life, but I had become that much closer to becoming a "man," and having direction and responsibility in my life. It was a defining time in my life.

The following weekend I received a pass, so I hitchhiked up to San Jose to visit mom and dad, and June. The following Monday I got a ride back down to Ft. Ord to my barracks. We remained in our barracks, pulling various details around post, while awaiting orders for AIT.

Details were exactly what the name implies. They were usually worthless tasks, meant to keep everyone busy. The best way to describe them was time-consuming and labor-intensive. It could include anything from raking pine needles, to picking up pine cones, to painting rocks.

YES, you read that correctly. Sergeants major and first sergeants were especially fond of having rocks as decoration, lining walkways and decorative landscaping. Ninety-nine percent of the times those rocks were painted white. Of course, inclement weather could ruin the cleanliness of those pristine white rocks, leading to — you guessed it — a rock painting detail.

There is another detail that ranks even higher in stupidity: All the old barracks were heated by coal-fired furnaces. The coal for each furnace was kept in a cement three-sided enclosure just outside the furnace. Rain tended to spatter coal dust onto the cement walls, in addition to the fact that coal would rub against the walls, making them a very dirty dark grey. The answer, in the minds of some sergeants major, was to paint the coal container walls white. Given that white gets dirty very fast, especially when in direct contact with coal, that led to plenty of details for the otherwise bored lowly enlisted man. Come up with any stupid idea for a "keep-the-troops-busy" detail, and I'm sure a first sergeant or sergeant major has already beat you to the idea.

On 30 April, Under Secretary of State George W. Ball predicted that the war in Vietnam would be a "long, slow, arduous" type of war that would not be "congenial to the American temperament."

Me as part of my Basic Training unit drill team. I'm sporting the dangerous hired killer look of someone who is still a somewhat rookie Army trainee. (my photo)

Me as part of my Basic Training unit drill team,
with the same look as the previous photo. (my photo)

Graduation Day podium in front my Basic Training unit barracks. (my photo)

CHAPTER 3

ADVANCED INDIVIDUAL TRAINING

D Company — 3rd BG — 1st Brigade

On 4 May I was assigned to D Company, 3rd Battle Group, 1st Brigade (aka D-3-1, or Delta-3-1), remaining at Fort Ord for Advanced Individual Training (AIT). As in Basic Training, we were quartered in somewhat modern looking three-story-high brick cement buildings, built in the early 1950s.

Since I had enlisted for "Airborne Unassigned" it meant that I was leaving my job selection up to the Army. Although that is usually considered to be a rather stupid thing to do, and I would advise anyone against letting the Army choose what you are going to do for the rest of your enlistment, I was happy with their selection. The infinite wisdom of the Army was to train me as an Infantry Indirect Fire Crewman during my next training phase (AIT). It helped me during my Vietnam service.

In AIT I had the "privilege" of being assigned to guard duty for the first time since entering the Army. It took second place as far as hated details to be assigned to went, right behind KP. Guard duty was generally performed between the hours of 1800 and 0600 Sunday through Thursday nights, and two 24-hour shifts, from 1800 Friday to 1800 Sunday, on weekends.

Guard duty began with a personal inspection, so it was important to wear your cleanest fatigue uniform and most highly shined pair of boots. You also needed to know your General Orders and Code of Conduct. Upon reporting for guard duty, each soldier was assigned one of three reliefs (shifts). There were three reliefs per guard duty detail. Each shift worked two hours, followed by four hours off.

At a designated time, the guard unit was ordered by the Sergeant of the Guard to fall in (form up) for inspection. We formed up, at attention, in three ranks (rows), each denoting a relief. The Sergeant of the Guard assumed the position of attention, centered in front of the guard formation. He then made sure all men were present, did an about face, and stood at attention in front of the formation.

When the guard was formed, the Officer of the Guard marched out to the formation and stood in front of the Sergeant of the Guard, at attention. The Sergeant of the Guard saluted the officer, stating, "Sir, the men are ready for inspection," at which time the officer returned his salute. The Officer of the Guard then marched to the first man in relief one, the Sergeant of the Guard following, to begin inspecting the men.

Upon reaching the first man, the officer came to attention, made a right face, facing the man, at attention. At that time, the guard came to "port arms," followed immediately by "inspection arms," at which time the guard pulled the bolt of the M-1 Garand back, looking down into the rifle chamber, to verify that there was no cartridge in the weapon, while still at attention. The officer then, snappily, grabbed the rifle from the guard, and inspected the entire weapon. While doing so, the officer asked the guard a question, usually asking the guard to quote a certain numbered General Order (there were eleven) or Code of Conduct paragraphs (there were six). The guard replied, by quoting the correct General Order (hopefully), or answering the question posed by the officer. The officer then handed the weapon back to the guard, who released the bolt, and returned to "order arms." That was followed by the officer making a left face, taking a couple paces, to a position in front of the next guard in line, followed again by a snappy right face.

The inspection continued, until all the guards had been inspected, and grilled. From that inspection, the supernumerary was determined. The supernumerary was usually excused from guard duty, deemed to be the sharpest man in the formation.

Depending on the object, or area, to be guarded, the guard either marched a guard route, or stood. The main thing to remember was your response if you were to spot a person in your area of responsibility. The first action was to immediately bring your weapon to port arms. Then, you were to, with authority, yell, "HALT, WHO GOES THERE?" After the subject answered (hopefully), you were to ask the subject to give you the password. After giving the password, the subject was authorized to pass.

Never did the Army assign a trainee to an area that really needed a knowledgeable, or experienced, guard. What the hell was a trainee supposed to do? We were only given one cartridge (bullet), and we weren't even permitted to have that cartridge in the weapon. If someone didn't respond correctly, and continued toward me, I guess my choice would have been to aim my weapon at him, pull the trigger, and shout, "BANG; YOU'RE DEAD!" Thankfully, I never had to test that theory.

All us paratrooper volunteers were placed in the same training platoon, to exercise us into shape before arriving at Jump School. That way (it was thought) the quit and drop-out rate would decrease at Jump School. The first thing they did was give us a physical exam and a special Airborne PT (Physical Training) Test.

I passed the physical examination with flying colors, learning I had 20/20 vision. I could have qualified to be an Air Force pilot after all, but, by that time it was too damned late. I was already in the Army. The Airborne PT Test was more difficult than that for regular Army personnel. It included pull-ups, push-ups, sit-ups, squat jumps, and a timed run. All the exercises had to be done to minimum Airborne standards, which I did. The Army PT test had been different, in that a soldier could make up on one test what he came up short on another.

We reviewed what we had learned about patrolling and land navigation in Basic, delving further into the subjects. We also trained a lot in infantry tactics, especially squad and platoon tactics in a combat situation. Included in infantry tactics was operations in and around minefields, including mine detection and removal. I paid special attention to the class on mine detection. The thought of dealing with enemy mines always made me a little nervous.

Because the infantry relied so heavily on maps and compasses for movement, a lot of time was spent in the classroom, and in the field, learning how to read and use a lensatic compass, and how to read and interpret a map, especially a contour map.

The compass training was somewhat easy, although some men still had trouble understanding the difference between grid (true) and magnetic north, and how to utilize that difference in the real world. You would have thought they would have learned enough in Basic, but I guess not.

For the map reading class, part of a large-scale military map stood in front of our class, as a training aid. The first thing we learned was what each symbol and line depicted. Many map symbols were self-explanatory, like a cross-hatched line representing a railroad line, a cross depicting a church, and the red cross symbol signifying a hospital. Heavy lines indicated roads, while light lines depicted elevations.

Some of the light lines were numbered, denoting the elevation for that line. We learned that the closer the lines, the steeper the slope, and the further apart, the shallower the slope. Once one became thoroughly familiar with the maps, it was easy to place mountains and depressions on the maps, as well as easy slopes and steep cliffs.

After the classroom training, we were taken outside for some practical use of our training, including revisiting and memorizing the length of our paces and how that would change based on different terrain. That information would become very important to us in the future.

Working with heavy weapons, we would be using map coordinates a lot. Since map coordinates included letters, we had to learn the military phonetic alphabet, which was used to denote the letters in the map coordinates.

The military alphabet had changed some since the World War II era. It was also different from the police alphabet, which I had heard on TV a lot. The phonetic alphabet was alpha, bravo, Charlie, delta, echo, foxtrot, golf, hotel, India, Juliet, kilo, Lima, Mike, November, Oscar, papa, Quebec, Romeo, Sierra, tango, uniform, victor, whiskey, x-ray, Yankee, Zulu.

Often, we had to spell out words. It was very important in the military, that all words transmitted be thoroughly understood. That was always done by spelling out the questionable words, by utilizing the phonetic alphabet; "right" would be "romeo india golf hotel tango." There were some numbers that were pronounced differently than civilians were accustomed to. That made sure the numbers were not misconstrued. Notable were thuree (3), fower (4), fiyiv (5), and niner (9).

When communicating large numbers, they were usually given as individual numbers. As an example, 129 would be communicated as one two niner, not one hundred and twenty-nine.

"The instruments of battle are valuable only if one knows how to use them." — Ardant Du Picq, "Battle Studies"

Interpreting a contour map gave some men fits. If understood, comparing the surrounding terrain features to that shown on a contour map could make determining map orientation and your exact position a snap, especially if there was terrain other than flat ground. That understanding made it a lot easier to determine the coordinates of the individual's and target's location. Some men just couldn't understand that. Knowing your exact coordinates on a map was extremely important in a combat situation. Without that knowledge it was impossible to report your location, or that of the enemy.

Incorrect coordinate location information had resulted in numerous incidents of friendly troops being bombarded by friendly air support and/or artillery support. Correct location information gave supporting units the information they needed to quickly send reinforcements in case of dire circumstances. It also ensured accurate air and artillery support on a much quicker basis. Outside, the instructor pointed out local terrain features, followed by pointing out that same terrain feature on our contour maps of the local area.

Map coordinates were usually given as eight number descriptions. Our military issued maps were lined, the distance between lines depending upon the scale of the map. A 1:50,000 scale map was lined every 1,000 meters, whereas a 1:250,000 scale map was lined every 100,000 meters. The 1:50,000 scale map was what we utilized. It was a matter of interpolating distances from left to right and bottom to top within a given square to determine the coordinates of a given location.

Besides infantry tactics, heavy weapons training consisted of training on the 60mm (millimeter), 81mm and 4.2-inch (107mm) mortars, as well as the 106mm recoilless rifle. Most of our mortar instruction concentrated on operating the weapons, but a large portion also included techniques of forward observing (FO) and fire direction control (FDC) for the mortars, as well as techniques for utilizing the weapons during offensive, defensive, and retrograde (Army speak for retreat) combat situations.

Because forward observation required the use of a radio, we also learned basic communications techniques. Forward observation was a technique whereby a soldier would go to a forward position (or a high position overlooking the battlefield, sometimes in aircraft), in order to observe the artillery (or mortar) strike, after which he would radio back to FDC his suggested change of distance and direction (always reporting the changes as he sees it from his position, i.e., left 50, add 20—meaning that from his angle of sight, the gun round needed to be aimed 50 meters to the left, and the range should be increased by 20 meters) to strike the intended target.

Note that all measurements were in meters, due to the ease in using the metric system, as opposed to inches, feet, and yards. In addition, when working with mortar gunnery, all directional measurements used mils rather than degrees. A complete circle is 6400 mils, the equivalent of 360 degrees. Therefore, one degree equals 17.7778 mils. Defined, a mil is the angle that equals one meter wide at 1,000 meters distant.

Fire direction control instruction taught how to determine (mathematically and through using charts) the azimuth at which to point the weapon, and the elevation and charge to utilize for correct distance to the target, using information obtained from a forward observer. Later, while serving on a Special Forces A Team in Vietnam, that training was to provide some great expertise for me. Mortars were in every A-camp I was assigned to, and since only the Heavy Weapons Leader of each team had any in-depth training on mortars, I was able to help tremendously with the mortars, especially the larger 4.2" mortar (my favorite).

Mortars were crew served, muzzle-loaded (rounds were loaded from the front of the tube), high-angle-of-fire infantry weapons used for indirect fire support; the larger the mortar, the larger the crew, the longer the range, and the larger the killing radius for the employed rounds. Mortars were known as "infantry's artillery" because of their ease of movement and artillery-like fire support, enabling heavier support than the traditional infantry small arms fire.

All three of the Army's mortars used at that time fired heavy explosive (HE) white phosphorous smoke (WP) and illumination rounds (which were attached to parachutes for slow descent). Our 81mm and 4.2" mortars could also fire smoke (FS) rounds that laid down dense white smoke. The WP rounds could be used to lay down smoke for screening purposes and/or anti-personnel and incendiary applications. Screening fire missions were timed, firing a certain number of rounds per minute, to maintain the screen. A smoke chart was available to determine recommended timing sequences. The chart factored in various weather conditions.

Another possible mortar fire mission was the "barrier of fire." The barrier of fire was a mission given to sections of mortars, not individual mortars. It was a barrier of exploding rounds, laid on a prearranged line in front of friendly troops. The fire mission was ordered for a given amount of time (until an alert is over) or until the ammunition is exhausted, whatever occurred first. The mission usually targeted approaches that could not be covered by heavier final protective fire. For mortar fire to be effective, it had to be of sufficient volume of fire and had to hit the target at the right time, with the correct round and fuse.

The different sized mortars were very similar in basic appearance and functioning. The mortar was a weapon that was fired at a high elevation (pointed skyward, aka indirect fire), with the shell traveling on a high arch trajectory. It made it possible to fire on targets that were not in sight due to hills or mountains between the weapon and the target. It also provided cover for the mortar crews. In fact, mortars placed in permanent defensive positions were usually protected by small protective walls around each weapon.

The distance the mortar projectile (shell) was propelled was determined by a combination of weapon elevation (degrees raised or lowered) and shell propelling charge (amount of measured explosive charges attached to the shell that launch the shell out of the mortar tube).

The 60mm mortar (so called because the inside diameter of the mortar tube was 60 millimeters) weighed 45 pounds, making it the easiest mortar to carry on operations. The normal crew for the 60mm mortar was three men, the squad leader, the gunner, and the ammunition bearer. Its rounds weighed between 3 (HE) and 4 (WP) pounds each. Unlike the heavier 81mm and 4.2" mortars, it could be hand fired by simply pointing the mortar rather than wasting time using the sight (of course that method of fire also resulted in markedly less chance of hitting a small target), although little time was spent on this technique or this weapon during AIT.

60mm mortars were more of an offensive and close-in defensive support weapon, having a maximum range of almost 2,000 yards (effective range 1,000 yards) and a minimum range of a mere 50 yards. The HE round had a bursting (kill or injure) radius of 17 yards. Also available for use with the 60mm mortar were illumination and WP (white phosphorus) smoke rounds.

Each round had fins for stabilization in flight and came with an ignition cartridge and four equal propellant increments, the equivalent of a full charge. The propellant increments were bundles of sheet powder, in waterproof cellophane bags, fitted into slots in the fin blades.

The desired amount of propellant was determined by the distance the round was to travel. The amount was prepared simply by removing the amount of increments needed for the desired range. An increment consisted of a square bundle of sheet powder. Once the correct propellant increment had been attained, the round's safety wire was removed, and the round was placed in the mortar tube, propellant end down.

Because mortar tubes always point upward, the round was simply released to slide down toward the base of the tube. Upon striking the firing pin in the mortar base, the ignition cartridge was ignited, causing an explosive flame. The flame ignited the propelling charge, which detonated a larger explosion, driving the round up and out of the tube, arming the fuse. The maximum rate of fire of the 60mm mortar was 30-35 rounds per minute, while 18 rounds per minute was deemed normal and safe for extended periods.

The 81mm mortar had a smooth bore, weighed 136 pounds, fully assembled, had a maximum range of almost 3,300 yards, and a minimum of about 75 yards. The 81mm mortar was usually manned by a five-man squad, consisting of the squad leader, gunner, assistant gunner, first ammunition bearer, and second ammunition bearer.

The rounds weighed between 6 (light HE) and 15 (heavy HE) pounds. The rounds were stabilized in flight by fins in the tail section. Supplied with each charge was a propelling charge, which consisted of a primer, ignition cartridge, and either four or six removable propellant increments. Propellant increments were removed to attain the desired propellant charge.

As with the 60mm mortar, the 81mm round was dropped into the tube, fins first. The round's primer hit the firing pin on the base of the tube, which detonated the primer and, in turn, the ignition charge, which then ignited the propellant increments. The ignition of the propellant charges forced the round out of the barrel.

The maximum rate of fire of the 81mm mortar was 30-35 rounds per minute, while 18 rounds per minute was deemed normal, and safe for extended periods. It was a crew-served weapon, although one man could operate the weapon if need be. When large deflection changes were required, the assistant gunner would have to kneel in front of the mortar bipod and lift it far enough to clear the ground. The gunner then shifted the weapon to the newly-desired position.

81mm Mortar at my second camp in Vietnam, Vinh Gia, Detachment A-422. (my photo)

Teammates firing the 4.2" Mortar at my first camp in Vietnam, Cai Cai, Detachment A-412. (my photo)

The 4.2" (107mm) mortar tube was rifled, resulting in the shell rotating as it left the tube. The shell continued rotating during flight, thus making it very stable. This also meant that the rounds did not require fins. The normal crew for this mortar was four men, the squad leader, gunner, assistant gunner, and ammunition bearer. The tube was sixty inches long, weighing 157 pounds by itself. The baseplate weighed 193 pounds, and the bridge and standard assemblies combined weighed 250 pounds. The assembled mortar weighed 673 pounds.

Because of its heavy weight, the 4.2" mortar was almost always transported by vehicle. It was also a very unwieldy weapon to manipulate if large directional changes needed to be made. It had a maximum and maximum effective range of 7,400 yards, and a minimum range of 840 yards. The rounds weighed from 22 to 27 pounds each, consisting of the fixed shell, fuse, and propelling charge.

The propelling charge was a combination of ignition cartridge and powder charges. Charges were adjusted by removing the desired amount of increments from the cartridge container. The charges were a combination of bags, bundles, and sheets. A bag was the equivalent of 5 increments, each bundle was 5 increments, and sheets came in one-increment sizes, which could be reduced to 1/8 portions of an increment.

For the first minute, eighteen rounds maximum could be fired, followed by nine rounds per minute for the following five minutes. The recommended maximum sustained rate of fire after the initial six minutes, was three rounds per minute. It called for a crew of four to eight men but could be operated by two people when needed.

A fire direction center (FDC) was not needed with the 60mm, while the 81 and 4.2 generally required a fire direction center to coordinate fire. The 81 and 4.2 also required the use of an aiming stake for aiming the weapon, and a forward observer (FO) for spotting results and reporting needed changes to the mortar crew. All three of the mortars were supplied with sights, which sometimes were not used with the 60mm mortar.

We learned all jobs on a mortar team, including those jobs that weren't necessarily in the general vicinity of the weapon, and spent quite a bit of time on the firing range. A mortar crew generally consisted of a gunner, loader, spotter (forward observer, aka FO), and plotter (Fire Direction Control, or FDC). After firing the weapons, we learned how to clean and maintain the weapons.

When setting up the 4.2" mortar, the baseplate was firmly set in the ground by firing a couple rounds, and the sight was placed on the mortar. After that was done, an aiming stake was placed in the ground at a known azimuth (direction) from the mortar.

When a deflection (direction) was given to the gunner, he rotated the sight to the given deflection reading. He then traversed the mortar right or left, until the vertical line in the sight unit was on the left side of the aiming post. If the deviation was larger than the traversing rod permitted, the entire mortar assembly had to be physically moved, by the assistant gunner, to a point close to the aiming post, followed by the sight being traversed to the aiming post.

The gunner, or assistant gunner, made sure the sight was cross-leveled, using the bubble level device on the sight unit. The gunner elevated and traversed the mortar tube as new firing directions were received from the FDC.

The spotter (FO) radioed his position (using eight-digit coordinates) to the FDC. The job of the FO was to detect the location of the target, radio in the grid coordinates of the target, observe subsequent round explosions, and make adjustments to guide the rounds toward the target.

The initial fire request by an FO included information that was appropriate, as well as required, for the fire mission. In order, that included:

(1) The identification of the observer (unit job description).

(2) Request (fire mission).

(3) Location of target (by grid coordinates) and azimuth from observer to target (compass azimuth in degrees or mils).

(4) Nature of target (target description).

(5) Type of adjustment to follow (either area or precision fire).

(6) Ammunition (type of round to be fired — if not specified, high explosive [HE] rounds would be fired).

(7) Fuse (type of fuse to be affixed to the round - proximity or delay fuses can be requested - if not specified, percussion [impact] fuses would be utilized).

(8) Type of control (usually the FO specified "will adjust," signifying that the FO would announce the adjustment to be made).

The FO communicated the adjustments to FDC in accordance with his position, not that of the gun. In other words, if the round exploded about twenty meters to the left of the target and twenty meters short, as he saw it, he would announce to FDC, not what he saw, but the adjustment required from his position to hit the target, right two zero, add two zero.

The basic method used to get the best results in target destruction was known as bracketing the target. Direction of fire was usually the easiest to accomplish, distance the most difficult. When bracketing a target, one round was over (or under), followed by a round under (or over). The FO then knew that the target lay between those two positions. The distance between the over and under was halved.

As an example, if a round landed an estimated 200 meters over the target, the FO reported it as such, and the gunner fired the equivalent of 200 meters less. If the round landed short of the target, the following round would be fired half as much further, or 100 meters added distance. Utilizing this method, the target would soon be hit.

When the round hit within approximately 100 meters, the next command was a change of 50 meters, followed by the command "fire for effect." The order "fire for effect" meant that the target had been zeroed in, and more rounds were to be fired, to annihilate the target.

The most mentally challenging job was that of the plotter (FDC). Our instruction included FDC organization and equipment, operating a plotting board, preparing observed firing charts, preparing surveyed firing charts, computing basic missions, using deflection conversion tables, determining and applying meteorological (weather) corrections, and special missions.

The FDC's job was to convert the calls for fire support into proper fire commands, to insure accurate mortar fire on the target. He marked (plotted) the FO and mortar positions on a map grid. As he received changes from the FO, he plotted the changes on his plotting board grid and computed a new azimuth and range for the gunner.

The range settings were determined by a combination of mortar tube elevation and number of charges, obtained from a tabular firing table. The FDC then communicated to the gunner the new tube azimuth and elevation, and the number of charges to be placed on the round.

An example of an initial, or follow-up fire order given to the mortar (or section) would be "HE (type of round), one round (number of rounds to be fired), deflection 2801 (direction in mils), charge six (amount of charges on the round), elevation 0919 (elevation in mils to be placed on the mortar."

When it was determined that the rounds were striking close enough to the target as to not require a change, the following firing order was given: "HE, fire for effect, ten rounds." At that time the mortar crew fired ten rounds, utilizing the same deflection, charges, and elevation as was used with the previous round.

Illumination rounds required more complex computations, including determining the range to burst (horizontal distance measured from the gun to the burst point), elevation (angle of the mortar that, used in conjunction with fuse setting, produces an air burst 600 meters above the target area), and fuse setting (number set on fuse that will produce an air burst 600 meters above the target area).

Before firing the four-deuce mortar, we were instructed on how to handle misfires. The first crewmember to notice a misfire was responsible for loudly announcing, "Misfire." At that point all crewmembers were to remain with the mortar but cease operations.

If the round could still be seen, protruding from the mortar tube, the gunner was responsible for removing it. If, however, the round slid partially or completely down the tube, the gunner was to position himself behind the mortar tube and kick it sharply with the heel of his boot, several times.

If that didn't work, the gunner had to wait until the barrel was sufficiently cool enough to grasp with his bare hands. The mortar tube was then dislodged from the base unit, and the rear of the tube was raised to a horizontal position. The rear was then slowly raised, enough so the mortar round slid toward the tube muzzle. The assistant gunner was to grasp the round, remove it from the tube, and place it a safe distance away from the weapon and other personnel. The round was later destroyed.

Upon receiving a new fire command from FDC or the section chief, the gunner repeated all commands. That reduced the possibility of error, especially important when the target was near friendly units. When the gunner announced the ammunition type and charge amount for the round, the ammunition bearer repeated the information, then prepared the round and charge for use.

Prior to firing the round, the gunner removed the sight unit from the mortar. The ammunition bearer handed the prepared mortar round to the assistant gunner. The assistant gunner grasped the round near the center, then guided it carefully into the barrel, tail first, being careful not to disturb the lay of the mortar tube. Upon assuring the round was inserted correctly, he then moved his hand away from the round quickly, in a downward motion, parallel to the mortar tube, thus dropping the round down the tube.

• • •

During AIT, a pair of Special Forces Green Beret recruiters gave a talk to our training unit. They impressed me very much. They also showed a short movie about Special Forces in action. I had never previously heard of Special Forces or of the Green Berets and, of course, had no idea what they did, or what their mission was, until those recruiters gave us their spiel.

I later learned that 1962 was the first year that Special Forces recruits were recruited from men just having enlisted in the Army. Prior to that Special Forces had only accepted non-commissioned officers (NCOs). The term "Green Beret" came about because Special Forces soldiers wore (and still wear) green berets as their official headgear.

The first Special Forces group (the 10th Special Forces Group [Airborne]) was formed in 1952. In the fall of 1961, when President John F. Kennedy approved the wearing of the green beret by Special

Forces soldiers. He called the green beret "a symbol of excellence, a badge of courage, a mark of distinction in the fight for freedom."

To become a member of Special Forces a man had to be a triple volunteer. First, he had to have voluntarily enlisted in the Army (or voluntarily extended for an addition year if he had been drafted into the Army), then volunteered for Airborne (paratrooper), and finally volunteered for Special Forces.

Keep in mind that the term Special Forces denoted, and still denotes, U.S. Army Special Forces units, not Rangers, Air Commandos, Navy SEALs or other special units. Some media have problems using the correct terminology. Units such as Rangers, Air Commandos and SEALs (as well as Special Forces) are officially designated as Special Operations units.

The more the recruiters talked about the mission and the qualifications needed to be a part of Special Forces, the more I wanted to be a part of such a great unit. I immediately volunteered, as did about twenty other men from my AIT class. That evening I called home to tell my mother and father. The immediate reaction was mom crying in the background and dad accusing me of having a death wish. They were very mad at me.

Shortly after volunteering for Special Forces our group of SF recruits were given a phalanx of tests, with required minimum standards for passage. We began with the Army Physical Readiness Test for Special Forces physical qualification, basically a PT (physical training) test.

The Army had four grading levels for PT tests. The easiest was the minimum score to determine qualification to be in the Army. If you were weak in one area of that test, you could make it up in another part. The next higher score was qualification for being part of a combat unit. The third highest score was qualification for Jump School and Airborne units. The toughest score was that used to determine qualifications for Ranger and/or Special Forces.

For Jump School, Ranger and Special Forces, there was no such thing as making up for a weak area. Every exercise had minimum standards, and every single repetition had to be done perfectly. Weakness on any exercise meant flunking. The tests included push-ups, pull-ups, sit-ups, squat jumps, and a timed two-mile run, all done while wearing combat boots and fatigues.

There was a difference between pull-ups and chin-ups. I had done lots of chin-ups before entering the Army. Chin-ups were done with the palms facing toward you, whereas pull-ups were done with the palms facing away. Pull-ups were a LOT HARDER to do than chin-ups.

Airborne push-ups also had strict rules as to form. Each repetition had to be accomplished with the head and eyes facing forward, hands in a forward position, a ramrod straight back during the entire exercise, elbows in the locked position at the top of the push-up, and no squirming while doing the exercise. Any imperfect repetition was not counted.

"The first and last essential of an efficient soldier is character; without it he will not long endure the perils of modern war." — Charles Wilson, First Baron Moran

Next were the Special Forces Selection Battery tests. These tests measured intelligence, reading and mathematical knowledge, foreign language aptitude, psychological makeup, self-location (determining your location from a series of photos), decision-making aptitude, and Morse code aptitude.

Special Forces had to have a special mindset. More was required for acceptance than just being physically fit. Special Forces was looking for men who could improvise at a moment's notice, respond well to tough ethical dilemmas, and were culturally sensitive. They also wanted men who could operate independently and react well to unpredictable situations, without direct supervision, and without a chance of the individual becoming unstable. In addition, they wanted men who were willing to take on dangerous, and sometimes lonely, missions without complaint.

"Ten soldiers wisely led will beat a hundred without a head." — Euripides

There was a saying that the Army was interested in men with a strong back and a weak mind. That could certainly not be said about Special Forces. Some volunteers had already been dropped from selection due to recorded medical deficiencies, and others due to their GT test (Army equivalent of an IQ test) scores being too low.

What a lot of people didn't realize is that the GT score required for selection into Special Forces was equal to that required to become an officer in the United States Army (110). That gives a pretty good indication of the intelligence of the Special Forces soldier. In fact, it was said by one general that the average Special Forces soldier's GT score was higher than that of the average Army general. All Special Forces soldiers were expected to be leaders, not just the SF officers. About 60% of the volunteers were immediately dropped from the list of potential "Green Berets," due to their test results.

Because of the many classified missions and activities Special Forces was involved in on a regular basis, I had to immediately initiate a request for a Secret security clearance, the minimum required to be in Special Forces.

The form I had to complete included listing every place I had ever lived, schools I had attended, personal friends' names and addresses (which included a few Swedes, a native-born German, and the kicker, a Russian-born exchange student from Kuwait [his parents were Russian]), any run-ins with law enforcement (clean as a whistle), and my basic financial status (there were times, I guess, that I mishandled my allowance, LOL).

A poor financial history or a criminal record was almost a guarantee that the application would be rejected. By the time all the ensuing training (including Special Forces training) was completed, I was the only one of the twenty-some volunteers from my AIT class to eventually graduate to a Special Forces unit.

I caught pneumonia. I was admitted to the post hospital on or about Friday, 8 June. Pneumonia was so prevalent at Ft. Ord that the hospital had a ward especially for pneumonia cases. The reason it was prevalent was the fog. Along the California coast, fog was almost a daily occurrence in the summer, especially during the morning hours. The cadre ran the trainees and conducted physical training (PT) in the morning while the trainees wore only a short-sleeved T-shirt for upper body cover. Between PT exercises the trainees were sweating while standing in the cold, damp fog, in their T-shirts. That was very conducive towards catching pneumonia.

I had an x-ray of my lung on Tuesday, to determine how my pneumonia treatment was progressing and they still didn't have the results on Friday. A couple of the men in my ward said they had x-rays done on Saturday, and still didn't have results, six days later. I spent over a week in the hospital. It took what seemed like forever before a doctor even saw me after I was admitted. I felt abandoned.

A PX (Post Exchange store) cart came around daily, selling items we might wish to buy. In addition, a Red Cross lady came through with a cart full of free books to choose from. During that time, on 14 June, I was administratively promoted to Private E-2 (the next higher pay grade) due to my four months of time in the service. I was still a slick sleeve (no rank stripes on the arm) but for some reason it felt good to be promoted. That same day they x-rayed me.

I had been bored silly. I kept occupied the last few days of my "incarceration" by doing paint-by-number acrylic paintings of horses. Paint-by-number paintings were white canvases that were lightly pre-lined, with numbers within the lined areas. The numbers denoted the paint color to utilize for that section. I completed two paintings during my last three days in the hospital. The truth is, I did a pretty good job with those paintings, enough so that I gave them to my then girlfriend, June, for a birthday present.

June came all the way down to Ft. Ord from San Jose to visit me on the 17th, along with my friend Ron from nearby Carmel, and Mom and Dad later in the day. By Monday, 18 June, I was really becoming stir-crazy. The staff had to wait for x-ray results before I could be released, and the results still hadn't come, a week later. The results had apparently been loaded on the slow boat, via China.

D Company-11th Battle Group-3rd Brigade

I was finally released from the hospital on Tuesday, the 19th. I sure was happy to finally get out of there. Army training couldn't, in any way, be compared to any civilian school system. Civilian teachers were allowed free rein as to how they taught a subject if it was effective and certain

106mm Recoilless Rifle. (Internet photo)

Typical Wooden Barracks. (my photo)

subjects were included.

Army training courses and schools followed rigid lesson plans, formulated by the Army, to be followed in sequence, as well as subject matter. In this way, if the trainee missed a portion of his training due to illness, or other problem, he/she could be re-cycled from one unit or class to another, without missing a beat, continuing right where he/she left off. Thankfully, I had just completed my mortar training before having come down with the pneumonia. In fact, I had completed mortar qualifying as an expert mortar gunner.

I was immediately re-cycled to another company to finish my training. My new training unit was D Company, 11th Battle Group, 3rd Brigade (Delta-11-3). Our barracks were the old World War II non-descript two-story wooden frame style. The bottom floor consisted of two small rooms at one end, designed to house cadre, a large "squad bay" in the center, and a community latrine (bathroom facilities) at the far end.

As was the case in the other barracks, the toilets were open stalls, so everybody could see you as you went about your business of dropping a load. Nothing like being on display while shitting, even though only men were permitted in the barracks. If I got an urge to shit, it waited until I had no choice.

I did everything possible to spend the least possible time sitting on that shitter. The same held true for the shower facilities (there were no bathtubs). They were communal. I had always been shy, even to the point of not liking to shit, piss, shower, or dress in front of other people. The Army, I will have to say, did a quick job of us getting rid of that shyness.

Although called a squad bay, the bay usually housed 16-18 metal double bunk beds, sleeping 32-36 soldiers. The second floor was similar, except there was no latrine facility on that floor. The head of each bunk was on the outside of the bay. Against the wall, behind each bunk, were our wall lockers, one per person. At the foot of the bunks, lining the bay corridor, were our footlockers, also one per person. On either side of the long corridor were vertical 4"x4" supports lining the corridor, each with a nail pounded in at a slight angle, upon which hung a red-painted #10 butt can. The building was heated during the winter by a coal-fed furnace.

On Monday, 25 June our unit went to the field, sleeping in pup tents. Upon arriving in the field two of us paired up, fastened our tent-halves together, and put up the tent that we would share. We trained in battle tactics and how to live in the field. An entire day was spent on Escape and Evasion, basically teaching us how to escape and evade, as well as how to act if we were captured.

That evening we put our training into practice. I was caught once but managed to escape before we arrived at the "prisoner of war (POW)" compound. Through it all I ended up with a badly skinned elbow and very sore knees.

We returned from the field late Friday afternoon, 29 June. We were immediately told to clean all our gear and have it ready for inspection Saturday morning. No rest for the weary. On 30 June, because of my promotion to Private E-2, I received a huge pay raise (let's hear a big cheer) of $5.20 a month, to $83.20 monthly.

Upon having returned from the field we began training on the M40 106mm recoilless rifle, on 2 July. Our training began indoors, with a static display of the weapon, as well as some training aids. The weapon did not actually have a 106mm bore; its bore was 105mm. It was called the 106mm recoilless rifle to distinguish its ammunition from other ammunition.

The M40 recoilless rifle was an approximately 460-pound crew-served direct fire weapon (targets were in sight of the weapon and aimed using a telescopic sight trained on the target) that was a little over eleven feet in length, and almost four feet high. It was originally produced as an anti-tank weapon but could also be used in an anti-personnel role.

The blast from the firing of the weapon escaped out the rear of the weapon, resulting in a much-reduced recoil upon firing. The danger from firing this weapon was from standing behind the weapon. The back-blast from the tube could cause much bodily harm to anyone who made the mistake of standing or walking behind the weapon when it was fired.

Rounds for the weapon included HEAT (high explosive anti-tank), HEP-T (high explosive plastic-tracer, and AP-T (antipersonnel-tracer). The weapon had a maximum range of about 8,000 yards, and a maximum effective range of almost 1,500 yards. M40s were normally employed in general support missions along the forward edge of the battle area, normally covering most likely avenues of support, and located to give mutual support.

We began firing the weapon on 5 July, known as "train-fire." The weapon sported an M8C .50-caliber spotting rifle on top of the tube, to aid with aiming the weapon. To aim the weapon, it would be basically pointed toward the target. Then the weapon was traversed left or right, using a traverse hand wheel located on the mount. The barrel was raised or lowered as needed to place the target on the gun sight crosshairs, using the elevating hand wheel on the left side.

Upon acquisitioning the target in the aiming scope, a round from the .50-caliber spotting rifle was fired, by pulling on the elevation wheel trigger. The weapon was then re-aimed according to the hit of the .50-caliber round. The hit location was determined from the white puff of smoke given off by its impact.

The .50-caliber round was not a normal machine gun round, rather being a specially manufactured round to as closely as possible simulate the flight path of the explosive round. In a worse-case scenario, the .50-cal. round could have been used as an anti-personnel round but was not designed as such.

The M40 round was fired by pushing in on the elevation wheel trigger mechanism. The 106 could be ground mounted or mounted on a vehicle, usually a jeep. We fired the weapon from both ground mounts and vehicle mounts.

We were constantly reminded of the hazard of standing, or walking, behind the M40 when it was fired. Another bad thing about the weapon was the decibel level of the fired weapon. We were not issued, nor temporarily given, hearing protection. The weapons were routinely fired without protective devices, resulting in personnel on 106s incurring clinically significant hearing losses.

We began qualifying on the 106 on Tuesday, 10 July. On that

first day of recorded firing, I tied the base record, with 240 points out of a possible 240 points. They announced my score over the range loudspeaker. By the end of qualifying I had earned my First Class Recoilless Rifle Gunner badge. I was told that the following Saturday, 14 July, a delegation of VIPs was coming to Ft. Ord to see what kind of training was conducted.

I was selected as one of three men to man a 106mm recoilless rifle for a live fire exercise. We arrived at the firing range Saturday morning, well prior to the VIPs arriving. I don't remember how many rounds were laid out for firing, but it was a bunch.

I had been assigned to be the recoilless rifle team's loader, responsible for loading each round into the weapon. The target was a burned-out, blasted-many-times tank hulk downrange. My position was on the left rear of the weapon. We fired numerous rounds, putting on a great, noisy, and explosive show, but were not equipped with earplugs. After the live fire demonstration, I could not hear ANYTHING until Monday.

After the demonstration, we had to clean the weapon. I couldn't hear a thing our instructor said. To this day, my right ear has significant hearing loss. I should have gone on sick call for my hearing problem, but I didn't. Going on sick call was frowned upon by the training cadre. I was also authorized a weekend pass, as a reward for participating in the exhibition. I wasn't about to lose out on that pass by going on sick call.

As with Basic Training, our AIT was eight weeks of intense training, generally Monday through Friday, 10-14 hours a day, with Saturdays dedicated to inspections and administrative purposes, and Sundays free. Unlike Basic, we were occasionally authorized to leave the company area but generally not go off post.

Our class had its last day of training on Friday, 27 July. On that day, each of us was awarded our first MOS, that of 112.0, Infantry Indirect Fire Crewman. For the first time in the Army, I had an official career, or job, designation.

MOS was the acronym for Military Occupational Specialty. The first number (1) designated that it was a combat MOS. The second number (1) identified the Career Group of Infantry or Armor. The third number (2) indicated the subgroup of Infantry Indirect Fire Crewman (also known as Heavy Weapons). The fourth number (0, after the decimal point) indicated that my Level of Skill was "entry level." I was a full-fledged, inexperienced, deadly (probably more-so to me, than others), killing machine.

Upon graduation, the following day, I looked even sharper in my Class-A uniform than I had after Basic Training, wearing my newly authorized, highly-polished, crossed rifles infantry brass, with light blue plastic discs behind, and surrounding, the branch and U.S. collar insignia.

On my chest, I wore my also newly awarded "First Class Gunner" Qualification Badges for 81mm and 4.2" Mortar and Recoilless Rifle, as well as my previously issued Rifle and Pistol "Marksman" badges, earned in Basic Training.

Because of being re-cycled due to my bout of pneumonia, my new orders had not yet been cut, or forwarded to my training unit. I therefore had to remain at Ft. Ord for a couple extra weeks, awaiting orders sending me to Ft. Benning GA for Jump School. During that time, I wore the infantry blue dickey under my fatigue uniform and was classified as temporary "permanent party." I felt very important, even though I had no specific job.

One day I was assigned to escort, on foot, a prisoner to the stockade. He had been AWOL. I was unarmed. I guess they figured the prisoner was not a flight risk. It was a very long walk to the stockade, over some parts of Ft. Ord that were devoid of people. As we neared the stockade, the prisoner told me he had a knife, but had decided not to use it in an escape attempt and turned it over to me.

I couldn't believe that nobody had inspected him before turning him over to me, especially since I was going to be unarmed. I was quickly learning to not trust the obvious being done in the Army, but to expect the unexpected, and possibly the worst.

On 3 August Australian "battle-hardened jungle fighters" arrived in South Vietnam at the request of the South Vietnamese government. They were there to teach anti-guerrilla tactics to the South Vietnamese

Army (ARVN). Quite a few of them worked with Special Forces teams in Vietnam.

I had to wait almost four weeks at Ft. Ord, doing all sorts of boring miscellaneous jobs. I also did some exercising and running, to keep in shape for my upcoming Jump School. I was finally notified, on Monday 20 August, that my orders had arrived, and I was to fly out on Friday, to report to Fort Benning, GA, and the Basic Airborne Course headquarters, that day.

Early Friday morning, the 24th, I woke up, and finished packing my duffel bag. I had packed most of my belongings the night before. I dressed in my khaki dress uniform and reported to our unit headquarters building. After a short wait, a bus arrived, and I loaded on, carrying my duffel bag. I was transported to the Monterey Airport, arriving a short time later to catch my United Air Lines flight to Los Angeles.

I had to wait about 45 minutes for my flight to be announced on the airport loudspeaker system. The boarding went quickly, since there weren't many passengers there for my flight. I located a window seat on the right side of the aircraft. I always enjoyed sitting next to the window because it afforded me a view outside, as I still do. I opted to sit on the right side, because that would offer the best view of the coast, as we flew south, to Los Angeles.

As soon as we passengers were loaded, and seated, the door was firmly latched shut, the wheeled stairway rolled away from the aircraft (there were no ramps at the Monterey Airport), and the engine start-up procedure began. When the engines were running smoothly, the pilot pulled out, taxiing to the active runway, Runway 10 (basically an eastbound takeoff). Being the low-traffic airport that Monterey was, we were cleared for takeoff as soon as we reached the west end of the runway. The pilot taxied to the far west north/south taxiway, turned right onto it, then another right onto the runway, eastbound.

While aligning the aircraft with the runway, the pilot applied full power. We were on our way! The aircraft picked up speed, pushing our backs against the seat backs. Upon reaching liftoff speed, the nose lifted, and we began our climb. Upon reaching a safe altitude, our aircraft banked to the right, continuing to climb. We flew down the coast. It offered a stunning view of the central and southern California coast.

About an hour later, we began our approach to LAX (Los Angeles International Airport). We had been heading southeast for a while, flying inland. I could feel the airspeed decrease, as we entered a "pattern" for landing. At about a thousand feet above ground, we turned slightly right, on a modified base leg. Shortly before reaching the axis of Runway 24, we banked to the right, and lined up with the runway. Our aircraft continued to descend, flying over the city suburbs. The touchdown was uneventful. Well before the end of the runway, our aircraft taxied off it, making a right turn, and headed to the terminal area.

Upon arriving at the tarmac, and offloading, I walked to the Delta terminal area, to check in and wait for my Delta connecting flight to Atlanta GA. I was only 19 years old, so I couldn't sit in the bar, or have an alcoholic drink. I therefore ordered a Coke and sipped on it while I waited for my next flight.

After a short wait, my flight number was called on the loud speaker. I got in the long line for my flight boarding. After what seemed like forever, I boarded the Delta Airlines Douglas DC-8 jet, and again found an empty window seat near the middle of the aircraft, just behind the wing. After an uneventful takeoff, from Runway 24, we made a slow climbing turn, over the ocean, to an eventual eastbound heading.

We were in the air for a little over three hours. The entire time, I was wondering what I had gotten myself into. I remembered, vividly, the misery I had gone through with my right knee after injuring it playing basketball at San Jose State, and the fact that the doctor had ordered that my orders to Jump School be rescinded.

I had no idea how my knee would hold up, fearful of not being able to complete some mandatory exercises, and even more fearful that I would not make the grade for something I had worked so hard to accomplish. And then, there was the Special Forces training following that. Suddenly doubts were emerging, and I was nervous about my future.

We finally entered the landing pattern of Atlanta Municipal Airport. That managed to temporarily curb my worries about what my near future was going to be like. After touching down, taxiing to the terminal, and deplaning, I walked to the gate from which my next flight would depart.

While there, I met a couple of the men from my first AIT unit, who were departing for another Army assignment. They both had been medically disqualified from Jump School. I found the gate for my next and final flight, a feeder airline, flying a short 45 minutes to Columbus, GA.

Meeting my former training mates rekindled my fears about Jump School, and the fears of my knee ruining my future. Thankfully those fears were short-lived; they faded as we approached the Columbus Airport. Upon deplaning I went to the baggage claim area to retrieve my duffel bag.

I followed the signs that led me to the Fort Benning transportation hub, and the bus that would take me to Fort Benning, GA. After a ride of a little over a half hour, I got off the bus at the 43rd Company, 4th Battalion, the Student Brigade headquarters, and proceeded to sign in.

CHAPTER 4

JUMP SCHOOL

Blood on the Risers

He was just a rookie trooper and he surely shook with fright.
He checked off his equipment and made sure his pack was tight.
He had to sit and listen to those awful engines roar.
You ain't gonna jump no more.

Chorus: Gory, gory, what a hell of a way to die.
Gory, gory, what a hell of a way to die.
Gory, gory, what a hell of a way to die.
He ain't gonna jump no more.

'Is everybody happy?' cried the sergeant looking up.
Our hero feebly answered, 'Yes,' and they stood him up.
He jumped into the icy blast, his static line unhooked.
And he ain't gonna jump no more.

He counted long, he counted loud, he waited for the shock.
He felt the wind, he felt the cold, he felt the awful drop.
The silk from his reserve spilled out and wrapped around his legs.
And he ain't gonna jump no more.

The risers swung around his neck, connectors cracked his dome.
Suspension lines were tied in knots around his skinny bones.
The canopy became his shroud, he hurtled to the ground.
And he ain't gonna jump no more.

The days he lived and loved and laughed kept running through his
*   mind.*
He thought about the girl back home, the one he left behind.
He thought about the medicos and wondered what they'd find.
And he ain't gonna jump no more.

The ambulance was on the spot, the jeeps were running wild.
The medics jumped and screamed with glee, rolled up their sleeves
*   and smiled.*
For it had been a week or more since last a 'chute had failed.
And he ain't gonna jump no more.

He hit the ground, the sound was 'Splat,' his blood went spurting
*   high.*
His comrades they were heard to say, 'A helluva way to die.'
He lay there rolling 'round in the welter of his gore.
And he ain't gonna jump no more.

There was blood upon the risers, there were brains upon the 'chute.
Intestines were a-dangling from his paratrooper suit.
He was a mess, they picked him up and poured him from his boots.
And he ain't gonna jump no more.

Army Airborne (Jump) School

I arrived at Ft. Benning by bus, for the Basic Airborne Course, on 24 August (the hottest time of the year). I signed into headquarters and was assigned to 43rd Company, 4th Student Battalion, The Student Brigade, in Class #9. The school was run by the 4th Airborne Training Battalion (Airborne), The Student Brigade, U.S. Army Infantry School. Although officially classified as a school by the Army, the Basic Airborne Course was more physical training than scholastic training. It was also a mental test as far as overcoming fear of heights. In fact, I can't remember any portion of the course that included indoor classroom instruction.

The mission of Jump School was to teach us how to don our parachutes and equipment correctly, and then correctly jump out of a perfectly good airplane in flight, descend toward earth, and land, without injury. Critical to those activities was knowing how to react to any unplanned problems that might occur during that activity.

Mental alertness, confidence in equipment and its reliability, and the ability to react automatically, quickly, and correctly, were of paramount importance. To those of us going through the training, however, it seemed as if the mission of the school was to give the drill instructors an outlet for their pent-up anger and rage, utilizing us as their targets. At least we all knew that after graduation we would be paid more, thus making our ordeal a little more tolerable.

As each of us arrived, we were sent to the unit supply room for issuance of our usual bedding: mattress cover, two sheets, two blankets, and a pillowcase. Our barracks was the old World War II non-descript two-story wooden frame style building I had lived in during the latter part of my AIT at Fort Ord.

Sadly, but not surprisingly, the barracks had no air conditioning. The temperatures for the time I was there (August and September) were in the 90s and 100s, with the usual southeastern miserable humidity to match. We sweated day and night. Whether it was 2200 hours or 0400 hours, we were sweating even while still. All our beds were double bunks, which lined each side of the open bay. As was usual with military barracks, the latrine facilities were totally open; no privacy whatever. The same held true for the shower facilities.

Upon arrival and recommended by friends (and cadre) already there, a group of seven of us began preparing for what lay ahead of us. Beginning on Saturday the 25th, we set aside free time to run (twenty-minute runs with no stopping) and exercise. At the end of each session sweat was pouring from every pore of my body, my T-shirt was solidly stuck to my chest, and my lungs were heaving from the exertion. That gave me an idea of what I was up against for the next few weeks.

I began wondering why, in my right mind, I really wanted to go through Jump School. I knew there would be a physical fitness test that

I would have to pass prior to beginning training. In fact, I knew it was scheduled for Tuesday, the 28th.

The only exercise I was truly worried about was the push-up, since that was my weakest exercise. All exercises, including running, were done in uniform and wearing combat boots. I quit smoking that week. I lasted all of 12 hours. That was an impossible place to even attempt ceasing dragging on the weed.

As soon as everyone who was scheduled to be assigned to our class number arrived, we were briefed as to how we would act and what was expected of us during our assignment to the Student Brigade. Greatly impressed upon us was the fact that Airborne troopers were better and sharper than any "legs," and we were to hold to those standards even though we were still "legs." The word "leg" was a derogatory term used to describe anybody who was not "jump qualified," or who had never jumped out of a perfectly good aircraft, in flight.

The "Black Hat" cadre (our Airborne instructors, also known as "Black Hats" due to the black baseball caps they wore) certainly made for good examples of what they described as sharp paratroopers. The Black Hats all wore highly spit-shined Corcoran jump boots, black baseball caps, highly-starched and tailored fatigue trousers bloused into their jump boots, as well as form fitting white T-shirts, with the excellent physiques to look good in those T-shirts. The officers wore highly-starched, tailored khaki trousers bloused into their jump boots, and form fitting white T-shirts. The NCOs were all "Master Blasters" (Master Parachutists).

The Black Hats warned us that any time one of them yelled "AIRBORNE!" we were to immediately reply "ALL THE WAY!" That exchange was an Airborne tradition that still holds. We were also told in no uncertain terms that our hair needed to be shorter, our fatigues needed to be cleaner, our boots needed to be MUCH shinier (i.e. spit-shined), and our bunks needed to be made MUCH tighter (so a coin would bounce off it) than when we were in Basic and AIT.

I spent a LOT more time spit-shining my boots there than I did in Basic or AIT. In fact, I added a step to the process, using my cigarette lighter to melt the Kiwi shoe polish and a torn-up T-shirt to rub it into the leather of the boot. The T-shirt seemed to do the application of the melted shoe polish the best. I then wet the T-shirt and rubbed the boot with it in circles, attaining a good "spit-shine."

While eating our daily breakfast, a member of the cadre went through the barracks and tore apart any bed that wasn't up to Airborne standards. That meant re-making the bed immediately, if returning to your barracks and finding your bedding on the floor. It also meant a gig on that trainee's record. Too many gigs in a week, and the trainee was re-cycled, having to repeat that same week again. NOBODY wanted that!

Many trainees voluntarily quit rather than repeat a week. The Black Hats were much tougher on us than we ever experienced in Basic or AIT. They were hard-ass and vulgar, and they seemed to delight in screaming at us. I will have to admit, however, that some trainees were more deserving of being a target of their wrath than others. Those who became the favorite target of the Black Hats generally did not last long and quit. It was not comfortable being a "target rich" individual.

Most of my complaining before beginning official training had to do with the awful heat and humidity and what I considered to be "rotten" food, the likes of which I wrote home was "the lousiest I've had in my life." We always went to the mess hall in formation, at a double time. While waiting in line, unless moving, we had to stand at a rigid parade rest.

The first week was basically "Detail Week," also known as "Zero Week." It consisted mostly of physical conditioning, harassment, and details. My schedule that week was basically:

0400 hours, reveille—dress, shave and wash up, make bed to Airborne standards, quickly clean designated area, and sleep on the floor until

0500 formation—daily information disseminated by drill instructors and double-time to mess hall for breakfast

0545 return to barracks—sleep on floor until

0630 police call and PT (Physical Training)

0700 return to barracks—sleep on floor until

0730 formation—assigned and sent to daily details

1130 formation—double-time to mess hall for lunch

1230 return to barracks—sleep on floor until

1300 formation—assignment to afternoon details

1630 formation—double-time to mess hall for dinner

1730 relax until

1800 mail call, the most important formation for mental stability. After mail call, run for exercise with friends, shine boots, polish brass, wash clothes (and place the fatigues between the mattress and cot bedsprings to press while sleeping), relax, read a book, write letters until

2230 lights out (bedtime) for the barracks.

Falling asleep wasn't difficult. As tired as we always were, we could fall asleep at the drop of a hat, and anywhere. A wooden floor for a bed might not sound comfortable, but at least it was a flat surface onto which we could stretch our tired bodies. If I had free time in the evening I would almost always go to the barracks where my AIT buddies were, in Class #6. I discussed with them what I could look forward to in my training, as well as some helpful hints. At 2100 hours I usually shined my boots, polished my brass, and took a shower. Then I would wash my clothes, get into bed, and read until lights out at 2230.

The details we could be assigned to varied widely: They could be anything as simple as cleaning, painting or guarding the barracks, to KP (kitchen police — peeling potatoes, washing trays, etc.), to serving officers in the Officers' Mess Hall. Details were almost always physical in nature.

Making the bed consisted of square corners, no wrinkles and making sure the covers were so tight that a dime dropped on the bed would bounce. From wake-up time (reveille) through the morning and afternoon, sleep was attained at any time possible. Sleep consisted of curling up on the barracks floor (don't you dare lie or sit on your bed, mussing it, at any time during the day) and sleeping, even if only for 10-15 minutes.

There were no chairs in the barracks. If you wanted to sit, you sat on the barracks stairways or on your footlocker. There were also no televisions in the barracks. Jump School became expensive when I had to buy enough new clothing to have the required amount of "serviceable" gear for passing inspection. The first week I had to purchase three pair of socks, three T-shirts, and two pairs of fatigue uniforms, to replace those in my possession that wouldn't pass inspection there.

The qualifying physical fitness test was tougher than I had expected. Out of 200 in our class, only 150 passed. We had to do 4 PERFECT "Airborne" pull-ups, 34 PERFECT sit-ups in two minutes, 80 PERFECT knee-benders (deep knee-bends), 22 PERFECT "Airborne" push-ups (fingers forward on the ground), and a 4-minute run – 2-minute walk – 4-minute run – 2-minute walk – 4-minute run. During all exercises (except the run, which was done in formation) a cadre member was watching the individual being tested.

During the first two weeks at Jump School, roughly half of the men quit or were drummed out due to physical reasons. Harassment and tough physical regimens, especially running and push-ups, during the first two weeks were the normal reasons for quitting. All running was done in formation and in step, with cadence being counted by your "Black Hat." During our entire time at Jump School we did not receive a single pass.

My next to last day of detail week (Thursday, 30 August) was spent pleasing officers. My detail began at 0800, moving beds and dressers from one floor to another in the Bachelor Officers' Quarters (BOQ). At 1130 I was switched to KP (Kitchen Police — working in the mess hall) in the Officers' Candidate School (OCS) Mess Hall.

OCS was the school that enlisted men attended to become officers in the Army. The school included foreign officers, there to obtain training in the ways of the U.S. Army. Most of the officers I saw there were from Vietnam and Iran. There were also several from the Philippines, Saudi Arabia, Spain, Austria, Thailand, and several South American countries. That same morning my friends from AIT in Class #6 graduated.

On 31 August, I learned a hard fact of military life: Your financial records do not always follow your movements on a timely basis. My financial records had apparently gone somewhere other than where I was, making it impossible for my duty station to determine my pay.

Thus, I learned another military necessity. I could request a "partial payment" to hold me over until my records were found and I could receive my full authorized pay.

The following day, unbeknownst to me, U.S. Army Special Forces, Vietnam (Provisional) was formed in Saigon. That signaled the official increased commitment of Special Forces in Vietnam. Prior to that, the 1st Special Forces Group on Okinawa had been supplying men and teams to Vietnam.

Ground Week

The Soviet Union had agreed to send arms to Cuba, believing that the United States intended to attack Cuba. Routine surveillance flights by American aircraft discovered missile sites being built on Cuban soil, as well as Soviet Ilyushin IL-28 tactical strike medium bombers parked on tarmacs, with a range of about 1,000 miles, and capable of delivering atomic bombs. Tension between Cuba and the United States increased in magnitude.

The Cold War was getting much closer to American territory. There was a lot of fear that communist guns and weapons in Cuba were way too close to our shores. On 4 September, President Kennedy announced publicly that we would not tolerate offensive weapons being placed on Cuban soil.

The first official week (Ground Week) didn't begin until Tuesday, 4 September (due to the 3rd being Labor Day), more than a week after arrival at Benning. The first week consisted of a lot of physical training to get us in shape and weed out the recruits who couldn't make the grade physically, in addition to being instructed in individual airborne skills to prepare us to make a parachute jump and to land safely.

Once training began each recruit was assigned a number, which was displayed prominently on the front and rear of the helmet, written on tape. Throughout Jump School, the recruit was identified and yelled (screamed) at by his number only, regardless of rank. If a Drill Sergeant yelled your number, you had better respond immediately. My number was 348.

The classes consisted of a mix of Army, Navy and Air Force

personnel, including officers. The Air Force personnel were mostly Air Commando recruits, while the Navy men were mostly SEALs. Trainee officers were treated the same as enlisted. That was true for us trainees also. We talked to them as equals, not even calling them "sir."

During training, the day always began with a very stringent personal inspection by the Black Hats. Their inspections were the definition of picky. The inspections included personal cleanliness, neatness and cleanliness of uniform, spit-shined boots, recent haircut, and clean-shaven.

It was amazing how many "gigs" (mistakes) the Drill Sergeants could find. One of their favorites was to gig a recruit for needing a haircut. A very short crew cut was required. To pass inspection it was wise to have a haircut twice a week. Some recruits decided the easy way out was to shave their heads. Not smart! If the head was shaved, it had better be shaved EVERY morning, because ANY stubble was a gig.

Another favorite ploy was for the Black Hat to ask a recruit to undo his belt buckle. He would then thoroughly inspect the belt buckle to make sure the INSIDE of the damn thing was spotlessly shiny. I have no idea, to this day, why a belt buckle had to be flawlessly shiny on the inside.

One poor recruit in our class pulled the all-time idiotic stunt: Before Jump School he had a jump-wings tattoo placed prominently on his arm for everyone to see. Jump wings were only awarded after graduation from Jump School. The Black Hats harassed that poor recruit so much that he quit. He didn't even last a week. Need I say he didn't earn his wings?

"The first virtue in a soldier is endurance of fatigue; courage is only the second virtue." — *Napoleon Bonaparte*

Push-ups were a fact of life at Ft. Benning. It seemed every time you took a breath you were told to "DROP, GIVE ME TEN." It began in the morning, before breakfast. All movement at Jump School was done at double-time (running). Jump School had its special type of double-time, called the "Airborne shuffle." In other words, running. All standing was to be at a rigid attention or parade rest. After inspection, we were double-timed to the mess hall for breakfast.

A short while after breakfast we were again put in formation, followed by being double-timed to our physical training area. Once there, we began an hour of very intense physical training, which included push-ups, squat jumps, sit-ups, pull-ups, deep knee bends, squat thrusts, followed by a three-mile run, all done while sporting combat boots.

The squat jumps, deep knee bends, and squat thrusts were especially murderous on my bad right knee. Each repetition of those exercises was excruciating. Because of the heat and humidity, we were constantly reminded to stay hydrated and ingest a lot of salt, to replace the salt that left our body when we sweated, which we did a lot. Almost everywhere we went were drinking fountains and salt pill dispensers. We were constantly admonished to take our salt pills. It seems incongruous to me now. Every time I see a doctor now, I'm reminded to drastically reduce my salt intake. I sure wish they'd get their stories straight. Sheesh!

All exercises had to be done to the instructor's count and PERFECTLY. If a Black Hat caught you doing a single push-up incorrectly, he would "invite" you to do the push-ups again, and again, just to make sure you were proficient at doing your push-ups. We wore no shirts. When we were not exercising, we would have to stand at attention. Any twitch — usually brought on by the Georgia state bird: the gnat — brought on the dreaded… you guessed it, "DROP, GIVE ME TEN" (or twenty-two, depending on the week of training). You immediately assumed the prone position and began pushing the state of Georgia away from you, perfectly, time after time. Once a Black Hat got you for one thing, you were one of his favorite targets for the remainder of the day.

During running (of which there was a lot) anyone who got out of step while running was yelled at, and told to "DROP, GIVE ME TEN." That meant the offender was to get out of formation, drop to the ground and push the state of Georgia away from himself 10 times. In other words, do 10 push-ups.

While the offender did the 10 push-ups, the other recruits had to run (in step and formation) around the offender until he completed his 10 push-ups. Because that caused the group to have to run longer, and further, offenders were not especially appreciated by the rest of the group. Repeat offenders were especially disliked.

The SEALs really earned our ire because they purposely got out of step, and when they were told to "DROP, GIVE ME TEN" they would immediately yell "which arm, sergeant" and proceed to knock out 10 one-armed push-ups. Each running formation was followed by an ambulance, picking up men as they fell, passed out from the heat or suffering from sunstroke.

Much of the time running included chants done to the tempo of the run. A couple examples were:

1. "Airborne, Airborne, have you heard?
   We're gonna jump from a big iron bird."

2. "If I die on the old drop zone
   Box me up and send me home."

3. "Stand up! Hook up! Stand in the door!
   Stood up, then collapsed on the floor."

4. "GI bowl and GI gravy
   Gee I wish I'd gone in the Navy."

5. "There's no use in going home
   'Straight leg's' got my gal and gone."

6. "Airborne, Airborne, where you been?
   Ran 'round the post and goin' again.

7. Where you goin' when you get back
   Off the tower with full field pack."

I began very inauspiciously. The first day (Tuesday), during physical training in the early morning, I passed out. I was fortunate. We had just finished the last exercise when I dropped. Had it happened earlier, I probably would have been set back a week. It was a monumental struggle just to stand up, followed by swaying on my feet while standing. At least I wasn't alone. Three other trainees were taken to the hospital after passing out from heat and sunstroke. Ten trainees quit that same day. From then on, I made it a point to down plenty of salt tablets.

As usual, the second day's training began with physical training. I received a physical training gig. Four PT gigs in any one week was rumored to be reason enough to be re-cycled, being set back and repeating the entire week again. I had been screwing around before PT, knocking off about 50 push-ups within about fifteen minutes before the beginning of PT. I was able to knock out the four-count push-up, plus some other exercises, including having to drop and do push-ups for a screw-up, but when it came to the eight-count push-up (which included deep knee bends), I didn't perform them correctly. In addition, my right knee was in some major pain.

I didn't have much free time during the evening hours once training began. We had only three hours free by the time dinner and mail call were over with. I kept busy those three hours by washing my fatigues that I wore that day (a nightly ritual), showering the stench off the body, spit-shining my boots, and polishing my brass (belt buckle, including the inside of it, and belt tip). That left little time for writing letters.

Ground Week also consisted of learning how to exit the aircraft (using a mock door at ground level), as well as the preparation for exiting. Onboard the wooden mock aircraft, the preparation for making an exit took just a few minutes, following the commands yelled out by the jumpmaster. The commands were as follows:

"GET READY!" That was the command yelled by the jumpmaster alerting everybody that the time to jump was near at hand. We were to prepare our bodies for the next command, holding the static line metal hook in our right hands.

"STAND UP!" That commanded all jumpers to stand up, facing the steel cable to which the static line hook would be attached. The cable ran the length of the mock aircraft.

"HOOK UP!" At that command, each jumper attached their static line hooks to the steel cable.

"CHECK STATIC LINES!" Each jumper pulled on his static line attachment device, making sure it was firmly and safely attached and locked to the steel cable.

"CHECK EQUIPMENT!" That was the command for the jumpers to double check their equipment, making sure the harness and other equipment was attached correctly. The man behind each jumper checked that jumper's parachute set-up; the last man in line (last man in the "stick") did an about-face, so the man in front of him could check his parachute and equipment.

"SOUND OFF FOR EQUIPMENT CHECK!" Each man had a number in the stick assigned to him, beginning with the number one, assigned to the lead man. Starting in the rear of the jump line, each man sounded off with his number, followed by the word "OKAY" (i.e., NUMBER TEN OKAY . . . NUMBER NINE OKAY, etc.).

"STAND IN THE DOOR!" That command was to be followed by the number one man (head of the stick) standing in the exit door, knees slightly bent, and both hands on the outside of the door, ready to propel himself out of the door upon the command.

"GO!" The command to jump. The number one man jumped out the door, followed one at a time by the remaining jumpers. Upon exiting the door, the exit position was assumed, that being chin drawn in against the chest, forearms and fingers extended as if holding onto the reserve parachute, elbows tightly held against the side of the body, and counting "one thousand, two thousand, three thousand, four thousand," which represented the amount of time, in seconds, that it should take for the parachute to open.

The focus of Ground Week's training was jumping out of a simulated aircraft door with your elbows tight to your side, the hands gripping the reserve parachute (which was in front of the body, just below the belly), and the feet and knees tightly together.

That brought another harassment technique to bear against us. At any time, while in a group, or alone, a Black Hat could bark, "HIT IT!" At that time, the individual, or group to which the order was directed, was expected to immediately hop approximately six inches off the ground, coming to the exit position immediately after the hop, and proceed with the four second count. Anybody who failed to react in the time or the manner deemed correct by the Black Hat would immediately be dropped for the going rate of push-ups. It was not unusual for a trainee to average a few hundred push-ups a day.

On day two I jumped four times out of the 34-foot tower. The 34-foot tower was an enclosed boxlike structure on legs, with a simulated door. It was utilized to train for exiting the aircraft door and reacting to the opening of the parachute. The bottom of the box was 34 feet tall because some overpaid psychologists determined that was the height men most feared.

The door of the 34-foot tower was approximately the height of a fourth-story window. In fact, a couple men couldn't bring themselves to jump off it. Each recruit wore a harness, which included the reserve parachute and fake main parachute with strap and hook attached. The hook was attached to a rolling pulley. The pulley, in turn, was affixed to a long steel cable that reached from the tower (near the simulated aircraft door) to a dirt berm about 150 feet from the tower and slightly lower than the tower height. All four of my jumps were perfect. I found that I enjoyed jumping out of the tower immensely... the first few times.

The recruit was ordered to "stand in the door," at which time he stood in the door with his knees slightly bent and his hands flat against both sides of the outside of the door. One of the cadre then yelled "SOUND OFF WITH YOUR NAME AND NUMBER!" At that command, at my turn, I yelled, as loudly as possible "JAMES, NUMBER 348, SERGEANT!"

At the command "GO," the recruit jumped outward from the door using his legs and arms, assumed the tight position of head down (chin on the chest), elbows against the side of his body, hands on his reserve, and knees and feet tightly locked together with legs straight. Upon jumping out the door, the recruit immediately began counting out loud (loud enough for the Black Hats to hear), "ONE THOUSAND, TWO THOUSAND, THREE THOUSAND, FOUR THOUSAND."

At about the end of "one thousand, two," the strap reached the end of its length, approximately eight feet, abruptly stopping the jumper's downward progress. At "four thousand" the recruit was to look up, simulating checking to see if his parachute canopy was open and in good shape and grab the risers (the straps that attached him to the cable), all the while keeping his legs and feet together. Near the end of the cable (at the berm) other recruits grabbed the jumper and stopped his momentum. At that time, the recruit was unsnapped from the cable, and a Black Hat (with a very firm voice) critiqued his jump and, if need be, yelled "DROP, GIVE ME TEN."

All during that training function (which lasted through a good part of the day), the recruit had to keep the harness on. It was very uncomfortable (especially in the crotch area) because the harness had to be so tight. That week also brought on other uncomfortable results. When jumping out of the tower, the harness' metal "quick release" dug into the middle of my chest, causing the skin to rub off and puss to form and run. I saw the field medics about it. They taped a gauze bandage onto it and told me there was nothing to worry about. In addition to that, the harness was making my crotch feel like it was rubbed raw.

The missing skin in the middle of my chest became prime playground for the gnats (aka official Georgia state bird) while I stood at attention between exercises during PT, and they would gather there and have a party. We had been warned not to swat at the gnats, being advised that at least the gnats were airborne, while we were not. In addition, we were warned that killing a gnat was illegal, since it was the Georgia "official state bird." That was extremely bothersome, but reaction to their playtime was a no-no, since it would result in "DROP, GIVE ME TEN."

Fifteen additional trainees quit the second day of ground week, including two men who bunked next to me. As was usual for me during Jump School, I was forced to ask for more money from home to cover expenses. The fact that my paycheck wasn't keeping up with me didn't help matters. The partial pays that I was drawing were just that: PARTIAL pay. I was constantly writing home for $10 or $20.

Incorporated during the week was learning to do a correct Parachute Landing Fall (PLF). We began by all entering a sawdust pit. A Black Hat told us to perform a PLF, either left front, right front, left side, right side, left rear, or right rear. We then hopped vertically, and upon the feet returning to the ground, executed the direction of PLF we were ordered to complete.

The position we had to assume on the hop was the position recommended when preparing to land; hands reaching up as if pulling down on the parachute risers, elbows tight into the sides of the body, chin tucked into the chest, knees bent slightly, and feet and knees kept tightly together, toes pointed ever so slightly toward the ground.

Upon striking the ground, the PLF was performed. The correct PLF was supposed to be a sort of roll, included touching earth with the balls of the feet (with knees slightly bent), the right or left outside thighs, upper right or left body below the arms, then the upper back (shoulder area). No bones (especially knees or elbows) were to touch the ground during the PLF.

The PLF was always to be done to the left or the right. Heels, ass, and head PLFs were the ultimate no-no's (as were standing landings). An easy explanation is that it is nothing more than a controlled (hopefully) crash landing. Upon perfecting the PLF on the ground, we graduated to making a PLF off a five-foot high wooden platform.

We graduated to the Swing Landing Trainer. It was nicknamed a lot of different monikers, some unprintable. It consisted of a steel frame hanging from a cable and was designed to give the trainee the closest possible sensation to landing. We stood on a six-foot high wooden platform, wearing a parachute harness. The risers of the harness were attached to the steel frame.

Upon orders from the instructor, we stepped off the platform and swung freely by the risers. The instructor controlled the swinging and released the training device at his pleasure. I really think they had evil on their mind when releasing the device, because it always seemed to be released at the most inopportune time for an easy PLF.

When the cadre released the harness, the recruit was required to do a left or right PLF, depending on which way he was swinging when the harness was released. It had to be an instantaneous decision. My PLFs were thankfully good enough to receive compliments. Incorrect PLFs were, of course, punished by "DROP, GIVE ME TEN."

At that point in our training, "DROP, GIVE ME TEN" meant we

had to knock out twelve push-ups or knee-benders. The knee-benders were required when it was deemed impossible to do push-ups, such as when wearing a parachute harness, or parachute (reserve and/or main), which was during most of our parachute training. The extra two were for the sergeant, and for Airborne. When finished with the tenth, we knocked out the eleventh yelling "ONE FOR THE SERGEANT," followed by the twelfth and yelling "AND ONE FOR AIRBORNE."

The Swing Landing Trainer probably replicated real landing conditions better than any other method. For some reason (maybe because I was right-handed), I preferred to execute a right-side PLF. Maybe that's why my right leg is now ¾" shorter than my left, or perhaps my leg was always that short and was the reason I preferred right PLFs.

PLFs were extremely important for health reasons. The descent rate of the T-10 was 22 to 25 feet per second. It was said that the speed at which a T-10 jumper would hit the ground was the equivalent of jumping off the roof of a one-story house (kids, don't try this at home). That could hurt if the jumper didn't cushion his landing somehow.

Thursday morning, I couldn't do any knee bends correctly, due to my bad knee, resulting in another PT gig. That afternoon I split my chin open in two places during my first jump from the 34' tower apparatus. I had apparently not tightened my harness enough, resulting in the "quick release" metal unit on the front of the harness striking my chin when I reached the end of the strap after jumping out of the tower.

The resulting sudden stop resulted in the "quick release" rising to the level of my chin. I bled profusely. The result was "DROP, GIVE ME TEN," then a trip to the hospital for six stitches, and missing the remainder of the day's training. The stitches had to remain in my chin for nine days.

Thinking that I was now going to be re-cycled and need to repeat the same week again, and the fact that I had a knee problem that was extremely painful (and made it difficult doing most required exercises) made me reflect on what I was doing. I marched myself down to headquarters and paced back and forth, debating about quitting.

Sanity (some people might respond with insanity) finally got the better of me and I marched myself back to my barracks to face the music and begin week two all over again, no matter what. I knew the knee would be the worst problem, but I was determined to tough it out. All my worrying was for naught. I was not re-cycled. Thursday and Friday the weather was perfect: The sun didn't shine AT ALL.

Saturday, I received my first Personal Gig for needing a haircut. I sometimes had the impression that they dreamed up gigs for us, not wanting anybody to go without one. I had a haircut just a week before being gigged that day.

I learned the hard way that I was going to have to get a haircut twice a week to pass inspection. Heaven only knows how they could tell if it had been over four days since our last haircuts. On that morning, part of our PT was a 25-minute no-rest run. That same day, at noon, we completed Ground Week. I was not re-cycled because I had done enough correct exits from the tower. I had received only one Personal gig (dirty brass, dirty clothing, improperly polished boots, stubble on the face, haircut, etc.) and four Physical Training gigs for Ground Week, all due to my aching knee.

Five more men quit Jump School that Saturday, and fifteen were re-cycled, having to repeat ground week, most of them because of not making enough satisfactory jumps from the 34-foot tower.

At any time, for almost any reason, factual or dreamed, a trainee could be dropped for push-ups. After returning from having my chin stitched, I reached into my pocket to retrieve my sick call slip and turn it in as instructed. A sergeant saw me with my hand in my pocket and immediately dropped me for ten push-ups.

After finishing the push-ups, I tried to give my sick call slip to another sergeant during roll call, as I had been told to do. He immediately dropped me for ten push-ups for doing so. A mere thirty seconds later a sergeant dropped me for ten more push-ups, telling me that I shouldn't have the sick call slip on my person. I had the feeling that I had just become a convenient, target-rich environment.

While in the training area, all trainees had to stand at attention or at a rigid parade rest. If seated, you had to be seated at a modified position of attention, ramrod stiff. Of course, any time you moved, you had to move at double-time. No walking was permitted. During that week, I averaged about 200 push-ups and 100 knee-benders a day.

I finally came to realize that the best way to deal with pain was to alter my mindset. I convinced myself that whatever I was doing that was causing the pain was almost over with. I didn't dwell on the time remaining in Jump School, just the fact that the activity that was painful was close to completion. It worked… most of the time.

It was amazing what head trips could do to you if you didn't have a way of combating them. It was mind over matter. That first training week did a great job of separating the men from the boys, the boys being re-assigned to leg (non-Airborne) units.

Tower Week

During the following week (Tower Week, beginning Monday, 10 September) the heat returned, big time (101 on Thursday, with humidity to match), we graduated to "DROP, GIVE ME TWENTY," jumped with full equipment (field pack attached) from the 34-foot tower, made our first jumps from the 250-foot tower, went through suspended harness training, and had three hours of wind machine training.

On Wednesday (the 12th) I finally received a partial pay. Whoopee! It was all of $25. I was also told I wouldn't get paid until I reached my next duty station, hopefully Ft. Bragg. The following day (Thursday, the 13th) we had three hours of training with the wind machine. The wind machine was utilized to train in procedures for handling the parachute once on the ground, in a high wind situation. It was one way of showing us that we weren't always safe, even though we had already touched down on land.

There were several methods to collapse a parachute in a high wind environment. The preferred method was to quickly recover from the landing and run around to the top of the inflated parachute, deflating the canopy by hand, making it impossible for the wind to drag you along the ground.

The next method was to have a fellow jumper deflate the canopy for you. The third method entailed removing the protective covers

34-foot tower at Fort Benning GA. (Internet photo)

from the two "parachute quick-release" snaps (one at each shoulder) that fastened the parachute straps to the harness, then pulling both snaps to release the harness from the parachute.

The wind machine was followed by the Suspended Harness apparatus (aka suspended agony apparatus). That was the swing landing trainer but used for a different purpose. We practiced in-air procedures, including turning right, turning left, speeding up our forward progress, and slowing our rearward progress.

Suspended Harness training (aka hanging torture) taught and tested reflexes in steering and control of the 35-foot T-10 parachute (the parachute in use at that time) while in the air. That exercise consisted of the recruit's harness being attached to a suspended device while standing on a platform.

The recruit then leaned forward, falling off the platform, held aloft by the harness. The recruit remained hanging from the contraption, the harness digging into the crotch area. If the harness was placed the least bit wrong the pain was awful (and there was no adjusting of the harness once the recruit was hanging there). Even if the harness was correctly placed there was constant pain in the groin.

While hanging in suspended agony, we learned the procedures we would be utilizing as soon as the parachute opened and we began our descent. We were taught to check our parachute after deployment, checking below us to make sure we weren't descending on another jumper, as well as physically checking to the left or right before turning. Checking beneath while descending and left or right before turning was drummed into us as being of paramount importance for our (and others') safety.

Next, we learned to steer our parachute while descending. Risers were the four straps that connected the jumper's two parachute harness straps to the parachute lines. To go any direction, the two risers on that side were pulled. Pulling on the risers pulled that side of the canopy down, creating movement in that direction.

Of course, wind had the most effect on direction of travel, but the parachute could still be steered, somewhat, by the jumper. A newer version of the T-10 came out in the mid-sixties. The new version was

250-foot tower at Fort Benning GA. (Internet photo

the T-10 Modified, which was much easier to steer.

During suspended agony training, we also learned tree, wire and water landing positions, as well as emergency procedures. When making a tree landing, the jumper straightened his legs as much as possible, toes pointed downward, placing both legs together tightly (so limbs wouldn't come up between the legs — making for a very painful crotch injury, which nobody wanted to endure), crossing his arms and holding them across his face, all the time praying.

Upon stopping, if it was not possible to climb down the tree normally, the jumper could release his emergency chute and climb down the reserve, depending on the distance from the ground. If that didn't work, it was a case of waiting for help. For a wire (power line) landing, the jumper placed his legs and feet together, pointed his toes downward and made himself as skinny as possible, once again praying with much gusto and sincerity.

For a water landing, the jumper (only after knowing a water landing is imminent, and the water was more than a foot, or so, deep) was to release his equipment, cross his arms in front of his body, strike the quick release strike plate to separate the risers from the harness, maintaining a grip on the harness with the crossed arms while still holding on to the risers. Just before hitting the water, the jumper then stretched his arms straight up (releasing the risers), keeping his legs straight and pointing his toes until entering the water.

It was important that the jumper was certain of a water landing before preparing for one. During one of my subsequent jumps in later years, one of the jumpers mistook a roadway for a river during a night jump. The results brought about a painful "splat" and an ambulance ride. At night, the moon shining off a macadam road could indeed look like a river.

We were also taught how to react to parachuting emergencies. There were several types of emergencies that could occur in the air: The worst was the collision with another jumper or parachute, in which one or both chutes could collapse. A parachute total malfunction, resulting in the chute not opening, was a given immediate reaction: pull the rip cord on the reserve parachute with your right hand, at the same time turning your head to the right to avoid the reserve chute slapping your face as it deployed.

A collapsed chute, or partially deployed chute, created possible major problems. The jumper had to be careful not to permit the reserve chute getting tangled in the main chute, as the reserve chute deployed. In that case, the reserve chute handle was pulled with the right hand, keeping the left hand over the reserve ripcord flap. Upon release of the reserve from the pack, it was grasped by both the left and right hands and thrown out and to the left as hard as possible.

Entanglements were the most dangerous circumstances. Some parachute deployment problems included the parachute opening to a Mae West (a suspension cord over the middle of the parachute, forming two small parachutes—much like a large bra, hence the description—resulting in significant loss of lift and subsequent increase of speed earthward), a panel torn in the parachute, or colliding with another jumper or his chute (either from above or at the same level).

Equipment jump landings were different from non-equipment (known as Hollywood) jumps. Preparation for landing with equipment first entailed releasing the tie-down for the pack or rucksack at first chance and letting it fall, to dangle below you (it was attached to the jumper by a long strap). Then the lower weapon tie-down was to be undone. The weapon was fastened to the body and the lower leg. Landing without loosening the weapon produced the same results as landing with a leg splint—bad news. The parachute landing fall (PLF) was done normally (hopefully).

The Black Hats had a cruel sense of humor when they gave us our initial demonstration of our next training apparatus. The 250-foot tower (the equivalent of the height of a 25-story building) had four long outward arms. A maximum of three of the arms were utilized at any one time, determined by the direction of the wind. The recruit was equipped with a parachute harness. The harness risers were attached to a special parachute that was, in turn, attached to a metal ring of the same circumference as the open parachute.

The parachute and recruit were slowly lifted by the tower arm (affording a great view of Ft. Benning if you weren't scared to death) to the top of the tower. For the initial demonstration, a "recruit" was raised to the top of the tower. "He" was then released. The parachute malfunctioned, and the "recruit" fell, slamming into the ground. Only after a lot of yelling, did we learn that the "recruit" was a dummy. The Black Hats had gotten our attention for their safety lecture, which followed.

The 250-foot tower was the second test of a recruit's fear of heights (the first being the 34-foot tower), and the closest training for the real thing. Upon reaching the top, there was a jolt, and the recruit dangled, swinging slightly, with a bird's-eye view of much of Fort Benning. It was unnerving, but a beautiful view.

When ordered by the instructor, the parachute was released, and the recruit began drifting down to earth. During that time, the instructor issued instructions to the recruit, using a bullhorn. The recruit was given instructions on which way to slip the parachute, to not crash into the tower.

We were warned, before being lifted aloft, that we should not look down just prior to landing. We were, instead, to look forward, to determine when to prepare for landing. Looking down could result in a tensing of the body or "reaching" for the ground with the feet. That was especially important when making a night jump.

The final test was, of course, the PLF at the end of the ride. The landing was as hard as if making the jump from an aircraft. Mistakes were awarded with (you guessed it!), "DROP, GIVE ME TWENTY." Even though the physical training exercises had increased in intensity, I didn't receive a single Physical Training gig during Tower Week.

"Failure is not defeat until you stop trying." — Unknown, I found it in a Chinese fortune cookie.

Sadly, on Saturday, the last day of Tower Week, I found out I had to repeat Tower Week. The Black Hats didn't feel I had qualified enough times on the 250-foot tower. That was a major morale deflator. I once again had to fight wanting to quit. In fact, once again, I walked solemnly down to the headquarters building again, thinking of quitting. When I got to headquarters, I paced back and forth in front of the building for

Posed photo of me wearing my paratrooper gear. (my photo)

quite a long time, as I had when I cut open my chin.

"You win some, and you lose some." — A common quote

Hell, NO! Only losers believe that. I'll be damned if I'm ever going to feel okay losing something. That isn't, and wasn't, a part of my mindset.

Once again, I finally convinced myself that I was not a quitter. I could make it if I just put my mind to it. I marched myself back to my barracks, head held a lot higher than when I had sullenly walked from the barracks to the headquarters building.

I was reassigned to Class 9a. I was also given a new roster number to place on my helmet, and to make sure to remember, since that would be how I was identified by the cadre while in my new class. Many classmates quit during Tower Week, and many others quit because they did not want to repeat Tower Week after being told they would have to repeat the week if they wanted to continue.

At about this time, on 14 and 15 September, the first sizable group of United States-based Special Forces personnel arrived in Saigon, Vietnam, for a six-month TDY (Temporary Duty) assignment in South Vietnam. The group consisted of seventy-two men; one C Detachment and four A Detachments.

I pretty much flew through my repeat of Tower Week. By the end of Thursday, I had already qualified on all the required apparatus. I was two for two on the 250-foot tower and five for five on the 34' tower.

Since a fifty percent success rate was passing, and I only had three more 34-foot tower jumps to make, I knew I had it made. Thankfully I had passed Tower Week the second time around. I finished the week with no Personal or Physical Training gigs for the week. My thought was "HOORAY, NEXT WEEK I WILL JUMP FROM THE BIG IRON BIRD!"

Jump Week

GET READY!
STAND UP!
HOOK UP!

CHECK STATIC LINES!
CHECK EQUIPMENT!
SOUND OFF FOR EQUIPMENT CHECK!
STAND IN THE DOOR!
GO!

The fourth and final week was (hallelujah!) "Jump Week." It began for me on Monday, 24 September. Preferring death to any further training, we were ready to put all our training into the real thing: a parachute jump. We were transported to the airfield on buses.

During jump week, each recruit made 5 parachute jumps onto Fryar Drop Zone (DZ), in nearby Alabama, using static-line-deployed T-10 parachutes (35-foot circular, non-steerable, canopy), from a U.S. Air Force C-119, flying 1,250 feet above the ground. We were also equipped with 24-foot circular non-steerable reserve parachutes for backup.

Upon arriving at the airfield and unloading, we were guided to a large building, in which there were rows of wooden benches. That building was known as the "Sweat Shed." The name was appropriate. There we sweated from the heat and humidity, and sat, "sweating" our first jump. The jumpmaster briefed us on the details of the upcoming jump. This was done before each jump we made at Fort Benning. The following information was given to us pre-jump, in the shed:

- Drop zone
- Type of aircraft
- Type of parachute
- Weather decision time (for GO, NO GO decision)
- Type of individual equipment and separate equipment with which troops will be jumping
- Load time
- Station time
- Takeoff time
- Length of flight (time from takeoff to drop)
- In-flight emergencies (possible emergencies that could be faced during the flight, and how they would be dealt with)

- Time on target (estimated time arriving over the drop zone)
- Direction of flight over DZ
- Drop altitude (distance above the ground from which we were to exit the aircraft)
- Predicted wind on the DZ, and direction of wind
- Parachute turn in point (location on the edge of the drop zone)
- Medical support plan
- Obstacles on or near the DZ (obstacles that may affect our descent and landing)

We donned our gear, which included our main parachute rigging and reserve parachute. The main parachute was carried on our backs, the reserve parachute over our stomach region, pull handle (for opening the parachute) located on the right side of the reserve parachute pack.

A yellow "static line" crisscrossed the back of the main parachute container. One end of the line was attached to the top of the parachute, the other attached to a metal clip that we would attach ("hook up") to the metal cable running down the length of the aircraft.

The C-119 was known as a "Flying Boxcar" because that is what it looked like. Paratroopers also called it the "Flying Coffin." It was a twin-engine propeller-driven cargo aircraft. It also had twin booms leading to two tails, and certainly didn't look like it could ever get into the air, much less stay there, and fly. Those aircraft certainly were not very aerodynamic, sounded like a bucket of bolts as they "flew," and were pre-Korean War relics.

We joked that we were better off than the Air Force crew flying them; we were at least able to jump out of them while they were in the air. The Air Force crew had to remain on that pile of junk until it landed back on terra firma.

Jumpers jumped out the doors near the rear of the aircraft. The drop zone (jumper landing area) was a VERY large dirt field (Fryar Field Drop Zone). At the end of each jump, each individual recruit was again critiqued by the "Black Hat." Sub-perfect performances were of course rewarded with (yep, it hasn't ended yet) "DROP, GIVE ME TWENTY" push-ups. The first parachute jumps were always

"Hollywood" jumps, meaning the jumpers were jumping with only the parachute gear (main and reserve parachutes).

The C-119 seated 42 paratroopers, 21 on each side. As in most Air Force cargo aircraft, the seating was against the outside of the interior, facing inward, with the back against the aircraft skin. The seating in almost all military transport aircraft consisted of nylon cargo netting stretched between pipes, forming an uncomfortable bench.

Before starting the engines, the pilot gave us a safety briefing. It didn't calm our fears about the aircraft at all. In part, he stated that, "If we have an emergency at a safe altitude, I will turn on the green light and ring the bell continuously. That is your signal to hook up and exit the aircraft as fast as possible." He then started the engines, which sounded like they were in bad need of maintenance. We taxied to the end of the runway, and rolled onto the runway, facing into the wind.

When we were cleared for takeoff, the pilot pushed the throttles in for full power. Ever so slowly, the aircraft picked up speed, rattling, shaking, and creaking down the runway. Like me, I'm sure everybody wondered if it would get off the ground. I guess you could compare it to riding a scary carnival ride, wondering if it was going to fall apart before it got to the drop zone.

Wonder of wonders, we got off the ground near the end of the runway, and our pilot proceeded to s-l-o-w-l-y climb to his designated altitude and place our aircraft in formation with the other 119s, as tail-end Charlie. Tail-end Charlie was the least preferred position for passengers onboard the aircraft, especially in that rickety thing.

Because the pilot was trying to maintain position in relation to the other aircraft, there was usually much more jockeying for position in the tail-end aircraft. We had to fly in this formation for quite a while, waiting for the winds to die down on the drop zone (DZ).

There was a maximum safe wind on the ground for safe parachuting, and it was above that limit. Riding in a C-119 in windy conditions was bad enough but being tail-end Charlie made it worse. We were bouncing all over the place, and the pilot was constantly trying to maintain position in the formation, making for a bouncy roller coaster ride of great proportions.

Most of the jumpers in our aircraft were spilling their guts on the floorboards of the aircraft. That plane STUNK on the inside. By the time the winds were down to acceptable speed, all we wanted to do was get the hell out of that airplane.

The Air Force Loadmaster finally opened the jump door. We knew then, that the time was near. The jumpmaster rose, hooked his static line to the cable, walked to the open door, and looked out the door, studying the terrain below. When he felt the time was right, he turned to face us, stomped his left foot onto the floor, forcefully pushed his hands and arms a little forward and up into the air, palms facing the jumpers, and shouted above the roar of the noisy C-119 twin engines, "GET READY!" At this command, we knew that the time to jump was getting close. The butterflies in the stomach increased a little bit. We unbuckled our seatbelts and prepared our bodies for the next command.

Shortly afterward the jumpmaster shouted, "STAND UP," lifting both his arms and hands in the universal signal to stand. All of us stood up, facing the steel cable to which the static line hook would be attached. The next command was "HOOK UP," as he raised his right hand in the air, forming a hook with his index finger and pretending to hook his finger to a cable.

We all detached our static line clips from the top of our reserve parachutes and attached them to the steel cable that ran the length of the aircraft. At "CHECK STATIC LINES," he pumped his right hand (with the hooked finger) up and down, simulating pulling on the connection. Each of us then pulled on our static lines, making sure they were firmly and safely attached and locked to the cable, and visually checked our line and that of the jumper in front of us.

The jumpmaster then shouted to "CHECK EQUIPMENT," as he patted his chest exaggeratedly with both hands, simulating checking equipment. We proceeded to double check our equipment, making sure everything was attached correctly, and there were no loose cords anywhere, the man behind each of us checking our parachute set-up on our back.

"SOUND OFF FOR EQUIPMENT CHECK," with the

jumpmaster cupping both hands behind his ears (as if trying to hear better), resulted in each man, from last to first, sounding off their stick number, followed by the word "OKAY" (i.e., NUMBER TEN OKAY... NUMBER NINE OKAY, etc.). I was number six, so when my turn came, I yelled out "NUMBER SIX OKAY."

Satisfied that his stick (group of jumpers) was ready, the jumpmaster returned to the aircraft exit, scanning the terrain. Being number six in the stick, I could see out the door, and see the ground passing by underneath us. At a designated point over the ground, he pointed to the open doorway and yelled "STAND IN THE DOOR."

Following that command, the number one man (head of the stick) stood in the exit door, knees slightly bent, body erect, and both hands on the outside of the door, ready to propel himself out of the door upon the command. I would be the sixth to exit the aircraft. In front of me, next to the door, was a red light.

A short time later the red light went off, and the green light lit. The jumpmaster slapped the ass of the number one man, yelling "GO!" The number one man immediately exited the aircraft. Jumping the C-119 consisted of shuffling rearward in the aircraft, to the open door on the side, near the rear of the aircraft. There was no fear in our minds, just a burning desire to get out that door, where there was fresh air and no smell of vomit.

We jumped one at a time, taking just enough time at the door (one second according to training rules) to assume a slightly bent knees attitude, with one foot forward on the edge of the doorway and both hands on the outside edge of the aircraft, to help push each of us out, as we leaped through the door, into space.

When it was my turn, I took position in the door momentarily, jumped up and out the door upon feeling the slap on my ass and the jumpmaster shouting "GO!" assumed a tight body position, with my feet and knees together and locked, my hands on the ends of the reserve chute, head down with chin tucked into my chest, and began counting, "One thousand! Two thousand!" The first feeling was the prop blast from the propeller, pummeling me backwards, making it hard to concentrating on counting.

As I fell, I saw the tail of the aircraft getting further away. I was in a momentary free fall. Very shortly thereafter, at about "two or three thousand," I felt a slight tug when the static line reached its full extension, pulling the cover free from the pilot (drogue) chute, which in turn pulled the main chute out of its bag. The still deflated main chute streamed behind, and above, me, filling with air (hopefully), deploying and giving me an opening jolt, like being pulled upward, just before "four thousand."

I looked up into the canopy, to ensure the parachute had deployed correctly, and there were no twists, tangles, or tears, followed by checking around to make sure there was no imminent danger of colliding with other jumpers.

Had I not been able to look up, due to the static line being wrapped around my neck (it happened sometimes), I would have had to check my rate of descent by comparing my rate of descent with that of the other jumpers. If I was dropping significantly faster than the other jumpers, I would have deployed my reserve parachute, as instructed during our training.

As soon as I had confirmed my parachute was satisfactory, I scanned the air around me again, as well as below, to confirm I wasn't in any danger of colliding with any other jumpers or coming down on somebody else's parachute. Silence prevailed. The only sounds were that of the aircraft flying into the distance and the instructors on the ground barking instructions through megaphones to the jumpers in the air.

The quiet serenity surrounding me was awesome. I was in another world. And the view from up there was awesome. I could see for miles. I had finally made my first parachute jump, and it was a magnificent feeling and a major adrenaline rush.

I could see the smoke from the smoke grenade on the ground, indicating the direction, and strength, of the wind on the ground. I knew I had to land in the opposite direction the smoke was blowing, to land into the wind.

As I approached the ground, I went over my landing in my mind. Legs slightly bent, feet and knees together, elbows in front of the face, hands even with the top of my helmet, holding the chute risers, and relaxed. We all hit at a speed of about twenty-two feet per second, a hard jolt. Then… the landing on the balls of the feet, bending the body slightly into the desired landing direction, to hit the calf, side of the thigh, ass, and back of the shoulder in a semi-rolling action. If you could get up, and walk away from a parachute landing, IT WAS A GOOD ONE.

Once on the ground, we had to rise quickly and run around the parachute after landing to collapse it. The wind was trying to drag the chute and us along the ground, so speed was essential. After collapsing the parachute, we gathered it in our arms in an S-roll, and returned to the parachute turn-in area, at a double-time.

The elation on our faces was obvious. That first jump was the easiest of all jumps I made. That was because I was reacting exactly as I had been trained, like a robot. After that jump, I thought more about what I was doing, interjecting a bit of fear into my mind.

On Tuesday we made two jumps, one in the morning and one in the afternoon. The morning jump was another instructional jump, with another perfect PLF on soft ground. The following jumps we momentarily took door positions and exited on our own. The Tuesday afternoon jump resulted in another perfect PLF, this time on very hard ground. On both jumps I was the eighth man out the door (stick number 8).

Wednesday morning, I knocked out 40 straight push-ups, wearing a helmet, first aid pouch, canteen, and four-pound kit bag, just to see how I could do. That was a major improvement over the only 28 I was able to manage when I arrived at Benning with no extra gear on me.

We had to wait again (this time on the ground) for the winds to subside, which they did in the afternoon for jump number four. For some reason, after takeoff for that jump, my brain said, "This is an unnatural act and a dangerous thing you are doing. Why are you jumping out of a perfectly good airplane?"

During that jump, and all following jumps I made, I had a healthy nervousness about every jump. An old Master Blaster (a paratrooper with hundreds of jumps) once told me that if I ever became blasé about a jump and wasn't at least a little nervous, I should quit jumping. He said nervousness was healthy and would ensure that I was careful and would not miss any safety checks before jumping. My jump went well. The only thing out of the ordinary was having to slip my parachute a lot while in the air to avoid other jumpers.

The last jump was an equipment jump. Equipment jump meant the recruit jumped with standard combat equipment. That consisted of both parachutes (main and reserve), a fully loaded pack and an M-1 Garand (World War II era) rifle. The pack was strapped to the jumper below his reserve chute and the rifle was tied to the body.

During the parachute descent it was up to the jumper to undo the tie-down for the pack, allowing it to hang down below the jumper (attached to the jumper by a strap) so it wouldn't interfere with the jumper's PLF. The rifle also had to be untied to free the body for a PLF. I was the number seven man in the stick for that jump.

On that last jump (full equipment) I had to slip away from a lot of other jumpers. The wind was strong on the drop zone. When I arrived at ground level, I went plowing into the ground, breaking my M-1 Garand rifle in two when I did my "PLF." The M-1 Garand rifle was a VERY sturdy and somewhat heavy (for a rifle) weapon.

I knew I was in deep trouble as I marched back to the assembly point with the rifle barrel group in my left hand, rifle stock in my right hand, and a sore hip. I knew for sure I was in for another re-cycle and more training, if not dropped from the school entirely.

The first thing to happen was (no guessing needed) "DROP, GIVE ME 20." I was overjoyed when that was the only punishment I received. Happily, I was not re-cycled or dropped. One thing that might have helped was the fact that nine other jumpers broke their rifles. It was mostly due to the strong winds on the drop zone.

I was sore for a few days after that jump. I had scraped and bruised my hip. The rifle had been between my aluminum canteen and the ground; I landed on the canteen, which in turn scraped my hip and broke the rifle. I WAS NO LONGER A LEG! "Legs" were non-paratroopers whom paratroopers considered to be the lowest form of soldiers, contemptuous military human beings who had no reason to

Jump wings authorized to be worn on our uniforms upon graduating from Jump School. (Internet photo)

C-119 Boxcar, the type aircraft we jumped from during Jump School. (Internet photo)

be proud of their station in life.

Jump School had a rule that there was to be a one second interval between jumpers exiting, for safety reasons. Once we arrived at our units, that changed. In our units we exited as close to each other as possible. There were several reasons for that. We wanted to get out the door quickly, reducing the thought process about jumping into open air.

The closer the men exit the door, the closer they would be upon landing, and the better the chance of landing on the drop zone, especially if you were toward the end of the stick. That was helpful in a combat situation, because it meant you wouldn't be spread out all over kingdom come.

And, lastly—but very important—the closer you were to the first jumper on a peacetime jump, the closer you were to the parachute turn-in location, saving a lot of steps lugging the ungainly parachute and, if jumping with equipment, the heavy weight of all your gear.

I had become in much better physical condition by the time I graduated. In high school I had major problems in PE with the rope climb. During Jump School I flew up the rope, one of the fastest in the class. I also went from 28 regular push-ups upon arrival, to 40 push-ups with equipment (helmet, first aid pouch, full water canteen and kit bag).

Upon graduation, on Friday, 28 September, the class was placed in formation, our new silver "blood wings" were handed to us for us to pin on ourselves, and each of our new orders were read off. We would now begin earning an extra $55 a month in jump pay. That resulted in a fantastic 66% pay raise for me. I was now up to $138.20 per month.

"Blood wings" were the first jump wings given to paratroopers. They were so named because in earlier days the wings (which had two metal pins about ½" long in the rear for going through clothing material) would be held to the new paratrooper's chest and pounded into the chest with a fist, thus causing the two pins to pierce the skin and cause bleeding.

I had no further use for the hated Army-issue low quarter shoes (Oxfords), except to have them ready for inspections when called for.

Our "new" dress uniform included our trousers bloused into our boots, the sign of the paratrooper. Also, I had a new number tacked onto the end of my MOS. My new MOS was 112.07, meaning I was still an entry-level heavy weapons infantryman, but I was a Parachutist (the fifth number, 7 denoted it).

I never felt totally comfortable jumping out of perfectly good airplanes, but it was a job, and I received extra pay for doing it, so I did it. It was also required if one was going to be a Green Beret. Although I was now "Airborne" and proud of it, I was also a "cherry jumper."

A "cherry jumper" was a man whose jump record only included his jumps at Jump School. I remained a "cherry jumper" until I made my first parachute jump at my next assigned location. Being a "cherry jumper" was, at least, better than being a "leg," also known as a "straight leg."

The term "leg" was originally "straight leg," referring to the lack of bloused boots on non-paratroopers' dress uniforms. Airborne troopers tucked (bloused) their pants in their boots, whereas non-paratroopers (aka "legs") did not, leaving their pants hanging straight down, over their low quarters (low-sided civilian-style shoes).

Of my graduating class, about 40 were assigned to Germany, 30 to Okinawa, 3 to Panama, 50 to the 101st Airborne Division in Ft. Campbell, KY, 10 to the 82nd Airborne Division in Ft. Bragg, and 50 of us to Special Forces Training Group, also in Ft. Bragg.

Old Airborne proverb: *"If you ain't Airborne, you ain't shit!"*

Airborne Creed by ????????

I am an Airborne trooper! A paratrooper!

I jump by parachute from any plane in flight. I volunteered to do it, knowing well the hazards of my choice.

I serve in a mighty Airborne Force—famed for deeds in war—renowned for readiness in peace. It is my pledge to uphold its honor and prestige in all I am—in all I do.

I am an elite trooper—a sky trooper—a shock trooper—a

spearhead trooper. I blaze the way to far-flung goals—behind, before, above the foe's front line.

I know that I may have to fight without support for days on end. Therefore, I keep my mind and body always fit to do my part in any Airborne task. I am self-reliant and unafraid. I shoot true, and march fast and far. I fight hard and excel in every art and artifice of war.

I never fail a fellow trooper. I cherish as a sacred trust the lives of men with whom I serve. Leaders have my fullest loyalty, and those I lead never find me lacking.

I have pride in the Airborne! I never let it down!

In peace, I do not shirk the dullest duty nor protest the toughest training. My weapons and equipment are always combat ready. I am neat of dress—military in courtesy—proper in conduct and behavior.

In battle, I fear no foe's ability, nor underestimate his prowess, power and guile. I fight him with all my might and skill— ever alert to evade capture or escape a trap. I never surrender, though I be the last.

My goal in peace or war is to succeed in any mission of the day—or die, if needs be, in the try.

I belong to a proud and glorious team—the Airborne, the Army, my Country. I am its chosen pride to fight where others may not go—to serve them well until the final victory.

I am a trooper of the sky! I am my Nation's best! In peace and war I never fail. Anywhere, anytime, in anything—I am AIRBORNE!"

CHAPTER 5

SPECIAL FORCES TRAINING GROUP

Those of us assigned to Ft. Bragg (for 82nd Airborne Division and Special Forces Training Group) were loaded Saturday morning (29 September) at 0800 onto a Trailways charter bus, for the 450-mile trip north to Ft. Bragg, NC, and another new chapter in our lives.

We went through Macon and Augusta, Georgia, as well as Columbia, South Carolina. The scenery, especially in Georgia, was beautiful. During the trip, I was shocked by the amount of old, broken down shacks that had people living in them. I had never seen such squalor. About halfway to Fort Bragg, we stopped to stretch and have lunch. We all had a lot of time to think while on that bus.

A lot of the men heading to Special Forces training decided that they had undergone enough harassment and hard training, and made up their minds to quit upon reaching Training Group. Of course, the rumor mill was going strong about how tough Special Forces training was going to be, some of it true, but a lot of it pure bunk. I was very tired of training and was harboring thoughts about quitting. I was certain my knees wouldn't last through physical exercise more difficult than I had already endured.

We arrived at Ft. Bragg at 2000 hours, having been on the road for 12 hours (remember, this was before the advent of the Interstate highway). The first stop on base for our bus that night was on Smoke Bomb Hill, in front of a sign that read: Headquarters Company, Special Forces Training Group (Provisional). Smoke Bomb Hill was where all the stateside Special Forces Groups and Special Forces Training Group were located. That was where SF (Special Forces) lived.

The front door opened, and out strode the CQ (charge of quarters for overnight hours), a Special Forces NCO with the obligatory clipboard, approaching the group of us who had offloaded, duffel bags in our hands. He greeted us and gave us a very short speech.

Apparently Training Group was used to quitters, because he announced that those of us who wished to quit would have that opportunity on Tuesday, so I had more than two days to ponder my future. I was later told that many men volunteered for SF and 82nd Airborne just to keep from being immediately assigned overseas duty.

I was thinking about opting for assignment to the 82nd Airborne Division, also at Ft. Bragg. The NCO then lifted his clipboard and proceeded to call out our names from the set of orders he had, giving each of us a chance to respond when our names were called. Everyone was accounted for.

Unlike Basic and Advanced Training, and Jump School, the greeting was civil when we arrived. Nobody yelled at us, or harassed us right off the bat. That was something new. We were being treated like human beings. We were immediately led to the unit supply room and given the usual U.S. Army initial bedding: mattress cover, two sheets, two blankets, and a pillowcase. We were then led to the barracks we would stay in for the weekend.

On Sunday morning our group was issued passes for the day. That was my first pass in over a month, and I was completely broke. I went nowhere. I stayed in the barracks all day. I figured the Army still owed me $110, but I had no idea when I would receive it.

On Monday we began the day the same way every other training day had been for me, before the crack of dawn. The first formation included roll call, followed by Police Call and PT, which included a run. That was followed by being dismissed and everybody walking to the mess hall for breakfast.

That was a change from Basic and Advanced training, where we were marched in formation to the mess hall, and Jump School, where we were run, in formation, to the mess hall. We were finally deemed trustworthy to find the mess hall without help.

After breakfast, we had a short period of time free until the second formation. The NCO read off the list of names on the orders he had for us, assigning us to companies as we responded to our names being called. I was assigned to B Company, Special Forces Training Group (Provisional).

An NCO from each of the Training Group companies was present to march us to our new assigned company barracks. Our barracks, like Jump School, were old two-story wooden barracks built at the beginning of the World War II era, with an anticipated lifetime of five years, and… no air conditioning. More than twenty years after they were built, we were living in them.

The barracks were heated by coal-fed furnaces. The toilet/shower facilities were on the bottom floor. Everything was wide open, no stalls. When you sat on the can, you were on display for all to see. There were two private rooms on the stairs end of the upstairs barracks, reserved for the highest ranking of the trainees.

The squad bays on the top and bottom floors were open, with single bunk beds (thankfully no more double bunks, I had graduated to better living conditions) and corresponding wall and footlockers lining each side. Each of the barracks housed about fifty trainees.

We were issued our field gear, which included a pack that was unlike anything I had ever seen. It was called a rucksack and was huge when compared to the military issue pack. I learned later why we were issued such "humongous packs." We would be spending a lot of time in the field, and once we were assigned to a unit, were expected to carry all we needed in our rucksack, for unknown periods of time in the field or foreign country. In Jump School, our equipment jump was made with a pack attached to us. In SFTG, as well as SF, we would be jumping with that huge rucksack.

We were not separated by training phase, rank, or SF MOS we were pursuing. Because of that we learned bits and pieces of the other MOSs during our stay at Training Group. That served well for our overall Special Forces training. In fact, I was able to learn bits and pieces of communications and weapons while attending Training Group.

Our company consisted of four of those old barracks, and two one-story buildings of the same construction. One was the combination orderly room, mail room, day room (the only place with a television), and arms room, while the other housed the supply room. At the time, all of Special Forces were housed in the old World War II era buildings. Most of us in Special Forces Training Group were there straight out of Basic, AIT, and Jump School, with just a few experienced NCOs from line units.

I was thankful I had decided to stick with Special Forces. In a letter home I gave five reasons for staying around for training: "(1) I signed up for it, and didn't feel right about backing down; (2) it will be a challenge; (3) the type of men in Special Forces are different than regular Airborne; (4) it sounds like interesting work; and (5) I want to begin learning new things again." I have always been interested in learning new things, even now (as I write this). Apparently, some of our guys who volunteered for SF did so only because they wanted to remain in the United States longer.

When Major James (the Training Group Commanding Officer) gave his welcoming speech, he told us that Special Forces had a way of weeding out those types, as well as the ones who came to SF for the rank and money. By that time, we had already lost 15 of the 55 in our group, and training hadn't even begun yet.

Unlike Jump School, where quitters were made examples of by the cadre, in Training Group quitters were not harassed or embarrassed, but they did receive some of the lousier details until finally receiving their new assignment orders. When a barracks-mate or classmate disappeared, we just figured they had quit or had flunked out.

Major James stated that only those who wished, from the bottom of their hearts, to become Green Berets would make the grade through the training course. That evening I wrote home, asking mom to send me some civilian clothing. I was finally going to be able to wear civvies on a somewhat regular basis during my free time.

"If we should have to fight, we should be prepared to do so from the neck up instead of from the neck down." — *General Jimmy Doolittle*

Once again, we were subjected to a battery of tests, this time to determine our psychological status. A man could be a perfect physical specimen, but that didn't assure he would qualify for Special Forces. Much more than physical strength was required to be a good Green Beret.

Special Forces wasn't looking for men who were good in a bar fight. They were looking for mature men of high moral character who could walk away from participating in a bar fight with their heads held high. They were also looking for men who could work without supervision, on their own, and could function well, working in any conditions, with any type of people.

A Green Beret had to be able to persevere and want to help the human race in times of trouble. There could be times that a lone Special Forces man could be called on to be an official representative of the United States government, ready to make snap decisions without guidance, and immediately act upon that decision, knowing full well that the action could have deep consequences on himself and the United States. It was not a position to be taken lightly.

One of the physical tests that worried me was the Combat Water Survival Test for Special Forces. It required us to be able to tread water for a somewhat substantial time, as well as swim about 50 yards in water, dressed in our combat fatigues and combat boots. I was highly challenged trying to tread water in high school, and I was only wearing swimming trunks. I had no idea how I would fare while fully clothed, and the thought of going through that test scared the crap out of me. I certainly wasn't a star performer in that test, but I passed it... just barely.

The commander of the Special Warfare Center was Brigadier General William P. Yarborough, a 1936 graduate of West Point. He had assumed command in January 1961. General Yarborough wasn't looking just for men who would be good guerrilla warfare combatants, he was also looking for men of higher than average intelligence and character, who had good judgment, maturity, and self-discipline, as well as being able to work closely with foreign nationals who were a far cry from Americans. He was also looking for men who had inherent ingenuity, capable of solving difficult, sometimes seemingly impossible, unexpected problems, quickly and practically. Those men had to be able to work in small groups, and sometimes alone, with no guarantee of aid from anyone else.

General Yarborough was not looking for rough, tough Ranger types. Rangers were a breed apart, and experts in their field. When you cut them loose in a combat situation, they were killing machines, ready to cut a swath in the enemy. Bloodletting was a part of their makeup. Yarborough wanted tough soldiers who could change with the situation; killers if need be, compassionate and merciful if that suited the mission better.

Tuesday morning's time schedule was the same as Monday's. At the second formation those who were undergoing training were dismissed to go to their designated training areas; those of us who were not training were given our assignments for the day, usually details of some kind. Unlike my previous training, Basic, AIT, and Jump School, those of us attending classes were not marched to their classes. We were expected to arrive at classes on our own time but be on time.

Details included, but were not limited to: cleaning the local area; work in the mess hall (unlike KP); ash and trash (our description of picking up garbage from unit areas); fireman (keeping the barracks coal burning heating systems running and stoked); demonstrations (carrying out various jobs in the Special Forces demonstration area, known as Area 2 at the time); being sent to the rifle range to help work the firing line for another unit; and working in the supply shack moving heavy items around for the ranking civilian while he sat on his ass giving instructions, etc. It was almost always very boring work.

The best and most cherished detail, which was also a great training aid for us, was being assigned to a field exercise as indigenous combatants in a guerrilla unit, or as an aggressor searching for guerrilla units. What more fun could a soldier have, than running around in the outdoors, searching for people or enemy groups?

The all-time worthless detail I heard of (besides painting rocks and cement coal bins white) was a group of SF trainees detailed to pick up all the pine cones in the Area 2 Demonstration Area. Shortly thereafter it was decided that pine cones were natural, and a detail was formed to return those pine cones to their natural environment, in the Area 2 Demonstration Area. Wow — talk about stupid!

Rank meant nothing in Special Forces when it came to details. Even if you were a sergeant, you had to participate in the details. The problem was that the post headquarters determined how post details were to be handed out by the amount of personnel in the units, not by the amount of personnel below the rank of sergeant. Special Forces was the only unit at Ft. Bragg that had almost all NCOs in the unit, virtually no privates, and very few PFCs and SP4s.

I noticed the first few weeks at Ft. Bragg that Special Forces men didn't particularly look special, other than the beret they wore. Some were a little overweight (not much though), some wore glasses, some were short, and some tall. The main difference between the looks of SF compared to others, was that the SF troops exuded an air of confidence. Then, as now, Special Forces doctrine specified that the man made the difference, not the equipment he carried, or the beret.

That same day we were interviewed to find out what MOS (Military Occupational Skill, aka job) we were most qualified to pursue in Special Forces. The interviewers went over our qualification tests, something I don't think the rest of the Army ever did. The officer who interviewed me told me that all my test scores were very high. Because of my extremely high test scores in radio Morse code aptitude (he said they were some of the highest he had seen), he tried his best to talk me into signing up for communications training.

I pretty much had my choice of specialty training. I had been in Training Group long enough before the interview to have witnessed the radio operator trainees coming to the barracks constantly rattling off dit-dahs (Morse code) and had decided that training to be a radio operator would drive me nuts.

We had the choice of radio operator, medic (which would require a minimum of one more year of intense medical training and dealing with a lot of blood and gore), light weapons, heavy weapons or demolitions (explosives). Since I was already trained in heavy weapons and held that MOS, I opted to request training as a demolition specialist (aka Combat Engineer, MOS 121).

Explosives sounded like something I would really enjoy. Besides, the field required a good knowledge of mathematics and I had always been good in math while in high school and college. The decision was made, and all I had to do was wait a couple weeks (I thought) for the next class to form.

The specialty training was scheduled to last six weeks, the first week consisting of mathematics training, which I figured would be a breeze for me. The following five weeks of training would be demolition training, which would be a blast (pun intended).

Special Forces came under the command of the U.S. Army Special Warfare Center when I arrived there. Basically, the Special Warfare Center (SWC) at Ft. Bragg consisted of the 7th Special Forces Group [Airborne] (7th SFGA), Special Forces Training Group [Provisional] (SFTG), Psychological Operations (PsyOps) units, Civil Affairs (CA) units, and the U.S. Army Special Warfare School (SWS), for U.S. and allied foreign officers.

Also considered to be part of the SWC chain of command were the 1st Special Forces Group [Airborne] in Okinawa, and the 10th Special Forces Group [Airborne] in Germany, along with their associated support units.

Special Forces was not only unlike any other U.S. military unit, its unit organization was just as unique. Generally speaking, a Special Forces Group, commanded by a colonel, consisted of a headquarters and headquarters company, a signal company (communications), and four Special Forces companies (A through D), consisting of A-, B-, and C-teams. Some groups also had an aviation company.

"A handful of men, inured to war, proceed to certain victory, while on the contrary, numerous armies of raw and undisciplined troops are but multitudes of men dragged to the slaughter." — Vegetius

We learned that Special Forces was basically centered on the twelve-man A-team, officially titled a Special Forces Operations Detachment A, or Alpha. It was a twelve-man team consisting of a Commanding Officer (calling for a captain), Executive Officer (first lieutenant), Operations Sergeant (aka Team Sergeant or Team Daddy, calling for a master sergeant), Intelligence Sergeant (sergeant first class), Heavy Weapons Leader (sergeant first class), Light Weapons Leader (sergeant first class), Radio Operator Supervisor (sergeant first class), Radio Operator (sergeant), Demolition Sergeant (staff sergeant), Demolition Specialist (specialist 5th class, similar in rank to sergeant), Medical Supervisor (sergeant first class), and Medical Specialist (specialist 5th class).

The basic Special Forces A-team make-up has existed for over fifty years. It has withstood the passage of time and numerous wars and conflicts, as well as training missions in foreign countries. In some cases, depending upon the team's mission, teams could be authorized extra personnel, or even operate as a split, or smaller, team. The founding fathers of Special Forces certainly knew what they were doing when they devised Special Forces.

It was incomprehensible to conventional units that a squad-sized team would be led by a captain and, especially, that the second in command would be another officer, a first lieutenant. In addition, having a master sergeant on a group that small was unheard of, particularly being as how he was on a team *commanded by* a captain and a lieutenant. To cap it all off, the remainder of the unit were NCOs. Not understanding Special Forces, conventional commanders considered this unit makeup as a waste of NCO expertise.

In conventional units the chain of command went from the top down, and the norm was for orders to be issued, and subsequently followed, no questions asked. On the other hand, on A-teams the norm was for the entire team to discuss the options, each man having a voice. Each man was just as important as the other men on the team. Each man was also an expert in his field, and cross-trained in the other fields.

I noticed that I had changed over the months since enlisting, both mentally and physically. My mental attitude and physical fitness were great. When I sucked in my stomach (which was pretty firm already), my rib cage was no longer obvious. In addition, my chest and arms had expanded some, and my legs were solid. When I first entered the service, the rear of my legs had been noticeably flabby. I had also gained some weight (I was kind of skinny when I enlisted), but no fat; it was more of a muscular weight gain.

There were three companies of trainees in Training Group (A [Alpha], B [Bravo] and C [Charlie] companies). Each company was assigned its own color band for the blocked fatigue caps we wore: green (Co. A), blue (Co. B), and red (Co. C). My company's color was blue, so we had thin blue adhesive bands wrapped around the base of our fatigue caps (we weren't authorized to wear the beret yet and wouldn't until after graduation). We called the colored bands "ghost bands." Every day an SFTG NCO would patrol the main post area, looking for people with colored bands on their caps. They were easy to spot, which made it harder to ghost (sneak away from working mind numbing and seemingly worthless details).

Up until about September 1962, a candidate had to be at least 19½ years old to be eligible for Special Forces. On or about that date the minimum age was changed to 20 years of age. I figured I was going to have no problem either way, as my 20th birthday was coming up in a few days, 7 October.

That first week we had some classroom training, consisting of classes to prepare us for upcoming training and responsibilities. On Wednesday, the 3rd, we were lectured on "The Meaning of Security," "The History of Special Forces" and "The Special Forces Insignia and Crest." We also watched a movie concerning Special Forces teams in action in Vietnam. As of that same day, 15 of our original 55 recruits had quit.

I found out we would only be required to have a haircut every ten days, not twice a week as in Jump School. I figured I'd try to grow a flat-top hair style. We were to wear clean, lightly starched fatigue uniforms and shined boots daily, so no more do-it-yourself uniform washing.

Security was extremely important at this stage of the game. We were told that we were not to permit anybody to take photographs of us, especially in uniform. We were also not to permit a newspaper to write an article about us or our training. The minimum security clearance needed, to be assigned to Special Forces was "Secret."

We were reminded that all military personnel were prohibited from keeping private records, diaries, or paperwork that contained statements concerning national security. That covered a wide spectrum of information. We were also informed that diaries should not be kept in a combat zone, due to probable inclusion of potentially classified information.

We were firmly reminded that military members were forbidden to carry on a correspondence with individuals we did not know, such as pen pals, chain letters, or round robins. We were advised that enemy countries had gained useful intelligence information in this fashion. Much of Special Forces operations relied on secrecy and surprise, especially since Special Forces units always acted in small numbers.

My Secret security clearance hadn't materialized yet, so I was a little worried about that causing a problem for assignment. Special Forces required a minimum security clearance of "Secret" because they trained and worked with "special" weapons and information, and were often involved in classified operations and missions.

I assumed that all my time residing in foreign countries, as well as having a German and a Russian friend in high school, and Swedish childhood friend as a pen pal, were reasons for the delay.

Special Forces Green Berets were very high profile anonymous soldiers. It had become somewhat widely known that Green Berets existed. What wasn't known was what they did, the extent of their operations, and where they operated. Even wives, at times, didn't know where their husbands were or what they were doing even during training.

Information was classified to protect national security. Levels of classification were based on the severity of the information, and the level of damage that could be done if the information was to get into the wrong hands. One thing we couldn't stop, however, was the "leaking" of information by politicians for political purposes.

There were four government classification categories of information. From lowest to highest level, these were For Official Use Only, Confidential (included Confidential—Modified Handling Authorized), Secret, and Top Secret. There were also several specialized classifications, such as NOFORN, which was not to be distributed to foreigners, and ORCN, which required tracking of the data dissemination. Some documents were marked with code words added to the classification. Documents so designated could only be seen by personnel authorized to access data of the classification, as well as the code word.

For Official Use Only classification, also known as Controlled Unclassified Information, normally was for administrative matters of interest only to Department of Defense personnel. Access to For Official Use Only data did not require a specific clearance, only that the individual have a need to know the information contained therein.

Confidential, also known as "public trust," classified materials usually included technical manuals and troop strength figures. It was for information that could be prejudicial to the national defense if disclosed. Documents and information classified as Secret could have resulted in serious damage to our nation if disclosed. Important intelligence information and technological developments for national defense were examples of Secret materials.

Top Secret was the highest classification, dealing with information that could cause exceptionally grave danger to the United States if divulged. Examples of Top Secret information included operations plans and strategic plans dealing with the conduct of war. Of all these classifications, only three required clearances: Confidential, Secret, and Top Secret. Of course, most important of all was the fact that without the need to know, it didn't matter how high your security clearance was, to be able to access information.

The Confidential clearance was, naturally, the easiest to get, as well as the clearance with the shortest waiting time for approval. Investigation of the applicant covered the most recent seven years of the applicant's life. It had to be renewed (along with another investigation) every fifteen years.

The Secret clearance could take as long as a year to investigate, and the clearance had to be renewed every ten years. Examples of events that would lengthen the investigation process were: numerous past residences (that described me—eleven different homes, not counting military moves), residence in foreign countries (also described me—five residences in two foreign countries), and ties with foreigners (me again—besides having had foreign friends while living overseas, I was in a pen pal relationship with one of my Swedish elementary school buddies). Unpaid bills, a poor financial history, and a criminal background were a few of the circumstances that could lead to denial of a Secret clearance.

Top Secret (TS) clearance was the most difficult, mainly because it permitted access to documents and information that pertained to national security, counterterrorism, or other highly sensitive data. It required a Single Scope Background Investigation (SSBI), which meant that government agents contacted employers, coworkers, and other personal contacts. It included background checks on immediate family. It often took 6-18 months to obtain, sometimes up to three years. The SSBI had to be renewed every five years. According to a Washington Post report approximately 854,000 people held Top Secret security clearances in the United States in 2010.

I would eventually attain a "Top Secret Crypto" clearance during my service time. That was a top attainable security clearance, basically denoting that I had the clearance to read, or be told, any classified information, so long as I had the "need to know." That was the defining phrase in the military. If you didn't have the need to know for a classified item of information, it mattered not what your security clearance was; you weren't permitted to have knowledge of the information.

Clearances for certain information went even further, requiring an additional signifier for the information. An example would be an operation with the security classification of Top Secret Tango. The only personnel authorized access to material dealing with this operation would require not only a Top Secret clearance, but an additional "Tango" clearance. That did not mean that a person with Top Secret clearance was more of a security risk than those with a Top Secret Tango clearance. It meant, instead, that people holding Top Secret clearances had no need to know anything about the Tango information.

A popular joke in the military was the term "Burn Before Reading," a "secret squirrel" clearance meaning the information was so secret that it shouldn't be read. Of course, another joke that went around the military and civilian world was the term "military intelligence," referring to the intelligence field in the military, but often the butt of jokes dealing with the intelligence of some military personnel.

As far as Special Forces history, it was of a short duration up to then, but did trace its roots back to World War II and the Office of Strategic Services (OSS). Special Forces had been created for waging unconventional warfare.

The Dictionary of United States Army Terms defined unconventional warfare as "the three interrelated fields of guerrilla warfare, evasion and escape, and subversion against hostile states." It also stated that "unconventional warfare operations are conducted within enemy or enemy-controlled territory by predominantly indigenous personnel, usually supported and directed in varying degrees by an external source."

Department of the Army Field Manual FM 31-21, Guerrilla Warfare and Special Forces Operations (September 1961 edition) defined unconventional warfare as "the interrelated fields of guerrilla warfare, evasion and escape, and subversion against hostile states (resistance).

"Unconventional warfare operations are conducted in enemy or enemy controlled territory by predominantly indigenous personnel usually supported and directed in varying degrees by an external source." Special Forces was tasked to participate in any mission assigned to it by the U.S. Army.

According to FM 31-21, the mission of U.S. Army Special Forces was "to develop, organize, equip, train, and direct indigenous forces in the conduct of guerrilla warfare." It added that Special Forces could also "advise, train and assist indigenous forces in counter-insurgency operations."

The missions would eventually vary immensely, mainly due

to the flexibility and highly trained men of Special Forces. The predominant missions included planning, conducting, and supporting unconventional warfare and internal security operations.

Special Forces troops were experts at training, advising, and providing operational, logistical, and monetary support for foreign military and paramilitary forces. The concept was that Special Forces would be "responsible for the conduct of all unconventional warfare activities within guerrilla warfare operational areas and may be called to perform other tasks associated with or in support of guerrilla warfare."

The expertise grew to include counterinsurgency operations, the prevention of guerrilla insurgencies. It made sense that men who were experts in guerrilla warfare and paramilitary forces, would also be experts in preventing or combating the same.

The most common methods of infiltration were by aircraft landing on a secluded landing zone, parachute, overland across borders, or sneaking in via submarine or boat. We could also pretend to be tourists, workers, or businessmen. Special Forces was trained to live in that same territory, through limited re-supply, living off the land. Thus infiltrated, we could attack strategic enemy targets deep in enemy territory, rescue allied troops, or collect intelligence. We were also trainers and advisors, able to form or aid guerrilla units within enemy territory.

Basically, Special Forces was expected to infiltrate into enemy territory, purposely placing ourselves in a situation in which we were surrounded by the enemy. Stateside, and on specialized missions to foreign countries, Special Forces trained American and friendly forces in military and Special Forces techniques.

On any given day, dozens of different countries' military uniforms could be seen around the Special Warfare Center, being trained by U.S. Special Forces personnel. Special Forces constantly had A-teams in foreign countries all over the globe, training the military units of those friendly governments, and on a few occasions advising those units during potential combat situations.

President Kennedy had shown much interest in Special Forces in the fall of 1961. He liked the idea of a unit based on a small, highly trained force that he felt would be very effective fighting in the small guerrilla-style wars he thought the U.S. was sure to play a part in. He became a powerful advocate for Special Forces at that time.

He visited the Special Warfare Center, home to Special Forces, at Fort Bragg, that same fall, and announced that Special Forces was to be authorized the wearing of its distinctive headgear, the green beret, by direction of the President.

Kennedy had countermanded orders that had been set forth by powerful generals within the Pentagon and conventional units. Those highly placed individuals were totally against any type of distinctive headgear, especially the beret. They were also against the concept of unconventional warfare. Special Forces was, from the beginning, an unwanted bastard child of the Army.

Special Forces became very conspicuous in Southeast Asia, especially for its part in the Vietnam War, due to the nature of that conflict. Who better to advise in the art of counterinsurgency than a unit trained to use unconventional tactics? Special Forces would eventually also have numerous small units in Vietnam that operated as unconventional units, gathering intelligence on the Viet Cong (a contraction for Vietnamese Communists), in their own territory.

It didn't take long to realize that Special Forces would play a different role than what was envisioned at its creation, acting as a counterinsurgency force opposing a guerrilla insurgency, as opposed to fighting as a guerrilla force. In fact, Special Forces units had been in South Vietnam since 1957, suffering their first casualty there on 21 October. Special Forces also sent units to Laos, in 1959, and Thailand in 1960. In all cases, the Special Forces units were acting as instructors and advisors on the fight against communist insurgency.

The insignia and crest had their own meanings and distinctions. Both were only worn by Special Forces personnel and were a source of pride, as was the green beret itself, of course. The shoulder insignia was, and still is, shaped like an arrowhead, which represented the basic skills of the Native Americans, who were experts at unconventional warfare. It was designed by CPT John W. Frye in 1956.

Inside the teal blue arrowhead was a gold upright knife, with three gold lightning bolts. The knife was a V-42 "fighting knife," represented the unconventional nature of Special Forces operations. The V-42 fighting knife was originally designed and issued to the 1st Special Services Force (SSF) during World War II. SSF (along with the OSS of WWII) were the forerunners of Special Forces.

The three lightning bolts represented the ability of Special Forces to infiltrate by air, water or land. Above the insignia was an arced black insignia, with gold lettering that read "AIRBORNE," signifying the fact that Special Forces and the wearer of the insignia were airborne qualified (paratroopers).

Now there is a second arced insignia above the arrowhead and "AIRBORNE" insignias, reading "SPECIAL FORCES," which denotes the wearer to be Special Forces qualified. In the '60s a further qualification was known as a 3-qualification. The number three was tacked onto the end of the MOS number, designating the fact that the soldier was Special Forces qualified.

Being qualified in three Special Forces MOSs was considered "cross trained." Being "cross trained" also meant that the individual was qualified to have a full flash on his beret at that time, rather than a "candy stripe" flash. In later years, every Special Forces qualified individual would be authorized the full flash.

The flashes denoted the Special Forces Group to which the individual was assigned. Gold was 1st SFG (Abn), black was 5th SFG (Abn), red was 7th SFG (Abn) and green was 10th SFG (Abn). White denoted personnel assigned to Special Forces Training Group as permanent personnel, not trainees.

Later active duty groups included the 3rd SFG (red, white, gold and black), 6th SFG (red, white and black), 8th SFG (teal blue and yellow) and several different reserve and national guard Special Forces units.

The crest (worn on the shoulder of the Class A uniform and on the beret [centered in the full flash or centered above the candy stripe]) consisted of the upright V-42 "fighting knife" over two crossed arrows and a ribbon flourish with the Latin words "De Oppresso Liber." The crossed arrows (as with the arrowhead insignia) represented the skills of Native Americans and the "fighting knife" with unconventional warfare. Army tradition says "De Oppresso Liber" meant "to liberate the oppressed" or "to free from oppression" in English. Literally translated, however, it means "from (being) an oppressed man, (to being) a free one."

The personnel at training group, including trainees, were unlike those I had been associated with so far. Everyone acted and looked professional and mature. Seriousness was a way of life. During basic, AIT and Jump School there had been a lot of clowning around by the trainees. At Training Group, the trainees acted much more mature and serious about their training and their life in general.

Another difference was that I rarely heard any complaining about the Army. I had become sick and tired of hearing all the draftees in Basic, AIT, and Jump School, complaining about the Army. Between ALL Special Forces trainees being enlistees, triple volunteers, screened mentally and physically to meet exacting standards, you could say that we were dedicated to the Special Forces concept.

By the time I was in my SF training group, I had become so attuned to Army life that I was beginning to enjoy it. If nothing else, I was kept busy.

Finally, on Saturday, I received pay. Wow! All of $80. The following day, 7 October, I had wanted to go to town to celebrate my 20th birthday with liquid refreshment. Lo and behold, North Carolina had "Blue Laws": No bars were permitted to be open on Sundays, except on military bases. Nor could you purchase or consume any liquor in any commercial establishment, or buy any liquor in a state-run liquor store, which was the only place one could purchase hard booze off base.

Celebrating at the enlisted club on base wasn't nearly as much fun as celebrating off base would have been. Since I was only 20, I couldn't drink anything except beer and wine. So much for any kind of a decent celebration.

Fayetteville was in a "wet" county, so you could have alcoholic beverages if you were 18 years of age or older. The bars were, however, only permitted to serve beer (a watered down 3.2 beer at that). Every bar had a bartender and at least one barmaid (waitress).

Because you were not permitted to stand while drinking, or even move your own drink from one table to another (because that would entail holding the beer while on your feet), the barmaid had to transport all beers. Even if playing pool or shuffleboard (a favorite local game in bars) you had to sit down at your table or in your booth to take a sip of your beer.

An interesting fact about North Carolina in the 1960s was the mixture of dry and wet counties in the state. Some counties chose to be "dry" (not allow the sale or consumption of alcoholic beverages in the county), while others opted for "wet" (sale of alcohol by the drink in bars and restaurants and by the bottle in State Alcoholic Beverage Control stores). You could always tell when you were traveling across a wet-dry county line. The wet county would have a line of bars right at the county line, even if there was no town there.

On base, you could purchase beer in the EM Club at age 18, but no hard liquor. At the NCO Club you could purchase and consume beer if you were over 18 and hard liquor by the drink if you were 21, but you had to have a rank of sergeant or higher.

In the late 60s Fayetteville permitted private clubs to operate. In the private clubs you paid a monthly membership fee. You purchased your bottle of liquor from the state ABC store, took it to the private club, where a label was put on it, denoting it as yours. The bottle was then placed behind the bar.

You ordered your drink from the bartender and paid the bartender for your drink, even if it was only a shot of YOUR liquor that he or she poured. If you were a regular at the club you could also pay rent for a locker to keep your bottle of liquor in, since liquor was not permitted in the barracks on base.

Many was the time my friends and I would travel outside of pass limits on a weeknight to attend a dance. When the dance was in a dry county we would carry plenty of Old Spice after-shave lotion with us. During breaks in the dancing we would go out to the car and take a hefty swig of the Old Spice. After all, it did contain alcohol and was not unlawful to have in your possession. We had the best smelling breath in the whole dance hall.

The chow (food) at Training Group was unlike any I had eaten elsewhere in the Army. It was GOOD. A couple days after our arrival we were issued our field equipment, including the good old stand-by M-1 Garand rifle.

Training Group was a far cry from the other training units. Upon arriving there my attitude changed significantly. I felt very positive about everything and was extremely happy. We finally had freedom. We could go into town after duty hours and on weekends if we wished. Heck, it was the first I was permitted to have civvies in my locker.

The transportation into town was the civilian bus, known by us as the "Vomit Comet." The nearest town was Fayetteville (also known by us as Fatalburg, and later as FayetteNam). The bus was nicknamed the "Vomit Comet" because by the time it had made its last run from town to the base, it reeked of vomit from the drunk GIs, especially on payday weekend.

There were generally two areas the GIs went to in town: One was downtown on Hay Street. One block of Hay Street was all bars, my favorite being the "Turf Club." The other area was "Combat Alley," which was on Gillespie Street near the bus station, and was where most of the fights occurred.

Fights were common, often due to the egos of the combatants. Ft. Bragg basically had three different breeds of Army personnel: Special Forces, paratroopers (82nd Airborne Division and XVIII Airborne Corps), and legs (non-paratroopers).

To add to the mix were Air Force personnel from Pope Air Force Base, which was right next to Ft. Bragg and furnished the aircraft that supported Special Forces and the 82nd Airborne. None of those four groups seemed to intermix very well socially, even though they were all "allies" on the real battlefield. "Combat Alley" was constantly awash with young, brawling, drunk, pissing, and puking 82nd Airborne paratroopers.

I couldn't understand it. What was the sense in fighting fellow Americans, men who could well be your backup in a future combat situation, against the true enemy, Communism? We had war zones we went to overseas, to fight and die. Why did we have to do it in Fatalburg? Hell, there were plenty of true enemies in the world without taking it out on our own soldiers and airmen. I went to bars to enjoy, and drink beer, not to fight. Some men just didn't have their priorities in order.

It was not wise to ride on the last bus back to base. It was especially not advisable to sit on a seat that was located under a luggage rack on that last bus. The luggage racks were constructed of metal tubing, with an open type of construction. When the seats filled up, the drunker of the GIs would climb up onto the luggage rack and lie down above the seated passengers. That made for a very good chance of the sitting passenger being the recipient of a face or head full of vomit when the drunk above could no longer keep it in, or didn't care to keep it in.

Soldiers were not permitted to go to town wearing their fatigue uniform. Class A uniform (dress uniform) was okay, but nobody in their right mind would be stupid enough to wear a Class A uniform to town, unless going to town for bus, train or plane transportation to other destinations. Civvies (civilian clothes) were the preferred dress. Even wearing civvies, the extremely short haircuts (ALWAYS neatly trimmed) made soldiers stand out like a sore thumb.

Most local civilians weren't very friendly with the soldiers unless they stood to make money. They were for the most part, however, tolerant of the soldiers. Generally, if you wanted to meet the opposite sex you traveled to outlying towns or cities (further away than Fayetteville).

Few, if any, females went to the enlisted men's (EM) clubs on base; a few would go into the E-4 Club (for enlisted men ranked the equivalent of Corporal or higher), and in the NCO Club (Non-Commissioned Officer's Club, for Sergeants or higher rank) you could find a few more, especially if it was a dance night. Myrtle Beach on the Atlantic coast of South Carolina was one of the favorite locations in the summer. There was always a large selection of female college students partying there.

Ft. Bragg was a sprawling base on 130,000 acres of sandy rolling hills dotted with scrub pines. It was the "Home of the Airborne." The base included the XVIII Airborne Corps, 82nd Airborne Division, and 5th and 7th Special Forces Groups, besides Special Forces Training Group.

I toured the main part of Ft. Bragg a few times, for lack of anything else to do, but it was a very boring base. There was nothing beautiful about the base. It was mostly sprawling, rolling sand hills. Even the pines were sparse and scraggly, and the oak trees were scrub oaks.

When not training, the 0800 formation usually consisted of the NCO in charge standing in front of us, clipboard in hand, assigning personnel to details. Many times, not all personnel were picked for details and would be dismissed from formation to go back to the barracks. If a person remained in the barracks, chances were good that an NCO would come through to find a body or bodies to fill a late-requested detail and the person could be assigned to the detail. That was known as the "Hey, you!" roster.

On Tuesday (the 9th) I learned that I finally had been granted an Interim Secret security clearance. I found out when I was detailed as a security guard for a secret Branch Training class that day. The job required a Secret security clearance. The following day I was assigned to be the Barracks Orderly. I had quickly learned two ways to avoid the "Hey, you!" roster.

The first method was to volunteer early in the morning for Barracks Orderly. I had become an expert at operating the buffing machine, and that was part of the Barracks Orderly duties — keeping the barracks and floor spick-and-span, ready for inspection at any time.

All the work would be completed in the morning, leaving afternoon hours as free time to be spent in the barracks acting basically as a barracks guard. It was great for sleeping off a hangover, writing letters home, studying, or reading a book.

The second method was known as "ghosting." "Ghosting" was an art form in Special Forces. With the fact that being able to think on one's feet and being creative was (and still is) a major prerequisite for Special Forces, it figures that "ghosting" would become a widespread and creative activity. I found that the "Hey, you!" roster could be avoided by riding the "ghost bus." The "ghost bus" was the name given to the base bus. A person could ride the bus around base, thus avoiding the "Hey, you!" roster.

Many men were so adept at "ghosting" that they could avoid menial details altogether, not just worry about the "Hey, you!" roster.

One of the more daring methods to ghost was to walk around with a clipboard, looking important. Clipboards were signs of people in charge or participating in inspections. If you stayed out of trouble, the cadre didn't seem to mind if you "ghosted."

The only thing I didn't like was the wait to begin training. Starting dates kept being pushed back. I was originally scheduled (I thought) to begin training on 22 October. Apparently, class dates weren't pre-determined, but began as the classes filled.

I had to wait more than a month and a half to begin training. I learned that never knowing what lay ahead, and waiting for training, was normal in Training Group. It was a psychological test of sorts. It was very frustrating at times.

One of the ways I made extra money during the time I was waiting for the beginning of training was to pull KP (Kitchen Police) on weekends for other trainees. The going rate for pulling someone's KP was $10 a day (a little less than $1 an hour). I could easily make an extra $20 a week by pulling KP on Saturdays and Sundays. That paid for a lot of beers.

When pulling KP, I always tried to be one of the first to report. The easiest jobs usually were assigned to the first person showing up in the morning for their KP, unless you were friends with the Mess Sergeant, and had talked to him the day before about assigning you to a cushy job. The easiest KP assignment was DRO (Dining Room Orderly), basically keeping the eating area of the mess hall clean.

Examples of other available jobs when assigned to KP were: dishwashing machine (required rinsing, running dinnerware through the machine, and drying the same), and pots & pans (the hardest work, a lot of scrubbing). A boring job was peeling potatoes. Some of the mess halls had automatic potato peelers that didn't always peel the potatoes entirely, so a little peeling was still required.

I hated "guard duty." There was a duty roster posted outside of the orderly room (basically, company headquarters). On it were posted the KP roster and guard duty roster for the following few weeks. I always dreaded seeing my name on the guard duty roster. The beginning of the guard duty tour of duty began with Guard Mount: an inspection in formation, and a grilling by the "Officer of the Guard."

The first thing I learned was to make sure my boots were highly "spit-shined." I also learned that a pair of Corcoran jump boots looked the sharpest. I had one pair of fatigues (just for guard duty) that were tailored to fit me well and extremely starched, to the point of being able to lean them against a wall and not have them bend or fall to the ground.

When I had guard duty, I took my jump boots and starched fatigues with me to the guard-duty barracks, changing into them just prior to the inspection formation. My fatigues were so starched that I had to physically force my body into them. I also made sure just before formation, that there was not so much as a speck of dust or bit of oil in or on my rifle.

The reason for so much care in preparation for the guard duty formation was that the guard selected as the sharpest of the group would be selected as "Colonel's Orderly" or "General's Orderly" (also known as supernumerary), depending on whether it was unit or post guard duty. "Colonel's Orderly" was always reported to the unit as an individual "well done," and the designee was dismissed from guard duty and given the remainder of the guard duty hours off. The designee was also awarded a three-day pass.

Upon forming in front of the guard duty barracks, the "Officer of the Guard" would (in stiff military fashion) go from soldier to soldier, checking the soldier from head to toe for neatness, then checking that soldier's rifle inside and out. The final test for making "orderly" was correctly answering whatever question the officer posed upon that individual's inspection. The officers usually asked the soldier to state one of the General Orders, by asking something like, "Private, what is your sixth General Order?" You were then expected, with no hesitation, to spout off the exact wording of paragraph six of the General Orders.

I quickly learned (from accidentally giving the wrong general order for the one requested) that most of the officers didn't seem to know which order was associated with a which paragraph. After wrong answers were accepted as correct a couple times, I formulated a plan. When asked for a specific general order number, if I didn't know which one it was for sure, rather than take time thinking about it, I would immediately spout out the general order I knew best. It worked every time. I had a very good record of making orderly.

The few times that I didn't make orderly and had to stand guard was a pain in the butt. Unless the guard duty came on a weekend, the term of guard duty was usually just the overnight hours (1800 hours until 0600 hours). The duty would consist of reliefs (shifts) of two hours on, four hours off. That usually meant each guard would work two shifts.

On weekends, the tour of duty was twenty-four hours (beginning and ending at 1800 hours) working four shifts. The guard posts varied. Some guard posts required constant walking, making the rounds of the facility to be guarded. Others were posts during which the guard would stand or sit for periods of time, with occasional "making-the-rounds" of the facility.

The company formed a flag football team for the on-post league. I tried out (despite my knee) and made the team. In fact, I was selected as the first-string offensive and defensive end. It didn't seem to bother my knee any more than usual. It was a good way to keep myself busy.

On Monday (the 8th), I had requested a three-day leave to visit Uncle Jerre, Aunt Dorie and cousins Mike, Pat, and Dan the following weekend in the Washington D.C. area. The answer was a quick no! I was supposedly going to begin training on Monday, the 15th.

When Friday arrived, and I was told my training would not begin in Monday after all, I talked the First Sergeant into a weekend pass. Early Saturday morning, 13 October, I took the bus to Fayetteville and boarded the train to Washington, D.C. (the round-trip ticket cost me $19).

Uncle Jerre and Aunt Dorie (and my male cousins) lived in Silver Springs MD, just outside of D.C. Uncle Jerre picked me up at the train station. That afternoon, he drove us to cousins Pat and Mike's high school Homecoming Game.

Pat sat a few rows above Mike and me during the game. After the game Pat said that some of the girls sitting next to him were talking about me and my uniform. The Class A Airborne uniform I was wearing looked sharp and was very popular among the female gender in that part of the country. That became even more obvious when I was wearing my green beret while attending Engineer NCO School outside of D.C. in 1965. That evening, cousin Mike and I attended his high school's Homecoming Dance. I was, once again, in uniform and danced quite a few slow numbers with some cute seniors, while Mike just stood and watched all night.

Mike later enlisted in the Army trying to become a Green Beret. It was a shame: he wasn't even accepted for qualification because of a medical condition. Instead he became a leg clerk-typist. When he was assigned to the 25th Infantry Division in South Vietnam he wanted to be in the action.

Mike finally talked his CO into permitting him to do so as a tunnel rat. Wow; talk about going from the frying pan into the fire. Tunnel rats were usually somewhat short and slim men. Their jobs were to enter any underground tunnels found by the troops. It wasn't a job for anybody with claustrophobia, for sure. It took a helluva lot of guts to do that job. You never knew what you were going to run into, down there in the dark, including booby-traps and armed VC troops.

Mike's parents had the latest Bedford, PA, newspaper (where may parents were from) and, lo and behold, I was mentioned in the paper as being stationed at Ft. Bragg NC, going through Special Forces training. Apparently, mom (or grandma) had sent the information to the newspaper. I wasn't happy about being written up in the paper (all Special Forces soldiers were supposed to keep a low profile), but at least there wasn't a photograph of me, and it was too late to do anything about it anyway.

On Sunday, 14 October, an American U-2 spy plane flight over Cuba took photographs of Soviet medium range and intermediate range ballistic nuclear missile (MRBM and IRBM) sites being installed. President Kennedy was informed of this discovery on the following day. Troubles on our shore were escalating at a very quick pace.

I returned to Ft. Bragg on Sunday evening. The next day, Monday, at the morning formation, I was informed that I was promoted to Private First Class (PFC, E-3 grade). I finally got to wear one lone stripe on my arm. That made me extremely happy. I was tired of being a "slick sleeve" Private E-2. According to *The NoNCOm's Guide, 1966 edition* "outstanding individuals may be appointed to grade E-3 upon attaining 4 months' time in grade of E-2."

I guess somebody figured I was a good soldier. I had also made E-3 in the minimum total service time of eight months. Another thing I liked about the promotion was the $13.57 a month raise that came with it. I was now making $99.37 a month, plus my $55 a month jump pay, for a grand total of $154.37. Yeah, time to party!

During that morning formation, I notified the NCO in charge that I would have to go on sick call for a dental problem. I had to go to the base dental clinic to make an appointment and spent half the day there just to get a November appointment.

The speed at which the military functioned was beyond description. I returned just after the after lunch (1300 hours) formation. I went to my barracks and asked the Barracks Orderly if he had something he wanted to do that afternoon. Since he did, I took over as Barracks Orderly, and proceeded to sleep all afternoon.

As I had mentioned previously, one had to be in excellent health to be accepted into Special Forces. Not long after I arrived at Training Group, one of my barracks mates (I believe his last name may have been James also) had an epileptic fit in the barracks. There was no way he could hide the fact that it had occurred, so he was medically disqualified from Special Forces and was gone in a couple days. He had been one of the men I really felt was going to make a good Green Beret. It didn't pay to make many friends in Special Forces Training Group because of the large turnover from various reasons, especially medical and not being able to satisfactorily pass the courses.

The following day (the 16th) I made my sixth parachute jump, known as my "cherry" jump, my first since Jump School (had to earn my jump pay, you know). We were to make a "tailgate" parachute jump from a U.S. Army de Havilland CV-2 Caribou. The Caribou was a twin-engine propeller-driven cargo aircraft with a range of about 240 miles, designed to transport 26 paratroopers and fly in and out of short, unpaved landing strips. It was a "Hollywood" jump (no equipment) onto Normandy Drop Zone at Ft. Bragg and I was 15th in the stick. The aircraft cruised at about 170 mph but slowed to 100 knots (115 mph) when jumping from it.

As we neared the DZ, I could hear the whirring of the hydraulically-operated ramp in the rear, as it was lowered. We were given the pre-jump commands. I was at about the halfway spot in our stick of jumpers. When the green light came on to designate exit time, the jumpers in front of me shuffled single file rearward, onto the ramp, and "hopped," one at a time, off the rear of the aircraft into the beckoning blue sky.

Because of that type of exit, there was no "prop blast" to speak of. I grew to love tail ramp jumps. They were a snap. It was a major change from the jumps we made at Ft. Benning. Except for the fact that my chest wound reopened when the chute opened, and I was kept extremely busy avoiding nearby jumpers in the air, the jump went perfectly.

The main problems about Caribou ramp jumps were: (1) men might jump too close together, thus being hit by the preceding jumper's parachute when it deployed, or becoming entangled in the other jumper's suspension lines; (2) there was an increased chance of tangling one's arm in the static line; and (3) because jumpers were so close together, there was an increased possibility of jumpers colliding while descending.

Paratroopers had to jump at least once every three months to collect their monthly bonus jump pay. That could be waived if the paratroopers were in a location where jumps could not be made. Rumor had it that members of the 1st Special Forces Group on Okinawa, who had broken legs, were parachuted into the ocean off Okinawa, so they wouldn't miss jump pay. I know for a fact, that a later CO of that group got his nickname "Splash" Kelly from preferring water jumps to jumps on land.

On the 17th I went on sick call. My right knee had begun bothering me again. As usual, the doctor checked the knee, said he didn't know what was wrong with it, placed another wrap-around bandage on it, and told me to return if it didn't get any better. The normal spiel.

That afternoon a large group of Special Air Service (SAS) troops from Great Britain was feted at Fort Bragg prior to their return to Britain. The SAS was the British version of our Special Forces. They had been in the States training with Special Forces personnel.

I participated in the parade, which was formed to show SF strength and the different uniforms worn by us, honoring the SAS troops. I was clothed in a white, cold-weather uniform for use in snow country, with a pack (snowshoes attached to it), and an M-2 Carbine rifle. Our Special Warfare Center Commanding Officer, General Yarborough, was the primary speaker.

I had been doing pretty good avoiding detail work until 18 October, when I found myself on the unit detail roster, sending my knack of avoiding work spiraling downhill. I had to do KP (Kitchen Police) in our unit's mess hall. Not knowing the ins and outs of KP yet, and the jobs to avoid, I got the pots and pans job. Basically, that meant I was to clean all the eating utensils, pots and pans. It entailed almost full-time scrubbing. I was on the job from 0800 until 2030 hours; 12½ hours of mind-numbing hard work. I learned from that detail, that mess hall cooks thought nothing of dirtying what seemed like every pot and pan in their inventory.

The following day (19 October) I caught a Security Guard detail, although that job was only for two hours. The Cuban Missile Crisis officially began on that same day, when Air Force Chief of Staff General Curtis LeMay advocated "direct military intervention." He felt that merely putting a blockade around Cuba would not work and would lead to war anyhow. He argued that the Soviet Union would not invade West Berlin if we acted in Cuba but would if we failed to act.

That evening I was sure I had once again contracted pneumonia. I felt like I had a fever, had a lot of chest congestion, a headache, chills, and an upset stomach. One of the medic students in my barracks told me to cover myself with a lot of blankets, to sweat the fever away. I slept with 5 blankets on top of me. The following morning, I still had the congestion, and went on sick call. The doctor gave me some nose drops and cough syrup.

He seemed more interested in my knee than my congestion, however. He was bothered by my knee problem and said that he was going to schedule a visit to a specialist for me. I told him I was detailed for Guard Duty that afternoon, hoping he'd sign a release stating I was to be excused from the Guard Duty. He was happy that I was to have guard duty. His feeling was that the Guard Duty might aggravate my knee, making it easier for him to diagnose the problem. Thanks a lot, doc!

Because it was a Saturday, it meant the Guard Duty tour of duty was 24 hours, 1700 hours Saturday until 1700 hours Sunday, two hours walking a post and four hours off, four separate tours. Doc stated that I should go to the hospital emergency room if the knee got worse. Well, it did! By the time of my second of four shifts, I was in agony. The trouble was, there was nobody to replace me, so I didn't go to the ER.

Unbelievably, the pain in my knee subsided some after my third shift. On 22 October I was off to sick call again. This time the doctor sent me to the hospital for an x-ray and made an appointment for me to see a specialist.

President Kennedy made a speech that same evening, telling the American people (and the world) about the discovery of the Soviet missile emplacements being erected in Cuba and proclaiming an "arms quarantine" on Cuba. He said, "It shall be the policy of this nation to regard any nuclear missile launched from Cuba against any nation in the Western Hemisphere as an attack by the Soviet Union on the United States, requiring a full retaliatory response upon the Soviet Union." He also announced a naval blockade of Cuba that had begun the day prior. The shit had hit the fan.

Many senate leaders and military advisers called for air strikes on Cuba, and some advisers even called for an invasion of Cuba. The Soviet Union and Cuba objected to the sites being described as offensive, claiming the missiles were only there for the defense of Cuba.

The next day our company was placed on alert. In fact, all our armed forces were placed on DEFCON3 on the 23rd because of the crisis. That meant we had to be ready to move out within three hours. It also meant there were no off-post passes issued. The Strategic Air Command (SAC) was placed on DEFCON2, an extremely high alert status, and was kept on that alert status until 15 November.[2]

The 5th and 7th Group headquarters areas had barbed wire placed around them and were heavily guarded. Among other units, all Special Forces groups and the 82nd Airborne Division were also on alert. A contingent of Special Forces was assigned the mission of destroying the Soviet ballistic missile sites on Cuban soil. They were to parachute in, destroy as much as possible, and exfiltrate by any means at their disposal. It was a dangerous mission but didn't lack for volunteers. The mission got so far as to take off and fly in a holding pattern outside of Cuban airspace for a few hours, before being told the mission had been called off.

During that period of high alert status, those of us awaiting training had to pull the guard duty and KP details for the Special Forces units, meaning I spent most of my time on details. On the 24th, Khrushchev told Kennedy that the U.S. blockade of Cuba was an act of aggression. He also stated that Soviet ships that were already heading for Cuba would be ordered to continue their journey.

The next day the Joint Special Unconventional Warfare Task Force (JUWTF) was established at Fort Bragg, a result of the Cuban Missile Crisis. It was subordinate to the recently renamed U.S. Army John F. Kennedy Special Warfare Center (JFKSWC).

On 26 October I had KP again. That same day Kennedy reported to his advisors that apparently the only means of removing the missiles would be for the U.S. to attack Cuba, but he still wanted to give some time for diplomatic reasoning to diffuse the situation.

Castro cabled Khrushchev on that very day, requesting that the Soviet Union launch a nuclear strike on the United States if Cuba was invaded. Khrushchev, in turn, notified Kennedy that they would remove the missiles in Cuba if the U.S. closed its Turkey military bases.

The following day an American U-2 spy plane was shot down by a SAM (surface-to-air-missile) over Cuba, killing the pilot. There was no retaliation, but Kennedy agreed to bomb all SAM missile sites if any more American aircraft were attacked.

The Joint Chiefs of Staff recommended an air strike against Cuba unless there was obvious evidence of the dismantling of the missiles by the 29th. That evening President Kennedy sent a message, promising

Khrushchev we would not invade Cuba in return for the removal of the missiles in Cuba.

The next morning (28th) Khrushchev publicly announced that all Soviet missiles would be removed from Cuba. A crisis had been averted, but the quarantine remained, with the stipulation that it would not cease until the Soviets removed their IL-28 bombers from Cuban soil.

The quarantine was finally ended on 20 November, almost a month after it had been implemented. Because of the delays in delivery of critical messages, and the fact that a nuclear war had come so close to fruition, a direct phone line was established between the White House and the Soviet Union, known as the "Hotline." Also, a result of the Cuban Crisis was a beginning of discussions dealing with the nuclear arms race. The world had survived a possible nuclear Armageddon.

On 29 October I was scheduled for Guard Duty but was excused because I had an appointment with a medical specialist about my knee. He looked at x-rays of the knee and said he couldn't see anything wrong with it. He told me to return if the problem persisted.

The cadre suggested that each of us study the tactics and tenets of Mao Tse-Tung (Red Chinese Army) and Che Guevara (Cuban guerrilla leader), both considered to be experts in guerrilla warfare. The PX (Post Exchange) carried *Mao Tse-Tung on Guerilla Warfare* and *Che Guevara on Guerilla Warfare*, so I immediately purchased them both and began reading.

Mao Tse-Tung had decreed that there would be three phases to any war: The first phase would entail the formation of a safe base, situated in an isolated area. This was to be where volunteers were to be trained and indoctrinated. Those same volunteers were to spread out from the base, agitating and propagandizing against the government in power. Once a protective belt of people sympathetic to the movement was formed — from which food, information, and recruits could be obtained — the second phase could begin.

During the second phase the violent part of the conflict would begin, with sabotage and terrorism increasing. Raids and ambushes on vulnerable targets would be used to procure arms, ammunition, medical supplies, and other essential materials. As the guerrilla forces grew in stature and quality, political activists could be sent out to nearby areas to indoctrinate and "liberate" the populace.

Phase three followed, wherein orthodox military operations were utilized to annihilate the enemy, with guerrilla warfare taking a subsidiary role. Mao always stressed that a guerrilla war would fail without a clearly defined political goal. He equated guerrilla warfare to revolution, admitting that it could not exist or flourish without the support and cooperation of the masses.

The communists in Southeast Asia were happy about the Japanese-allied war during WWII because the war weakened government forces in countries fighting the Japanese. They were confident that the allies would win and knew that taking control of the weaker governments would be much easier after the war.

Mao Tse-Tung was known as the world's foremost authority on guerilla warfare. His publication *Red Star Over China* originally came out in 1939. In the publication, his "Rules for Conduct" was thought to be one of the best lists of tenets to be followed by guerrillas or soldiers wanting the civilian populace to be supportive of their presence. The rules were, in fact, put to music and became a daily official Red Army song.

Special Forces used their own version of Mao's rules when interacting with indigenous personnel. We would be formally taught to treat the indigenous people with respect, as our lives would be in their hands. It's a shame our country's conventional troops weren't taught the same credo, as it might have led to a different outcome in the Vietnam War.

Mao's rules were to be memorized by all his troops, and were strictly enforced to the point where violating them would result in severe punishment, and in some cases execution. Mao's Rules of Conduct included:

1. All actions are subject to command.
2. Do not steal from the people. Pay for everything you purchase.
3. Be neither selfish nor unjust.
4. Confrontation is not permitted with the poor peasantry.

He explained further with eight remarks:

1. Replace the door when you leave the house. (They often used doors as beds.)
2. Roll up the bedding on which you have slept.
3. Be courteous.
4. Be honest in your transactions.
5. Return what you borrow.
6. Replace what you damage or break.
7. Do not bathe in the presence of women.
8. Do not without authority search the pocketbooks of those you arrest.

Mao borrowed many of his ideas and tenets from another warfare expert, Sun Tzu. It was Sun Tzu who wrote, "Guerrilla strategy must be based primarily on alertness, mobility, and attack. It must be adjusted to the enemy situation, the terrain, the existing lines of communication, the relative strengths, the weather, and the situation of the people. In guerrilla warfare, select the tactic of seeming to come from the east and attacking from the west; avoid the solid, attack the hollow; attack; withdraw; deliver a lightning blow, seek a lightning decision. When guerrillas engage a stronger enemy, they withdraw when he advances; harass him when he stops; strike him when he is weary; pursue him when he withdraws. In guerrilla strategy, the enemy's rear, flanks, and other vulnerable spots are his vital points, and there he must be harassed, attacked, dispersed, exhausted and annihilated."

Che Guevara was the son of a left-wing Argentinian. He had been part of several unsuccessful attempts to depose Argentina's dictator, Juan Perón. In 1954 he was part of Arbenz's Guatemalan Communist government until its overthrow. After that he went to Mexico, where he met Fidel Castro in 1955. Che was an expert on Marx and Lenin, prominent Communists. He was also anti-American.

Che Guevara became Fidel Castro's prime strategist and Central American Communist revolutionary. He was generally considered to have masterminded the Cuban revolution, as well as being a prime advisor to Central and South American communist revolutionaries.

Che's forces entered Havana, Cuba in early 1959, taking control of the Cuban government for Castro. Another book I purchased was *150 Questions for a Guerrilla* by General Alberto Bayo, a top Fidel Castro advisor and instructor.

Payday was on the 31st. I got paid a grand total of $36, with a promise that I would get the rest of my pay the following month. $36 to last a whole month? Fat chance! The only good thing about it was that I would be due $220 the next payday. That would give me some spending money for my upcoming planned Christmas leave.

The following day (Thursday, 1 November) the Soviet Union began dismantling their Cuban missiles, bringing a sigh of relief to the whole world. I had guard duty that day and the next. I had to guard a water tank. During the overnight hours the temperature got down into the 20s. I wore long johns, two pairs of socks, a field jacket with wool liner and hood, gloves, and a heavy scarf. I still froze.

Between playing football on the unit team, and all the details I was having to pull because of the alert status everyone was on, I didn't have any time to waste money drinking in town. That was good! As of 2 November, our team was undefeated in eight games so far. The team had been formed prior to me arriving in Training Group, so I hadn't been playing during a lot of the games. I played offensive and defensive end. It was strange, but my knee didn't bother me while I played football.

On the 3rd I had to pull another day of KP. I got Sunday (4 November) off, followed by CQ Runner from 1600 Monday until 0800 Tuesday. Each unit was covered during non-duty hours by a Charge of Quarters (CQ). The CQ was usually an NCO, responsible for the unit area during the off-duty hours.

The CQ remained in the Orderly Room (unit headquarters), answering phone calls and maintaining order in the area functioning in the absence of the first sergeant and the company clerk, in general acting as the representative of the commanding officer.

The CQ Runner was sent to various places within the unit, under orders from the CQ. Most often, the runner's duties were to let someone in the barracks know there was a phone call for him in the

Orderly Room. After only 6½ hours rest, I was back on Guard Duty again from 1430 Tuesday until 1700 the following day.

Thankfully, I got paid part of what the government owed me on the 9th. It wasn't much ($30), but it at least gave me some spending money. I also received a letter from my main girlfriend at the time, Cindy. It was a "Dear John" letter. Thankfully another girl, who lived in Modesto, CA, was writing to me pretty regularly, as well as sending cookies occasionally.

On Saturday, the 10th, as if I hadn't already pulled enough non-voluntary KP, I voluntarily pulled KP for one of the guys for $7. It doesn't seem like much, but back then every little bit helped. Two days later (Monday) I had to pull guard duty again, on Veterans Day.

Wednesday was a new detail. I was on a crew that picked up explosives from the base ammo dump at 0600. We delivered it to one of the demolition ranges on post, waited around while they had their fun blowing up most of it, then delivered the remainder back to the ammo dump. I didn't get off that detail until 2100 hours.

The next day I was on KP. It began at 0400 and was supposed to continue until 2300, but I managed to bang my head badly, dumping a lot of blood all over the place. Because of that I got off at 1400 to recuperate. Talk about a glutton for punishment!

The next day (Friday, the 16th) I stayed in the barracks to recuperate from my head injury. That same day we were downgraded to DEFCON5 (a lower alert status). It meant that we were changed from 3-hour alert status to 5-hour alert status. It also meant that we could travel as far as 50 miles from the base if we left a contact phone number at the orderly room. The following day we were taken off alert status completely.

When the training roster came out on Friday my name hadn't been on it. I had understood that the last demolition class of the year would begin on Monday (19 November). I was not happy! I had been sitting around for a month and a half waiting for training and got skipped.

The following day I complained to the First Sergeant. He pulled some strings and got me scheduled for the demolition pre-math class beginning the 19th. He told me, however, that the next demolition class wouldn't begin until the following year. To add to my frustration, I was scheduled for KP all day on Sunday the 18th. My mind was being messed with big time.

There was a lot of talk in Training Group about Special Forces training in skydiving (known in SF as HALO, or High Altitude-Low Opening). Rumor had it at the time that they were hoping to train all SF in HALO jumping. As it was, HALO training was available for Special Forces personnel, but like the waiting list for Ranger training, the HALO training waiting list was LONG.

HALO was used to deliver, or insert, military personnel, equipment, and supplies from transport aircraft flying at a high altitude (15,000 to 35,000 feet). When making a HALO insertion, the parachutists free-fell until reaching their preferred altitude (usually a couple thousand feet above the ground), at which time they opened their parachutes

In March 1957, some members of the 77th Special Forces Group attended the first "Basic Body Stabilization Free Fall Parachuting Course, at Fort Bragg. Later that year, course #2 was held, with students coming from the 77th Special Forces Group, the Airborne School, and the 82nd and 101st Airborne Divisions. The following year, FA Team 25 of the 77th Group became the first detachment to qualify as "Military Freefall" (MFF) parachutists.

On 12 September 1961, a few Special Forces soldiers made a demonstration HALO jump for President Kennedy during his visit to Fort Bragg. Shortly before my arrival at Training Group, in September 1962, the Advanced Training Committee was formed, to develop infiltration methods for Special Forces. A six-week course was conducted by them, titled "High Altitude Low Opening Advanced Parachute Techniques."

At a later date, HAHO (High Altitude-High Opening) was introduced to military use. On a HAHO jump, the parachutists exited the aircraft at a high altitude, similar to a HALO jump, but opened their parachutes a few seconds after exiting the aircraft. HAHO permits the parachutist to travel long distances after exiting the aircraft, thus limiting engine noise from giving away the location of the parachutist landing.

CHAPTER 6

DEMOLITION TRAINING

Demolition Training

I finally began my one-week pre-math class on 19 November. My mathematics education in high school and college really came in handy. The course was a snap for me, almost to the point of being boring. Most of the class dealt with computations that included formulas (basically algebra) because so many demolition jobs involved computing the quantity of explosives required to do the job effectively. I graduated at the top of the class with a final score of 98%. More men dropped out of SF training, or in some cases were able to select other MOS training, due to not passing this short course.

On the 21st the Soviet Union agreed to withdraw bomber aircraft from Cuba, and President Kennedy officially ended the blockade of Cuba. Through all this we still had the daily barracks and personal inspection rituals. The inspections almost seemed like old hat after a while, but they did cause extra work, and thereby reduced our leisure time. Leave it to Training Group to get me right back on KP after finishing pre-math training. I had it on Tuesday, the 27th. Supposedly, I was now scheduled to begin demolition training on 3 December.

The 3rd of December came, with no training cycle listed on the bulletin board. Instead, a bunch of us went to the field. We had been told on Friday to prepare for going to the field on Monday, returning on Friday. We were also told that we would be acting the part of a guerrilla band, to undergo training by a trainee Special Forces A-team.

Our instructors would be soon-to-be (or, at least, hopefully so) Branch Training graduates. It was their final exercise, to prove their ability and worthiness to be a Green Beret. We were told that our uniform would be our most rag-tag civvies, since they were bound to get wear and tear, and dirty.

I packed two pairs of jeans and warm shirts since we were going to be in the mountains of North Carolina, in the winter. We departed early Monday morning on deuce-and-a-half trucks. We arrived in the hills of North Carolina, in a fictitious country known then, and still, as Pineland, about 75 miles west of Ft. Bragg. I made my own little hooch out of a couple of ponchos and some branches. I got very cold and wet, but learned a lot. It rained Monday night through Tuesday afternoon, and again on Wednesday night.

Thursday morning, we awoke to snow on the ground and snow still falling. When I awoke, I had to pee. As cold as it was, as much as I needed to pee, as far away from my hooch as the pisser was, and as few clothes as I had on, I didn't pee at the authorized pisser, using a nearby tree instead. Hey, trees need water too.

We were there to act as indigenous guerrilla warfare troops, being advised by Special Forces Branch Training trainees. They were teaching us, and advising us, how to fight the invaders, and take back our country. It was part of their final test for finishing their advanced training, before graduating, and being assigned to a Special Forces unit. They were there to "mold us into a fighting unit," give us training, and take us out on operations.

A few months later, I would be in those same woods, but acting the part of a Special Forces advisor, training a group of indigenous guerrilla fighters. It would be my graduation test. My time in Pineland helped me understand what I would be expected to do when it came time for me to be tested. It was great training for me.

Every Green Beret goes through the "Pineland" scenario, even to this day. It is the final test before graduating and earning the Green Beret. Upon returning from the field on the 7th, I checked the company bulletin board. Surprise, surprise, out of nowhere, demolition training was to begin for me that following Tuesday, 11 December.

We were transported out to the demolition range for our first four days of training. "FIRE IN THE HOLE! FIRE IN THE HOLE! FIRE IN THE HOLE!" That was the warning cry any time explosives were going to be detonated on the firing range. The first day was a fantastic demonstration of what different explosives looked and sounded like.

That first day we also suffered through SNOW. Wednesday the temperature didn't exceed 17 degrees in the morning and 32 degrees all day. Thursday the temperature didn't get above 5 degrees in the morning. Even the sand and dirt were frozen, not to mention us. We were learning that weather did not stop Special Forces from operating.

All that week was spent outside on the demolition range. It was a reminder that, unlike civilian schools that had snow days, during which schools were shut down due to snow, weather did not stop military training unless it was deemed extremely dangerous conditions. In fact, the opposite was true in the military. Bad weather was a good training aid; wars didn't stop because of bad weather, therefore training didn't stop either.

Bad weather could also be an asset to operations. During bad weather, aircraft sometimes couldn't fly. That made it possible to move large amounts of men and materials without being detected by enemy aircraft. The same was true for certain small unit operations. With no enemy reconnaissance aircraft in the air, small unit tactics could be accomplished without detection.

Bad weather could also result in reduced visibility and increased noise, during which visual and noise detection by the enemy forces could be severely affected, making ground movement safer. Normally, bad weather was an asset to aggressors on the move, and a hindrance to static defenders.

Unlike training I had gone through previously, Special Forces training wasn't as regimented. We were permitted to discuss the lessons, rather than just sit and listen. It was a much more relaxed atmosphere. Our instructors were Special Forces NCOs, many with Special Forces experience in Southeast Asia, especially South Vietnam.

One of the first things we learned in demolition training was what it takes to produce a firing train. As a very basic example, a typical fire train began with a match, with which to light a piece of paper, which in turn produced flame from wood, and finally caused coal to burn. The match would not light coal. It needed the in-between igniters to finally produce fire from coal.

With explosives, an initiator such as a firing pin or electrical charge was needed, which set off the detonator, which in turn ignited the booster that detonated the main explosive charge. Unlike previous training where we worked for hours on dummy equipment, at Training Group we were able to set off charges on the first day.

The first example shown to us was detonating cord (det cord), aka detonating fuse. Det cord has a very fast burning (explosive) rate — known as detonating velocity — of about 21,000 feet per second. Det cord had been strung around the outside of the firing range. When it was ignited, the det cord looked as if it had exploded all at one time, rather than beginning at one end and ending at the far end. It was an excellent way of showing how powerful, and dangerous, the cord was.

Det cord contained a small round core of explosives known as PETN (pentaerythritol tetranitrate), covered by white material. PETN was one of the most powerful of military explosives, almost equal to nitroglycerin and RDX.

Det cord looked exactly like white plastic clothesline. Because it was an explosive (rather than burning) cord, it could be used to detonate high explosive charges if it was wrapped around or wound through an explosive charge. It had to be initiated by a blasting cap or similarly suitable booster. Det cord was very safe to work with, due to its insensitivity to shock, spark, or friction. It was commonly used as a trunk or branch line to connect a group of explosive charges located in different places. It was also used in trench blasting.

On the second day, each of us set off four different types of explosives. The instruction included non-electric and electrically induced explosive trains. For the non-electric system, we utilized fuse lighters or matches to light the time fuse, which in turn ignited the non-electric blasting cap (containing a flash charge, priming charge, and base charge), which detonated the main explosive charge.

Setting up an electrical system required a blasting machine or battery attached to the wires that led to and that set off the electric blasting cap (containing a priming charge and base charge), followed by the detonation of the main explosive charge. Safety was highly stressed, including testing the time fuse (as well as homemade time fuse) before use. An incorrect burning rate or an incorrect length of fuse could be deadly to the good guy.

Most military explosives were de-sensitized, making them somewhat safe to handle and transport. The military certainly didn't want men transporting explosives that could be detonated by the mere striking of a bullet. Because of that, it also required a somewhat powerful shock to detonate most military explosives. Unlike Basic and AIT (where we practiced and practiced, much of the time without the real thing), here we were told ONCE what to do, and proceeded to do it with the REAL THING.

Each of us was issued a copy of the official Department of the Army field manual, FM 5-25 Explosives and Demolitions — 202 pages of important information for the professional explosives expert. Our training basically followed what was included in the field manual, and then some. I still have that manual. It was my bible throughout my career as a demolition specialist in Special Forces. Demolition training was extremely interesting, helped in large part by being able to blow things into smithereens. What a rush!

The manual (dated May 1959) defined explosives as a "substance which, when subjected to heat, impact, friction, or other suitable initial impulse, undergoes a very rapid chemical transformation, forming other more stable products entirely or largely gaseous, whose combined volume is much greater than that of the original substance."

My mathematics skills came in handy. It was easy to think that one needed only place a stick of dynamite or a pound block of TNT on an object to destroy it, but it could mean too much peripheral damage.

(We always referred to military explosives in terms of pounds.) Also, the stick or pound block might not do the job, due to improper placement of the charge.

When used in a military application one had to remember that someone had to carry all those explosives. Therefore, the most effective use of explosives was extremely important. You didn't want each team member carrying five to ten pounds of explosives, time fuse, detonating cord, blasting caps, etc., when five to ten pounds total would do the job.

Contrary to most people's opinion, explosives were used just as much for constructive purposes as well as destructive. When used for construction, the use of mathematical equations was very common. By constructive purposes I'm talking about quickly digging a deep ditch or foxhole utilizing dynamite or a cratering charge, using the "Monroe effect" of a shape charge to produce a large post-hole, blasting rock or a hillside to make way for a road, using explosives to fell trees, etc.

There was a different formula for each different use of explosives, so mathematical expertise was a must in demolition utilization. It was easy to think to oneself that additional explosives would do the job just as well, if not better. Hogwash! An over-abundance of explosives in a charge, or a poorly placed charge, could destroy a project.

Safety was highly stressed. Explosives were nothing to fool around with. Procedures were in place for handling and using military explosives. So long as those procedures were followed to the letter, demolition work was generally a safe activity. We were reminded that there were no old, fearless demolition men. You were to always treat explosives carefully and with your mind focused on the job at hand. You were never to take shortcuts and you were to not just double-check, but triple-check everything.

The uses of explosives were numerous. Different types of explosives were used for different outcomes. The low explosives were slow burning (called deflagration) and tended to push or shove objects (such as dirt, boulders, etc.). The burning rate for low explosives was 400 meters (1,300 feet) per second or less. Black powder and smokeless powder were examples of low explosives.

High explosives were very fast burning (called detonation) and used to cut or demolish objects (such as train tracks, trees, bridges, etc.). Heat or shock was usually required to detonate high explosives. The burning rate was 1,000 meters (3,300 feet) per second or greater. Examples were TNT and dynamite.

An explosion generally resulted in pressure, accompanied by heat. The main effects were fragmentation (of any container used), blast (aka concussion), and incendiary (fire). Fragmentation would, of course, be best when using a heavy metal container to house the explosive. A good example was a pipe bomb. That was constructed using a piece of metal pipe, into which explosives were packed. The addition of bolts and/or nails (or other suitable metallic fragments) inside the pipe increased the fragmentation significantly.

Blast was most noticeable inside a building. The blast effect was caused by expanding gasses, creating a concussion wave. Incendiary action is instantaneous, but would last longer if combustible materials were present, causing a fire.

The detonating velocity of different explosive materials was one of the important qualities to consider when selecting the correct explosive for the job at hand. It also determined the classification of the explosive. Velocity was measured in feet per second that the detonation wave travels through a column of the explosive material.

As a rule, the slower the velocity, the greater the moving action (such as in ditch digging) of the charge. On the other end of the spectrum, the faster the velocity, the greater the shattering action of the explosive.

Explosives were classified as (1) low explosives, (2) primary-initiating explosives, and (3) high explosives. Low explosives burned slowly and were mainly used as propellants; two examples were smokeless and black powder explosives.

Black powder burned rather than detonated. The burning speed of black powder was determined by the grain size. Finely granulated black powder burned much faster than larger grain. The chief use of black powder was in quarrying, fireworks, and time fuse. It was one of the first explosives used by man.

Primary initiating explosives were extremely sensitive and detonated without burning. They included mercury fulminate (an initiating explosive that was extremely sensitive to heat, friction, spark, flame, and impact, and used in detonators and blasting caps) and lead azide (an initiating explosive that was sensitive to flame and impact and used in blasting caps).

High explosives had a very fast, or high, detonating rate, and detonated in a violent action. Examples were dynamite, nitroglycerin, and TNT. We worked with several basic military explosives, including TNT (21,000 fps detonating velocity), Tetrytol (23,000), Compositions C-3 and C-4 (both 26,000 fps), ammonium nitrate (11,000 fps), and military dynamite (20,000 fps).

There were numerous different commercial dynamites, each having a different purpose. Commercial dynamite came in three types, straight dynamite, ammonia dynamite, and gelatin dynamite. Each type was further broken down by the amount of nitroglycerin content, which determined the strength or force of the resulting explosion. Commercial dynamite varied in detonating velocity from about 9,000 to 19,000 feet per second.

Numerous factors came into play when selecting the correct dynamite for the job at hand. Among those considerations was the material that was targeted, desired fragmentation, and condition of the target (wet or dry). Strength, when used in conjunction with dynamite, referred to the energy, which in turn, determined the power it developed, hence the work it could do.

When rating the nitroglycerin or straight dynamites, they were referred to according to the percentage by weight of nitroglycerin. In other words, a 20% straight dynamite contained 20% nitroglycerin by weight. The percent didn't indicate the relative strength, however. 40% dynamite was not twice as strong as 20%. In fact, a 60% dynamite was only about 1½ times stronger than 20% dynamite.

In other types of dynamites, the nitroglycerin was substituted with other powerful ingredients, such as ammonium nitrate. That made for an even larger selection of dynamites and dynamite strengths. Commercial dynamite was initiated by either electric or nonelectric blasting caps. Military dynamite was unlike commercial dynamite in many respects, especially its makeup, moisture retention, and safety factors.

Because military dynamite was destined for use in battlefield conditions and under all possible weather conditions, it contained no nitroglycerin, and was much safer to transport, store, and handle, than the commercial variety. Military dynamite also did not absorb or retain moisture, making it usable in almost all weather conditions. Its detonating velocity was about 20,000 feet per second. Military dynamite was detonated using electric or nonelectric military blasting caps, or detonating (det) cord. Military dynamite also had great heaving ability, making it extremely useful in ditching and quarrying.

TNT (Trinitrotoluene), one of the least sensitive explosives in the Army inventory, was also one of the most used, especially for steel cutting, concrete breaching, and underwater demolitions. TNT was a mixture of toluene, sulfuric acid, and nitric acid. It could be burned, without detonating. It was often used in the field to heat coffee (although not as often as C-4), using a small chunk lit with a cigarette lighter or match. It was also impervious to water.

Because of its higher detonating speed, Tetrytol was more effective for cutting and breaching. Tetrytol was a mixture of about 70% tetryl (Trinitrophenylmethylnitramine) — which had a very high shattering power and was used primarily as a booster — and 30% TNT. Composition C-3, and especially the newer, better, C-4, were plastic explosives that were even more powerful than TNT and Tetrytol. C-3 and C-4 were ideally suited for cutting steel and timber, as well as breaching concrete. Their pliability made it possible to shape the charge to place it in close contact with the target object. C-3 and C-4 imitated putty and molding clay in their consistency. C-4 consisted of 91% RDX and 9% plastic binder.

Like TNT, C-3 and C-4 were very insensitive and were waterproof. Because it burned with a very intense heat (without detonating) and gave off no discernable scent when burning, we often used C-4 to heat our coffee, even in Vietnam. It burned so hot that it only took seconds to boil water with it. In fact, because of the versatility and safety of handling C-4, it was our favorite explosive. It was easy to mold, which made it the best explosive for many jobs.

There were precautions to take when using C-4 for heating or cooking. We were warned not to breathe the fumes, since doing so could cause brain damage. In addition, dousing the flames by stomping on the burning glob of C-4 was not recommended. That detonated the explosive and ruined a good cup of coffee, not to mention the intended drinker of said coffee.

Ammonium nitrate was the least sensitive of the military explosives. Its shattering power was low, about 55% as powerful as TNT, but it was excellent at pushing or heaving, making it great for ditching or quarrying. Ammonium nitrate was packaged in cylindrical metal containers.

• • •

On 17 December, after our day of training and dinner at the mess hall, we made a night "Hollywood" jump onto Normandy Drop Zone. We jumped from a U.S. Air Force Fairchild C-123 "Provider." The C-123 was a propeller-driven cargo aircraft powered by two engines. Its cruise speed was about 185 mph and it was first flown in 1949. The C-123 was exited from the rear side door, near the tail of the aircraft. I was fifth man in the stick for the jump, and other than the strong prop blast which pushed me backward harder than usual after exiting, the jump went smoothly.

I received a Christmas pass. It was a two-week pass, to include New Year's Day. It began at one minute past midnight on Saturday morning, 22 December, and ended at midnight Friday, 4 January 1963. A good thing about being an airline brat was the fact that I was able to fly almost anywhere on an airline pass. The airline my father worked for had reciprocal agreements with quite a few other airlines for pass privileges. I could fly round trip nationwide for $20.

It meant having to fly on a stand-by basis, during the airline industry's busiest season, which sometimes resulted in being bumped off flights at inopportune times, but it was affordable on military pay. I used the pass to fly TWA from Washington, D.C. to San Francisco and back. Christmas was always considered dicey for stand-by flying. The trip was interesting, as well as "iffy."

I took an early morning "Vomit Comet" bus from near my barracks to the train station downtown. Either the bus I was on had not been on duty on the same route the night before, or someone had thoroughly cleaned the bus during the early morning hours. I didn't smell the usual early morning stench of the inside of the nighttime "Vomit Comet." I got off the bus at Hay Street in downtown Fayetteville, walked across the street to the railroad station's ticket window, and purchased a round-trip ticket from Fatalburg to Washington, D.C.

I didn't have long to wait for the northbound Southern Railroad passenger train to arrive. As soon as the conductor announced, "All aboard," I — and a few dozen more passengers — loaded onto the train. About halfway back in the coach car I had entered, I was able to see two adjacent empty seats. I sat down in the window seat. All my life, I have always opted for a window seat while traveling. I enjoy being able to watch the scenery.

Hearing a loud whistle, I knew we were preparing to power up and depart the station. We moved slowly through the city, but as soon as we hit the city limits, the train engineer poured on the coal. Besides enjoying the scenery on a train ride, I also loved to hear, and slightly feel, the clickety-clack of the iron wheels when they crossed the iron rail joints. It could almost lull a person to sleep.

We made several stops on our route northward, including Dunn, Wilson, Rocky Mount, and Weldon, North Carolina; Emporia, Petersburg, Richmond, and Fredericksburg, Virginia; and Washington D.C. We followed alongside the Potomac River for the greater part of the trip between Fredericksburg and Washington. D.C. It was some beautiful scenery.

I knew we were close to my D.C. stop when we slowed significantly and entered a huge rail yard. We were switched from rail to rail as we entered the heart of the rail yard and the station. We finally pulled into Union Station, in downtown Washington, D.C. Upon arrival, I gathered up my duffel bag, and found a bus destined for the Dulles International Airport.

Shortly after we were on the road to Dulles, I was wishing my flight had been out of Washington National Airport, instead of Dulles. National was in downtown Washington, D.C., whereas Dulles was a pretty good distance out of town, in Virginia. Dulles seemed to be in the middle of nowhere. In fact, it was a 35-mile ride from Union Station.

Dulles was a new airport, having been named after former Secretary of State John Foster Dulles. It had been dedicated on 17 November 1962. The first flight out of the airport was on 19 November, just a little more than a month before I arrived. It was a strange looking airport, especially compared to the many airports I had flown into and out of. The airport had one terminal, a very large, reversed arch roof, and three long runways, all parallel.

When we arrived at the terminal, I grabbed my duffel bag, and walked to the TWA ticket counter, duffel bag and carry-on bag in tow. I presented my airline pass and identification to the ticket agent. Fortunately, she advised me that the flight had numerous unsold seats, and I wouldn't have any problem boarding the flight. I had a couple hours to wait for my flight to depart, so I nursed a couple Cokes while waiting (since I was still under-age for drinking the hard stuff in most places).

I finally heard the announcement that my flight was loading. We all boarded a "lounge coach," a large, wide, and very tall "bus." The coach drove us to our aircraft, which wasn't even parked at the terminal. In fact, none of the aircraft at the airport were parked at the terminal. The "lounge coach" pulled up to the open passenger door of a Boeing 707 jetliner. Being on stand-by, I had to wait until all the paying passengers had boarded the aircraft, after which time I was given permission to load.

I entered the cabin of the large 707 and was immediately told by the stewardess who greeted me, that I could sit anywhere I wanted in the First Class section. Wow! Now, that made me feel important. There were only three other people in First Class. I naturally took a seat next to a window.

I was the only person in that row of seats. I was going to be able to stretch out my 6-foot, 2-inch frame as much as I wanted. I noticed

222

right off the bat that all the stewardesses on my flight were young and beautiful, nothing new. There were two stewardesses to wait on the four of us in First Class. It was going to be an enjoyable flight.

As we neared San Francisco, I noticed what appeared to be fog covering the Bay Area. That was not a good sign. We were cleared for a straight-in approach to San Francisco International Airport. As we descended, on the runway approach path, we were engulfed in fog. I could see absolutely nothing out my window. We continued the approach. I was hoping the crew knew what they were doing.

Suddenly, I felt a power surge, and we began climbing. Missed approach! The pilot announced that we were going to try again. Upon reaching a safe altitude, the pilot turned the aircraft around, and began flying a downwind leg of the airport traffic pattern. A few minutes later, he turned the aircraft again, until we were on another final approach, slightly above the fog.

Down, and down we went, into the fog until, once again, we had to execute a missed approach. The pilot had attempted to land at San Francisco twice, but neither time was he able to see the runway to land. After the second missed approach, he announced that, due to the thick, low, fog covering the entire Bay Area, we were forced to reroute to Las Vegas.

I had all of $15 in my wallet, which wasn't enough for a hotel room, so I was a little nervous. The flight, and approach, to Las Vegas were smooth. It was nice to be able to see the airport as we descended. I had no idea what I was going to do after deplaning. My best guess was to sleep in the terminal, since I was almost broke.

When I checked in at the airline counter, I was pleasantly surprised when I was told that TWA would pay for a room for me and provide two meal tickets (dinner and breakfast). That cost them more than I paid for the airline pass. One of the stewardesses invited me to have dinner with the crew, which I was only too happy to do.

After dinner, we went our own separate ways. Although I was only twenty years old and the age limit for even entering the casino was twenty-one, I got away with it. My uniform probably helped. I ended up winning money on the nickel slot machines. Because of the amount of flights diverted to Vegas, I was a little fearful that I might have problems getting to San Francisco the next morning. Thankfully, I had no problem. I was able to take the first TWA flight to San Francisco.

It took me a little over 24 hours, but I finally managed to reach San Francisco late Sunday morning. As soon as I was in the terminal, I called mom and dad, then collected my duffel bag from baggage claim. Mom and dad drove up to San Francisco and picked me up in front of the terminal.

My ex-girlfriend, Phyllis, arranged a blind date for me. My blind date was a good-looking blonde girl (she had been recently featured in a nude magazine), about my age, and the mother of a toddler still in a crib. We went on a couple of enjoyable dates. I also spent a couple of nights with her. My father managed to get a few days off while I was on leave, so we played a couple rounds of golf, with me getting clobbered, as per expectations.

Being as I was only twenty years old, I didn't even bother trying to go to any bars, since you had to be twenty-one to drink in California. It didn't seem right. Our government could entrust us with weapons that killed people and equipment that cost tens of thousands of dollars. We were also risking our lives for our country. In addition, we were so trusted, that we had secret security clearances, yet we couldn't be trusted to drink alcoholic beverages until we were "of age."

On the Thursday before my departure, 3 January, the evening news was all about a big battle in South Vietnam on the previous day, in which the VC had claimed a major victory. The battle was in the Ap Bac village vicinity, a Mekong Delta village, only about thirty-five miles southwest of Saigon. Apparently, an outnumbered force of enemy troops was able to annihilate a much larger Army of the Republic of Vietnam (ARVN) force. I would learn more about the battle when I returned to Fort Bragg.

Early Friday morning, on 4 January, my folks drove me to San Francisco to catch an early return flight to Dulles International Airport via Denver. My return flight was also on a Boeing 707. Returning to Ft. Bragg upon the culmination of my leave was a snap. I was able to get transportation from Dulles, to Union Station, and my train back to Fatalburg. From there, I boarded the "Vomit Comet" bus back to Smoke Bomb Hill. I signed back into my unit late that evening, as planned.

There were about 11,000 military personnel in South Vietnam at the end of the year, including 29 U.S. Army Special Forces detachments, operating under the command of the U.S. Military Assistance Command, Vietnam (US-MACV). It was estimated that 30,000 communist Viet Cong and civilian sympathizers were in South Vietnam fueling the insurgency at that same time.

Information about the Ap Bac battle in South Vietnam was filtering into our unit. We heard that the South Vietnamese had suffered a major loss, including three American advisors killed, even though they had outnumbered the Viet Cong, four to one. In fact, the South Vietnamese troops were supported by artillery, armor, and helicopters, unlike the Viet Cong. The battle had included units of the ARVN 7th Division.

When questioned by American reporters, General Paul Harkins stated, "We've got them in a trap, and we're going to spring it in half an hour." However, no such event transpired. As reporters tend to do, they couldn't understand why no other combat transpired.

The following day, they asked the American advisor to the ARVN 7th Division, LTC John Paul Vann, what had happened. He was not hesitant, answering that the fighting had ended the day before, unsuccessfully. In fact, he was quoted as saying, "It was a miserable ******* performance. These people won't listen. They make the same ******* mistakes over and over again, in the same way."

The battle at Ap Bac bothered Americans, causing them to lose faith in the Vietnamese ability to fight their own battles. It was becoming more obvious that American troops were going to have to be involved in the war. It was also becoming obvious that the military under Diem was not living up to expectations.

Much of the problem came from the fact that the military hierarchy was mostly populated by men loyal to and appointed by President Ngo Dinh Diem. They weren't being appointed because of their expertise. Many of the appointments were not up to the task of commanding a military unit. They were also scared. They were afraid their unit would suffer casualties. Therefore, they were reticent to take it to the enemy, preferring to remain out of the action. Diem rated successes by casualties, especially low casualty figures for his ARVN troops.

My Demolition Course continued, on Monday, 7 January, immediately after the Christmas break, with instruction about the different American explosives and their characteristics, and the most commonly used foreign explosives. We then set about learning how to use them — mostly for destructive purposes, but also for offensive and defensive purposes. Offensively, explosives could be used to cause damage or destroy enemy assets, as well as kill enemy personnel.

The longest and most difficult training entailed learning the tactical uses of explosives, which included a lot of training in mathematical formulas and placement of charges to do maximum damage. That training caused more men to be dropped from training.

An interesting specialty explosive device we learned about was the "shaped charge." The shaped charge worked on the principle of the Monroe effect. In other words, the open cone formed on the bottom of the charge forced the explosive surge, seeking the path of least resistance, to meet in the middle of the empty cone, forming a stronger thin jet, strong enough to penetrate armor. That principle was utilized in anti-tank weapon rounds and specialized explosives.

I used several 15-pound shaped charges later in Vietnam when digging a deep ditch. I used the shape charges to "dig" bore holes in the ground, the perfect size to lower dynamite into, to finish the cratering job. It worked perfectly.

The shaped charges had to be on stands of a computed height, or the explosive jet would not do the job correctly. Those charges could be military issue or homemade. Military issue shaped charges were available in two sizes: the 15-pound M2A3 (11½ pounds of pentolite [PETN and TNT] or Composition B) and the 30-pound M3 (50/50 pentolite or Composition B with a 50/50 pentolite booster). Both charges had the correct standoff distance built in. Composition B was a high explosive with a higher relative effectiveness and sensitivity than TNT, composed of 59% RDX (cyclonite), 40% TNT, and 1% wax.

Another pre-made explosive device we learned about was the Bangalore torpedo, even though most of us would never use it, except in training. Bangalore torpedoes were lengths of explosive-filled metal pipes that were connected using a connecting sleeve, to eventually make a torpedo of desired length. Its primary use was to clear a 10- to 15-foot-wide path through barbed wire entanglements, which is especially useful when attacking a fortified position. It could also be used to clear a path through a minefield, but the safe width of any such path was much narrower than that of the path through barbed wire.

An expedient Bangalore could be fashioned utilizing pipe of an approximate inside diameter of two inches and a wall thickness of at least .025 inch (24 gauge), packed with two pounds of explosives per linear foot. Bangalore torpedoes could also be used as anti-personnel devices by planting them in the earth vertically. The portion of the Bangalore that was above ground would spray its fragments 360°.

Of course, no explosives course could be taught without stressing the importance of safety when dealing with such a dangerous subject. It was stressed that most military explosives were safe, as a rule, but that safety precautions had to be followed religiously. We were warned not to carry explosives and blasting caps in the same vehicle, or on the same person.

Blasting caps had to be handled with kid gloves. We were also warned that any explosives containing nitroglycerin should be turned regularly during the storage process. If an oily substance appeared on casings or stains appeared on packing cases, the explosive was to be considered extremely sensitive, and destroyed immediately, preferably by burning. The oily substance indicated that the nitroglycerin had separated from the remainder of the explosive charge. Nitroglycerin was very susceptible to shock of any kind.

Blasting time fuse (aka safety fuse) contained black powder wrapped with several fabric and waterproofing layers, and came in 50-foot rolls. The cover of the fuses I used were smooth and a very dark green, although it came in many different colors. Time fuse conveyed flame at a slow, continuous, uniform rate. The burning rate of time fuse varied, basically from about 30 seconds per foot to 45 seconds per foot, hence requiring testing prior to each use, to determine the actual burning rate of the roll being used.

Outside factors (altitude, weather, storage conditions, etc.) had a lot to do with the burning speed. In addition, time fuse burned faster in an enclosed space than in the open, and it burned slower at higher altitudes. Even if that same roll had been tested the day before, it had to be tested before using again. That was the only safe way to determine how much time fuse was required for a selected burn time prior to detonation of the final object in the firing train.

Although time fuse could be lit using matches, it was much quicker and easier to light time fuse utilizing a fuse lighter. That was especially true if there was so much as a strong breeze, or rain. There were several types of fuse lighters, but the type that we used most often were the plastic pull type of fuse lighter.

The fuse lighter was attached to the time fuse. At the time for beginning the firing train, the operator only had to pull the ring on the fuse lighter to begin the process. When using electric blasting caps, a blasting machine was used to detonate them.

There were two basic types of blasting machines: the twist and the plunger type generators. We always used the lightweight twist-type hand generator machines. They were simple to use and easy to pack. When ready to detonate the charge(s), all one had to do was connect the two wires (leading to the detonator) to the generator, place the handle in the socket, and give a hard twist clockwise to the handle, thus generating the required electricity to fire the system.

Also available for use was the delay firing device. Those firing devices were available in delays anywhere from 3 minutes to 23 days. They were, however, not totally accurate, thus not to be used if exact timing was required. Those firing devices worked on the principle of a corrosive solution dissolving a section of restraining wire, which in turn released the striker.

There were two types of blasting caps: nonelectric and electric. The blasting caps we used were small copper tubes, closed at one end (the business end), and filled with one or more very sensitive explosives. Blasting caps, on their own, were dangerous explosive objects, requiring extreme care when working with them.

Nonelectric blasting caps were open at one end for the insertion of time fuse, and were utilized to detonate larger bodies of explosives, such as blocks of explosives or specialty explosive containers. Time fuse was used to initiate the firing of the nonelectric cap. One end of the time fuse was pushed gently into the open end of the cap.

Non-spark hand-operated cap crimpers (Army issue) were always used to attach the blasting cap to the time fuse. Those tools were similar in looks to pliers. Using your teeth to crimp the cap (a stupid don't-try-this-at-home-kids Hollywood trick) was stressed as a no-no. It was an excellent way to destroy teeth, mouth, and nose, making for a very ugly face.

Electric caps came in instantaneous firing and delayed firing. They were fired using electric current. Two electric lead wires emanated from the rear, to be attached to the firing device wires. They made it possible to detonate any number of high explosives simultaneously, and to ensure instantaneous detonation.

When detonating several explosive charges at the same time, an electric firing system was recommended, especially if a delay was required. Delay electric caps were like regular electric caps, but had a delay element within the cap. They were much more accurate than attempting a delay detonation with time fuse. Delay caps were used to detonate charges of explosives in rotation. They were useful in large building demolition, mining operations, and equipment destruction when camps were being overrun.

There were numerous ways of priming an explosive charge, the most popular being to place the blasting cap into a pre-supplied cap opening, making a hole in the charge for the cap, or making several holes through the charge and lacing det cord through those holes, always ensuring that the cap could not accidentally fall out of the hole.

Det cord burned (detonated) at a rate of 21,000 feet per second, making it an explosive in its own right. It could be used to prime explosive charges, and to connect explosive charges in a line, making detonation almost simultaneous.

We next covered calculation and placement of the four main types of demolition charges: steel cutting, timber cutting, breaching, and pressure. Mathematical calculations were used to determine how many pounds of explosives to use for each type.

The basic formulas were for TNT. The amount had to be adjusted when using other explosives, determined by the relative strength of each explosive in relation to TNT. As an example, C-4 had a relative effectiveness of 1.34, when compared to TNT's 1.0 effectiveness. Therefore, less C-4 was needed to accomplish the same task computed for TNT.

Tamping an explosive increased the destructive power of the charge. Tamping was defined as covering the charge with a somewhat heavy material, such as tightly packed sand, clay, mud, or other dense material. Maximum tamping effect could be obtained by making the tamping thickness at least the same thickness as the object to be destroyed. Because an explosive charge would detonate with the same force in all directions, the tamping was effective in directing the blast effect toward the target object, thus increasing its destructive force.

There were three basic classes of steel: structural, high-carbon, and alloy. Structural steel was the type that was most often found in targets for demolition. Structural steel included I-beams, wide-flanged beams, channels, angle sections, structural tees, and steel plate. They were used in buildings and bridges, as well as some other applications. That type of steel had its own formula for computing the size of the charge required to destroy the object.

High-carbon and alloy steel required a separate formula. Cutting railroad rail required either a half-pound C-3 or C-4 charge (80-pound or lighter rail) or a one-pound charge (heavier than 80-pound rail). Rail weight was determined by the weight of one yard of the rail.

Rail that measured more than 5 inches from the top to the bottom of the rail was 80-pound rail. C-3 or C-4 was the recommended charge for rail cutting because it could be molded against any irregular shaped steel (such as rail), thus increasing the effectiveness of the charge.

We discussed numerous ways to cut rail and disrupt rail transport. The recommended methods of disrupting rail transport routes were covered. Although cutting a rail would harass the enemy and be a nuisance, that method of disruption was very short-lived.

We were advised that removing a length of rail at least as long as the fixed wheelbase (driving wheels) of the locomotive pulling the train would cause the most damage and result in lengthy repairs. That was most likely to derail and damage the locomotive and rolling stock behind it.

Experience showed that removing 20 feet of rail would most likely result in derailment. In addition, cutting the outside rail on a curve was most effective. It was also suggested that if the route included parallel tracks, derailing the train on the inside of a parallel track curve would damage both the inside track and outside set of tracks. When attacking straight parallel tracks, it was suggested that the inside rail be cut, increasing the chance of damage to both rail lines. It was recommended that the derailment charges be detonated just prior to the locomotive reaching the length to be cut, not under the locomotive.

"In preparing for battle I have always found that plans are useless, but planning is indispensable." — *General Dwight D. Eisenhower.*

There were formulas designed for the removal of stumps and/or felling timber, dynamite being the explosive of choice. There were also different methods of charge placement depending upon root structures.

Charge sizes were generally dependent upon whether the stumps were dead or alive, and 50% was added if the target was a standing tree. Formulas for timber cutting using explosives, were designed to cut all woods, no matter the hardness. In all instances, ⅓ more TNT was required than C-4, given the choice. The formulas were used for cutting trees, as well as wooden piles, posts, beams, etc.

Cutting trees of more than 36 inches in diameter was not advisable, due to the large quantity of explosives that would be required. When felling trees to act as a roadblock or obstacle to the enemy, it was recommended that the trees remain attached to their stumps to create more work for enemy forces when clearing the obstacles. A different formula was used to determine the charge required for such an operation.

Breaching charges were usually used to gain entrance to something, such as a building, or to destroy bridge piers, bridge abutments, or field fortifications. Snaking det cord back and forth on a wooden door and securing it with tape worked great, but the same system was worthless when faced with a metal door. Breaching charges used for concrete, masonry, or rock created a shock that broke or shattered the material.

Pressure charges were used to drop a simple span on a concrete T-beam bridges. The explosion partially breached and overloaded the span, causing the bridge to break mid-span, and separate from the abutments or piers. These charges were placed over the centerline of each stringer, on the roadway. Tamping was recommended. Pressure charges usually blew out the concrete across the roadway.

In addition to the previous types of charges, instruction included the use of explosives for cratering, ditch blasting, stump removal, and boulder removal. The military issued a standard 40-pound cratering charge that was perfect for blasting craters. However, if the cratering charge was not available, dynamite or C-3/C-4 could be used. Dynamite was perfect because it had a slower burning speed than the C composition explosives, thus being able to "move" dirt easier.

There were three different methods normally used for the removal, or destruction, of large rock boulders. Those were "snakeholing," "mudcapping," and "blockholing." Snakeholing was an easy way to send a boulder flying.

With the snakeholing method, a hole was dug underneath the boulder, long enough to push however much dynamite was required to blow the boulder away from its current position. Tamping was then pushed into the hole, against the charge. The tamping directed the explosive force away from the hole, and into the boulder.

Mudcapping was best used to destroy the boulder in place and worked best if the boulder had an existing crack in it. Using that method, the dynamite was placed against the existing crack. Dirt was then gathered and mixed with enough water to form thick mud. The mud was then packed around the explosive charge, the more, the better. The mud was used for a tamping effect, directing the explosive force into the boulder at the location of the crack. That tended to break the boulder into smaller pieces.

Last, but not least, was the blockholing method. That method required the most work to prepare the boulder for extermination. It also required equipment that was not usually available in the field. A deep hole was drilled down into the boulder, the explosive charge placed in the hole, and tamping placed over the charge. That was the best method to obliterate a boulder that didn't have an existing crack. Of course, in all methods, the fuse or lead wire was extended out into the open before tamping occurred.

We spent quite a bit of time learning about bridge destruction techniques. Bridges, especially across large rivers or chasms, were perfect places to wreak havoc with enemy supply routes. Because of the many different bridge construction techniques and different materials used, the use of explosives and the placement of explosives could vary significantly.

Most of the time the destruction techniques involved the dropping of one or more bridge spans, plus damage to abutments to slow — and make significantly more difficult — the rebuilding of the bridge. Destruction of entire bridges was generally not required. What was suggested was to create a large enough gap in a bridge so that no existing prefabricated bridging could be used to span the gap.

Because it was important to be knowledgeable about bridge design and construction when planning to destroy a bridge, we learned a lot about the different types of bridges, as well as how they were constructed. The instructors described a lot of different bridge substructures (abutments, footings, end dams, and intermediate supports) and superstructures (lower chords, upper chords, stringers, decks, and treads), explaining the strengths and weaknesses of each, and how best to demolish them.

When dealing with a multi-span bridge it was suggested that the most effective method of doing the most damage was to demolish one or more of the intermediate supports. Destroying one support resulted in the collapse of the spans on either side of the support, so destroying alternate supports was the most economical way to drop larger portions of the bridge.

When dealing with single span bridges, it was more important to understand the construction techniques and materials before planning the destruction of the bridges. Among the many types of bridges were stringer, slab, T-beam, concrete cantilever, truss, cantilever truss, arch span and suspension bridges, each with their own idiosyncrasies when it came to their destruction.

Even among the different types of bridges were variations. When planning the destruction of a bridge it was always very important to do an in-depth reconnaissance of the target bridge, making a situation map sketch and a detailed drawing of the bridge, known in the demolition field as a demolition plan.

The situation map sketch should show the relative position of the objects to be demolished, the surrounding terrain features, and the coordinates of the object on existing maps. The demolition plan should include a side-view sketch of the bridge to be demolished. It should show the dimensions of critical members. Cross-section sketches should also be made, containing dimensions of each member to be cut. The quantity and kind of explosives required should also be shown. Unusual features of the site should be listed, as well as an estimate of time and labor required for the demolition projects and to bypass the site.

Transportation and communication system disruption was another important part of our instruction. With the fact that Special Forces was tasked with behind-the-lines missions, that was a very real mission for SF.

Targets of opportunity included highway and railroad bridges, road craters, cuts and defiles (blocking with destroyed equipment or manmade landslide), abatis (barricade of trees across a road, such as in a forest), railroad tracks, telephone and telegraph wires, radio stations, and airfields. The list was infinite.

Other subjects of instruction included mines (U.S. and foreign) and the preparation of a demolition ambush, the ambush being a principal tactic taught to and used by Special Forces. The Demolition Sergeant was the head honcho for a defensive minefield and was also responsible for rendering mines and unexploded ordnance (such as bombs and artillery rounds) safe, which, since they weren't explosive ordnance disposal technicians, usually entailed the destruction of such items in place.

In a demolition ambush, explosives were used in tandem with lethal projectiles (such as glass fragments, nails, roller bearings, etc.) and/or Claymore mines (including those built from scratch) to cause maximum personnel destruction of enemy patrols, etc. Rifles and machine guns were also usually employed during a demolition ambush.

The M18A1 Claymore antipersonnel mine was directional in nature. It was used more as a defensive weapon than as a mine. The Claymore was a rectangular fiberglass narrow box, shaped in an arc, with the lethal sector being the outward facing sixty-degree arc. It proved to be one of the most lethal mines in the U.S. Army inventory, and a great defensive weapon. It weighed 3½ pounds and contained more than seven hundred ¼" diameter steel ball bearings, propelled by 1½ pounds of C-4 plastic explosives.

The results from firing a Claymore were like what a target would look like after being fired upon by twenty 12-gauge shotguns all at once. It was usually used as a controlled mine, fired by friendly personnel at enemy personnel, unlike most mines that await the enemy accidentally setting off the charge by trip wire, pressure plate, etc.

The Claymore was used for both offensive ambush operations and for camp defense. The Claymore was placed on the ground, supported by two pairs of folding metal legs, and aimed using a built-in sight, in the direction the enemy was expected to approach. It was best to angle the mine so the deadly ball bearings would be propelled parallel with the ground.

One of the first things we learned was to make sure the marking "FRONT TOWARD ENEMY" faced toward the expected enemy, NOT toward friendly personnel. The kill zone was a sixty-degree fan in front of the mine, with a casualty radius of about 100 meters (109 yds).

There was also a danger area behind and to the side of the mine. There should be no friendly troops within 16 meters to the rear of the weapon, and within 100 meters all friendly personnel should be behind cover. The instructors stressed caution in making sure the Claymores weren't turned around by the enemy, resulting in the power of the

Claymore striking friendly personnel, rather than the enemy.

A Claymore placed to the front of an anticipated enemy column would produce a world of hurt to the enemy, with more than 700 metal balls ripping through the length of the column. Watching a Claymore in action was fun. When it detonated there was a loud CAROOMPH. At the same time a heavy dust cloud arose around the mine. When it was aimed at a cardboard target, checking out the cardboard target elicited a lot of oohs and aahs. The target was usually decimated.

We were taught that the recommended method of signaling the initiation of the demolition ambush was setting off the Claymore mine, while also shouting "Fire" in case the Claymore did not detonate as expected. Sometimes the generator would not generate enough current for detonation, in which case the order "Fire" would initiate the ambush.

An "automatic" demolition ambush could also be employed, so friendly personnel could be far from the ambush when initiated. In this type of ambush, a Claymore could be fitted with a tripwire (thus making it a mine) and set up with detonating cord so that the initial detonation would initiate detonation of numerous other emplaced mines.

The Claymore was primed by placing a blasting cap into one of the mine's cap wells. After placing the device, if the device was to be detonated by hand, the supplied 100-foot long electric firing wire was run back to the protected firing position. Each Claymore was also supplied with an M57 firing device. The firer's end of the firing wire was fitted into the M57, also known as a "clacker." The M57 hand-operated electrical generator looked like a staple gun, being operated by pressing down hard on the lever (about the same as operating a staple gun), thus generating a three-volt electrical current that immediately detonated the blasting cap, and thus the mine.

Because the M57 had a reputation of not generating enough electricity on the first attempt, it was always a good idea to squeeze the actuator several times. Detonation was supposed to be instantaneous. In case of emergency the Claymore body could be taken apart and the C4 removed for constructive or destructive purposes, including heating our morning coffee or our meal. It was also possible to rig the Claymore mine with a tripwire, for use in an enemy-activated "automatic ambush."

Another deadly anti-personnel mine was the M16A1 anti-personnel mine. It was copied from the "Bouncing Betty" mine invented and used by the Germans in World War II. It was activated by tripwire or pressure. In later years, one was devised that was activated by ground vibration.

After being taught about military explosives, the instruction moved on to the interesting, unconventional world of sabotage and improvised (homemade) demolitions. Sabotage was a wide-ranging field, covering many subjects.

Targets of sabotage were numerous. They included anything that could affect enemy morale, disrupt enemy supply lines, or destroy enemy infrastructure. A saboteur should never select targets or materials that are beyond his capacity. Certain targets were very valuable prior to a military offense, while others were valuable during the offensive. Transportation and communications facilities were valuable prior to, as well as during, a military offense. Transportation facilities of all kinds were ripe for sabotage.

Because explosives could be difficult to obtain in a guerrilla warfare environment behind enemy lines, our instruction included the use of mines, aerial bombs, and artillery shells in making expedient demolition charges. We were also taught how to obtain the ingredients on the civilian market (in enemy held land) for the construction of explosive devices from scratch. That especially included products obtained from agricultural stores and drug stores.

It was amazing to learn how easy it was to find materials to make explosive devices. As an example, the materials to produce black powder could be found in your neighborhood drug store, no signature required. The major problem with black powder was its ease in detonating.

The training went so far as to teach us how to produce explosive material from human feces; a smelly project for sure. Another possible source of explosive devices was unexploded artillery rounds and bombs, so we had to know their nomenclature and how to utilize them. Homemade weapons included pipe bombs, pipe and nail hand grenades (all of which could be utilized in a demolition ambush).

We were also taught how to construct our own time fuses and booby trap devices. The booby trap devices included various time-delay, trip wire, and trigger devices. There were various commercially available and military electric and non-electric time-delay devices.

Time pencils were non-electric time-delay devices that came in various delays. They were copper and brass devices shaped like pencils, with a glass vial containing acid, and a fuse at one end. They were actuated by crushing the vial, releasing the acid. When the acid ate through the restraining wire, the attached striker would hit and detonate the percussion cap.

The manufacture of incendiary devices for starting fires was also taught. Not to be left out was the construction and placement of assassination devices, to be used against individuals or groups of personnel.

Trigger devices included pull, pressure, release of pressure, and tension triggers. All devices could be utilized with an electric or non-electric system. The pull trigger was normally used as an anti-personnel device. It required a pulling action to activate. Examples include opening a door, moving an object to which the pull device is attached, or striking a tripwire. The pull action would release a cocked firing pin, causing it to strike a primer, which in turn would set off the blasting cap, thus detonating the explosive charge.

The pressure trigger initiated an explosion, or fire, through the addition of weight. It was used as both an anti-personnel and anti-vehicle device. This method had a myriad of methods for activation. An example would be something as simple as an ordinary mousetrap. It could be used for electric or non-electric firing, relying on something or someone stepping on the pressure pad of the trap.

The release-of-pressure trigger activated the system through the removal of weight. Like the pressure trigger, there were an infinite number of possible release-of-pressure systems. The tension trigger was activated through the release of tension, i.e. cutting a taut cord or wire that was holding the firing pin in the cocked position. Cutting the line released the firing pin to strike the system activator.

The easiest booby traps to produce were made from military issue hand fragmentation grenades and mines, since those were generally readily available. The simplest grenade was the "grenade-in-a-can," wherein the grenade was placed in either its shipping container or a can that was just a slight bit larger than the grenade and spoon assembly. The container was affixed to a permanent object, such as a tree, horizontally.

The grenade pull ring was removed from the grenade, and the grenade placed in the container, which held the arming spoon in place. A string, or wire, was wound around the head of the grenade, and stretched across a frequently travelled path or trail to act as a tripwire. When the victim tripped the wire, it pulled the grenade out of the container, releasing the firing spoon, and detonating the grenade.

Anything from simple explosive charges rigged with triggering devices, to mines, rockets and bombs rigged with triggering devices were brought up as weapons we could use against the enemy.

We also were taught expedient methods of firing weapons, especially the 3.5-inch rocket. If there was no available rocket launcher device, the rocket could be fired utilizing the rocket's shipping container or a self-built V-shaped wooden trough. The expedient wooden trough launcher was preferred due to better accuracy.

An experienced demolitionist could hit a target the size of a 55-gallon drum from 40-50 yards, while a tank could be hit from 150 yards. The firing of those expedient devices could be powered by a blasting machine or dry cell batteries. If need be the rocket could also be fired non-electrically.

We learned the many ways to make an expedient hand grenade, which included such easy to obtain materials as a tin can, bolts, nuts, metal scrap, commercial or improvised black powder, and commercial or improvised fuse cord.

Also included in the training was how to make homemade delay fuses and/or firing devices (including homemade switches for electrical systems, such as for use in the destruction of objects or locations after safely departing the area, or the assassination of an enemy military leader.

Time delay triggers could be produced utilizing either mechanical or chemical delay mechanisms. Clock mechanisms were the most popular mechanical systems. The possibilities were endless, especially when used for delay purposes.

We then went on to learn a ton of different improvised explosives and incendiaries. The first thing we were warned about was the inherent danger involved with working with homemade explosives and incendiaries. Homemade mixtures were much more dangerous than working with conventional explosives. And unbelievable as it may seem, as I mentioned earlier, explosives can be made from human feces. It wasn't easy but was possible if warranted.

One of the most popular incendiary devices was the Molotov cocktail. It was also one of the simplest weapons to make and use. Basically, it consisted of a glass bottle filled with a flammable mixture, such as napalm or jelly gas, with a wick or fuse in the bottle opening. Just prior to use, the bottle was turned upside down, so the wick could absorb the flammable mixture. The wick was then lit, and the bottle thrown.

The bottle broke upon impact, causing the acid to ignite the rags and the fuel, and sending the flammable mixture in all directions, lit by the burning wick. The fire bottle was made with sulfuric acid, gasoline and/or kerosene, water, potassium chlorate, sugar, and rags. It was very similar to the Molotov cocktail.

Fire was a simple way to sabotage enemy buildings. Sample targets for fire included buildings, such as warehouses, barracks, offices, and factories. Fires were easy to start anywhere there was an accumulation of flammable materials. It was advisable to start any fire after you had departed the area. That could be done using any improvised delay devices.

Some of the easiest delay devices for initiating a fire included a lit candle, with strips of paper wrapped around the bottom of the candle. That method worked with easily ignitable material, whereas more difficult to ignite material might require rolled and twisted gasoline-soaked paper wrapped around the bottom of the candle. The amount of paper used would determine the size of the resulting initial fire. A second simple fuse was a length of string soaked in grease.

It was unbelievable how many different types of improvised incendiary mixtures existed, as well as how easy it was to obtain chemicals that could be so dangerous. Even such common items as sugar were useful in making improvised incendiaries. In fact, when mixed with potassium chlorate (preferred) or sodium chlorate, the mixture could be used as an explosive or an incendiary.

If the mixture was enclosed, such as in a tightly capped pipe, a spark would detonate it. That was known as a pipe bomb, a good casualty-producing device. Unconfined, the same mixture was a great fast-burning incendiary. Concentrated sulfuric acid was a good igniter for the substance. Concentrated sulfuric acid could be obtained by draining liquid from wet cell batteries into a glass, pottery, or ceramic container, then heating it to a boil. Sulfuric acid could be obtained from a garage, machine shop, or hospital. To introduce a delayed ignition, placing the acid in a balloon, gelatin capsule, or similar container, worked well.

Another fast burning incendiary, that used sugar, was a mixture of potassium permanganate (obtained from a drug store, hospital, or gym) and sugar, burning somewhat hotter than the chlorate mixture, and ignited by adding a few drops of glycerin (obtained from a drug store, soap, or candle manufacturer). A pipe bomb could also be made by placing match heads into an enclosed pipe, with a fuse as an igniter.

An extremely easy incendiary to make, with materials that were extremely easy to obtain was a mixture of sawdust and wax. That mixture made for an incendiary that burned for a long period of time. All one had to do was add hot molten wax or tar to the sawdust to ignite it.

Of course, even easier to use for a long-lasting and very hot incendiary was Composition C-3 or C-4 explosive. Both were very easy to ignite and didn't explode unless an explosive device was used to initiate a reaction.

We also spent a lot of time learning about advanced demolition techniques. Advanced techniques involved explosive charges that were constructed for special purposes. Although those techniques produced charges that resulted in more productivity than conventional charges, and usually required less explosives, they also took more time to construct, and were more fragile.

The saddle charge was used to cut mild steel cylindrical targets up to 8 inches in diameter. It was made using Composition C3 or C4, shaped like an isosceles triangle, and primed (detonated) at the apex of the long axis. The thickness of the charge was determined by the circumference of the target.

The diamond charge was used to cut hard or alloy steel cylindrical targets of any size, including ship propeller shafts. The functioning of the charge was such that both points of the short axis were primed to detonate at the same time. The detonation traveled inward from the initial detonation, to the middle of the charge. When the detonating waves met at the exact center of the charge, they were deflected downward, cutting the shaft cleanly at that location.

As with the saddle charge, it was constructed using C3 or C4, and had the shape of a diamond. Both charges worked better if wrapped and constructed off-site. The best wraps were wrapping paper or aluminum foil. Neither charge was reliable against targets that were not solid, such as gun barrels.

The ribbon charge was used to cut flat or non-cylindrical steel targets, resulting in the use of much less explosives than with conventional charges. The charge was only effective for targets 2 inches or less in thickness but didn't require any tamping to be effective.

We also learned how to make a special charge for breaching fuel containers, which would also ignite the contents. The charge, called a platter charge, could also be utilized to destroy small electrical transformers, or similar targets. The charge could be set up as far away as 50 yards from the target. The platter could be glass or ceramic, but the best material was steel or other metal, weighing between two and six pounds. The platter didn't have to be concave but was more effective if it was concave. It could also be round or rectangular. The explosive was placed on the rear of the platter as a propellant to send the platter towards its intended target.

Another expedient charge for use against fuel containers was the soap dish charge. Unlike the platter charge, the soap dish charge was placed directly on the target. A standard GI soap dish could be used. C-4 explosives and thermite (or any other incendiary mixture) were placed in the dish. The basic rule was that a soap dish charge would destroy a container up to 100 gallons capacity; a thin cigar box would work on up to a 1,000-gallon container; and a charge twice that size would do the job on a 2,000-gallon container or smaller.

For destroying reinforced concrete up to a maximum of four feet thick, we learned about the earmuff, or opposed, charge. Because the earmuff charge had to be placed on both sides of the concrete target (hence the name "earmuff"), both sides had to be accessible.

Expedient shaped charges were not nearly as effective as manufactured shaped charges. The homemade charges utilized a high density, high strength explosive, and a conical liner of metal or glass. Perfect for the job were large wine bottles, emptied of course, because of the conical cavity on the bottom of most wine bottles.

We were also shown the expedient method of cutting the neck off the bottle cleanly. The size and type of explosive utilized in the shaped charge determined the recommended stand-off distance between the bottom of the charge and the target itself. The stand-off distance was extremely important for maximum efficiency.

Like the shaped charge, if it was not possible to be supplied with cratering charges, expedient ones could be made. Improvised cratering charges generally compared very well with the manufactured charge, especially when making large holes, or when putting several charges in a line to form a ditch.

Instruction also covered the construction of satchel and pole charges. Satchel charges were large charges used, for instance, to destroy a bunker. Because it was easier to carry and place a pre-packaged charge of the appropriate size and shape, charges were packaged in advance of an attack and carried to the target in convenient "satchels."

"Satchels" could be as simple as taping or tying the required number of explosive blocks to a board, or wrapping them in canvas, cloth, or paper. An improvised satchel charges could also be made by filling a #10 can with ammonium nitrate and melted wax and priming it with a small charge of C-4 or TNT.

Pole charges were designed for use against pillboxes (so the demolitionist didn't have to take unnecessary risks in placing the charges) and difficult to reach targets, such as bridge stringers or underwater bridge piles. The usual makeup of the pole charge was a pole, explosive charge, detonating cord, non-electric blasting cap, time fuse, and fuse lighter. The charge itself could usually be constructed similarly to the satchel charge.

Although Claymore mines were an issued item, they weren't always available to SF units in the field, especially behind enemy lines. We were therefore taught how to produce expedient Claymore mines and grapeshot charges in the field.

The field expedient Claymore and grapeshot charge was made with C-4 and any number of different projectiles, small steel fragments being the best. A #10 can worked great for a container, but almost any material placed between the projectiles and the explosive worked. We had to keep in mind that we would want to work with a small amount of explosive, enough to send the projectiles flying, not to demolish them.

Enclosed spaces (such as boxcars, warehouses, and other mainly windowless structures) were good targets for the dust initiator charge. The recommended initiator charge included powdered TNT or C-3 and an incendiary mix (such as a mixture of ferric oxide and aluminum or magnesium powder, obtained from an auto manufacturer, machine shop, or chemical shop). Surrounding the initiator charge was fine material (coal dust, cocoa, bulk powdered coffee, confectioners' sugar, powdered soap, etc.) or a volatile fuel, such as gasoline. The initiator charge sent the surrounding material outward, also igniting that material, which in turn destroyed the target.

The reason for that type of training was to make it possible for a team to function and accomplish missions if re-supply was not possible. Because guerilla warfare usually meant the team was well behind enemy lines for long periods of time, re-supply could be difficult and sometimes impossible.

Special Forces A-teams were autonomous units, able to function as a twelve-man team without higher echelon intervention or leadership. The A-teams trained as independent units, unlike regular army small units that trained as part of larger units.

During the last week of demolition training we went to the field for three days, beginning 21 January, on our final demolition tactical exercise. It was in a very remote location of North Carolina, Camp Mackall, in marshlands. Even though it was still winter, we had to be wary of poisonous snakes. We were told that some were not hibernating as they should have been. Most of our operations were done at night, in a tactical mode, so no flashlights could be used to spot snakes.

The operation went off without any incidents. We returned to Ft. Bragg on the 24th, and I graduated from Demolition Training on the following day, 25 January 1963, with an 82% average, placing well up in the top half of the graduating class.

Like most demolition experts, I had grown very fond of very loud noises, and became very proud upon accomplishment of a difficult surgical demolition job done perfectly. Of a beginning class size of 63 men, only 35 of us graduated.

Graduation meant I had two Special Forces Military Occupational Specialties (MOS's): Heavy Weapons (MOS #112) and Combat Engineer (MOS #121). Graduation also meant that my new primary MOS was Combat Engineer (or Demolition Specialist), while my secondary MOS was Heavy Infantry Weapons.

In fact, I had MOS's that qualified me for three separate slots in an A-team (25% of a team — Demolition Sergeant, Demolition Specialist, and Heavy Weapons Leader), although my knowledge of heavy weapons was not nearly as in depth as Special Forces-trained Heavy Weapons Leaders. Upon graduating we were advised that our names would be sent to our hometown police department, to be included on their list of local individuals considered to be explosive experts.

"There is no situation in the human condition that cannot be solved through a properly sized, shaped, packed, placed, timed, and detonated charge of high explosive!" — *Military Engineering Axiom*

Sometime in January, we heard about a 13 January attack on the Plei Mrong Special Forces camp in Vietnam that was on the border and manned by indigenous Jarai tribesmen. The camp had been infiltrated by Jarai Viet Cong sympathizers who had signed up as CIDG trainees. During the hours of darkness, many of them cut a twelve-foot gap in the camp perimeter barbed wire, permitting a swarm of VC to enter the camp, armed with satchel charges and Bangalore torpedoes.

During a period of two and a half hours, one hundred Jarai CIDG soldiers were killed or missing and four SF were wounded. Because of the amount of VC sympathetic infiltrators, it became difficult to determine friend from foe. It underscored a constant problem Special Forces had during the Vietnam conflict: not being able to fully trust the soldiers they were working, and living, with.

Other Specialty Training

Weapons Corse (Light & Heavy Weapons Leaders)

Considered to be the least demanding and least technical of all the Special Forces specialties (I'll hear complaints about that from SF weapons men, I'm sure), it was, nonetheless, a difficult course, and an extremely important position on the team. In the '60s each team had a Heavy Weapons Leader and a Light Weapons Leader. Basically, the Weapons Leader had two missions on the team — both, of course, involved weapons.

The weapons leaders were taught and expected to be able to expertly utilize and teach utilization, as well as repair, of their assigned weapons (light weapons [pistols, rifles, shotguns, or machine guns] for the Light Weapons Leader and heavy weapons [mortars, recoilless rifles, etc.] for the Heavy Weapons Leader), as well as the more popularly used foreign weapons. When speaking of heavy weapons for Special Forces, the weapons trained on were generally any large weapons that were smaller than an artillery piece.

Artillery weapons were not normally in a Special Forces camp. The Weapons Leaders were also responsible for training teammates and indigenous personnel in the use of their specialty weapons and expected to be experts in the use of weapons carried by indigenous personnel, as well as the enemy. In addition, they were proficient in all commonly used weapons of the world, especially the Communist AK-47 and Israeli Uzi submachine guns (which were popular worldwide, especially with guerrillas and insurgents).

Because of the possibility of being in locations where resupply was impossible, weapons men were also trained how to make homemade guns out of the most rudimentary supplies (such as a pipe and rubber bands) and how to fire bazooka rockets without the aid of a bazooka barrel.

The most common heavy weapons in the SF camps of Vietnam were 60-mm, 81-mm, and 4.2" mortars, as well as 57-mm and 75-mm recoilless rifles, with an occasional 106-mm recoilless rifle being present. Weapons trainees spent a lot of time on the range.

Tactics were also a large part of the training for a weapons trainee. The Weapons Leaders were the primary advisers and instructors for offensive and defensive conventional and unconventional tactics, as well as being able to assist the operations sergeant in operational and training planning (including infiltration, exfiltration, and route planning).

Medical Course (Medical Specialist)

The Green Beret Medical Specialist was, without a doubt, the best-trained medic in the world. Each A Detachment was authorized two medics: a Medical Supervisor and a Medical Specialist. Many was the time he had to act as physician, dentist, and veterinarian in some of the remotest places on earth, where any kind of medical care, or even evacuation, was not available.

Being an SF medic could be a very daunting responsibility. Unlike medics in the regular Army, an SF medic had to be just as adept a warrior in combat as the remainder of his team, just as skilled as an Infantry soldier.

At 39 weeks in length, the medical course was the longest, most difficult, and challenging training in Training Group. The training began with a basic course at Ft. Bragg, advanced course at Ft. Sam

Houston (outside of San Antonio, TX), on the job internship at any of several Army base hospitals, followed by surgical training back at Ft. Bragg. They were deeply involved in practical medical exposure while going through the internships in the hospitals and medical centers. That wasn't the end of it.

After "completing" their medical training, just like doctors, they had to go through very difficult oral boards (questioning by doctors), followed finally by Special Forces Branch Training. Many was the medic trainee who didn't make it and opted to train in another SF field instead. It was because of the extreme difficulty and long duration of medical training that Special Forces teams always seemed to be short of medics in the field.

There isn't even close to enough space here to describe what the medical field trainees went through, and what they learned. When they graduated from medical training, they were the best combat medics in the world, bar none. They were qualified as paramedics and emergency medical technicians (EMT) and were authorized to perform surgery. Many was the time they performed major surgery, including amputations, in the field.

Although our medics were not supposed to open the chest cavity, they could certainly stuff the contents back in, if necessary. They were even qualified to do dental work, to include tooth extractions, and veterinary medicine, which was utilized on many an occasion in Vietnam.

Their training included classroom studies in anatomy, physiology, pathology, patient assessment, and pharmacy practices. They also attend classes in the EMT and paramedic fields. After that they participated in clinical rotations in hospitals and emergency rooms. The trainees rode along and assisted paramedics on emergency calls. They also participated in life-saving trauma situations and assisted in births. They saw plenty of blood during their training, which led to some men deciding not to become medics. At the same time, they had to show that they were warriors, able to fight equally alongside the rest of their teammates.

Special Forces medics had to be the best, and had to be experts at their job, as well as be able to do their work in the worst of conditions, including bullets flying about. Where Special Forces operated (especially if in a guerrilla warfare environment behind enemy lines), medical help of any kind was usually not available. The medics were needed to keep the team, and the indigenous personnel, in top fighting form.

Each medic was an independent general practice healthcare provider, with emphasis on combat care. They were superb trauma physicians. They had to be able to diagnose and treat diseases that most people never even heard of in the States. I would come to trust their expertise, as much, if not more at times, as I would a doctor's.

The Bible of the SF medic was the *Merck Manual.* It was one of the world's most trusted medical references, a concise and complete medical reference for doctors, medical students, and healthcare professionals. I doubt that an SF medic ever went on a mission without it in his possession.

A lot of negative publicity eventually came out of SF medic training. The on-the-job training for gunshot wounds was done at the "Dog Lab." Dogs that had been scheduled to be put down by the local pound, were obtained by SF. The dogs were drugged, then wounded. They were then given the best care an animal could receive, including love and attention.

It was much better for a medic to have training on a living being, rather than do his first real emergency trauma care ever, on a human. Everybody in Training Group was told never to discuss Dog Lab, knowing the danger of objection.

It no longer exists, but it did, at one time, serve a very important purpose. So now that Dog Lab no longer exists, due to pressure put on the program, the dogs no longer serve a humanitarian purpose; they just die at the hands of the pound.

Communications Course (Radio Operator)

Communications training was probably the second most difficult of the Special Forces training regimens, as it was very technical in nature. It was also one of the more important, as the radio operators were the life link between the detachment and the remainder of the world, especially higher headquarters. Their course was also the second longest, at sixteen weeks, mainly due to the length of time that was spent learning and drilling in international Morse code.

Unlike conventional radio operators, Special Forces operators had to be true experts in the field of radio communications. Detachments in the field, especially behind enemy lines, had to be able to communicate long distances, using low-powered equipment. That required expertise beyond the norm, including being experts at antenna theory, to get the most range with the least equipment.

SF radio operators were expected to (1) have a thorough knowledge of communications procedures and commonly used operating signals; (2) have a thorough knowledge of the operating procedures particular to Special Forces operations, and understand how to prepare an SF SOI (Signal Operating Instructions); (3) be able to send and receive Morse code; (4) understand cryptography, and be able to utilize primary and alternate cryptographic systems; (5) have a basic understanding of radio transmitter and receiver theory, as well as organizational radio maintenance repairs; (6) understand the principles of radio transmission in the HF and UHF bands; (7) understand the construction and principles of field radio antenna operation (antenna theory); (8) understand communications security; (9) and have sufficient knowledge about other means of communications to be able to advise on their employment.

The SOI was required for radio communications security and dependability. The SOI provided a schedule and instructions for periodic scheduled communications contacts and blind transmission broadcasts (BTBs) from the SFOB, as well as emergency contacts with the SFOB. That reduced the possibilities of the enemy being able to intercept messages and/or locate transmitting sites.

To graduate, a radio operator had to be able to send and receive a minimum of eighteen words per minute in Morse code. I can still remember arriving at the Training Group barracks as a brand new trainee and hearing the radio operator trainees constantly murmuring dits and dahs, trying to learn the code. I swear they dreamt in dots and dashes.

In later years, when I cross-trained seriously in communications and became an SF Radio Operator, I would constantly read signs on highways in dots and dashes. I still do it at times. I also practiced by reading a page or two from a book, using Morse code. There was also a one-time pad interpretation chart that was a good thing to memorize, if you wanted to encipher and decipher messages quickly.

Additionally, the students had to learn how to set up, operate, and repair all U.S. military and commonly used foreign communications equipment, as well as communications theory, antenna theory, radio wave propagation, SF cryptographic procedures and, basically, be able to communicate in the field. That included a lot of mathematical knowledge and formulas. They had to be able to communicate on a radio anywhere, anytime, and certainly under extreme conditions.

Because Special Forces teams usually operated far from any other friendly force, communicating was a must, and getting the longest range possible out of your gear was of paramount importance. Expertise in antenna construction and antenna theory was a must when it came to attaining the maximum range from a radio.

Among the specialized studies were the military communications oddities, which included message formats, authentication procedures (methods of assuring the sender is who he says he is), operational procedures, abbreviations, acronyms (the military is loaded with them), prowords (terms with specific meanings to shorten a message), the many forms of clandestine communications (basically spycraft), and how to sabotage radio communications. In addition, the Radio Operator had to be able to teach his skills to allied military and civilian personnel (in their respective language).

Operations & Intelligence Course (O&I Operations SGT and Intelligence [INTEL] SGT)

The O&I field was not taught in Special Forces Training Group, being only available to staff sergeants or higher. The training was known by SFers as the "Team Sergeant Course" because it was a precursor to becoming one. Personnel were usually promoted to team operations or intelligence positions from within the framework of the A Detachment.

Upon promotion to that position, the personnel were sent to Operations & Intelligence School at Ft. Holabird, MD, for their formal training. About 90% of O&I students couldn't pass the course.

The Operations Sergeant (aka Team Sergeant) was the leader of the NCO/enlisted personnel on the team. He was trained in tactics, operations and intelligence gathering, in both conventional and unconventional warfare scenarios. He wrote the operational plans and combat orders for the A Team.

Intelligence Sergeants were the detachment experts for collecting, determining the importance and reliability of, and disseminating intelligence information. Much of the safety of the detachment and the planning of detachment combat operations relied on the expertise of the Intelligence Sergeant. The Intelligence Sergeant was responsible for setting up the spy network for the team, when deployed.

Officers (Commanding Officer [CO] and Executive Officer [XO])

Officers held the team leadership slots, even though when assigned to their team, they were usually the least experienced men on the team. Once assigned to their team, the CO should have realized that everyone else on that team was intelligent enough to have been an officer, just like him, even though he outranked them.

Training to be a Special Forces officer focused on operations, planning, tactics, techniques, and intelligence. It included conventional and unconventional warfare, as well as "dirty tricks." The SF officer trainees learned how to conduct raids and ambushes, guerrilla organization, how to set up drop zones and landing zones, and how to conduct underground operations (such as kidnapping, assassination, escape and evasion, intelligence nets, section and handling of intelligence gathering and reporting agents, fingerprinting, counterintelligence, and security). The subject matter went on and on, and it had to be taught, by those same men, to the allies and indigenous personnel they would be advising and training.

Miscellaneous

All those men had to learn to impart their specialized knowledge to the other team members, as well as any indigenous troops they were working with. Team members had to be cross-trained in all facets of the A Team expertise. Teaching was a vital part of the mission of all A Team members.

Between Training Sessions

On the Vietnam front, as of the end of 1962, troop strength was at more than 11,300. 31 men had been killed and 78 wounded, and 11 aircraft had been lost in combat.

After graduating from Demolition Training, I again had to wait for training, that time before being assigned to a Branch Training class. The Green Beret was not awarded, nor authorized for wear, until graduation from Branch Training.

In fact, even after graduation, the unit (group) full flash was not authorized for wear on the beret. Until a Green Beret was "3-qualified" (cross-trained in two Special Forces specialty fields besides his primary field) he was only authorized a "candy bar" (small strip with the group color) flash.

I found a book that had been recommended by my Training Group cadre in the PX entitled "The Guerrilla—and How to Fight Him," edited by LTC T.N. Greene, USMC. I read the book while I waited to begin Branch Training.

Besides describing recommended ways to fight the guerrilla, the book delved into the minds of the guerrilla leaders and covered a lot of areas that would be of assistance in operating as a guerrilla. It was my belief that studying the book would aid in understanding the guerrilla and his techniques and might give me some helpful information for my upcoming Branch Training.

Much of the book covered the theory and politics of unconventional warfare, describing how best to counter them. Of much interest to me was the beginning of the book, in which Mao Tse-Tung's primer on guerrilla warfare was discussed. As I mentioned earlier, his views on guerrilla warfare were thought to be the Holy Grail, and his writings on the subject were almost thought of as the encyclopedia describing how it should be done. They were required reading during Branch Training.

I spent too much time doing KP and guard duty details, as well as trying to "ghost" from the "Hey You" roster. Waiting for training in Training Group was frustrating. I think part of the test to see how much we wanted to be in Special Forces centered around keeping us frustrated and uninformed about our near future.

Details were numerous, varied, and boring (as well as frustrating) as hell. They included "ash & trash" (garbage man), police calls, firing and demolition range work, custodial (so the civilian high-paid office management people in the building could continue sitting on their asses, practicing supervising underlings—us), and other menial jobs around the base.

On 13 February I celebrated a year in the Army (and still in training) with a night "Hollywood" jump onto Normandy DZ from a U.S. Air Force Douglas C-124 "Globemaster." It was my first and only jump from a "Globemaster," which was a double-decker cargo aircraft powered by 4 radial engines. At the time it was the largest cargo aircraft in the Air Force's inventory.

Like the C-119 and C-123, the C-124 was exited from a rear side door and had a pretty good prop blast upon exiting the door. A favorite joke among paratroopers describing jumping from the C-124 was "everybody downstairs, outside; everybody upstairs, downstairs."

I was selected as a member of the company basketball team, and on Saturday our team began practices. The next week-and-a-half we were kept busy with daily basketball practices. Because of my college basketball experience, I was selected to be the coach-player. We were signed up to enter the Ft. Bragg Basketball Tournament, scheduled to begin on the 25th. We were very confident. It's a shame that confidence didn't result in skill.

We were never in the game for the first one. We got clobbered. The second game we came away with a close win, 54-52, but lost the third game 57-49, even though we played well. That ended our tournament experience. Not surprising, since it was the first time our team had ever played together, and almost all the other teams consisted of players who were used to playing together.

During the week of Monday, 25 February through Saturday, 2

March, I was assigned as a member of the Area 2 Demonstration. Three of those days the ground was covered with four inches of snow. The demonstration area was later named the Gabriel Demonstration Area.

In April 1962 a Special Forces advised unit was overrun and four SF were captured. George Groom and Francis Quinn had been captured unharmed, but SSG Wayne Marchand and SP5 James Gabriel had been wounded. The VC almost immediately executed Marchand and Gabriel, on 8 April 1962. Groom and Quinn were later released, unharmed.

The demonstration and demonstration area were renamed in honor of Gabriel. Many of us referred to the area as "Disneyland." It was interesting duty, and I didn't mind it, especially if I was assigned to a demonstration venue.

The demonstration was designed to showcase the Special Forces tools of their trade, expertise, and methods of operating to visiting dignitaries, who were guided, in small groups, through the demonstration area, stopping at each station for short descriptions of what Special Forces expertise the station depicted. The dignitaries could be anything from high-ranking military officers (from almost any nation), to congressmen, to world leaders (including American Presidents), to people off the street.

There were several stations set up for the demonstration, including the introduction station, which was set up with bleachers for the seating of spectators, demolition area, survival area, rappelling, hand-to-hand combat demonstration, a replica Vietnamese village with secret VC underground tunnels, and several fixed displays. Sometimes the demonstration included a HALO skydiving-type jump. Another highlight of the show was a demonstration of the Fulton Surface-To-Air Recovery (STAR) system, better known to us as "Skyhook." It was a joint Special Forces-Air Force venture.

The way the operation worked was that a kit was air-dropped (parachuted) to the personnel or person on the ground to be set up for extraction. The kit consisted of an 8-foot diameter, 23-foot long balloon; a 500-foot long nylon lift line (250-pound equipment/one-man strength, or 500-pound equipment/two-man strength); two helium bottles to fill the balloon; an insulated nylon coverall/harness suit for wear by the person to be extracted; and marking methods for day or night. (By the way, this same system was shown in the movie "Green Berets," starring John Wayne, where they were extracting an important captured enemy officer.)

The individual to be extracted donned his suit, was attached to the nylon lift line, and then sat on the ground, facing in the direction of the approaching aircraft — usually an Air Force MC-130 or Army "Caribou" aircraft with a 20-foot long metal yoke sticking out to the front of the aircraft, at an angle, looking somewhat like a hook.

The balloon was then inflated and released, to float skyward. The aircraft approached at about 500-800 feet above the ground, into the wind, with its yoke arms (hook) extended. The yoke snagged the lift line attached to the balloon at about 125 miles per hour.

After snagging, the individual was lifted by power winch into the tail of the aircraft over the opened tail ramp. There was, of course, a time at which the individual was flying at the speed of the aircraft. If you're into scary theme park rides, that would have been the ultimate thrill. Seeing the operation unfold is not unlike seeing some of the stunts in a James Bond movie. Hundreds of extractions were executed over the years, with only one fatality (as far as I know).

At the introduction station a Special Forces A-team was lined up on the stage, with full equipment (rifle, rucksack, web gear, etc.). Again, if you have seen the movie "The Green Berets," you will have seen the introduction scene. The men stepped forward, one at a time, beginning with the commanding officer (CO) of the team. Each man described his job title and job description in the foreign languages (or one of the foreign languages) he spoke. That was followed by the same individual repeating what he had just said, in English.

Occasionally one of the men would get the crowd laughing by saying that one of the foreign languages he spoke was "Southern" or "Hillbilly," and that he had a working knowledge of English. Next to the stage were areas in which tools of the trade were displayed, such as demolition equipment (explosives and booby traps), weapons (including foreign), communication equipment (various radios and antennas), medical gear, etc. After the introductory spiel, the team members would file off the stage and take up positions among their specialty displays, ready to answer any questions the audience may have had.

A dirt trail wound through the woods of the demonstration area. I worked at two different stations for the demonstration. The first was not a station, as such. At a midway point between two stations, I was hidden in a camouflaged hole in the ground, dressed in civilian clothes (jeans and sweatshirt) and armed with an M-1 Garand rifle loaded with a clip of blank ammunition. When a guided group would walk by, I would pop out of my hidey-hole, emptying the clip of blank ammo at the group. It scared the crap out of some people, which I loved.

My favorite station was the Survival Station, which showed methods of survival in the wild. My uniform included boots, jeans, a beat-up San Jose State sweatshirt and a Swedish beanie I owned. Quite the look. Part of my job consisted of being the snake handler. I also demonstrated how to prepare a live chicken for eating in the field. It began by strangling the chicken by hand or chopping the head off with an axe. Another member of our group did that. Then we skinned them (rather than plucking) and prepared them for eating on site.

One of the reasons Green Beret soldiers were given the moniker of "snake-eaters" was because we also showed how to prepare snakes for eating in the field. One of the favorite ways to kill the snake was to bite the head off. It made for a lively reaction by the onlookers. Two of the snakes we didn't kill were the boa constrictors.

During my assignment at Area 2, I adopted the boas as my pets. One was 6½ feet long, while the other was 5 feet in length. They were very harmless unless teased or bothered. I was taught a way to put them to sleep. It worked. That made it a lot easier to transport them around my neck to and from where they were kept, about a mile from the demonstration area.

Speaking of snakes, one of the other trainees, an American Indian named Shenandoah, had a pet boa constrictor that he kept in the barracks. When Shenandoah made a parachute jump, the boa went along. After the boa's first jump he was christened "Airborne," and a set of jump wings was attached to his cage. We also always took him to town with us. Most of the barmaids were very unhappy about his presence.

CHAPTER 7

BRANCH TRAINING

"The purpose of all war is peace." — *Saint Augustine, 354-430*

I finally began my more than six weeks of Branch Training on Monday, 11 March. It was a great feeling, knowing that it was the final hurdle before finally earning my "Green Beret," and being assigned to a Special Forces unit. Branch Training was where Special Forces techniques were taught, among them being counterinsurgency, guerilla warfare, tactics, land navigation (determining where you are and which direction to go using a lensatic compass and contour map) and survival. It consisted of a mix of classroom and field training.

Because Special Forces missions touched on so many types of warfare, the training was multi-faceted. Most people associate warfare with front lines, and military units going head-to-head across those front lines. Those were the methods with which World Wars I and II were fought, and the methods best known by the civilians who weren't in the fight. The larger the battle, the more the people back home knew about it.

Unknown to many was the importance placed on the unconventional warfare going on behind enemy lines, especially during World War II. Guerrilla warfare tactics were being used by the Allies on the Western Front and the Pacific Front. Those tactics were usually relied upon to disrupt enemy lines of communications and supplies, gather intelligence, rescue downed pilots or allied agents, or just to harass and confuse the enemy. That type of warfare required special men and special training. It wasn't a mission that an ordinary soldier could step into expecting to accomplish. It was because of the importance, and the positive results coming out of those behind the scenes battles during WWII, that Special Forces was envisioned and formed. As in the Demolition Course, our Branch Training instructors were Special Forces NCOs, many with Special Forces experience in Southeast Asia, especially South Vietnam.

When I arrived at Special Forces Training Group, Special Forces activities mainly dealt with unconventional warfare (UW, which includes guerrilla warfare, training indigenous personnel, intelligence systems, sabotage techniques, operational planning, and escape and evasion), but also included foreign internal defense, direct action, and special reconnaissance. Added to that, for Vietnam especially, was civic action (CA, mainly the responsibility of the team medics and engineers).

Direct action missions were the activities we looked forward to. Satisfaction and proof of accomplishment was immediate. On the other hand, FID required finesse and lots of patience on the part of the SF soldiers, and the obvious sense of accomplishment wasn't present. It also required a knowledge of, and willingness to abide by, the constraints inherent in working with a different set of values and laws.

Methods of Instruction

When I had volunteered for Special Forces, I figured I was going to be in the toughest, meanest outfit there was. I thought all our training would involve learning how to kill the enemy, any way possible. I never expected that so much of the training we received at Special Forces Training Group would be academic. The last thing I would have expected at that time would have been me being turned into a teacher.

But that's what they had in mind.

The first major course of instruction was Methods of Instruction (MOI), learning teaching skills, and it lasted a full week. There was even an Army Field Manual for it, FM 21-6, *Techniques of Military Instruction*. It was one of the most difficult non-physical classes in Branch Training. A man had to be comfortable in front of a large group of strangers, and able to express himself to those same strangers. It caused one of the largest drop-out and flunk rates in Branch Training and Special Forces, especially for trainees who had no real Army NCO experience. Many men didn't even try to get up in front of the class, quitting instead. Some others got in front of the class and froze, suffering stage fright.

There were no lessons on how to conquer stage fright. You either conquered it, or you flunked. Flunk MOI, and you were out of SF. Everybody on a Special Forces team had to be capable of instructing, as well as leading. My major problem was my shyness and fear of being in front of a group of strangers as the center of attention.

Thankfully I had a couple of teachers in high school who stressed public speaking, so I was able to squeak by my shyness, even though I was extremely nervous. The truth is, being shot at in a future conflict didn't scare me nearly as much as the thought of having to stand in front of a group of people and speak to them.

The fact that I had participated in high school and college sports should have dispelled my shyness in front of people, but it did no such thing. None of the sports I participated in (baseball, track, and basketball) helped to control my fear of being in front of total strangers. Those were not high attendance sports.[3]

There were five basic steps to instructing. The MOI instruction began with step one, instruction in the preparation of the lesson plan. The Army was a stickler for lesson plans: For each class given in the military, a lesson plan had to be formulated and typed, or in writing. At least one copy was delivered to company headquarters, to be filed for future reference. There was a lesson plan form, formulated and printed by the U.S. Army. That standardized outline had to be adhered to when planning a period of instruction, and it was minutely detailed. Every step had to be spelled out in excruciating detail. On it were supposed to be listed all the references used for the period of instruction. The usual was to list the field manual (FM) from which the material was gathered.

The Army had a field manual for almost any subject under the sun except, maybe, how you should go to the bathroom. Although I'm sure there was a manual explaining, in detail, how the latrine (military bathroom) was to be built. The class planning process was as important as the class presentation. The major reason for that intricate detail was so that other team members could take over the class if the primary instructor became incapacitated or was absent for some reason.

Step two was the presentation to the class. There were three methods of presenting a course of instruction, according to the Army. Those were the lecture (usually presented along with visual aid, if possible), conference (in which the class is expected to participate), and demonstration (especially useful in motivating the trainee).

We were introduced to methods of expediently making training aids, especially an easy-to-make field training aid known as the "sand table." The "sand table" was basically a 3-D map, made from any available materials, including dirt or sand to show terrain elevations. Most of the time the "sand table" was not even a table; it was a mosaic on the ground, with piled dirt signifying a hill and a line made in the dirt signifying a road, trail, or river.

Objects, such as buildings, could be as simple as a piece of wood, while vehicles could be ammunition cartridges. The instructors taught us how to use various easy to find objects to construct those do-it-yourself training aids. I later learned that those classes on field expedient training aids would come in handy.

Many was the time I had to teach a class on a subject or piece of equipment that I did not have on hand to show the student soldiers. That called for field expediently producing one from whatever was handy. That also included making fake explosives from scratch. I always enjoyed making my own training aids.

It was stressed that we had to be able to teach people who had a very limited intelligence. We had to be able to teach from the very basic premise that our students knew absolutely nothing about the way a piece of equipment functioned. To do that we basically had to "dumb" ourselves down, attempting to think like our students might think. We also had to be able to impart incentives for the personnel to learn the subject we were teaching.

When applicable, the presentation was usually followed by the students applying what they had learned, thus giving the students practical practice and demonstrating their understanding of the lesson.

Step four was an examination, which could be included with the third step (application). The fifth step was a review, during which the instructor would answer any questions the students may have had. This step could also be done as a critique of how the students applied their newly learned subject material.

It became obvious why we needed to be good instructors. If we were sent to a country to act as advisors, we would have to be able to teach the indigenous personnel how to use the equipment we were supplying for them, in addition to teaching them the basics of combat as we would expect them to operate, keeping in mind that they may know nothing about the subject to begin with. We had to expect that the indigenous personnel with whom we were working were untrained in the subject matter, which, much of the time was the situation we encountered.

I had to give a twenty-minute course on electrical firing of demolitions toward the end of MOI week. That was to prove that I was capable of instructing in my specialty field. We took our first Branch Training exam on Friday. I passed, figuring I got a minimum of an 82% on the test.

You would have thought that the company and unit details would have stopped once training began. That certainly was not the case. Saturday evening, 16 March, I was put to work as the company orderly room CQ Runner, from 1700-0800 hours.

History of Guerrilla Warfare

I cannot be certain that the following is everything we were taught, or the order of instruction, but I'm including this history because it was part of our training, and it was covered in pretty good detail during our course on the history of guerrilla warfare, all the way back to the very beginning of such warfare.

Because Special Forces was, at the time, mainly tasked as an unconventional (guerrilla) warfare unit, our training began with a four-hour class on the history of guerrilla warfare. Guerrilla warfare was basically any warfare that didn't fall into the category of "conventional" warfare.

Guerrilla warfare was characterized by infiltration, sabotage, propaganda dissemination, and psychological warfare. Basically, unconventional warfare could be classified as any war that does not feature large unit actions. Guerrilla warfare was thought by many to be a dirty form of warfare, because rules of conduct were not always strictly adhered to, and normal methods of fighting battles were not adopted.

Guerrilla warfare goes back to the beginning of time. Now guerrilla warfare is known "officially" as unconventional warfare, and has changed with the times, becoming more sophisticated. Recorded guerrilla tactics date back to 512 BC, when the Persian king, Darius, crossed the Danube River into land occupied by barbarians called Scythians.

Outnumbered, the Scythians resorted to guerrilla warfare, including a scorched-earth policy, to drive Darius' army from their lands. More recently, Alexander the Great was met by Bessus, who was waging guerrilla-style war on Alexander's eastern front. The action lasted 2 years, before Bessus was captured and executed by Alexander in 329 BC.

Modern day instances of guerrilla tactics included World War II, by the allies and the enemy. World War II was not the war to end all wars, instead resulting in the beginning of many small brush wars. Before the war ended, Greece had its own problems, with a Communist insurrection that began in 1944.

The military branch of the Greek Communist Party (KKE) managed to organize scattered groups of insurgents into a secret army, training them in Yugoslavia and Albania. By 1946, that army, known as the Republican Army, was carrying out raids in villages, to obtain supplies and recruits. By the end of the year, they were killing village policemen and citizens who were pro-government, also kidnapping villagers to attain village cooperation.

The Greek government responded poorly, giving police, national guardsmen, and paramilitary organizations free reign in fighting the insurgency. Rather than that reaction, the government should have tried to work with the villagers, to protect them and alleviate their suffering.

In December 1946, the world learned about the insurgency, when the United Nations Security Council began an investigation. American advisers were sent to Greece to help quell the insurgency. The main problem was that the Americans were advising the Greeks to use conventional tactics against a guerrilla force.

The war became protracted, causing misery to all Greeks. The Communists screwed up, however, by forcing men to join their units, using threats of reprisals against their fellow villagers and families. Deserting recruits resulted in reprisals. The Communists quickly alienated the citizens. In March 1947, President Truman began a large military-economic aid program to the Greek government. In October 1949, a cease-fire ended the bloodshed. It was estimated that 158,000 Greeks died, the result of a guerrilla war gone bad.

After World War II, Communists worldwide tried to capitalize. The Philippines had been ravaged by the war. The Huks were a Communist group that had grown in stature and strength during WWII, because of helping to fight the Japanese. The Filipino government was in disarray, which also aided the Communist Huk movement.

The only reason the Huks didn't try to overthrow the government immediately after the war, was the proliferation of American troops in the Philippines. The fact that the American troops were popular with the Filipino population was a strong detractor for a Huk rebellion. However, when the government ousted Communists from their Congress, the Huks took up arms.

After the war, the Huks had buried their weapons, with the thought that a time might come when they could use them. It was easy for them to dig up their WWII weapons and set up relatively secure bases in the wilderness of central Luzon. The Filipino government, like the Greeks, was more intent on defeating the Huks than trying to console and help the citizens.

An army was formed at the suggestion of the U.S. government and its military advisers. The army was well armed and well trained, but they tried to defeat the Huk guerrillas using conventional means, rather than counterinsurgency tactics. The American military advisers were, by the way, very instrumental in the conventional tactics being used.

The army all too often disrupted and antagonized the native population, while trying to root out the Huks. The Huks knew the army was coming well before they arrived. The Huks, however, infuriated the people by ambushing and attacking the wrong people, and killing many helpless people. The army finally perfected some excellent counter-guerrilla tactics.

A new Minister of National Defense came to power in 1950. He was a born leader and became a beloved hero of the Philippines. Within eighteen months of taking charge, the Huk insurrection was controlled. The Huks are still active to this day, although bands of communist rebels have generally replaced them.

Shortly after the Japanese surrendered, strife began in Malaya, again caused by a Communist faction, known as the Communist Party of Malaya (MCP). Like the Huks in the Philippines, the MCP turned in their arms and "disbanded" in 1945. Most of their weapons were buried in caches, to be dug up when needed, and the group maintained a sizeable cadre.

After the war the British made the mistake of forming the Union of Malaya, a colonial state that included Malays, Chinese, and Indians. It was not a popular setup, especially disliked by Malayan sultans and the Malayan civil servant organization. The Malayan Communist Party (MCP) began spreading propaganda, which in many cases spawned strikes and demonstrations.

By 1947, the Malayan People's Anti-British Army, manned mostly by Chinese, numbered about 4,000 guerrillas. Their method of warfare consisted of sabotage, assassinations, arson, bombings, and terrorism. Their mission was to capture arms and supplies, as well as attract recruits. However, they badly underestimated the reaction of the populace and the resolve of government officials.

The popular uprisings didn't live up to expectations. Also, the British were able to devise a military plan that would work. In 1950, a retired British general, Sir Henry Briggs, began service as the director of operations for Malaya. He formulated a plan that became known as The Briggs Plan, predicated mainly upon the notion that key to victory was popular support and depriving the enemy of that support.

The enemy was deprived of civil support by the resettling of outlying populations, moving them to protected villages. By autumn of 1951, more than 250,000 had been moved. Security forces had also been strengthened, numbering 84,000 auxiliary and special police, 60,000 Home Guard troops, and 55,000 regular army troops. An amnesty program was also instituted, resulting in 300 Communists surrendering and signing on to fight against their former comrades.

By 1950, the Communists had already been forced to abandon conventional tactics and convert to guerrilla tactics. Pacification and small unit tactics won the day, slowly but surely, defeating the Communist insurgency. Although progress was maddeningly slow, it was positive progress, wiping out 2/3 of the enemy during the two-year period from 1952 to 1954.

The war lasted twelve years but was successful. The Malayan campaign was thereafter used as an example of how to defeat a guerrilla insurgency. It was a shame that the French didn't learn anything from the successful counterinsurgencies of the time. The French were just bound and determined not to pass political reform.

The world, and especially Southeast Asia, was learning the hard way about Communist intentions of enlarging their sphere of influence, no matter how it was done. They were also learning the realities of guerrilla warfare, because that was the only way Communists could gain a foothold. The weaker the country, the larger the toehold attained by insurgent Communists. That reality came close to home turf also, festering in the nearby turf of Cuba in the Cuban Revolution.

A band of 82 men, led by Fidel Castro, set out from Mexico in a leaky old cabin cruiser called the *Gramma*, on 25 November 1956. Soon after landing, the group was attacked by Cuban forces, under dictator Fulgencio Batista. Many of the band were killed or executed upon capture. Only 22 members of the band were able to reunite after the slaughter. The survivors re-grouped and hid out in the Sierra Maestra mountains, receiving support from an urban guerrilla network and other small groups.

Three years after the failed revolution, Ernesto Che Guevara was named by *Time Magazine* as "Castro's brain," at the same time being promoted by Castro to Comandante (commander) of one of Castro's army columns.

We learned a lot about Castro and Guevara. After "Che" was promoted, he became a brutal and ruthless disciplinarian. He considered deserters to be traitors, having them tracked down, and executed by his men. He was also known to have informers and spies immediately executed, sometimes doing the dirty deed himself. Guevara was an expert at guerrilla style hit-and-run attacks in Cuba, followed by fading into the countryside, before Batista forces could retaliate.

In late December 1958, Che marched across Cuba, with a column of revolutionary soldiers, cutting the island in half. The final battle his men participated in was the Battle of Santa Clara, during which he and his men won a decisive victory, although outnumbered ten to one at times. On 2 January 1959, the day after Batista fled to the Dominican Republic, Che Guevara entered Havana. Six days later, Fidel Castro arrived in Havana, declaring victory.

A total of 2,000 people died during the two-year revolution. During the rebellion, the rebels had ruled with the penal law known as the "Law of the Sierra," which imposed the death penalty for serious crimes. Che was tasked by Castro with purging the Batista army, which he did, utilizing "revolutionary justice." It was estimated that several hundred people were executed nationwide.

Che was assigned numerous official positions within the new government, to which he devoted boundless time and energy. He was a devout follower of Marxism-Leninism and believed in leading by example. For that reason, he expected the population to follow suit. He termed that to be *"el Hombre Nuevo"* (the New Man). That new man was expected to be selfless, hard-working, non-materialistic, anti-imperialistic and gender-blind. Che believed in self-sacrifice, abhorred economic inequality, and wished to eliminate materialistic incentives, to be replaced by moral incentives. He viewed capitalism as greed, constantly preaching socialism in its stead.

In his quest to eliminate "social inequalities" Che — as the new Finance Minister and President of the National Bank, in addition to his position as Minister of Industries — nationalized factories, banks, and businesses. He also outlawed raises for good work, instead issuing certificates of commendation.

All workers were issued a quota, which they were expected to meet. Workers who failed to meet their quotas were punished through a pay cut. The results of this new system were a massive drop in productivity, as well as a rise of absent workers. His programs were a huge failure.

Critics of Guevara, including a former deputy of Che's, accused him of being "ignorant of the most elementary economic principles." Because of Guevara's nationalization of businesses, Cuba lost all its commercial ties with Western nations. To make up for that loss, Cuba turned to Eastern bloc nations, signing numerous trade agreements with them.

Cuba became the center of attention in the United States again, on 17 April 1961, when an army of 1,400 U.S.-trained Cuban exiles invaded Cuba, in what became known as the Bay of Pigs Invasion. The invasion was a huge boondoggle. The invading army was expecting some support, which did not arrive. During an economic conference in Uruguay, in August, Che sent a note to President Kennedy. The note said, "Thanks for Playa Girón (Bay of Pigs). Before the invasion, the revolution was shaky. Now it's stronger than ever."

A lot of people never knew that Che Guevara was wounded during the invasion, and he wasn't even close to the action, having been lured to the opposite coast by a fake invasion by U.S. Marines on the West Coast of Pinar del Rio the previous day. He shot himself when his pistol fell out of its holster, accidentally discharged, and grazed his cheek. Guevara later became a large part of the relationship between Cuba and the Soviet Union, as well as bringing Soviet nuclear weapons to Cuba, almost causing a nuclear war in October 1962.

"Laws are inoperative in war." — *Marcus Tullius Cicero (106-43 B.C.), "Pro Milone"*

While in Basic Training, I had attended a class on rules of warfare. The instructor had covered the basics of what a conventional soldier should know. Being as how Special Forces were unconventional units that would fight an unconventional, very possibly guerrilla, war, there were further rules that we had to learn, also spelled out by the Geneva Conventions.

According to the "rules," a guerrilla had to be wearing a distinctive uniform or other distinctive item, recognizable from a distance. The guerrilla also had to carry his weapon in the open and conduct all operations within the guidelines set forth in the rules of warfare. All guerrillas had to be under the command of a responsible person, who was the liable party, should any unacceptable behavior occur. Unbelievably, the wearing of the enemy's uniform, to avoid being detected, was legal, but participating in an armed conflict while wearing that same uniform was not.

Miscellaneous Training

Land Navigation:

Land navigation was another tough course, especially for those men who came from urban areas. Land navigation is the art of knowing where you are, and where you are going. Thankfully, my Boy Scout experience helped me in that class. We were taught land navigation (on differing terrains) during daytime and nighttime hours.

The nighttime course was, of course, the most difficult. Even though we were going to be able to use our compasses to navigate, we learned how to find the North Star, if we were in the Northern Hemisphere, or the Southern Cross, if we were in the Southern Hemisphere. That way north or south could be found, no matter what hemisphere we might be in.

We were tested by being run through a difficult compass course, over varying terrain and ground cover (bushes, trees, etc.) during the day and at night. We were given three grid coordinates, which we then plotted on a map. We then plotted azimuths (compass directions) and distances to each of the target posts. It was best to set an azimuth and find easy-to-identify intermediary points along the azimuth, heading towards that point, rather than trying to keep your compass on a setting, and following that setting.

It required expertise to read a compass and to interpret paces into meters while pacing the course. A few men had to go through the compass course a couple times before passing, and a couple couldn't hack it at all, resulting in them being dropped from training, and thus their chance for a Special Forces assignment. What we had learned about land navigation in Basic and Advanced Infantry Training wasn't anywhere near as in depth as SFTG training was.

Besides the difficulty of finding a target at night, night movement was a test of wills and fears. If you've ever walked through the woods at night, without benefit of a flashlight, you know what I'm talking about: There are sudden depressions to fall into, tree branches striking your face, and spider webs to walk into.

Training and testing nighttime movement was extremely important, however, because SF preferred infiltration and reconnaissance during the night because of the reduced chances of being spotted by the enemy. Light of any kind was forbidden. Any light made it possible for the enemy to locate you and eliminate you immediately. Moonlight and starlight help. When there are no stars or moon, it's pitch black.

As a teen living in Carmel-by-the-Sea CA, I walked to a friend's house after dark on numerous occasions. If you've ever been to Carmel, you know that their trees are almost considered to be sacred. Streets are built around trees. To add to the danger of walking at night in Carmel, there are NO street lights. Many were the moonless nights that I almost strode headfirst into an unseen tree.

The remainder of the week, we were given classroom training on aerial operations, survival, and escape and evasion, in preparation for practical training in those subjects in the field.

Aerial Operations:

Air support was next on the agenda. The location at which a team might be assigned had a lot to do with whether air support might be available, as well as how much, or what kind of support might be available. In some locales air support might have been only of the logistical air support nature, such as covert air drops of supplies, while other locales might have offered the opportunity of tactical air support (bombing, strafing, etc.). We spent more time learning about the logistical part of air support, because that was the type of air support we would expect the most during a guerrilla warfare scenario.

There were numerous considerations to account for when selecting an acceptable drop zone (DZ). There were basically two types of air drops, personnel and supplies. Especially important when dealing with drop zones was terrain features, both on and near the DZ. We had to keep in mind that the aircraft would be approaching and departing the DZ at low altitudes, so we had to make certain the general area surrounding the DZ was relatively free of obstacles that might interfere with safe flight. Flat or rolling terrain was preferred, with 360° obstacle-free terrain, so that the aircraft could approach from any direction. The minimum open quadrant for an approaching aircraft was 90°.

If drops had to be made in hilly or mountainous terrain, a level plateau was preferred for a DZ. Valleys and terrain surrounded by hills were inadvisable, due to the difficulty of locating from the air. For night drops, if there were any hills or obstacles more than 300 feet above the DZ elevation it was recommended that they be at least 3 miles from the DZ, whereas anything over 1,000' elevation above surrounding ground level should be at least 10 miles from the DZ.

If the recommended minimums were not met, it was to be noted in the DZ report, and aircraft could be expected to be flying and dropping their loads higher than desired for a parachute drop. Drop sites had to be located so that the aircraft remained well clear of enemy air defenses and installations when on final approach for the DZ. The size of the selected DZ had to be predicated on the amount of personnel and/or supplies to be dropped, the longest leg of which should have been the same direction as the flight path of the dropping aircraft.

The surface of the DZ needed to be selected keeping the articles to be dropped in mind. If personnel were to be dropped, a DZ with many rocks, shrubs, fences, etc., was a very poor choice. Pastures were, of course, preferred. Water DZs were acceptable for personnel and supply drops if the minimum depth was four feet. The water also needed to be clear of underwater obstructions to a depth of four feet.

It was recommended that when selecting a DZ, an initial point (IP) be selected for the aircraft to be making the drop. The IP was always to be a point that was recognizable from the air, 5 to 15 miles from the DZ. The IP was the final navigational checkpoint before reaching the DZ. At the IP, the pilot of the aircraft was to turn the aircraft to the predetermined magnetic heading designated by the team on the ground to take him directly over the DZ.

For drop zones, wind direction and speed had to be determined, to assess where the aircraft should begin releasing the load to ensure the entire load would land on the designated drop zone. The initial release point was designated by a "T" on the ground, visible to the pilot and crew of the aircraft. The "T" was placed in the location at which it was determined that all objects or personnel dropped from the aircraft would impact on the DZ. The placement of the "T" was determined by wind drift.

Since we were utilizing the T-10 parachute at the time, the formula we had to learn was: drift (in yards) = altitude (in hundreds of feet) x wind velocity (in mph) x 4.5, a constant factor. When using any parachute besides the T-10, the constant factor was 2.8. The wind direction, of course, determined in what direction the object would fall.

Many factors came into play determining the location of the "T." Among them were the distance forward that a body/object would travel upon exiting the aircraft, prior to the parachute opening (known as forward throw). For the forward throw, the release point was moved an additional 100 meters in the direction of the aircraft flight.

After parachute deployment the next factor was the drift of the object. Drift was determined by the wind speed and direction, as well as the vertical distance the object had to descend. The final factor was the expected dispersion of the objects to be dropped. We learned the formula for determining dispersion. It was a rule-of-thumb formula: ½ speed of aircraft (mph) x exit time (seconds) = dispersion (yards), where elapsed exit time is the time between the first and last exit. When personnel were dropped, a safety factor of 100 yards was added to each end of the drop zone.

At night, drop zone markings were in the form of some sort of light, while during the day the preferred markings were large colored panels, tilted at a 45° angle, toward the incoming aircraft. It was best to have the lights pointed at the approaching aircraft, in a position such that the lights could be seen by the aircraft but *not* be spotted by enemy forces.

It was recommended that, when jumping personnel on a DZ of 6,000 feet or more above sea level, the DZ material be soft, such as snow or grassland, because the parachutist would be dropping at an increased rate of descent. Although making landings more difficult, swamps, marshland, dry rice paddy fields, and water were all acceptable DZs. We were reminded that the minimum depth for the safe landing of personnel in water was 1½ yards. We were also warned that a water DZ must be clear of floating debris and protruding boulders, ledges, and pilings.

Specific minimum information was required when reporting drop zones. Those included: The code name of the DZ, and indicating whether it was a primary or alternate DZ; location, using complete military grid coordinates; open quadrants, in magnetic azimuths, indicating acceptable aircraft approaches; track, given as required or recommended, approach; obstacles, listing all obstacles over 300 feet elevation above DZ level, within a radius of 5 miles, and not shown on issued maps (reported by description, and magnetic azimuth and distance from the center of the DZ); reference point, as a landmark shown on the issued map (again reported by name) and magnetic azimuth from the center of the DZ (all magnetic azimuths, except that of the aircraft track, are measured from the center of the DZ); requested date/time of drop; and supplies requested.

For all aerial operations there were SOIs (standard operating instructions) for authenticating to the aircrew, proving that you were the friendly force, not the enemy. Signals for daytime and nighttime operations were also important. Keep in mind that we were training for combat and resupply in an enemy held area. Drop zones and landing zones had to be marked well enough for friendly aircraft to find at night, but not enemy aircraft or ground personnel. The DZ was usually small and isolated.

You had to also keep in mind that the resupply aircraft had to first penetrate enemy airspace undetected, find the location, and arrive within a five-minute window. If he could not find your DZ or LZ in that five-minute window, there would be no resupply. If the resupply was successful, haste was required to remove all lights and signals, load up the supplies, and get the hell out of there. In fact, the best night signals, if acting clandestinely in enemy territory, were flashlights pointed toward the approaching aircraft.

Generally, the same requirements needed for situating a DZ were used for locating an LZ, except they were a little more stringent, with little room for error. As with DZs, LZs were best located on flat or gently rolling terrain.

We were warned that LZs located at high altitudes required significantly longer landing area, due to decreased air densities at higher altitudes. The same applied to LZs located in high temperature locations. For every 1,000-foot gain in elevation above 4,000 feet mean sea level (MSL), 10% of the minimum length for a given aircraft had to be added to the runway. In addition, 10% had to be added for temperatures over 90°F, and 20% if over 100°F.

If the LZ was to be selected for a fixed wing aircraft, terrain surrounded by hills was unacceptable. If the LZ was in an area that had hills on three sides, it was mandatory that landings and takeoffs be with the aircraft headed upwind. That meant that the hills had to be at least far enough away from the LZ that the aircraft in use could make a level 180° turn in either direction before landing or after takeoff, at a safe altitude above the ground.

Of course, one of the mandatory deciding factors for the location of an LZ was the type of aircraft that would be utilizing the site. The larger the aircraft, the longer and wider the required landing area had to be. In addition, the terrain clearance on the approach and departure routes had to be within limits of the aircraft in use. Each type of aircraft had its own glide and climb ratio.

We did not necessarily need to know those figures for each aircraft but had to be familiar with the general ratios for medium and light aircraft. For medium aircraft, the LZ had to be at least 3,000 feet in length and 100 feet in width. For light aircraft it had to be a minimum of 1,000 feet in length and 40 feet in width. During the nighttime hours the width had to be at least 150 feet for both types of aircraft. In addition, safety factors were added. The following were advised: an additional 10% of the runway length added in both directions, as a cleared surface capable of supporting the aircraft, and a 50-foot strip extended to each side, cleared to within three feet of the ground.

As with DZs, panels were used for daylight marking, and lights for nighttime marking. The maximum allowable crosswind was 15 mph for medium aircraft, and 17 mph for light aircraft. When determining approach and takeoff clearance, the rule of thumb used was the glide-climb characteristics of the aircraft to be used.

Medium aircraft were assumed to have a glide-climb ratio of 1 to 40 (one foot gain or loss of altitude for every 40 feet travelled horizontally), while light aircraft had a 1 to 20 ratio. In addition, no obstruction taller than 6 feet was permitted at or near either end of the LZ. Also, no 50-foot high obstruction was permitted within 2,000 feet (1,000 feet for light aircraft), or 500-foot high within four miles (2 miles for light aircraft), or 1,000-foot high hills within 8 miles of the LZ for medium aircraft.

There was a lot more to airborne operations than is obvious to the onlooker. There were protocols to those operations. For instance, knowledge of the aircraft to be used was important when setting up a landing zone. Much less landing surface was needed when using a STOL (short-takeoff-and-landing) aircraft, than was required for a large transport aircraft. It was also important to know the usual direction of the wind.

As much as possible, aircraft should land and take off into the wind to minimize landing and takeoff rolls. There was absolutely no room for error. When the real thing came along, resupply flights would be planned well in advance of the specified time. The pilot would probably never have used the landing zone before, thus being totally unfamiliar with the location and the surrounding territory. He had to rely entirely on the information from, and the expertise of, the team on the ground.

Landing zone restrictions were totally different for rotary-wing aircraft (helicopters). They were able to land on relatively small cleared spaces, ascending and climbing almost vertically, if necessary. Their main limitation was range and limited payload weight. Except for noise, helicopters were great for insertion and exfiltration. They could, in fact, hover slightly above the ground, not even touching the ground, and load or discharge personnel and supplies.

Even though capable of almost vertical landings and takeoffs, the safest approach and departure involved the helicopter being able to approach and depart the landing pad while flying into the wind, albeit at a steep angle, especially compared to fixed wing aircraft. It was recommended, for safety's sake, that the landing area be cleared to 90 meters in diameter.

Specific minimum information required when reporting landing zones included: The code name of the LZ; location, using complete military grid coordinates; long axis, in magnetic azimuths, indicating probable landing direction; description, including surface type, length, and width of runway; open quadrant, indicating acceptable approaches, by magnetic azimuths from the center of the LZ; obstacles, listing all obstacles reported by description, and magnetic azimuth and distance from the center of the LZ; reference point, as a landmark shown on the issued map (again reported by name, and magnetic azimuth from the center of the LZ; requested date/time of arrival; and supplies requested and/or items to be evacuated. All magnetic azimuths, except that of the aircraft track, were measured from the center of the DZ.

The quality of the helicopter landing pad was more important than one might have thought. It was important that the landing pad be relatively level and clear of obstructions. The landing area had to be firm enough to support the weight of the aircraft. A minimum of heavy dust or loose snow had to be present, due to the possibility of such items making for dangerous vision interference during lift off, and just prior to touchdown. A helicopter could land in water, so long as the water depth didn't exceed eighteen inches and the ground under the water was firm.

We were reminded that the helicopter normally had a climb ratio of approximately one to five, or one foot of climb for every five feet of horizontal distance. For its LZ, the preferred light/panel marking system (day or night) was the "Y." The bottom marker of the "Y" was placed 50 meters in front of the front edge of the LZ, as the aircraft approached. The next marker was placed at the front edge of the LZ. The remaining two markers were placed 50 meters from the front edge marker, on the left and right sides of the LZ, 50 meters apart.

From the air, the markers looked like a "Y," when approaching the landing zone. The "Y" also acted like a wind arrow, pointing (as much as possible) into the wind (since helicopters "should" land and take off into the wind). The helicopter touchdown area was delineated by the triangle formed by the three lights on the top of the "Y."

Survival on the Ground:

Being as it was the Army, the first survival tip came in the form of an acronym: SURVIVAL. The acronym spelled out important points to remember when survival became your main option. The "S" stood for "Sizing up the situation." That included understanding your own situation and finding a safe place to hide as soon as practical, determining your location, and thinking like the enemy was thinking. "U" was "Undue haste makes waste." Eagerness to escape could lead to taking unnecessary risks. "R" reminded us that it was important to "Remember where you are." "V" cautioned us to "Vanquish fear and panic," because those reactions could lead to making major mistakes. It was suggested that understanding the causes of fear and panic could help overcome the reactions. "I" recommended that we "Improvise," an action that was nothing new to any Special Forces trooper. "V" was a rejoinder to "Value living." Conserving our health and strength was of paramount importance. Planning our escape and eating and drinking as healthy as possible would help us maintain a healthy mental attitude. "A" advised us to "Act like the natives," another activity that Special Forces was famous for. "L" touted the importance of "Learning all we could about the techniques and procedure involved in surviving," before we had to use them. The survival techniques we learned were mostly predicated on surviving in a situation where the enemy could be seeking to find us.

There were several guidelines about how to handle ourselves when requesting assistance from local natives. Those included:

(1) Show yourself, and let the natives approach you.

(2) Deal with the recognized chief.

(3) Do not approach groups.

(4) Do not display a weapon.

(5) Do not risk being discovered by children.

(6) Treat the natives well.

(7) Respect local customs and manners.

(8) Take their advice on local hazards.

(9) *Never* approach a woman.

Our health was, of course, paramount to surviving. Given the fact that if we were in survival mode, we would probably be by ourselves, we were reminded that we would be our own medics, therefore we were taught some basic first aid, as well as given tips about how to remain healthy. Of major importance to our health was to keep hydrated, with potable water, and by feeding ourselves. Of course, that meant finding water and food, methods of which were included in our training.

I had no idea there were so many places water could be found, especially in arid lands and from some plants. I was amazed at the many ways of attaining water, no matter how dry the scene. We were reminded that sick looking water and ugly looking animals were not necessarily damaging to our health.

There were ways of making most water safe, and fixing foods to make them palatable and safe. Warnings were included, dealing with dangerous types of water, as well as game and plants that were poisonous. For example, water could be obtained from vines. After cutting the vine all the way through, a nick could be cut in the vine, about three feet from the cut. Potable liquid would drip out. We were warned to avoid any milky juice from vines, plants, or trees, as well as to never let the vine touch your lip.

We were warned that if we could only find a minimal amount of water, we should eat sparingly. Eating made a person thirsty. Surprisingly, we were told that more than one-third of all known classified plants were edible, and that if we saw any animals eating them, or signs of animals eating them, they were generally safe to try. There were safety concerns with eating foods that were not normally a part of our diet. Mushrooms were to be avoided, because there was very little nutritional value in them, and a great many of them were poisonous.

Grasshoppers, ant eggs, hairless caterpillars, larvae and termites were good when cooked. Surprisingly we learned that the tiny ant was almost 100% protein, and that it was a delicacy in many areas of the world. When dealing with snakes, rats, mice, frogs, and lizards, the heads, skin, and intestines had to be removed. When preparing rats for consumption, we had to be certain to boil them until all the flesh was completely separated from the bones.

Snakes brought on concerns also. Some snakes were both hemotoxic (destroy red blood cells and tissues) and neurotoxic (dangerous to one's nervous system). Just handling some of those snakes could be dangerous. There were also some snakes that, if they bit you on a small extremity (finger, toe, etc.), you'd better be prepared to self-amputate that extremity.

We were reminded to check our surroundings while in a survival mode. A lot of our needs could be found within sight of our location. Some examples were thorns being usable as needles and strips of vines for thread. Vines could also be used as rope. We were advised never to sleep on the ground, if possible. Riverbeds, dead trees, ant nests, and bat caves were also to be avoided. The best location was elevated ground.

• • •

The following Monday, 1 April, we were transported to nearby Camp Mackall, in the sand hills just west of Ft. Bragg, for our practical training in aerial operations, survival, and escape and evasion. That same day, the 8th Special Forces Group (Airborne) was activated for duty in Panama.[4] We were to "camp out" at Mackall for the week.

It was a perfect area for our type of training. It had been a military base during World War II. It was like a piece of history in arrested decrepit decay. There were some old buildings, equipment, and even an old airfield that was usable, but without any of the usual airport lighting or facilities. It was a runway, period, and not very large at that. The airfield was only used for training purposes.

The headquarters building consisted of a tarpaper shack. We used the old airstrip when being trained in the art of setting up drop zones and landing zones in enemy territory, for resupply aircraft. During that field exercise we also set up a drop zone (DZ) and landing zone (LZ) during nighttime hours, during which the parameters were totally different.

During the nighttime landing zone part of the field exercise it felt strange holding my light for the pilot while the aircraft's propeller was whirling so close to my body in the darkness. We learned the expedient method of setting out runway lights. Numerous C-ration cans were gathered. A mixture of gas and dirt was placed into each can, filling about half the can. Once lit, the markers remained lit for a goodly amount of time. The upper half of the can also acted somewhat like a windshield for the flame.

On the 3rd we began escape and evasion and survival training, still at Mackall, which included learning to live off the land and surviving in the wild. That part was almost like an extremely advanced Boy Scout campout, except with higher stakes and instructors who didn't treat you with kid gloves. The cadre had set up some great examples of shelters, beds, traps, snares, etc., for us to gaze upon. That gave us a good idea about how creative we could be in the field.

Instruction included lessons on ropes and knot tying, what was safe to eat, and what wasn't, and how to make and set up snares, traps and field shelters from items found in the wild, as well as identifying snakes. Of course, if you were going to be eating wild animals, you had to also know how to prepare that game, and build and start a fire, with no matches or lighters, so that was also included in our training. Where Special Forces operated sometimes included many poisonous snakes, some deadly. In fact, there were poisonous snakes at Mackall.

Because escape and evasion could include a situation where we had limited equipment to work with, we learned how to navigate in the wild, with no compass to guide us. Being able to read the sun's location, nighttime constellations and important stars was paramount to that situation. We slogged through the swamplands of Mackall, and set up survival camps, including different types of shelters, traps, and snares, as well as fireplaces and latrines.

I think I found some of the deeper sinkholes in the marshland while slogging around. I came back a muddy mess. We were tested on survival that evening. I learned that I passed with a grade of 83%. We also spent a lot of time at Mackall hiking around with heavy rucksacks, practicing patrol and patrol leadership procedures.

"So in war, the way is to avoid what is strong and to strike at what is weak." — *Sun Tzu, "The Art of War"*

We returned to Ft. Bragg for the next phase of Branch Training, instruction in unconventional (guerrilla) warfare (UW), and how to succeed in a guerrilla warfare scenario, including the politics associated with it. Training somewhat followed FM 31-21 (Field Manual titled "Guerrilla Warfare and Special Forces Operations").

Guerrilla warfare was a valuable asset in supporting other military operations, and was usually the result of a resistance, rebellion, or civil war caused by political, sociological, economic, or religious disputes. Guerrilla operations were usually conducted by relatively small groups, using unconventional offensive tactics.

U.S. Army publication ST 31-180 (Special Forces Handbook) described the primary mission of guerrilla forces as interdicting enemy lines of communications and enemy installations and centers of war production, as well as conducting other offensive operations in support of conventional military operations. Among the supporting tasks of a guerrilla force were intelligence, psychological warfare, evasion and escape, and subversion against hostile states.

Special Forces had numerous capabilities, when it came to utilization of guerrilla units, as well as some limitations. Among the many capabilities were missions in support of battlefield theater commanders, including interdiction of communication lines and harassment of enemy key areas and military and industrial installations; psychological operations; special intelligence tasks (especially target location and damage assessment of prior operations and artillery and bombing missions); escape and evasion operations; and cover and deception missions.

Additional missions included support of local tactical commanders' combat operations, including taking control of key terrain (to enable airborne and amphibious operations); use as a reconnaissance or security force; capture of key installations to prevent enemy destruction; diversionary attacks against enemy units to support cover and deception plans; and operations to isolate portions of the battled zone, airborne target area, or beachhead. Missions also included working with allied forces, to include reconnaissance and security operations, conventional combat operations (if the guerrilla unit was properly trained and supported); rear area security missions; counter-guerrilla operations; and support of civil affair operations.

Among the limitations were limited capabilities for static defense or holding operations; lack of adequate training, equipment, weapons and supplies to participate in large-scale combat operations during the initial phase of unit operations; dependence upon the indigenous population and an outside power for supplies and equipment; restrictions on friendly supporting fires into operational area due to frequent movement of the guerrillas and necessity of local population safety; need for precise, timely, and accurate intelligence; often spotty communications systems between guerrilla units and higher headquarters; and reaction time, often delayed by dispersion of forces for security reasons.

We went through all the different methods of infiltrating and/or exfiltrating into, or out of, our operational area. The main methods used by Special Forces were by sea, air, and land. There were numerous methods to infiltrate by sea, including by aircraft (parachute jump into the water, a water landing by an amphibious aircraft, or a rappel or free-drop into the water from a helicopter), surface craft (PT boats or cargo ships) or submarine (especially useful if making a clandestine insertion or recovery). By air we could parachute in, utilizing either regular parachuting methods or HALO, or fly in using STOL aircraft onto rough airstrips or rotary-wing (helicopter) aircraft. Ground methods included stay-behind (remaining hidden while the enemy overran the position) and clandestinely sneaking through enemy lines.

The initial link-up with the indigenous personnel was of paramount importance, as were the best and safest methods of doing so. It was imperative to begin the initial meeting on the best possible terms, while also adhering to security measures. One of the main tenets taught concerning successful guerrilla warfare was winning the hearts and minds of the population. Without the indigenous personnel supporting a guerrilla movement, it would surely fail. An additional asset was that the present government be disliked by the populace.

Guerrilla forces generally lived in the countryside. If the indigenous population was willing to report sightings of the guerrillas to the government in power, the guerrilla was at a major disadvantage. Guerrilla units almost always moved about in small mobile units, making movement easier and stealth more possible. The guerrilla relied on mobility, elusiveness and surprise.

We were warned never to trust the indigenous personnel we worked with, but also, never to let them know we didn't trust them. It was impossible to run thorough background checks on those individuals. It was stressed that we should never turn our backs to them.

Resistance movements were normally made up of personnel with varying motivations. Some of the personnel might be motivated by a strong desire to survive, whereas others might join because of deep ideological convictions, either religious or political. Religious convictions could result in a very strong motivation in certain instances. Other motivations could include economical, personal gain, hatred, security, ego, and fear of reprisal.

Economical motivation was usually driven by fear of losing one's livelihood, or a fear of starvation. Those motivated by personal gain were those who could not always be trusted. Being offered more to fight or collect intelligence for the enemy could easily sway the motivation of a questionably motivated resistance fighter.

Although those motivated by hatred had a very strong motivation, care had to be taken to keep those individuals focused on the target at hand, rather than pure hatred of the enemy. Hatred could, at times, be a detriment. Fear of reprisal included personnel who feared for themselves and/or their families under the current regime.

The preceding motivations were usually inspired by a government that violated rights or privileges, oppressed a group, threatened the life or freedom of its populace, or an invading force that has drastically altered their lives. Regardless of the reasons, those personnel were united against what they viewed as a common enemy. They fought those perceived injustices in many ways. Some of them assisted the resistance movement by serving as fighters with the guerrilla force; others served as part-time guerrillas or civilian support groups known as auxiliary units; while still others were members of the underground.

There was no way a guerrilla movement could succeed without support, especially the moral and logistical support of the local civilians. There were numerous types of indigenous support that were mentioned. Among those were recruitment, delivering needed supplies, volunteering information, acting as early warning informants, and aiding in escape and evasion when needed. Additional support could come from outside sources, such as a sponsoring government.

No matter who, or what, the support was, a guerrilla force had to realize that it had to adhere to the rules of the Geneva Convention, just as conventional armies must. If abiding by those rules, any captured guerrilla was entitled to treatment by his captors that at least equaled that of a regular army soldier captive.

Because guerrilla fighters were irregular soldiers, they could not be expected to go head-to-head with enemy units of similar or larger sizes. Some conventional unit commanders in Vietnam made the mistake of considering a unit of South Vietnamese irregulars to be as capable as a similar sized American unit. Mistaken assumptions of that sort made for some hard lessons learned. It wasn't the fault of the Vietnamese unit; it was due to the nature of the unit, as well as the lack of training. They were never trained to be as effective as regular units.

Keep in mind that Special Forces was initially trained to be experts in guerrilla warfare, behind enemy lines. If an operation went sour, team members could not expect the help of any artillery or air support, or even an immediate air evacuation. Escape and evasion were the name of the game. The indigenous personnel could easily blend in with the population, but that wasn't always a choice for American Special Forces men in a foreign land.

To be effective, and not be wiped out, the guerrilla unit had to be equal, or superior, to the enemy in the field of intelligence gathering, cover and deception, the use of time, and the use of propaganda. There were three types of propaganda, all useful to know, understand, and utilize. Propaganda was broken down into white propaganda (correctly attributed and the source correctly identified), gray propaganda (unattributed and the source was concealed), and black propaganda (falsely attributed and the source was falsely named, usually to embarrass the named source). To be successful, the unit had to be mobile, quick, and able to surprise the enemy. We were taught how best to accomplish that.

There were three scenarios in which Special Forces was expected to be used in the early 1960s. Those were general, limited, and/or cold war situations. During a general war Special Forces was expected to be able to organize guerrilla forces in enemy territory. Our operations were supposed to support conventional military operations (as an example, by harassing the enemy from the rear as they tried to concentrate on their front).

When involved in a limited war, Special Forces could infiltrate behind enemy lines and make small raids or destroy important enemy targets. We could also train personnel (in friendly territory) indigenous to the enemy territory, to be later infiltrated into enemy territory.

During a cold war (as in the '50s and '60s) we were capable of training military personnel in the art of combating guerrilla and terrorist activities, and subversion. We also taught foreign military personnel (in locations all over the world, as well as at Ft. Bragg) the techniques of guerrilla warfare.

Of strategic importance in a guerrilla warfare situation was the terrain upon which the guerrilla force lived and operated. We learned that mountains, swamps, forests, and jungles offered the best terrain for acting covertly.

We were taught that prior to beginning an operation we should make an estimate of the situation. That was accomplished by delineating the situation and possible courses of action. Important information included considerations affecting courses of action, enemy capabilities, and your own courses of action. Important questions to ask when formulating the plan were "Who, What, When, Where, Why, and How?" During the analysis one had to determine enemy capabilities and list the advantages and disadvantages of any plan of action.

Instruction then moved on to describe and teach how the Special Forces Operational Base (SFOB) was set up and operated. That was the Special Forces Group operational and administrative location for guerrilla warfare activities, located in friendly territory. The SFOB was normally activated prior to area hostilities. It was not necessarily in one specific location but could be dispersed in several locations.

When units were deployed, the SFOB was the main source of administration, communications, logistics, planning and direction of operations, intelligence, training, liaison, coordination, briefing and infiltration. The SFOB consisted of two main elements: operational and administrative, which included training.

The operations center was where the representatives of the unit and special staff sections, and other commands with operations in the area were located. There were isolation areas in the SFOB, in which Special Forces detachments received their mission descriptions and conducted final preparation prior to infiltration.

A large part of the SFOB was the communications complex, containing all the communications equipment needed to communicate with higher headquarters and subordinate units. Communications were tantamount to the success of the Special Forces mission. The administrative center contained unit and special staff sections. That included logistics support (supply, motor, parachute rigging, medical, and any other required support elements.

It was amazing how much went into the operational planning of something as small as an A Detachment operation. The SFOB Operations Center was responsible for that preparation, as well as the success of the mission.[5] The SFOB Briefing Center was responsible for briefings and debriefings of the detachments involved in operations, detachment studies, special training, and the staging of detachments to departure sites.

Methods of infiltration were studied. When possible, contact with a guerrilla unit was preferred prior to infiltration, but infiltrating "blind" (no prior contact) could become necessary. There were four accepted methods of infiltration: air, water, land, and stay-behind.

The preferred method was air. That was, however, impossible to accomplish when adverse weather conditions existed. Teams could be infiltrated by parachute drop, STOL aircraft inserting teams into areas that contained unimproved dirt airstrips, helicopter insertion, and amphibious aircraft landing and taking off on bodies of water.

Water infiltration could be done via surface or underwater means.

Stay-behind infiltrations were accomplished by pre-positioning teams in proposed operational areas and hiding during enemy advances. Once the enemy had passed the stay-behind teams, they prepared to operate behind the lines.

The least desirable method of infiltration was by land. It was least desirable because of the exposure to the enemy being lengthy, and the limited amount of supplies and equipment that could be carried.

Resistance elements came in different forms. The basic unit was the guerrilla force. That was the military-style combat unit of the area command. Special Forces detachments were expected to unite and control those guerrilla units. Auxiliary forces were responsible for organizing and providing for civilian support of the resistance movement.

Guerrilla units were mobile, moving from place to place to conduct combat operations. Unlike guerrilla units, auxiliaries were not mobile.

They remained in their area of residence, supporting the guerrillas. Support included physical security and advanced warning of enemy movement, intelligence gathering, counterintelligence (reporting about enemy agents and locals supporting the enemy), logistical, recruiting for guerrilla units, psychological warfare (spreading of rumors, leaflets, etc.), civilian control (terrorizing or eliminating collaborators, etc.), aiding downed pilots and other friendly personnel in evasion and escape, and many other missions of support. The underground was formed to conduct operations on targets that were not reachable by guerrilla units.

Security of the guerrilla base of operations was extremely important and covered by our instruction. With the fact that a guerrilla unit was a small band of irregular troops, they had to be mobile and very security conscious. Large-scale operations by enemy regular troops were always a possibility, and early warning systems, hasty evacuation plans, as well as rear area delaying actions were of paramount importance.

Among the many means used for security were: patrols, outposts, a sentinel system, warning devices, dispersion, mobility, camouflage, communications security, counterintelligence activities, records safeguards, and cover and deception.

Patrol procedures were also a very important aspect of guerrilla warfare. We had to learn how to patrol during both day and night, and how to impart that knowledge to indigenous personnel, as well as the different types of patrols. We learned all aspects of patrolling, including the preparation for and missions of patrolling, and the makeup of a patrol.

Patrolling was not a case of just deciding to go out, hoping to meet the enemy, and returning. A lot of what made a patrol successful was the planning that went into it. Without intelligence, the patrol would have no idea where the enemy was and how to deal with him the best. After that was determined, one had to make the determination as to the size and makeup of the unit to be utilized. Once that was decided, a plan had to be organized, delineating procedures and responsibilities. The planning included coordinating with other friendly combat units in the operation area.

Once the mission and time of departure were spelled out, an intricate plan was formulated, delineating all actions, possibilities, and individual responsibilities. Tasks had to be assigned to each patrol member. In addition, timing of travel and actions were discussed. Primary and alternate routes were reviewed, including utilizing a different return route from that used in going to the objective.

All patrol members had to be briefed on the important items of the operation and reviewed in detail before the patrol moved out. This included: the signals to be used, challenge and reply passwords, locations of leaders within the patrol structure, actions upon any enemy contact, contingency plans, rally points if the patrol was somehow dispersed, actions on the objective, and the rally point for reassembling after actions on the objective.

Upon returning from patrols, and/or after the end of being involved in a combat situation, it was required that an After-Action Report (AAR) be filled out and submitted to higher headquarters. After-Action Reports had an official format of questions/statements.

We received a short training period on the importance of the AAR, and instructions on how to properly complete an AAR. The initial portion of the AAR included a chronological (by time and date) list of events, while the second part was for an explanation of the entire operation, stressing important points. We were reminded that AARs were classified documents and should be handled as such.

"The essence of war is violence. Moderation in war is imbecility." — *British Sea Lord John Fisher*

The ambush and the raid were the most common and important tactics used by guerrillas. They were both surprise actions, designed to kill as many of the enemy as possible within a short period of time. Both also consisted of two elements: the assault force and the security force. The major difference was that the ambush was an attack on a moving or temporarily halted target, while the raid was an attack on a stationary target. We spent time in the field practicing and improving our tactics, honing them to near perfection. Trains, truck convoys, individual vehicles, and troops on the move were good ambush targets.

In an ambush, the assault element conducted the main attack against the enemy, which included halting the ambush target, killing or capturing personnel, recovering supplies and equipment, and destroying the vehicles or supplies that were unwanted or immovable. The security element isolated the ambush site by erecting roadblocks or taking under fire any local outposts or enemy reinforcement units. They were also responsible for the security of the withdrawing assault element. The ambush was an excellent method for the guerrilla to obtain stashes of weapons, ammunition, and supplies.

The key to an ambush was firepower and surprise. It had to be a short, violent attack. A high volume of rifle and machine gun fire, as well as hand grenades, and, if available, Claymore directional antipersonnel mines, made for a very deadly ambush.

It was imperative that the enemy be totally surprised by the ambush. That meant total concealment and silence. There could be nothing at the ambush site that looked like people had been in the area. The ambush site had to have, however, clear fields of fire, which meant no branches, bushes, trees, etc., that would hamper the ambush. We practiced a lot of different ambush techniques.

There were two categories of ambushes — deliberate and hasty — as well as two types of ambushes: the point ambush and the area ambush. Deliberate ambushes were conducted at predetermined locations and were usually set up on suspected enemy routes of travel. It was the task of the patrol leader to select the location and extent of the kill zone and assign sectors of fire for each man. The enemy basically set the time of the attack, while the attacker picked the location.

The second type of ambush was the hasty ambush, or ambush of opportunity. The only difference being that there was no time for planning an ambush of opportunity because it was a last minute, unexpected opportunity. Patrol members were rehearsed on actions to take in case of an ambush of opportunity even before departing the home base. Each man had to know his job should the opportunity arise.

Hasty ambushes, as the name implied, had to be set up as quickly and quietly as possible. Therefore, each patrol member had to know his assigned location and duty during the ambush. It was critical that the hasty ambush not be initiated until most of the enemy were in the kill zone.

Planning was crucial when considering ambush options. Intelligence wouldn't always be available on an ambush target but was an asset if available. Of importance would be the probable size, strength, and composition of the enemy force to be ambushed. A reconnaissance needed to be done to determine the best site for the ambush, as well as determining the best approach and exfiltration routes, preferably concealed. Smaller units could defeat larger units utilizing successful ambush techniques.

Terrain was a major consideration. The perfect terrain for an ambush would be a site where the terrain funnels the enemy into the killing zone. Clear fields of fire for the ambush force was also important, with concealed firing positions if possible. During an ambush, the deadliest results occurred if the rifle and machine gun fire were aimed between the hip and chest of the enemy.

Ambushes conducted during periods of darkness resulted in a larger choice of positions and better opportunities to surprise the enemy while also confusing them. The downside was that control during the ambush and movement to and from the ambush site was degraded. On the other hand, ambushes conducted during daylight hours were easier to control, and offered the choice of continuing the action for a longer time.

There were also two accepted formations used in an operation depending upon the terrain. A linear ambush was one in which the assault and support elements deployed in a long line, subjecting the enemy to deadly flanking fire. The linear ambush was possible if the ambush site was in terrain that restricted the enemy's ability to maneuver against the ambush party, or in open terrain wherein it was possible to keep the enemy confined to the kill zone.

The second acceptable formation was that of the letter "L," known as the L-shaped ambush. With the L ambush the assault element formed the long leg of the formation, parallel to the target's line of movement. The short leg at the end, and at a right angle to the assault element, was manned by the support element. The L-shaped ambush permitted flanking, as well as enfilading fire against the enemy. The L-shaped ambush was not to be used if the short, perpendicular leg would have had to cross a straight road or trail.

Of course, ambush training meant counter-ambush training. The immediate action drill (reaction to an ambush) was pressed firmly into our minds. If you tried running away, you were toast. The only reaction that resulted in a chance of survival was to immediately react to the ambush, returning fire at the same time and with the maximum possible firepower. The best defense was to be on the offensive.

There was absolutely no time to think. Taking time to think was deadly. The first reaction was to immediately assume the prone position, or seek cover if available, and throw concussion, fragmentation, or smoke grenades toward the attackers. The soldiers in the kill zone were then to return fire and assault the ambush position. The men not in the kill zone were to fire on the enemy, shifting fire as the men in the kill zone assaulted.

"The God of War hates those who hesitate." — *Euripides, 480-406 BC*

A raid was a surprise attack upon an enemy installation or force, therefore requiring stealth on the part of the raiding force. It consisted of a quick, violent attack, with rapid cessation of combat, and a swift withdrawal, usually by a small force of platoon size or larger.

The raid could have one of several objectives. It could be to destroy or damage supplies, equipment, or installations; capture supplies, equipment, and key personnel; cause casualties among the enemy; a ruse to draw the enemy's attention away from other operations; and/or to keep the enemy off balance, forcing him to deploy units to protect his rear areas.

Before a raid could be planned, a target had to be selected, and a target analysis performed. There were numerous criteria used to determine target selection. When selecting a target, the objective was to inflict the maximum possible damage, with the minimum expenditure of men and materiel. The criticality of the target was important.

A target was critical if its destruction or damage would result in a significant loss of ability to conduct and support enemy operations. Among those targets, bridges, railroad rights of way, tunnels, ravines, and mountain passes were critical for lines of communications, while train locomotives, vehicles, and POL stores were critical to transportation.

Once the criticality of a target was determined, the vulnerability, accessibility, and recuperability had to be assessed. Accessibility included security around the target and location of the target. If the target could be repaired and brought back into operation quickly, destruction was a wasted effort.

If the mission was to destroy a target, several factors were involved. Among those were gathering detailed target intelligence, doing extensive ground reconnaissance, having a sound plan with alternates, participating in detailed rehearsals, and finally, achieving maximum destruction of the target(s) with minimum effort, time, material, and personnel.

One of the most important segments of a raid was the reconnaissance. The target had to be observed for a long period of time. Activity (such as sentries and guard posts) and target defenses (perimeter fencing and minefields, as well as strong and weak points in security) had to be studied in detail. Upon returning to camp, the information was then reviewed in detail and a plan was formulated. Part of that planning entailed making a basic terrain model of the target area. That gave those involved in the raid a good idea of what they would be facing, and how the raid was to be conducted.

During the pre-operation briefing, every movement and pertinent piece of information from departure to return was covered in great detail, leaving very little to chance and ensuring that everybody knew in fine detail what their jobs were and how those jobs would be accomplished. Any emergency that might be expected was also covered in detail, including any action to be taken if the unit was spotted en route or ambushed. Radio communication frequencies and call signs were also assigned, and communications SOP (standard operating procedures) were gone over in detail.

Prime targets for raids included transportation (railroad, highway, water, and air); communications (telephone, telegraph, radio, and television); industry (manufacturing facilities—especially weapons, aircraft, vehicles, ammunition, shipping, etc.); power (electric, nuclear, and chemical); fuel (gas and oil); and military installations and personnel.

If possible, the following suggestions were paramount to the success of a raid or ambush.

(1) Maintain twenty-four-hour surveillance on the target or objective area until the time of attack.

(2) Rehearse the elements of the force.

(3) Use a mission support site (MSS) if the distance to the objective area is problematic.

(4) To maintain surprise, strike quickly.

(5) Withdraw quickly, using a different route than used to approach the objective.

The instructor went over the recommended ways to do the most damage to certain targets. Quite a bit of time was spent on the destruction of railroad systems, mainly because of the profitability and ease of destruction by guerrilla units. Because rail lines were so difficult to guard, almost anywhere along the line was a safe target.

When destroying track it was recommended that breaks in the tracks be made in several locations. Destroying track just as the train was entering a sharp curve or downgrade was the best, because it would destroy the locomotive and derail the train, thus creating quite the mess. The best place to destroy a rail line (as well as highway systems) was on a bridge or in a tunnel or narrow railway passes. Repair work would take much more time than merely cutting the rail on level ground.

To disrupt waterways, the recommended methods were to sink ships and/or drop bridges into the waterway by using explosives. When mining a waterway was not possible, fire from recoilless weapons was a close second. Firing at the engine room area, waterline, or boat's bridge were recommended.

The easiest method for destruction or delay of communications was the destruction of antenna sites and/or transmission lines. Similarly, power systems could be disrupted by destroying transmission lines and/or towers, as well as transformer stations. Pipelines were the easiest targets for the disruption of fuel supplies. They could be blown up, or contaminating agents could be injected into the pipelines.

It was always stressed that any operation, even any bivouac or RON site, should have an emergency rendezvous (aka rally point) location, in case of unexpected negative consequences, and even in the cases of raids in which the forces would be purposely divided and bugging out in different directions.

• • •

An important part of our coursework dealt with Area Studies and Area Assessments. We would be spending a lot of time reading and discussing Area Studies prior to any deployment. Each area study contained a myriad of information and was extremely long and detailed, covering all possible scenarios in the target country or area.

Area Studies included: information about general subjects (political, geographic positions, population, national economy, and national security); geography (climate, terrain, and major geographic subdivisions); people (basic racial stock and physical characteristics, standard of living and cultural [education] levels, health and medical standards, ethnic components, religion, tradition and customs [especially taboos], rural countryside, political parties or factions, dissidence, resistance movements, and guerrilla groups); enemy (political, conventional military forces, and internal security forces [including border guards]); targets (railroads, telecommunications, POL [fuel], electric power, military storage and supply, military headquarters and installations, radar and electronics devices, highways, inland waterways-canals, seaports, natural and synthetic gas lines, and industrial plants).

The political aspect of an Area Study included the government itself, including the international political orientation of the government and the degree of popular support for the government; the attitudes of the indigenous personnel toward the United States, its allies, and its enemy; the historical background of the nation; how much the country depended upon foreign countries for its existence and/or its alliances with foreign countries; and significant political, military, and economic concentrations.

The geographic positions described the location and size of the country, climate, general utilization of its land, and its strategic location reference to neighboring countries, including the natural defenses along its borders, points of entry into the country, and strategic routes within the country.

Knowing the population was extremely important to SF teams entering a country. The Area Study told us how many people resided in the country, as well as the religious, ethnic, and nomadic groups within it. It also discussed any division between rural and urban groups, and the locations of population centers and large cities.

Knowing the national economy gave us an idea of critical targets within the country, and how self-sufficient the country was. The indicators included technological standards; natural resources and how self-sufficient these resources were; financial structure of the country, and how much of the country's financial well-being depended upon foreign aid; the agricultural and domestic food supply; industry and its level of productivity; the manufacturing of and demand for consumer goods; foreign and domestic trade and facilities; fuels available, as well as power facilities; its system of telecommunications and radio; transportation systems, including railroads, highway, waterway, and commercial air, and how they compare to our standards and adequacy.

Knowing the country's national security, of course, was of primary importance to us before deploying to a country or region. Paramount would be the country's military forces, as well as the organization and strength of any security and/or paramilitary forces. It was also important that we knew the center of political power and national defense organization.

Geography would give us an idea of what type of equipment and supplies we would need, and what we were to expect. It included the study of the local climate, including normal, minimum and maximum rainfall, snow, and temperatures in the different geographic areas of the country at different times of the year. The terrain had a lot to do with how we would train prior to deployment.

Coastal areas and rivers would require waterborne training; deserts would require weather operations training; jungles would require jungle training and survival; while mountainous terrain would mean training in mountain operations and possibly skiing. Terrain and climate would also be a large factor in aerial operations, including re-supply and support.

We underwent a review of how to read relief maps of the country and area of operation. That was important so that we could determine the general direction of mountain ranges and ridgelines, and whether they were solid or broken. It was also good to know the average degree of slope, characteristics of the valley and plains, as well as any natural routes or obstacles for cross-country movement.

It was also important to study where the rivers were, and in which direction they flowed, as well as the location of large lakes and whether they were suitable landing zones for amphibious aircraft. A study of the coast was important for determining re-supply points, exfiltration, and infiltration routes, as well as secretive hideaways such as coves, estuaries and inlets.

If possible, we also would need to study areas that might be potential landing zones for light aircraft. Important to our survival, in case of emergency, was also the availability and potable quality of water sources, as well as the availability of cultivated (vegetables, grains, fruits, nuts, etc.), natural (berries, fruits, nuts, herbs, etc.), and wild food (animals, fish, and fowl).

Since we would be spending a lot of time working with the local indigenous personnel, it was imperative that we study and understand the people of the country in all regions. Knowing the standards of living (especially the extremes from the norm) and education levels would prepare us for being able to communicate better, as well as know how deep (or bare basics) we could delve into technical subjects.

Knowing the general health and medical standards of the operational area gave us an insight into what our team medics should expect in the way of common diseases, as well as how careful we would have to be when it came to cleanliness, etc. It also gave us an idea of the level of care and equipment at medical facilities, as well as how many, and where, medical facilities existed. Equally important was the quality of the water, especially for drinking.

If the operational area was undergoing conflict it was extremely important to know the ethnicities involved if the strife was ethnically driven. We would need to know the locations and/or concentrations of the group(s) involved, as well as the basis for their discontent and motivation to bring about change, especially if they were opposed to the majority ethnicity and/or the regime in power. We would also want to know which, if any, foreign influences were present.

We would possibly be working with personnel of different religious backgrounds, so it was helpful to know any religious divisions in the operational area, especially if those divisions were part of a reason for strife. Locations and concentrations of specific religious groups were delineated in the Area Study.

Of utmost importance when working in third world countries, especially, was the existence of taboos, particularly if they were strong and established, possibly influencing individual actions or attitudes. Knowing of taboos would also be helpful in keeping us out of trouble, which could at times have deadly consequences. Any broken taboo broken would result in possibly irreparable damage to working relationships. Especially in rural areas, indigenous personnel could very well have different customs and habits. It was important to realize those differences.

Political parties (authorized and unauthorized), as well as their affiliations with foreign entities, should be known. Their policies and goals needed to be understood, as well as any violent opposition factions within the parties. Dissident and resistance factions, as well as guerrilla groups, were to be studied in depth, noting locations, activities, strengths, motivations, leadership, outside support, etc.

The enemy had to be understood, to neutralize and defeat it. The area study would point out any outside power within the enemy, including the number of non-national personnel, their influence with the indigenous personnel, and their organization. If there was a dominant national party within the enemy ranks, it was advisable to know its dependence upon, and ties with, outside powers.

Any evidence of dissension within any level, were indications of weaknesses to be exploited. If the enemy was a foreign conventional military force, important facts about those forces included: morale, discipline, personnel strength, organization and basic deployment, uniforms (including unit designations and ordinary and special insignia), leadership, training, doctrine, equipment, facilities, logistics, and effectiveness (especially strengths and weaknesses).

Besides knowing the enemy, a war cannot be won without knowing the locations and vulnerabilities of targets within the enemy's zone of control. The Area Study gave us a list of targets, their importance, and their vulnerabilities. Generally, the Area Study listed targets in the order of priority.

Railroads were a vital link for delivery and movement of men and supplies by the enemy. Railroad lines were broken down by importance, locally and generally; possible bypasses, and ease of bypass usage; number of tracks; electrification (many foreign railroads were powered by electricity); location of maintenance crews, repair supplies and equipment; types of signal and switch equipment; vulnerable points, including unguarded small bridges and/or culverts; cuts, fills, overhanging cliffs or undercutting streams; key junctions or switching points; tunnels; and security systems.

Being the major means of communicating between combat units and headquarters, telecommunications systems were also valid targets for destruction. Targets included: POL facilities, power stations, military storage and supply, military headquarters and installations, radar and electronics devices, highways, inland waterways and canals, seaports, natural and synthetic gas lines, and industrial plants.

Last, but certainly not least, was the inclusion of an intelligence report on the assigned operational area. It basically covered the same subjects as the general Area Study, except it narrowed the subject matter to a relatively small and specific area, focusing on operational plans within the team's operational area. During that phase as much crucial information to the planned operations was amassed.

Locations and significant terrain features were plotted on the map or located on map overlays. That information could include, but not be limited to: recommended bases and alternates for the guerrilla force; primary and alternate DZs and LZs; possible landmarks for use in direction and orientation for infiltration vehicles (aircraft, boat, etc.); possible routes from the infiltration point to the likely guerrilla base(s), with stopover sites; points at which contacts with friendly elements can make contact; anticipated or known enemy forces, including location, strength, capabilities, and estimate of operations and movement; settlements and scattered farms, etc.; railroads, highways, telecommunications, etc., located in the operational area; all major installations and facilities; distances between key points; and the recommended point of attack on assigned targets, as well as selections of other possible targets.

After arrival at a guerrilla base, it was recommended that detachments continue the intelligence gathering procedure. The gathered information was stored in what was known as an Area Assessment. Area Assessments were vital for the continued operations and security of the detachment. It was also helpful information for use in an orientation for any new personnel or allied units entering the area of operation. Any time information was collected that was not included in the initial Area Study or was a deviation from that information contained in the Area Study, the information was to be transmitted to the SFOB.

"Wars may be fought with weapons, but they are won by men." — *General George Patton Jr.*

One of the main reasons Special Forces was such an asset was, and is, its highly trained men. It's amazing how much damage a very small unit can do when it is well equipped and manned with superior soldiers. Special Forces was, and is, is a force multiplier, able to accomplish much more than conventional units of the same size, especially when working with indigenous guerrillas or troops.

Among the many things we learned was doing the best with what we had. We would be taken to a location where there were just a few items on hand and told to accomplish a mission with them. It took a lot of common sense, creativity and teamwork to accomplish the task at hand. It was an excellent way to teach the need for teamwork, and to test a trainee's ability to work with other people. Teamwork is essential in Special Forces, as is creativity.

That was one difference between Special Forces and conventional units. Creativity was accepted, and, in fact, looked for in a Special Forces trooper, whereas simply obeying orders was acceptable and recommended in conventional units. Although SF wanted tough men who were smart and got along well with others, they also needed men who could adapt well and be flexible.

Besides searching for men who were intelligent and tough (physically as well as mentally), Special Forces training was one of very few military training programs that looked for people who could readily get along with others, bonding with teammates. That bond was the glue that held A-teams together and made them so valuable and capable. High on the qualification list were those men who were adventurous, extroverted, and type A individuals. Mental maturity and a sense of responsibility were also a plus.

A scary thought about guerrilla tactics was the fact that a guerrilla unit had to remain highly mobile. Wounded personnel could severely hamper that mobility. In those cases, wounded personnel sometimes had to be left behind, hidden from the enemy as much as possible and returning later to retrieve them, if possible.

On the other hand, it was also taught that badly wounding enemy personnel, rather than killing them, could hamper the enemy's movement, as many more men were required to treat and transport the wounded than the dead. A morbid thought, but useful when needing to slow an enemy advance. Of course, that strategy was only helpful if the enemy cared about its wounded; some enemies could care less.

All during Branch Training I was having to go through tooth and nerve surgery, once every ten days. We were tested at least once a week on what we had learned during the different phases of training. We were never told the test results. I could only guess that I had gotten in the 80-90% range on all my tests.

"The South Vietnamese themselves are fighting their own battle." —
U.S. Secretary of State Dean Rusk, April 1963

On Monday, 15 April, we were all gathered in a briefing room, and briefed on the field exercise we were about to embark on. It was to be our final Branch Training eight-day field training exercise (FTX). That FTX was designed to test our newly learned skills, as well as everything we had learned while attending Special Forces Training Group, in as realistic conditions as possible.

Key to the exercise was being able to work with the local indigenous populous, helping them, while they, in turn, hopefully helped us. It was an attempt at duplicating what could happen if we infiltrated into a foreign country with the mission of helping to defeat an invading force. We were to put everything together that we had learned, proving that we could utilize that expertise in an operational environment.

We either passed and went on to a Special Forces assignment, or we were booted, flunked out, possibly with a chance to repeat, or sent to a conventional airborne unit for assignment. The FTX wasn't named when I experienced it. Over the years, and decades, it has gone through numerous transformations and names.

Some of the names were Gobbler Woods, Cherokee Trail, and currently Robin Sage. Over the years the local civilians became very involved in the exercise, looking forward to working with the Special Forces trainees, as they came in to "save" their precious homeland. Some of the civilians even formed guerrilla bands, with identifying armbands and flags, and waged "war" on the enemy. The "enemy" was often units from the nearby Ft. Bragg-based 82nd Airborne Division.

We were given the warning order for a parachute jump that evening. We were to jump from a U.S. Air Force Air Commando-piloted C-46 "Commando" cargo aircraft.[6] Our jump altitude would be 1,000 feet above ground level (aka AGL) rather than the usual 1,250 feet AGL. We were to jump into a small, difficult drop zone in mountainous terrain. That, coupled with all the equipment we were jumping with was going to make for an interesting jump. Jump time was to be at 2330 hours.

The People's Republic of Pineland had been invaded and overrun by an aggressor force. The exiled government had requested our aid, to train and advise their guerrilla fighters in their battle to win back their homeland. The end objective of the guerrilla war was to restore the U.S.-friendly government that had been legally elected to power. (Pineland was actually in the Uwharrie National Forest, about seventy-five miles northwest of Ft. Bragg, near Oak Grove, in western North Carolina.)

Once on the ground, we would travel overland, using night land navigation techniques, to meet with a small welcoming group of Pineland guerrillas, who would then lead our teams to their guerrilla band headquarters. From there, we would begin our training and advisory missions. The People's Republic of Pineland was a fabricated country located, for this scenario, in western North Carolina.

Any time our personnel were out in the field in civilian territory (which was often) for a simulated war exercise) we were warned about the possibility of accidentally running across a still. We were warned about that in Training Group and later in group. The people who operated moonshine stills in the mountains of North Carolina, and other southeastern states, were very protective of their livelihood and carried loaded weapons to protect them. If fired at, we couldn't count on our blank rifle cartridges to be much protection. If we ran across a still, our instructions were to "get the hell out of there as quickly as possible."

The equipment I gathered together for our final field problem included everything I would need for 8 days (including food) in the field. Special Forces used nylon, aluminum frame jungle and large canvas rucksacks rather than packs. Rucksacks were a staple of and unique to Special Forces, and could carry a lot more than a pack, which was important when going on missions during which no re-supply was expected. Our rucksacks weighed a minimum of 65 pounds loaded. We also carried M-1 Garand rifles, which weighed 9½ pounds (one of the heaviest and most cumbersome rifles in the U.S. Army).

A partial list of equipment I loaded in my rucksack was: a blanket and a quilted camouflage poncho for sleep gear (I decided against a sleeping bag because of its weight and bulkiness); two Army-issue ponchos (used to make the tent, as well as rain protection); a set of Army-issue fatigues; a set of civilian field clothes (a lot of our time would be spent mingling with and pretending to be civilians while operating as a guerilla warfare unit); extra socks and underwear; a pair of field boots; "meal, combat, individual," (C-rations) and other assorted essentials.

Attached to my load bearing web gear were: a collapsible canteen; a normal Korean War-era metal canteen; a field dressing packet carried in an olive-green first aid pouch; and a lensatic compass carried in a compass pouch, among other equipment. I didn't carry a mess kit because it was extraneous weight. There was a metal drinking cup included in the canteen pouch, and I ate my meals out of the can, so why carry a mess kit?

I had learned quickly that ponchos were worthless as raincoats in the warm climate of the south. It served better as a sauna than protection from the rain. Sure, it kept the rain off you, but you'd get just as wet from perspiration as the rain if you donned it — there were no air holes, so the heat would gather and intensify within the poncho.

I did find, however, that the poncho worked great when used to build a hooch in the field. Conventional (aka "regular army") soldiers carried shelter halves or "pup tents" into the field. Special Forces troops were issued two ponchos, which made it possible to erect a pretty good shelter. There were times my shelter looked like a miniature cabin, very comfortable.

That evening we formed in front of Training Group headquarters, with our packed rucksacks. Roll was taken, after which we loaded onto the rear beds of deuce-and-a-half trucks, our rucksacks in tow. It was dark as we were transported to Pope Air Force Base.

We were all just a little bit nervous, as this would be our first night jump into a small DZ with a heavy rucksack in mountainous terrain, knowing that this final training exercise would be the make or break point for graduating, and being authorized to don the coveted Green Beret of Special Forces.

Our trucks pulled onto the tarmac, and we offloaded. There wasn't a moon to be seen. We were going to be jumping into that small DZ on a moonless, very dark night, at a lower altitude above the ground than usual. Up went the pucker factor.

In front of us was the C-46 air transport from which we would jump. The C-46 had very small doors toward the rear of the aircraft, near where the tailwheel of the aircraft was situated. With our rucksacks on our backs, we proceeded to a nearby hangar to don our parachutes, rucksacks, and helmets under a bank of spotlights.

We were shown how to rig our rucksacks when jumping. When jumping, the rucksack was attached, upside down, just below the reserve parachute (which was attached in front of the stomach area). We were also shown what to do with the rucksack, prior to landing. We were not to ride the rucksack into the ground.

About 200 feet above the ground the rucksack was to be released, dropping fifteen feet, to the end of the fifteen-foot long nylon tether strap it was attached to. The lowering of the rucksack was done to prevent the jumper from injury when landing.

We partnered up with another team member, to make sure our equipment was correctly and securely in place. When all was completed, we filed (a better word might be "waddled") to our designated aircraft. Because of all the equipment we were carrying, we needed help getting into the aircraft, climbing a short ladder to do so.

If you've ever seen photographs or movies of the paratroopers on their aircraft, seated like packed sardines along the inside of an aircraft, that's what we looked like. We were all as close together as possible, seated with our backs against the aircraft skin, with our hands and lower arms resting on top of the reserve parachute.

Final Field Exercise

The engines were fired up, one at a time, with a cough and a rumble. We could clearly hear the engines as they warmed up. When the pilot was satisfied with the sound and pitch of the engines and propellers, he called into the tower and received taxi instructions. We began taxiing to the active runway.

Upon reaching the runway, we sat for a while, awaiting clearance for takeoff. Pope AFB was a large, busy base, with a lot of arriving and departing cargo aircraft. When we received clearance for takeoff, the pilot taxied onto the runway, turned the aircraft to head down the length of the runway, and pushed the two throttles forward to full power.

The two engines came to life, roaring, gradually powering the aircraft to a faster speed. We were forced backward, against our neighbor toward the rear. Part way down the runway, the pilot pushed the yoke forward slightly, the tail came off the ground, and shortly was gradually lowered again, to attain takeoff angle. The aircraft slowly left the ground and began climbing.

We headed westward as we climbed in the darkness. When we reached our designated altitude, the pilot pulled back on the throttles, and the engines came to a loud droning sound as we attained cruising speed. There was mostly silence from us; just the loud sound of the droning engines as we neared our destination.

At about 2315 hours, the jumpmaster rose, reached up, and hooked his parachute static line to the overhead cable running the length of the aircraft cabin. He then took a step to the open door, and looked out the door, studying the dark terrain below.

When he felt the time was right, he turned to face us, stomped his left foot onto the floor, forcefully pushed his hands and arms a little forward and up into the air, palms facing the jumpers, and shouted above the roar of the noisy C-46 twin engines, "GET READY!" At this command we knew that the time to jump was getting close.

We unbuckled our seatbelts and prepared our bodies for the next command. Shortly afterward, he shouted "STAND UP," lifting both his arms and hands in the universal signal to stand. All of us stood up, facing the steel cable to which the static line hook would be attached.

The next command was "HOOK UP," as he raised his right hand in the air, forming a hook with his index finger, and pretending to hook his finger to a line. We all detached our static line clips from the top of our reserve parachutes and attached them to the steel cable above our heads.

At "CHECK STATIC LINES," he pumped his right hand (with the hooked finger) up and down, simulating pulling on the connection.

Each of us then pulled on our static lines, making sure they were firmly and safely attached and locked to the cable, and visually checked our line and that of the jumper in front of us.

The jumpmaster then shouted to "CHECK EQUIPMENT," as he patted his chest exaggeratedly with both hands, simulating checking equipment. We proceeded to double check our equipment, making sure everything was attached correctly, and there were no loose cords anywhere. The man behind each of us checked our parachute set-up on our back, while we did the same for the jumper in front of us.

"SOUND OFF FOR EQUIPMENT CHECK," with the jumpmaster cupping both hands behind his ears (as if trying to hear better) resulted in each man, from last to first, sounding off their stick number, followed by the word "OKAY" (i.e., NUMBER TEN OKAY . . . NUMBER NINE OKAY, etc.).

Satisfied that the jumpers were ready, the jumpmaster returned to the aircraft exit, scanning outside. At a designated point over the ground, he pointed to the open doorway and yelled "STAND IN THE DOOR." Following that command, the number one man (head of the stick) in front of me, stood in the exit door, knees slightly bent, and both hands on the outside of the door, ready to propel himself out of the door upon the command.

Given the amount of equipment attached to us, it was more like we fell out the door. I was the number two man in the stick, meaning I would exit the aircraft right after the man in the door. As such, I could see the darkness outside. In front of me, next to the door, was a red light.

A short time later the red light went off, and the green light came on. The jumpmaster slapped the ass of the man in the door, yelling "GO!" The first man exited the aircraft. I followed, waddling to the open doorway, taking position in the door momentarily, then "jumping" out the door.

I immediately assumed as tight a body position as I could, with my feet and knees close together and locked, my hands on the ends of the reserve chute, head down with chin tucked into my chest, and began counting, "One thousand! Two thousand!"

The first feeling was that of the prop blast pushing at me. I was in a momentary freefall. Very shortly thereafter, at about "three thousand," I felt a slight tug when the static line reached its full extension, pulling the cover free from the pilot (drogue) chute, which in turn pulled the main chute out of its bag, filling it with air (hopefully), deploying it and giving me an opening jolt, like being pulled upward, at about "four thousand."

I looked up into my canopy, to ensure the parachute had deployed correctly and there were no twists, tangles, or tears. As soon as I had confirmed my parachute was satisfactory, I scanned the dark sky around me and below, to confirm I wasn't in any danger of colliding with any other jumpers or coming down on somebody else's parachute.

I tried to make out any kind of a horizon in the darkness. It wasn't going to happen. It was just way too dark. The only thing I could make out was the light on the DZ, and I knew I had no chance of landing there. I tried steering my parachute toward the light by pulling the risers down as far as I could on the side the DZ was located, trying for a maximum slip in that direction. There was too much of a breeze blowing the other direction.

Silence prevailed. The only sounds were that of the aircraft flying into the distance. The quiet serenity surrounding me was awesome. I was in another world. I was also not where I wanted to be. Heaven only knew where, and when, I was going to crash-land onto, or into, whatever was below me.

We had no idea the jump was going be as interesting as it turned out being. As much as I admired Air Force crews, especially Air Commandos, the pilot (and possibly co-pilot) of this jump mission blew it big time. I don't know if they might have been imparted with incorrect information by our Special Forces training personnel or not (I seriously doubt it), but it was always up to the commander of the aircraft to double check all information dealing with altitudes, etc. I tend to doubt it was an SF fault because this drop zone and location was the usual training area for the final Branch Training FTX.

We were supposed to exit the aircraft at 1,000 feet above ground level (AGL), even though training jumps were supposed to be conducted at 1,250 feet AGL. Instead we were given the green light exit signal at 1,000 feet mean sea level (MSL). With the fact that we were jumping in the hill country of North Carolina, that made for a potentially dangerous circumstance.

Since the ground at the drop zone was 400 feet MSL (plus or minus a few feet), it meant we were exiting the aircraft at only 600 feet AGL, lower than even the published lowest safe exit altitude for a combat jump (900 feet AGL) at that time. Add the fact that there was a slight wind, a small drop zone, and a moonless (VERY dark) night made for danger ahead. A descent of only 600 feet left very little time to think or act before hitting the ground or whatever.

The exit point for a jump was determined through a mathematical formula that considered wind direction and speed, coupled with vertical distance between exit and landing. That computation was used to locate the lit "T" on the ground, marking the exit point.

With the fact that the wind was across the drop zone, with no time to steer the parachute once all equipment was loosened for landing, it meant the landing would be to the side of the drop zone instead of on it. That happened because the "T" was set for the wind affecting us through 1,000 feet of falling and drifting, not a mere 600 feet of falling and drifting. This difference in altitude meant that we would only drift about 60% of the distance, leaving us off to the side of the drop zone.

It so happened that the side of the drop zone we would now be touching down on was where the deep ditch, roadway, trees and power lines were. We hit solid and not-so-solid objects (trees, ditch, power lines, etc.) much earlier than anticipated, resulting in quite a few injuries, and one man hanging from the power lines.

I remember that as soon as I had loosened and dropped my rucksack to the end of its tether line and untied the lower tie-down for my rifle, I saw the very faint horizon directly in front of me, meaning I was going to hit ground (or whatever) pretty damn quick. Some of the men hadn't had the time to undo their rifles and/or lower their rucksacks. I prepared for my soon-to-be collision with Earth. My PLF was more like a "pray, crash, and melt"; it was impossible to plan my landing fall for any particular direction after touching down.

I crashed into a dry creek bed. How I avoided injury, I don't know. I was sore, but still able to function. Thank God! What a way to begin the final training exam! The drop zone was a scene of chaos.

Had it been a real infiltration into enemy territory, one of the first actions would have been to bury the parachutes somewhere off the drop zone after gathering up the injured jumpers so the chutes couldn't be spotted. The parachute became worthless once behind enemy lines, and was too cumbersome to carry, but was a clear sign (from the air and ground) of the location of a group's infiltration if spotted by the enemy.

Instead of burying the chutes (since it was just an exercise and parachutes were costly), we turned them into the parachute turn-in location next to the DZ. We immediately packed our steel pots (helmets) in the rucksack and placed our field caps on our heads. The field cap wasn't nearly as cumbersome or heavy on the head as was the steel pot. Special Forces during that era never wore helmets (except during parachute jumps, range firing, demolition use, or when our camp came under artillery or mortar fire).

We tactically moved off the DZ to our previously designated rally point, formed into our teams, and began our night land navigation to our first objective. Unlike modern days, with personnel having night vision equipment and GPS locators, we had to use our night navigation, map reading skills and compass to reach our objective. Because we had also been trained how to determine direction utilizing the stars (especially the Big Dipper and North Star in the Northern Hemisphere, and Cassiopeia in the Southern Hemisphere) shining above us, those were used as backup navigation.

We proceeded overland to link up with a forward representative of the guerrilla group (G's) we were to support and advise during the exercise. Upon meeting with the representative, there was an exchange of passwords (to determine the fact that this individual was, in fact, a member of the G's). After a few formalities, the representative led us to the hidden G encampment.

Upon arrival, a few more formalities were discussed before we were finally able to bed down. One of those formalities was our team leader forming a professional relationship with the G Chief and talking him into the fact that we had a lot to offer him and his small band of guerrillas.

When morning broke, we were immediately up and at it. The first order of business was for our commanding officer to discuss what the G commander expected of us, and what we expected of the G's. This began the problems we would encounter working with the G's throughout the exercise. Naturally, the first request made by the G chief was supplies, weapons, and ammunition, with no kind of commitment on his part, in return.

The "guerrilla chief" was, in fact, a senior Special Forces NCO, and the guerrillas were also mostly Special Forces men, or SF trainees awaiting training, all in civilian clothing, many times purposely acting with attitude, and trying to test us in all ways possible, especially our tactfulness, skill in working with, teaching and advising "indigenous" personnel, ability to teach classes in the field, and maintenance of "cool."

We were to work as advisors/trainers to those guerrilla unit members (almost always referred to as "G's" by SF). Those guerrillas/cadre, who were always purposely hard to work with, threw in a lot of hypothetical difficult situations, which we had to work around or defuse. They made life interesting while we were in the field and threw in a lot of surprises and head games.

The norm was when the team wanted the G's to do a job or mission, and the G chief, for one reason or another, didn't want to or came up with a reason not to. They would come up with different reasons not to, including "religious beliefs." It was amazing how many weird "religious beliefs" those G chiefs could come up with. It was our job to find a way to work around those "religious beliefs" to get the job done.

We were being tested on our creativity and willingness to find a way to work with the G's. It was almost comical at times. The difficulties we encountered with the G's were much more than any team would be expected to encounter in a real situation, but it opened our eyes as to what might happen on a mission.

Lose your temper on this field problem and you were out. Although not always assigned in a leadership position, all Special Forces trainees had to display their ability to be leaders and, as such, be able to remain calm in the worst of situations.

The exercise was not a test of physical strength. Part of the reason for the field exercise was to evaluate each of us as to our ability to work with a team, in a team environment, with indigenous (foreign) personnel in an unconventional warfare situation. Special Forces training put a premium on teamwork, since teamwork was the backbone of Special Forces.

The United States Constitution forbids the U.S. military from carrying on operations within the United States, but we were participating in a training exercise, not an "operation," and the local "Pineland" civilians got a big kick out of "playing the game" with us and worked with us hand-in-hand.

To this day, the "Pinelanders" look forward to the FTX, taking sides and getting into the spirit of the training exercise. In the early days some of them even formed their own little guerrilla band, harassing the invading army, and leading them astray.

All different types of military personnel were also assigned to the exercise, in job assignments totally different from their usual fare. The exercise has expanded, now covering a large part of North Carolina, in territory that still goes by the name "Pineland." In return for their assistance, Special Forces helps the "Pinelanders" mend fences, repair barns, etc. It's a win-win situation, unless you are a trainee who can't pass muster.

After the initial problems with the G's, things settled down a little, and we scheduled training for the G's. We began by instructing the guerrillas in our field of expertise, as well as helping each other demonstrate to the class and help run firing ranges. It was a team effort. I gave a course on how to destroy bridges with demolition charges, since part of the exercise was going to be that very mission.

Team instruction included reconnaissance and combat patrolling (which included reaction to an ambush), land navigation, day and night ambushes on various targets, and air resupply. We taught and demonstrated how to plan and conduct air resupply missions, day and night.

Problems came at us right and left, and we had better respond in the correct manner, or we were toast. That tested our ability to think quickly and logically, and to accomplish our mission(s) with what was on hand, but we did it, successfully completing our FTX mission.

Those of us who graduated, did so on 26 April. We received the treasured 3-suffix on our MOS (mine changing from 121.17 to 121.13), which signified Special Forces qualification, although we were still treated as if we were not yet qualified. It may be hard to believe, but it took longer to train a Special Forces soldier than to train a fighter pilot. When you reached that pinnacle, you knew you deserved the new headgear, new shoulder insignia, and new assignment that went with them.

What a glorious day! After more than a year in training units (14+ months) I had finally earned my "beret, men's, wool, rifle green, army shade 297," aka the "Green Beret." And it was all worth it, a hundred times over. I graduated in the top 10% of the class (14th in a graduating class of 150) with an 89% average.

Physical conditioning had been secondary to mental toughness and determination, as well as emphasizing our abilities to adapt to changeable situations. I was psyched, and ready for new challenges. Recently, a fellow Special Forces veteran did a great job of describing the Green Beret we wore. He stated that "the beret is IN the head and heart, not ON the head."

While on our final Branch Training exercise, Secretary of State Dean Rusk stated on 22 April, "The Viet Cong look less and less like winners.... The South Vietnamese are on their way to success."

Rather than going directly to a group, as I thought I would, I had to stick around Training Group until orders came down for me. It was back to details again. The day after graduation I had KP, and two days later, guard duty. They were really piling it on, a proper send-off from Training Group. On Sunday the 28th, a few of us were transported to Raleigh, North Carolina, to act as an honor guard for the funeral of a Special Forces man. The next day I had guard duty.

On 1 May, the 6th Special Forces Group (Airborne) was officially activated and designated as a Special Action Force, commanded by

Colonel Charles L. Kasler. On 3 May I was told I would be assigned to the 7th Special Forces Group (Airborne), at Ft. Bragg on the 8th. On 7 May I finally received those orders, with a reporting date of 8 May 1963.

The Special Forces Creed

I am an American Special Forces soldier!

I will do all that my nation requires of me.
I am a volunteer, knowing well the hazards of my profession.

I serve with the memory of those who have gone before me.
I pledge to uphold the honor and integrity of their legacy in all I am—in all I do.

I am a warrior.
I will teach and fight whenever and wherever my nation requires.
I will strive always to excel in every art and artifice of war.

I know that I will be called upon to perform the tasks in isolation, far from familiar faces and voices.
With the help and guidance of my faith, I will conquer my fears and succeed.

I will keep my mind and body clean, alert, and strong.
I will maintain my arms and equipment in an immaculate state befitting a Special Forces soldier, for this is my debt to those who depend on me.

I will not fail those with whom I serve.
I will not bring shame upon myself or the Special Forces.

I will never leave a fallen comrade.
I will never surrender though I am the last.
If I am taken, I pray that I have the strength to defy my enemy.

I am a member of my nation's chosen soldiery.
I serve quietly, not seeking recognition or accolades.
My goal is to succeed in my mission—and live to succeed again.

De Oppresso Liber

Me wearing my first green beret, with 7th Special Forces "candy stripe" flash below the Special Forces crest. I'm sporting my supposedly fully-trained "snake-eating Green Beret" hired killer look. (my photo)

"The Ballad of the Green Berets"
by SSG Barry Sadler

Fighting soldiers from the sky,
Fearless men who jump and die,
Men who mean just what they say,
The brave men of the Green Beret.

Silver wings upon their chest,
These are men—America's best.
One hundred men will test today,
But only three win the Green Beret.

Trained to live off nature's land.
Trained in combat, hand to hand.
Men who fight by night and day.
Courage speaks for the Green Beret.

Silver wings upon their chest,
These are men—America's best.
One hundred men will test today,
But only three win the Green Beret.

Back at home a young wife waits,
Her Green Beret has met his fate.
He has died for those oppressed,
Leaving her this last request.

Put silver wings on my son's chest.
Make him one of America's best.
He'll be a man they'll test one day.
Have him win the Green Beret.

Sadler was one of us, but I would like to have seen some slightly different wording in the song. That only change would be to change "win the Green Beret," to "earn the Green Beret." The beret was not something you won; it was something you earned through extremely hard work.

317

CHAPTER 8

SPECIAL FORCES HISTORY

History of Unconventional Warfare

Unconventional warfare, commonly known as guerrilla warfare, is not a new form of doing battle. It has existed since the first caveman ambushed another. The difference is that it has become a precise art. Unconventional warfare includes many forms of guerrilla fighting: infiltration, sabotage, propaganda, and psychological warfare — basically, anything but vast battlefield warfare fought by large bodies of troops.

It's unknown how early guerrilla warfare got its start in North America, but the credit goes to the Native American population for expertise in unconventional warfare. Early American settlers quickly encountered the heretofore unseen tactics of the hostile Native American warriors. The settlers learned in time that the best way to combat the Indians was by using similar tactics, a form of guerrilla warfare. They learned to operate quickly, in loose, small formations. They also learned the need for fire discipline, ambush, and surprise actions.

Over time, as more settlers arrived, and the danger of hostile Indians subsided, those guerrilla tactics became a thing of the past. By the time the French and Indian War began, in 1754, George Washington wrote, "Indians are the only match for Indians; and without these we shall ever fight upon unequal terms."

Special Forces traces its lineage back to Rogers' Rangers, a small combat unit during the French and Indian War and the American Revolutionary War. Rogers' Rangers was formed during the French and Indian War (aka Seven Years War) as a British Army provincial company that came from the New Hampshire colony.

The unit was trained and led by Major Robert Rogers, who had organized it as a mobile light infantry unit with the main mission of reconnaissance, but available as a long-range special operations force, being capable of remaining afield for long periods of time, living off the land. The company became known for their unusual daring and exceptional frontier warfare skills.

While conventional French and British units slugged it out using traditional European style combat, Rogers' Rangers fought an extremely successful and deadly hide-and-seek mode of warfare. The British wasted no time classifying it as an independent ranger company. The unit proved so effective that it was enlarged into a corps of more than a dozen similar companies, numbering more than 1,200 men at its largest.

By the late 1750s the unit had become the main scouting force for the British, gathering much needed intelligence about enemy forces. In 1757, during the French and Indian War, Rogers formulated a list of rules and recommendations for his 600-man ranger company, to be used as a manual for guerrilla warfare. They were called "28 Rules of Ranging." Rogers combined Native American tactics and his own techniques to make the list. Following is a simplified and edited version of the list, containing one "extra" rule, extracted from his 1759 journal, and obtained from Wikipedia online:

1. All Rangers are subject to the rules of war.
2. In a small group, march in single file with enough space between so that one shot can't pass through one man and kill a second.
3. Marching over soft ground should be done abreast, making

tracking difficult. At night, keep half your force awake while half sleeps.

4. Before reaching your destination, send one or two men forward to scout the area and avoid traps.

5. If prisoners are taken, keep them separate and question them individually.

6. Marching in groups of three or four hundred should be done in three separate columns, within support distance, with a point and rear guard.

7. When attacked, fall or squat down to receive fire and rise to deliver. Keep your flanks as strong as the enemy's flanking force, and if retreat is necessary, maintain the retreat fire drill.

8. When chasing an enemy, keep your flanks strong, and prevent them from gaining high ground where they could turn and fight.

9. When retreating, the rank facing the enemy must fire and retreat through the second rank, thus causing the enemy to advance into constant fire.

10. If the enemy is far superior, the whole squad must disperse and meet again at a designated location. This scatters the pursuit and allows for organized resistance.

11. If attacked from the rear, the ranks reverse order, so the rear rank now becomes the front. If attacked from the flank, the opposite flank now serves as the rear rank.

12. If a rally is used after a retreat, make it on the high ground to slow the enemy advance.

13. When laying in ambuscade, wait for the enemy to get close enough that your fire will be doubly frightening, and after firing, the enemy can be rushed with hatchets.

14. At a campsite, the sentries should be posted at a distance to protect the camp without revealing its location. Each sentry will consist of 6 men with two constantly awake at a time.

15. The entire detachment should be awake before dawn each

morning as this is the usual time of enemy attack.

16. Upon discovering a superior enemy in the morning, you should wait until dark to attack, thus hiding your lack of numbers and using the night to aid your retreat.

17. Before leaving a camp, send out small parties to see if you have been observed during the night.

18. When stopping for water, place proper guards around the spot making sure the pathway you used is covered to avoid surprise from a following party.

19. Avoid using regular river fords as these are often watched by the enemy.

20. Avoid passing lakes too close to the edge, as the enemy could trap you against the water's edge.

21. If an enemy is following your rear, circle back and attack him along the same path.

22. When returning from a scout, use a different path as the enemy may have seen you leave and will wait for your return to attack when you're tired.

23. When following an enemy force, try not to use their path, but rather plan to cut them off and ambush them at a narrow place or when they least expect it.

24. When traveling by water, leave at night to avoid detection.

25. In rowing in a chain of boats, the one in front should keep contact with the one directly astern of it. This way they can help each other and the boats will not become lost in the night.

26. One man in each boat will be assigned to watch the shore for fires or movement.

27. If you are preparing an ambuscade near a river or lake, leave a force on the opposite side of the water so the enemy's flight will lead them into your detachment.

28. When locating an enemy party of undetermined strength, send out a small scouting party to watch them. It may take all day to decide on your attack or withdrawal, so signs and countersigns should be established to determine your

friends in the dark.

29. If you are attacked in rough or flat ground, it is best to scatter as if in rout. At a pre-picked place you can turn, allowing the enemy to close. Fire closely, then counterattack with hatchets. Flankers could then attack the enemy and rout him in return.

Rogers' Rangers company was formed again during the American Revolutionary War, that time as an American loyalist force against the British.

The American Civil War is famous for its battle technology and new deadly weapons, as well as pitched battles and units moving forward en masse, to be mowed down by the enemy, until the larger force prevailed. Less well known is the fact that guerrilla warfare was utilized with deadly results throughout the war, especially by the undermanned Southern forces.

One such unit was led by Captain John Mosby, under the command of Jeb Stuart. Mosby led 29 volunteer rebel troopers into Union territory, to the location of Union General Stoughton's headquarters. He strode into the general's bedroom, awakened him, and announced that the general was his prisoner. Mosby became feared by Union leaders, raiding at will with a small band of men, and wreaking havoc on Union forces and supplies.

In 1874 an international conference convened in Brussels, Belgium. The conference was convened to make "civilized rules" for warfare. Their stupidity bounded forth. They declared that the only way guerrilla warriors would be "legally" recognized was if they were under the command of one commander, wore distinctive badges, carried their arms openly, and followed the "laws and customs of war." All well and good, but the only forces who adhered to those rules were the "good guys."

During World War II England formed a secret service that was to act independently of any other unit. It was known as Special Operations Executive (SOE) and was under the department of Economic Warfare. Soon after it was established, Winston Churchill told the Minister of Economic Warfare to "set Europe ablaze."

The SOE mission was to form a nucleus of personnel to act as resistance in Nazi-occupied countries and assist as a "fifth column" in the liberation of any country invaded by the British. When the United States entered the war in Europe, Major General William J. "Wild Bill" Donovan wanted to form a military unit like the SOE, that would specialize in guerrilla warfare. He was met with intense opposition from the Army and Navy Chiefs of Staff, as well as the FBI. Realizing the overwhelming opposition from such important government agencies, he went directly to president Franklin D. Roosevelt. Roosevelt loved the idea and, despite cries of indignation from government agencies, issued orders to form the OSS.

Donovan met with "Intrepid," code name of the leader of the British SOE, to get help in forming his own unit. Donovan formed the Office of Strategic Services (OSS), based loosely on the British SOE. Once trained, they immediately began individual and joint operations (with the SOE). The OSS worked clandestinely, infiltrating (usually by parachute) small groups of men and women into enemy territory (mostly in France and Burma, in the Pacific Theater). There they organized and directed resistance groups. Even General Douglas A. MacArthur opposed the OSS, barring the OSS from acting as a unit in his Pacific Theater. Despite that, OSS personnel in Burma ran highly successful missions.

It was amazing that any successful anti-German missions were accomplished in Europe, especially in France. The de Gaulle backers refused to associate with the Giraud backers, and vice versa. In addition, the terrain wasn't conducive to guerrilla operations in most of Europe. Trying to coordinate underground and guerrilla activities was also a challenge.

Communist-leaning groups struck out at the enemy any time they could, while other groups tended to act with more care and planning. The pro-communist groups tended to be less liable to coordinate with other groups and units. Despite that, the guerrillas and underground had a great effect on the Nazis force, physically and morale-wise.

Jedburgh teams, acting as special command units, were sent into France to aid the French underground. Each team usually consisted of two officers and a sergeant acting as radio operator. All three were trained in guerrilla tactics, with the mission of coordinating operations and arranging for resupply of the guerrilla bands.

In September 1943 General von Rundstedt, the German commander-in-chief in France, wrote to Hitler that "there were 534 very serious rail sabotage actions, as compared to a monthly average of only 120 during the first half of the year." Sabotage was so damaging, in fact, that the Germans had to divert SS units from the front to guard the rail system, day and night.

In early 1944 the guerrilla actions against the Nazis became so overwhelming in southern France that German commanders were reporting a general revolt, with German troops being surrounded by guerrilla bands for days at a time and killed off in locations that were isolated.

Prior to and during D-Day in June 1944, signals were sent out by SOE, calling for a general insurrection. Over a thousand rail lines were cut or destroyed, which resulted in German reinforcements not being able to reach the invading hordes of allied troops before they gained a foothold in France.

Guerrilla units on the Eastern Front were deadly in their fight against the Germans. They did not generally operate in harmony with conventional operations, but acted on their own, striking as often as possible. Unlike guerrilla bands on the Western Front, however, the Soviets were not prone to arm and supply the partisans on the Eastern Front because of a fear of peasants being armed, and eventually turning on the Soviets. Even with that in mind, the Soviets were eventually forced to form and supply partisan guerrilla bands.

The European Theater of Operations (ETO) was not the only theater to see effective guerrilla engagements. When Corregidor fell in early 1942 not all American-Filipino garrisons surrendered to the Japanese, opting instead to retreat into the jungles and mountains to continue the fight against the Japanese using guerrilla tactics.

The Cold War

Few people realize the long-term effects World War II has had on the world and Special Forces. One only needs to delve a little deeper than most people wish to. On 13 June 1942, a Presidential military order directed by President Franklin Roosevelt established the Office of Strategic Services (OSS). Its mission was to collect and analyze war-related intelligence, as well as conduct special operations against the enemy. When the war ended, the OSS was dissolved.

When Germany fell, and the Allies declared victory, the Soviet Union occupied Central and Eastern Europe, while the United States and Western allies occupied Western Europe. The Yalta Conference was held by allied nations in February 1945 to determine the fate of Germany.

Eventually German zones of occupation were delineated, with the eastern zone of Germany being assigned to the Soviet Union, and the remainder of Germany being split between the United States, Great Britain, and France. The same fate befell Berlin, which would eventually cause problems.

Tensions built between the Eastern Bloc (which included the Soviet Union and its satellite states) and the Western Bloc (the United States, Great Britain, and several other nations aligned with the U.S.). It became known as what we termed the "Cold War."

Although never resulting in armed warfare, both sides did, however, arm as if they intended to do battle. It became a nuclear build-up and showdown, each side trying to build the strongest nuclear arsenal. The thought was: the stronger and scarier the arsenal, the better to discourage the other side from attacking. It was a doctrine known as "mutually assured destruction" (MAD), and went by the theory that each side was strong enough to annihilate the attacker. Nuclear dominance was sought by both sides. In the U.S. it was normal to have air raid sirens blaring as tests, and frequent "duck and cover" drills in schools for fear of "The Big One" being dropped.

After World War II, in 1945, the OSS was disbanded (by President Harry S. Truman, at the insistence of the Army, Navy, and FBI), as were the Rangers. That left the military with virtually no unconventional warfare unit to call on if needed. In the late '40s and '50s the mindset about Europe focused on "when" the Russians would invade the non-communist countries of the continent, not "if" the would invade. Some military men felt that when that happened, the U.S. should have an unconventional unit to lead a guerrilla army against the Russians in their rear areas.

In 1947, tired of Soviet-backed communist insurgencies, the U.S. government adopted a mission of containment to stop the spread of Communism. In June the Marshall Plan was enacted, pledging economic assistance to European countries willing to participate in economic rebuilding. In September 1947 the CIA was formed, but it wasn't authorized to act completely clandestinely until 1949.

In early 1948, Western European nations and the U.S. declared the western German zones to be merged into a federal government system and re-industrialized the country. Shortly after that, the Soviets announced the formation of the Berlin Blockade, beginning 24 June 1948. The purpose of the blockade was to stop food, materials, and supplies from reaching West Berlin. The response was a massive "Berlin Airlift," carried out by numerous allied countries. On 12 May the following year, the Soviets gave in and lifted the blockade.

On 25 June 1950, tens of thousands of North Korean troops, supported by Red China, invaded South Korea. The horde was unstoppable. Thousands of North Korean guerrillas got behind allied lines and created havoc.

It was widely thought that allied guerrilla forces could do the same to North Korea, but there was no such unit. A quick reaction was to form the United Nations Partisan Infantry Korea and several smaller guerrilla units, United Nations Partisan Forces, Korea. They hadn't had much training, so they weren't as effective as they could have been. Also, in 1950, the U.S. Army developed the Psychological Warfare (PSYWAR) Division of the Army General School, in Fort Riley, Kansas.

The political climate changed in the United States and the Soviet Union in 1953. Newly elected President Eisenhower was inaugurated in the U.S., and Nikita Khrushchev became the Soviet leader following the death of Joseph Stalin. In November 1956 Khrushchev was reported as saying, "Whether you like it or not, history is on our side. We will bury you." That caused a stir in world opinion.

Secretary of State John Foster Dulles recommended relying on nuclear weapons for protection against our enemies. He also called for "massive retaliation" against Soviet aggression.

Enter Special Forces, based loosely on the old OSS. Special Forces was formed in June 1952, becoming officially known as the 10th Special Forces Group.

The Creation

And the Lord spake forth unto the heavens and said, "Let there be Airborne." The earth then did tremble and quake and the waters did rise up and the clouds did part and there came forth a multitude of parachutes that filled the sky. God looked down and saw that this was good—and they were good—they were Airborne!

God then spake forth unto the land and said, "Let there be Rangers." And all at once the day turned to darkness and the winds did howl, mountains crumbled into the sea and the great rocks did part and there sprang forth a horde of Mephistopheles' disciples wearing Ranger tabs and carrying all sorts of deadly weapons. God looked down and saw that this was bad—and they were bad—they were Rangers!

Then God spake forth thrice — unto the sky, the earth and the sea — and said, "Let there be Special Forces." Lightning did flash and thunder echoed across the sky. Mountains spewed molten rock and rained fire unto the land. Tidal waves surged against the shore. Despair, disorder, and turmoil did prevail. Forthwith, there did appear a band of twelve extraordinary men. A few came from beneath the waves, others jumped from the sky and more still silently stalked from the dense forest. Each one was in camouflage battle dress wearing a Randall knife, star sapphire ring, Rolex watch and a green beret. Working together they brought peace unto the land. God looked down and saw that this was amazing—and they were amazing—they were Special Forces!

Beside himself, God now spake forth again and commanded, "Let all ye that are weak in mind and body arise and go forth." And lo from the abyss they crawled forward with indecision and limped weakly upon the earth. God looked down and shook His head for this was pathetic—and they were pathetic—they were legs!

The Birth of Special Forces

There were bitter battles with the Pentagon (which never really ended) over the concept of forming Special Forces, as a special operations unit. The generals, who thought only in terms of conventional warfare, wanted nothing to do with unconventional military units.

The birth of Special Forces came about on Ft. Bragg, North Carolina's Smoke Bomb Hill in 1952, brought about by Colonel Aaron Bank, who became known as the father of Special Forces. Colonel Bank had been an "operator" for the OSS behind German lines in France.

Officially, the lineage of Special Forces is traced to the OSS and the U.S. Army Rangers of World War II. SF was fashioned, in part, from the OSS concept. The 1st Special Service Force was also considered to be a Special Forces antecedent. It was a joint U.S.-Canadian combat force organized during World War II, with a mission of conducting raids and strikes on the enemy. The force was nicknamed "The Devil's Brigade," and made a name for itself running very successful operations in the Aleutians (Alaska), North Africa, Italy, and southern France. It was deactivated near the end of the war.

In his memoirs, *From the OSS to Green Berets: The Birth of Special Forces*, Colonel Bank wrote that traditional conventional soldiers considered unconventional warfare to be "something slimy, underhanded, illegal, and ungentlemanly. It did not fit in the honor code of their profession of arms." As if the enemy was going to play fair. Despite their complaints, a plan was approved for the Psychological Warfare (PSYWAR) Division school to move to Smoke Bomb Hill, at Fort Bragg, NC, on 14 April 1952. The unit was renamed the Psychological Warfare Center. PSYWAR at Fort Bragg initially consisted of the 6th Radio Broadcasting and Leaflet Group with the 10th Special Forces Group (Airborne) added to it. The center also consisted of the PSYWAR School, PSYWAR Operations Department, and Special Forces (SF) Department.

The mission of the unprecedented Psychological Warfare Center, according to the center's Table of Distribution (TD), was "to conduct individual training in Psychological Warfare and Special Forces Operations; to develop and test Psychological Warfare and Special

Forces doctrine, procedures, tactics, and techniques; and to test and evaluate equipment employed in Psychological Warfare and Special Forces Operations."

On 19 June, seven men (five private E-2s and a warrant officer led by Colonel Aaron Bank) officially activated the 10th Special Forces Group (Airborne) at Ft. Bragg, NC, loosely based on the Special Operations branch of the OSS. Its mission was to wage unconventional warfare. Most military commanders were bitterly against the idea.

The 10th was the first Special Forces unit, beginning a storied history of accomplishments and heroism worldwide. Within nine months, the unit numbered 1,000 hand-picked men. Many of the men assigned to the new hush-hush unit were Ranger and OSS combat veterans, as well as Lodge Act soldiers, so long as they could pass a security check.

The 1950 Lodge Act gave displaced foreigners from World War II the opportunity to enlist in the U.S. military and, after serving five years, be considered for American citizenship. It didn't guarantee citizenship but did expedite the citizenship process. The premise was that those personnel from countries now situated behind Russia's "Iron Curtain" would have the needed expertise of the area if American forces were ever to become involved in a conflict with Russia and needed to send troops behind Russian lines. At the time, the European theater being the theater in which trouble was expected, plans called for the new Special Forces to recruit partisans in Eastern Europe and conduct guerrilla warfare, during a war with the Soviet Union.

Work progressed on a training program for the new unit. An eight-week training program of instruction was devised, with priority given to teaching the Unconventional Warfare (UW) mission now assigned to the 10th SFG. Subjects included guerrilla warfare, escape and evasion, and subversion of a hostile state. Only one Army Field Manual of those subjects existed, at the time, that being FM 31-21, *Organization and Conduct of Guerrilla Warfare.*

The original mission of Special Forces was to wage unconventional warfare, trained to infiltrate behind enemy lines, during either a conventional or nuclear war scenario. In the beginning unconventional warfare was defined as warfare well behind enemy lines, as was done by the French Resistance during World War II. Special Forces teams were to infiltrate enemy lines by air, sea or land and organize guerilla units using the local populace.

The original mission envisioned a Soviet invasion of allied countries in Europe, during which Special Forces personnel would infiltrate into Eastern Europe, forming partisan forces to fight the enemy behind their lines. Before long, the mission would be expanded. SF personnel were trained to live and work with indigenous civilian forces of other countries. They were to organize, train, supply, and advise these units, leading them in raids on enemy forces and supply lines behind enemy lines. Those guerrilla units could reduce the need for more allied regular troops and raise havoc with the enemy at the same time.

Special Forces troops were force multipliers, experts able to do great harm to the enemy by using a minimum of manpower. Although both units were the cream of the Army crop, and Rangers are part of Special Forces lineage, Special Forces and Rangers had one major difference: Rangers were expected to accomplish their assigned mission, no matter the cost in lives. Special Forces, on the other hand, were trained to accomplish their mission with little or no loss of life. We were deemed too valuable to be blown away.

Because of its mission, Special Forces was designed to be self-sufficient, whether linked with a foreign/indigenous force or used as a stand-alone unit. SF troops were expected to be able to be deployed over long periods of time. Because of that, learning the language of the country in which it operated, as well as learning as much as possible about the country into which they would be infiltrated, was required.

The basic tenet of Special Forces doctrine was that Special Forces teams would live with, fight with, work with, and die with the indigenous personnel they were assigned to train, assist, and advise. Because the field manual relied heavily on the experience of Army officers in the Pacific during World War II, classified documents from the OSS experience were in high demand, as were personal experiences from OSS personnel, and OSS lesson plans and After-Action Reports (AARs).

Colonel Bank was insistent that the unit be manned by volunteers only (no draftees), that all of them would be paratroopers, and that the volunteers also be on at least their second enlistment, thus assuring that they were experienced soldiers. That was mainly due to draftees only serving two years, counting down the hours until they were discharged. By April 1953, the group numbered 1,700 officers and enlisted personnel.

The first formal Special Forces course began on 10 November 1952, attended by 51 officers and 52 enlisted men. That first class, #1-53, graduated on 17 January 1953. The following class, #2-53, graduated on 31 March 1953. Special Forces was on a roll.

The unit attracted most of the Army hardcore "weirdoes" who hated playing by the rules of the conventional military units. Those nonconformists got their chances to get back at conventional units. The SF unit was often utilized as adversaries during war games, acting as "guerrilla" units. They used every ruse and disguise possible to infiltrate the conventional units, often "capturing" or "killing" the unit's general. That, of course, managed to turn conventional officers against Special Forces even more, but it sure was fantastically enjoyable.

Being that the 82nd Airborne Division was stationed at Ft. Bragg, it received most of the abuse from SF. From its inception, Special Forces was seen by conventional high-ranking officers as manned by unconventional, undisciplined, irresponsible, nonconformist rabble who didn't fit in with Army rules of conduct and regulations; square pegs who couldn't fit into the round holes the Army wanted them to live in. That belief holds true to this day, I'm proud to say. I'm also very proud to admit that I was a part of that group of men. Special Forces men believed then, and still do, that accomplishing the mission was much more important than how it was accomplished.

Special Forces soldiers hated uniformity and regulations, and outwardly proved that fact on a regular basis. When conventional units went to the field for a training exercise, they were told what equipment and which uniforms they were to include in their gear, and what they would wear while in the field. In Special Forces, before going to the field, we were given an Area Study, to familiarize us with what to expect, and how we might want to dress.

We took the equipment we as individuals thought we would be utilizing, and packed the clothing, military uniform and civilian clothes we thought would be apropos for the mission at hand. Sometimes the clothing included no military uniform, just civilian clothes, especially if we were to be acting as unconventional guerrilla personnel, which was often the case. We could be seen wearing just about anything in the field, including a mix of military and civilian clothing, or just civilian clothes. Conventional commanders would have had conniption fits had they seen our attire. In fact, when they did see our attire, they became livid, confirming to them that we were all misfits, not worthy of being called U.S. Army soldiers.

As originally designed, Special Forces was organized around A-Teams (FA Teams, aka Field A-teams), initially manned by two officers and fifteen enlisted men (the team nomenclature called for non-commissioned officer [NCO] enlisted men). Not long after inception, the amount of enlisted men was reduced to thirteen. The highest command within Special Forces was the Special Forces Group Headquarters.

The operational detachments consisted of A-teams at the lowest level, followed by B-teams (FB teams) and C-teams (FC teams). The B-team was organized to control two or more A-teams and their guerrilla forces. The C-team was, in turn, organized to control up to three B-teams, operating within a theater of operations. The A-teams eventually would become manned by twelve men, two officers and ten NCOs.

The unit was so secret that even most career officers knew nothing of it. At first, men came to Special Forces because of recommendations and trust. Then, as has been the case forever, the men had to be enlistees to be in the group. No draftees were allowed, unless the draftee voluntarily extended his service time to that of an enlistee.

The wearing of the green beret (although not authorized) began by Special Forces personnel from the onset. The wearing of the beret in Special Forces has so many stories attached to it, that it would be impossible to trace the true history of the "Green Beret," but I will do my best here. As Special Forces grew, the covertness of the unit disappeared, and the best of men wanted to be associated with the unit. As it became better known, most regular Army commanders considered Special Forces to be an unwanted, unneeded, hair-brained idea.

A second Special Forces group was activated at Ft. Bragg on 25 September 1953, designated the 77th Special Forces Group (Airborne). On 11 November, the 10th SFG was ordered to relocate to Bad Tolz, Germany. Shortly after, in December, they made the move. The 10th Group's area of responsibility was Europe, while the 77th Group (later renamed the 7th Special Forces Group) was responsible for the remainder of the world.

In 1954 the Viet Minh (Communist Vietnamese) began spreading Communist propaganda and fomenting opposition to the South Vietnamese government. That same year U.S. Military Assistance Advisory Group (MAAG), Vietnam, sent advisors to South Vietnam.

The idea about wearing distinctive headgear, mainly berets, began in the 10th Group in 1954. In fact, the CO of the 10th, Colonel William Ekman, approved the wearing of the beret by his troops that year. The idea caught on in the 77th. The first berets in the 77th, teal-blue with gold piping around the sweatband, were loudly complained about. The idea was put forth that a rifle green beret be worn. The only such berets that could be found were berets that looked like Girl Scout headwear complete with the half-inch long pigtail on top.

Despite the men suspecting the berets might actually be Girl Scout berets, they proceeded to cut off the pigtail and wear the new berets, which the PX began selling. Although berets were not usually worn by people in the U.S., the men probably figured nobody was going to take the chance of poking fun at them for wearing the beret.

The first time the berets were worn at an official event, the comments began, questioning who the foreign troops were. From then on, the men considered their berets to be their image. That began the "Battle of the Green Beret." Higher headquarters demanded to know who authorized the wearing of the berets and voiced their opposition to the new headgear. The conventional Army brass considered the wearing of the beret to be elitist.

The Army always had problems with any personnel or units considering themselves to be "elite," or even acting in such a fashion. The conventional brass also considered those men to be oddballs and nonconformists who hated regulations. To countermand the opposition, Colonel Edson F. Raff II, the new commander of the U.S. Army Psychological Warfare Center (home of the 77th Group), declared the berets as troop-test items, thus qualified to be worn.

Post command first banned the wearing of the beret off post, then declared it could only be worn in the field. In the meantime, members of the 10th SFG continued wearing them in Germany, where there was no higher-up opposition to speak of. A Canadian company was found that could supply real military berets, so they were imported and sold by the local chapter of the Airborne Association.

The 82nd Airborne Division saw the berets and decided they wanted berets. They requested Department of the Army (DA) approve red berets for their troops. When DA disapproved the request, the 82nd complained that SF was wearing green berets. DA ordered the 77th SFG to quit wearing the beret.

Over in Vietnam, the U.S. Military Assistance Advisory Group, Vietnam (MAAG) numbered 342 personnel in July of 1954. In October, President Dwight D. Eisenhower made a promise to the government of South Vietnam, led by Premier Ngo Dinh Diem, that the U.S. would send direct aid.

In July 1955 the Peoples Republic of China announced they would aid the Viet Minh, and the Soviet Union announced they would do the same for North Vietnam. In October Premier Diem proclaimed South Vietnam to be a republic, with Diem as President.

The first Special Forces reserve unit was formed on 31 March 1955 at Fayetteville, NC. It was designated Special Forces Operational Detachment 300 and was assigned to the Third Army. It trained with the 77th Special Forces. The following year the PSYWAR Center was enlarged and renamed the U.S. Army Center for Special Warfare/U.S. Army Special Warfare School. The school's mission was to develop the doctrine, techniques, training and education of Special Forces and PsyOps personnel.

The dispute over the wearing of the beret came to a head in 1956. The Commanding General of XVIII Airborne Corps, LTG Paul D. Adams, relieved the Commanding Officer, Psychological Warfare Center and School, in April because of Special Forces soldiers wearing the green beret. LTG Adams permanently outlawed the wearing of the green beret, although the men still wore them during off-post training.

LTG Adams firmly believed that nobody could be any more elite than paratroopers. His successor, MG Robert F. Sink, wrote a communication to LTG P. Hickey, Commanding General Third Army, in 1957 stating, "I do not consider wear of a beret by U.S. soldiers to be in keeping with the American tradition, and its inclusion would give our uniform a foreign accent."

As the Cold War heated up, and belief spread that the Soviet Union and its Warsaw Pact allies were poised to attack Western Europe, it was believed that NATO defenses were powerless to stop the Soviet hordes. The U.S. military came up with a plan to at least blunt the attack.

In 1956, plans went forward to form a top secret clandestine Special Forces detachment, to be stationed in Berlin. It was designed to be a modified company-sized unit, containing six Special Forces "A" Detachments. Special men were recruited to serve in the unit. Men who spoke German, or at least an Eastern European language, were especially sought. The men were not to let anyone know they were SF or assigned to an SF unit, or that such a unit even existed.

The unit was sent to Berlin, in small groups of three to four men, in July 1956. Each man had their own cover, for what their purpose of being in Berlin was. Over time, a lot of the men began looking like locals, dressing and grooming themselves as Berliners. The unit was there to "support the Berlin Brigade" and was attached to headquarters, 6th Infantry Regiment, as the "Security Platoon." The teams specialized in unconventional warfare, intelligence tradecraft, and counterterrorism.

If Soviet forces invaded, about fifty A-teams of the 10th Group in Germany were to stay behind, or infiltrate behind enemy lines to conduct UW operations. The teams from Berlin would conduct operations against infrastructure in the Berlin area, before infiltrating behind enemy lines, and conducting UW operations. Berlin teams were also trained on the SADM "backpack nuke" described later in the book. The nukes were to be detonated where they were deemed to be of most use.

The unit went by many names. It began as "Security Platoon," renamed in 1958 as "Detachment A," and finally "Physical Security Support Element." Officially, the team's classified descriptions were 39th Special Forces Detachment in 1963 and 410th Special Forces Detachment in 1984. The unit wasn't disbanded until 1990, 34 years after its inception. During that time, it had a distinguished, although mostly unheard of, history.

The 77th Special Forces Group handpicked sixteen men (three officers and thirteen NCOs) to form the 14th Special Forces Operational Detachment. In June 1956 the detachment was sent to Hawaii. They stayed busy running missions to Thailand, Taiwan, Laos, and Vietnam. Shortly after that another detachment, the 8231 Army Special Operations Detachment (five officers and seventeen NCOs) was formed in Ft. Bragg and sent to Japan.

In June 1957 both detachments were moved to Okinawa, where they became the nucleus of the 1st Special Forces Group (Airborne), which was activated on 24 June, and was augmented by personnel from the 77th SFG being assigned to the 1st SFG. The unit was assigned the responsibility of being the primary unconventional warfare unit for the Pacific region, especially Southeast Asia.

That same month the 14th Special Forces Detachment, from the 1st Special Forces Group, went to Vietnam to train 85 Vietnamese Army troops of the counterespionage 1st Observation Group, at the Commando Training Center in Nha Trang. Three years later, those same Vietnamese troops would become the nucleus for the Vietnamese Special Forces (Luc Luong Dac Biet, aka LLDB, officially designated as the 77th LLDB Group).

U.S. Army Special Forces was uniquely qualified for the mission. They were combat-oriented, able to perform in the field relatively independently, experts in the field of guerrilla operations, and extremely capable of working with indigenous personnel. On 21 October 1957, CPT Harry G. Cramer of the 1st Special Forces Group became the first

SF soldier killed in the Republic of Vietnam.

First Sergeant John Hollis of the 77th Special Forces Group Rigger Detachment became the first man to make a military freefall HALO parachute jump on St. Patrick's Day of 1958, thus beginning a long history of HALO operations and training in Special Forces.

The following year Special Forces sent a B Detachment sized unit to Laos, disguised as civilians, and known in small circles as Operation White Star, to aid and assist Special Guerrilla Units of the Forces Armée Laotienne.

No military uniforms were worn by the Americans. They spent the least possible time in combat areas, limiting the dangers of casualties and the resulting uproar that would cause. Finding and recognizing the Pathet Lao enemy was difficult.

The opposite was true for the Pathet Lao knowing the location of the allied Laotian troops and their American advisors. The enemy was blessed with excellent intelligence. Of help to the enemy intelligence effort was the fact that the Laotian units were riddled with Pathet Lao infiltrator spies, able to keep the Pathet Lao abreast of every move the allies made.

Even the exact location of important structures within Laotian camps was known by the Pathet Lao. Infiltrated Pathet Lao made maps of the camps by the simple method of pacing off distances throughout the camp and recording those distances.

The same would happen in later years in Vietnam. Viet Cong infiltrators (hired as CIDG troops or camp laborers) were able to make exact maps of allied camps. Those maps acted as tour guides during an assault on allied camps and military installations. The 77th SFG also sent a C Detachment to work with the Laotian Forces Armée Royale (FAR). By summer, SF personnel strength in Laos had reached 107.

In 1959, and especially 1960, the Viet Cong (short for Vietnamese Communists) increased in size and combat activity, spreading throughout South Vietnam's countryside, as well as terrorizing the Vietnamese population.

More Special Forces advisors were sent to Vietnam, from the 1st SFG and from Ft. Bragg, NC. In May of 1960, the 7th Special Forces

Group sent a small contingent to South Vietnam to teach Vietnamese counterinsurgency tactics at the South Vietnamese Ranger training centers.

In 1959 a takeover of Laos by North Vietnam was a very real fear, with the communist Pathet Lao being directed and supplied by the Viet Minh. The U.S. wanted to strengthen Laotian forces, so they would be able to defeat the Viet Minh and Pathet Lao attempted takeover of Laos.

Special Forces teams were sent to Laos. Their mission was to train the disorganized remains of the Forces Armée Laotienne (FAL). Because the 1954 Geneva Accord granted Laos its independence and forbade overt military intervention or assistance, the mission was classified as an "aid" program. The U.S. was barred from having military troops in Laos, although it was not barred from funding the Laotian army. The CIA managed to get around the military troop stipulation by arranging for the Special Forces teams to be designated "civilian contractors," uniformed in civilian clothes.

White Star continued until 1961, with individual teams being sent to Laos on TDY (temporary duty) missions. Eventually the mission was altered to train local Kao and Meo (aka Hmong) tribesmen. The Special Forces mission teams were finally in their sphere of expertise, teaching guerrilla warfare and intelligence gathering to the indigenous tribesmen. During that time the U.S. Army Special Forces Reserve was reorganizing, spreading SF Reserve detachments throughout the U.S.

"It is clear that war is not a mere act of policy but a true political instrument, a continuation of political activity by other means." — From a translated version of "On War" from 1976

In the early 1960s communists around the world began "Wars of Liberation," mostly in the underdeveloped areas of Africa, Latin America, and Asia. Americans classified them as insurgencies. It grew to epidemic proportions. Most of the insurgencies were basically indigenous, caused by deep dissatisfaction with the government in power, and were sponsored or supported by the Communists.

On 6 January 1961, Khrushchev announced that the Soviet Union would support "just wars of liberation and popular uprisings." That led the United States to study ways to counter Communist supported insurgencies. The Communists made selective use of terrorism, knowing it looked as if the sitting government was unable to govern and protect its people.

From April 1960 to April 1961 (one year) the Viet Cong assassinated about 4,000 minor officials of the Diem government. That included village and hamlet chiefs, schoolteachers, and health officers. And that was the "quiet" era of the Vietnam conflict. Armed clashes between Vietnamese army units and Viet Cong increased from 180 in January 1960 to an alarming 545 in September.

The first Special Forces team to serve in the Republic of South Vietnam was from the 77th SFG, going over in 1960. On 6 June the 77th was re-designated the 7th Special Forces Group (Airborne). Special Forces then began a surge, with groups sprouting up and Special Forces actively recruiting new men for those units. The 5th SFG (Abn) Training Detachment was activated at Nha Trang in 1960.

In 1960, the Special Warfare School's mission expanded to teach counterinsurgency operations. That same year about four hundred graduates came out of the Special Warfare School. That number increased quickly in the years to come, as Special Forces began being assigned more overseas missions in allied countries, and the communist threat became real.

In February 1961, nine more SF teams were deployed to Laos. On 9 March, President Kennedy announced an expanded American role in Laos, authorizing Mobile Training Teams (MTTs) to be sent to that country. The 1st and 7th SFGs supplied the teams.

On 22 April, Captain Walter Moon's four-man Field Training Team (FTT-59) from the 7th Group, was advising the 6th Battalion d'infanterie (Lao). They came under heavy artillery fire and became outflanked. The Laotian troops ran, and the position was quickly overrun by the Pathet Lao. CPT Walter Moon was captured, attempted to escape a couple times, but was badly wounded the last time he tried. He was then tortured and eventually executed on 22 July.

SFC John Bischoff (Medic) and SGT Gerald Biber (Radio

Operator) were killed while attempting a breakout. SGT Orville Ballinger (Demolition Sergeant) escaped but was captured a few days later. SGT Ballinger was released from captivity in August 1962.

By May, SF was actively involved in counterinsurgency operations against the Pathet Lao, who were controlling the Ho Chi Minh Trail within the borders of Laos. The trail was a vital lifeline for the North Vietnamese insurgency in the Republic of South Vietnam.

Although pushed by President Kennedy to form a military unit capable of fighting the newly emerging global unconventional guerilla style warfare, the Pentagon in its infinite stupidity and hardheadedness continued to believe in their reliance upon conventional warfare, leaving the United States bereft of units trained and equipped to fight a counter-guerilla warfare.

Special Forces existed at the time, but the Pentagon continuously fought supporting, and especially enlarging, the unit. The United States military, and the Pentagon in particular, had always looked with disfavor upon elite units of any kind, and just the words Special Warfare or Special Forces sent very negative vibes through the upper ranks. Elitism in the Army was thought to be the same as oddballs and reformers, at the bottom of the food chain.

General William Yarborough, the commanding general of Special Forces, was tasked to build Special Forces. He was authorized to get the men he needed from other conventional units. And that he did, making many enemies along the way, for him and for Special Forces. He "raided" the combat units for the best men he could find. Even at that, some of those men selected did not pass muster for Special Forces.

1961 was a banner year for Special Forces with a lot of reorganization. Brigadier General Yarborough assumed command of the U.S. Army Special Warfare Center. He was to become a driving factor in the acceptance and growth of Special Forces. The 7th SFG continued dispatching B Detachments to Laos, as part of the White Star MTT mission, control of which had been transferred to the Military Assistance and Advisory Group (MAAG) Laos.

During the year, the 2nd, 9th, 11th, 12th, 13th, 16th, 17th, 19th, 20th, 21st, and 24th Special Forces Groups (Airborne) were activated as U.S. Army Reserve units. They were not full-sized groups, but small, scattered detachments. Over the years those units were deactivated and reactivated with different numerical designations and locations, basically constantly changing.

That same year, the Command and General Staff College, in Fort Leavenworth, KS, began to study the responsibilities of the U.S. Army during the Cold War. Its primary focus was on the Communist Wars of Liberation. The study analyzed communist strategy and assessed Army capabilities, especially the resources available for resisting communist insurgencies. Each department of the military was tasked with presenting a list of units they felt was best for countering the insurgencies.

The U.S. Army named Special Forces as its best prepared unit for the task, at the time numbering about 2,000 highly trained combat specialists in the field of guerrilla operations. An assessment of the Vietnamese insurgency pointed to U.S. Army Special Forces as the best unit for that type of insurgency. SF was selected because it was combat-oriented, independent of other units, and well trained for guerrilla warfare. The fact that they were also considered to be knowledgeable in the field of working with foreign units and dignitaries was a major asset.

On 21 September President John F. Kennedy announced the U.S. intention of providing additional military and economic aid to Vietnam. On that same day, the 5th Special Forces Group (Airborne) was activated in Ft. Bragg, NC. Special Forces teams were assigned missions of not only training but giving advisory assistance to South Vietnam's minority groups, to form them into paramilitary forces which became known as Civilian Irregular Defense Groups (CIDG).

Special Forces became a favorite of President Kennedy. President Kennedy incurred the disfavor of the Pentagon brass and other conventional unit commanders when he authorized the wearing of the green beret by Special Forces units, actually dispatching a telegram "ordering" that SF be authorized to begin wearing the green beret with their uniforms.

President Kennedy visited the Special Warfare Center on 12

October 1961. Special Forces marched past the reviewing stand, wearing the green beret that they had fought so hard for. Special Forces troopers then put on a demonstration of their capabilities, all wearing their green berets. Prior to that authorization, Special Forces personnel had been wearing the beret in the field, but not at official functions.

Later that day, President Kennedy sent a message to General Yarborough stating, in part: "My congratulations to you personally for your part in the presentation today.... The challenge of this old but new form of operation is a real one and I know that you and the members of your command will carry on for us and the free world in a manner which is both worthy and inspiring. I am sure that the green beret will be a mark of distinction in the trying times ahead."

How prophetic Kennedy's statement would become! The Army finally officially authorized the green beret for wear by Special Forces on 10 December. In a message to the Army on 11 April 1962, President Kennedy described the green beret as "a symbol of excellence, a badge of courage." Most regular Army commanders disliked Special Forces and despised the beret. It was a great victory for all Special Forces personnel.

The beret sucks as far as headgear goes. As proud as we were of wearing the beret, it was an impracticable headgear. It didn't shade the eyes from the sun, it got wet very easily and took forever to dry out, it didn't protect much of the head in the winter, and it was hot and uncomfortable to wear in the summer, making the head sweat. It had an air hole on the side of it but leave it to us Americans to fold the beret to the right side, over the right ear and the air hole, which was on the right side. You would think that cooler heads would prevail (pun intended) and request the air hole be moved to the left side, but that never happened. It's not like the air hole was a large, unsightly hole. Oh well! The beret was also very uncomfortable to wear.

Even personnel of other units disliked our berets. One time, when a couple of us were in Washington D.C. on pass, a group of Marines just out of boot camp taunted us from the other side of the street, calling us girl scouts. As was the tradition of Special Forces (when we were sober, at least), we let the comments slide.

There were a few things the beret was good for. It impressed the women and was great for starting fights. Also, when the urge hit while on a bumpy airplane ride, it made a great barf bag. After all the headaches of finally getting authorization to wear the beret, you hardly ever saw it worn during military operations. That is, unless a journalist asked for you to put it on for a photo shoot. After all, who's to know you were a Green Beret unless you wore one?

Special Forces numbered about 2,000 highly trained combat specialists in 1961. Throughout the year, Viet Cong activity had increased at an alarming rate. South Vietnamese units were being pressured, some beyond their limits. Afraid that Montagnard tribal groups might jump ship and support the Viet Cong, the U.S. Mission in Saigon sponsored several programs designed to increase counterinsurgency efforts in late 1961.

"Montagnards" was the term used for more than a hundred minority Vietnamese, most of whom resided in the highlands areas of South Vietnam. Those tribes shared a desire to be left alone in their scattered villages. Because the Vietnamese treated them as "subhuman," the Montagnards hated Vietnamese.

The U.S. Central Intelligence Agency (CIA) worked on plans to include minority groups, tribal and religious, in the fight against the communist insurgency. The efforts centered on paramilitary minority groups, eventually becoming known as the Civilian Irregular Defense Group (CIDG) program. That became the primary mission of Special Forces in Vietnam, mainly because of the history of Special Forces being capable of understanding their culture, and living within their primitive society, no matter the adversities.

The original targets of the program were the Montagnard tribes of the Central Highlands but grew to a nationwide effort over the years. The years 1961-1965 were learning years for Special Forces in Vietnam. Because that was not the mission for which SF was originally trained, there were some let's-try-this-and-see-how-it-works decisions made. If it worked, it was accepted as new policy, if it didn't, it was scrapped. New how-to pamphlets came out as lessons learned became policy.

It certainly became clear that our mission had changed since that foreseen when SF was formed in the 1950s. Instead of fighting a guerrilla warfare in enemy territory, we were fighting a counter-guerrilla war in "friendly" territory. Not that any of the Vietnamese countryside was really "friendly territory." In fact, enemy-controlled area was basically the countryside of South Vietnam, especially during the hours of darkness.

In October 1961, meetings were begun with Rhade leaders in the Central Highlands. The meetings went well, resulting in Special Forces being authorized to form a village defense system. The first Special Forces "camp" was established in Buon Enao, near Ban Me Thuot, as an experiment. The camp was the first of what would become many future camps, in which Special Forces played a significant advisory role. The Special Forces personnel at Buon Enao were assigned on a temporary basis (TDY).

The program was originally organized with area development in mind, to provide an area in which the indigenous population could be safe from Viet Cong influence and terrorism and could develop their own self-defense and security force program in local villages, similar to a successful program in Malaya by the British in years past. The program, known as the Village Defense Program, was organized for defensive purposes, not to hunt the enemy. The program was completed by mid-December. Darlac's province chief decided to expand the program, leading to forty more Rhade villages joining the project.

Many of the early programs originated with the Montagnard tribes of the Central Highlands, where local indigenous personnel were trained in the basic rudiments of warfare, with the ultimate hope that they could be a paramilitary force to be reckoned with.

Vietnamese government forces and officials were almost non-existent in the area, pretty much because the Montagnards considered them to be almost as much of an enemy as the VC. Much of that feeling was due to the discrimination the Montagnards endured from the Vietnamese. The Special Forces troops, on the other hand, were trusted by the mountain people. For once the Montagnards had the feeling that they were being treated with respect.

In the Spring of 1962, the program was designated as the Civilian

Irregular Defense Group (CIDG). CIDG troops were Vietnamese civilian soldiers, made up of local indigenous personnel employed by the U.S. Army Special Forces, not the Vietnamese government.

In 1962, the Special Warfare Center established the Special Forces Training Group (Provisional), to train enlisted volunteers for assignments to SF groups. The Advanced Training Committee was formed to explore and develop methods of infiltration and exfiltration.

In February 1962 GEN Paul D. Harkins took command of the newly-organized Military Assistance Command, Vietnam (MACV), formerly known as Military Assistance Advisory Group, Vietnam (MAAG). One of the staff positions was held by COL George C, Morton, commanding the Special Warfare Section.

On 23 July, the U.S. Department of Defense (DoD) ordered the CIA to turn over responsibility for the CIDG program to MACV in September 1962, of U.S. Army Special Forces Vietnam (Provisional), which would act in an advisory capacity. DoD retained the power to designate the SF commander.

Commanded by COL George Morton, USASF Vietnam consisted of a Headquarters and Headquarters (Hq & Hq) Company, a C Detachment permanently assigned from the 5th SFG in Bragg, four B Detachments on temporary duty (TDY) from the 1st and 5th SFGs, and 36 TDY A Detachments from the 1st, 5th, and 7th SFGs (six-month tours). This whole restructuring was named Operation Switchback. The entire operation was finally completed on 1 July 1963.

On 4 April, the Viet Cong overran a Vietnamese Republican Youth patrol base, capturing four Special Forces advisors, killing two and eventually releasing the other two. Specialist 5th Class James Gabriel, Jr. was one of the killed SF men. The Special Warfare Center's Area 2 Demonstration would later be renamed in his honor, known as the Gabriel Demonstration Area.

In June, the CIA instructed Special Forces to initiate a Trailwatcher program, designed to do reconnaissance of the border areas. By August, Special Forces numbered 21 teams, with five A-teams overseeing 60,000 natives from more than 200 villages. The other sixteen teams were in Vietnamese training and area-development centers. By September,

26 Special Forces A-teams were scattered throughout South Vietnam, controlled by three B-Teams.

Because of the spate of communist inspired and supported rebel activity in Central and South America, some elements of the 7th SFG, including Hq & Hq Company, were transferred to Fort Gulick, Canal Zone, Panama, in May 1962, to eventually become the 8th Special Action Force, Latin America (SAF).

The move to Panama was followed in August 1962 by the main body of Company D arriving, to become the nucleus for the 8th Special Forces Group (Airborne). The unit was re-designated and activated as the 8th Special Forces Group (Airborne), Special Action Force, Latin America on 1 April 1963. The mission of the 8th Special Forces Group was to give counter-insurgency training to allied Latin American countries.

A new Geneva Agreement was agreed to in 1962. It called for all foreign troops to leave Laos no later than 7 October 1962. All 666 American troops were removed, while 402 North Vietnamese troops were evacuated, leaving approximately 10,000 North Vietnamese troops in Laos.

By October 1962, about two hundred Rhade villages were included within the Village Defense Program's safety net. That success resulted in the chief being instructed by the Vietnamese government to include the Jarai and Mnong in the program. The success also resulted in more Special Forces action in South Vietnam, as more A-teams were sent TDY for six-month tours of duty.

"For to win one hundred victories in one hundred battles is not the acme of skill. To subdue the enemy without fighting is the acme of skill." — *Sun Tzu*

Special Forces and Its Personnel

Special Forces was trained not to react quickly to actions that could create trouble. There are times to be diplomatic and avoid a fight, while there are other times when fighting is required. Fighting of any kind should only be against the enemy, and then it is to the maximum extent, with extreme prejudice, meaning deadly.

COL Charles M. Simpson III, U.S. Army (Retired) wrote in his book *Inside the Green Berets, the First Thirty Years* that "retired SF men are an extremely peace-loving group with no desire for further combat.... Any group that comprises thousands of men who have been highly trained for violent combat can be expected to have a few bad apples. The SF is no exception, but the renegades are rare and atypical." Special Forces men understood the dangers of abuses that created enemies and alienated the indigenous population. That had been drilled into us in Special Forces Training Group Branch Training.

Conventional thinking always involved movement of troops, armor, artillery, and airpower in massive groups, with all parts of the equation under the protective umbrella of the others. Unconventional warfare, on the other hand, involved small, well trained, highly mobile units operating behind enemy lines, training and supporting small indigenous guerrilla forces, and conducting raids, reconnaissance, sabotage, and assassinations. The unconventional units were also great at harassing the enemy and using psychological warfare against them.

Helping the local indigenous population had to be a strong point for the small units, for self-preservation, if nothing else. SF units went on operations carrying *everything* we needed on our backs, usually with no armor or artillery support. For that reason, we packed our rucksacks very carefully, carrying no extraneous equipment. Sometimes our rucksacks weighed more than we did. Rucksacks were a part of our uniform in the field because they carried a lot more than Army-issue packs.

Because we had to carry everything we needed on our backs, even though we were effective warriors, we went into combat with only light weapons and light ammunition loads, keeping combat needs in mind. For that reason, Special Forces missions weren't expected to meet with heavy resistance. In fact, we usually tried to avoid head-on enemy contact, relying instead on stealth and outsmarting the enemy, and always keeping an escape route in mind.

One of the missions of Special Forces required us to walk a fine line. Friendly countries would request the services of Special Forces to help defuse uprisings. That put us into the counterinsurgency role.

The friendly governments weren't always perfect for the local populace but might be good enough for the U.S. to support them against an insurgency. When that occurred, the teams sent to help had to act with finesse and tact, backing the government and, at the same time, building rapport with the indigenous population. That required Special Forces men who had the maturity, judgment, and self-discipline to handle the problem with the utmost in professionalism.

Because Special Forces teams and men were expected to act in very small units and, sometimes, as individuals, not under the direct supervision of their chain of command, those men had to be able to make quick and thoughtful command decisions on their own. Most Special Forces missions were small, usually involving only very few (one to three) A-teams and a partial B-team for command and control purposes.

In the beginning, Special Forces managed to remain somewhat anonymous. Even Vietnam was basically a small operation to begin with. Then came Roger Donlon receiving the Medal of Honor for his valorous actions in Vietnam, Robin Moore's book *The Green Berets*, John Wayne starring in the movie version of Moore's book, SSG Barry Sadler's hit song *The Ballad of the Green Beret*, and escalation of the war and Special Forces involvement.

Wham! Special Forces came into the spotlight with a vengeance. It wasn't the fault of the Special Forces troopers. All we had done was to do our job the way we were expected (although many times more-so). We had not sought the publicity. We had become heroes to the public and, at the same time, despised by the rest of the military.

Then came Rambo! Rambo was a character with a bad case of post-traumatic stress disorder (PTSD) with a penchant for going out looking for trouble. Hollyweird never even came close to depicting a true Special Forces soldier. It was strange that they would characterize an American Special Forces "hero" as Rambo, and in the same breath characterize the British "hero" as suave and debonair James Bond.

Special Forces men were not macho, muscular men, nor did they always look tough. They also were not ruthless killing machines. There was no distinct or unique look in Special Forces. You weren't going to look at a Special Forces team and say, "those men look dangerous," although Special Forces A-teams were capable of death and destruction.

Special Forces looked for somewhat rugged men who could learn and master the critical skills needed on an A Detachment. The men had to be comfortable with being inserted into any location in the world, by any means, and be able to survive and work as a member of a small team, in a very hostile and harsh environment. They had to be reliable under the severest of pressures and be able to survive isolation. Those same men had to be independent thinkers, able to innovate with the few materials at hand.

If, by some small chance, a man had made it past the weeding out process of training, without being really motivated to be a good SF man, he didn't last very long. He would either quit or be transferred to a unit other than SF.

The men had to be capable of learning about the people in the region into which they were sent, as well as learning their language. And, of utmost importance, Special Forces soldiers had to be intelligent and tactful, understanding the ins and outs of working with indigenous personnel of highly varying intelligence and education.

If it were not for the fact that the word "politician" has become so nasty, I would characterize SF A-team personnel as warrior politicians. Green Berets were too valuable to be put in a situation of great risk. In fact, when behind enemy lines, unless on a mission to do so, they avoided the enemy, blending into the scenery when possible, to live another day.

Pete Blaber described Special Forces men very well in his book, *The Mission, the Men, and Me*. His book was about his time with Delta Force, as an operative and commander of the elite group. He described the Special Forces soldier as "a unique breed of cat, a breed that doesn't lend itself to any specific psychological profile." He also wrote that there was a "pattern of common individual traits such as mavericks, adventurers, and patriots; one or more of which are almost always present in the pedigree."

In the Army, the typical soldier was a single 18-year-old Private First Class (one stripe) with one year of army service under his belt, including training. The average Green Beret was a married 30-year-old Staff Sergeant (three stripes with one "rocker" underneath) with ten years of service time under his belt.

Paramount to Special Forces' success was team integrity. Although SF looked for men who were strong individualists, they also had to be capable of teamwork, fiercely loyal to one another, and their unit. A good description would be "one for all, and all for one."

When preparing for missions, besides language training, entire teams had to take in every available resource (classified and unclassified) to learn about the subject country, to include demographics, tribes, politics, religion, history, terrain, infrastructure, power grids, water supplies, agriculture, and economy. The teams were often isolated during pre-mission training, which was intense, and as realistic as possible. When possible, during pre-mission training, teams lived, ate, and worked as they expected to during their upcoming mission.

The teams trained as one and deployed as one, maintaining team integrity throughout. When returned from the mission, the pre-mission training was conducted in reverse. Teams were pumped for as much information as could be learned about the mission, the indigenous people, and the country in general. That was then used to train future teams going to that same location.

First hand "lessons learned" information was always considered to be extremely valuable for training teams for missions, and Special Forces became experts at utilizing this type of intelligence. To this day Special Forces teams use "lessons learned" from Special Forces activities in South Vietnam. Our problems with enemy sympathetic soldiers in camps in 'Nam were very comparable to the same problems encountered by Special Forces teams working with indigenous personnel in Iraq and Afghanistan during those conflicts.

Special Forces had a primary mission of unconventional warfare, consisting of half diplomacy and half combat. There was a common intelligence and work ethic. We were experts in our fields, expected to impart that knowledge to other individuals, including fellow teammates and foreign personnel who were our allies. Above all, we were instructors.

Secondly, we were advisers, followed by the uncommon instances where teams would act on their own. Special Forces was not a group of individuals, but of teammates. Teams had to be prepared to move out at a moment's notice — anytime, anywhere, anyhow. Even the method of transportation was flexible, anywhere from going in by submarine to skydiving into the target was possible. Because we practiced our trade discreetly, without fanfare, most people (including some of us) did not know about most of our exploits.

Special Forces consisted of teams, all of which acted as a cohesive group. Although time spent at Ft. Bragg many times meant different training and assignments for team individuals, when it came time for team training or pre-deployment training, the teams would get into the team mindset very quickly. That teamwork could be compared to a family.

The CO was an officer, but he was also part of the "family." Our teams were probably the most clannish units in the military. Conventional leadership courses in the Army taught that leaders should not get close to their men. That did not hold true in Special Forces. After all, while on a mission, the entire team lived together 24/7. There was no separate housing for officers as there was on a military base.

We treated our officers as equals, who were, however, our leaders. They often bore the brunt of teasing and practical jokes just as enlisted teammates did. Officers and enlisted NCOs also drank together. Unlike conventional units, the difference between officers and enlisted, especially NCOs, was blurred. In a conventional unit officers and enlisted men didn't dare intermingle. It was unheard of and against regulations. In SF it was a fact of life.

Teams lived for deployment. We didn't necessarily want to go some specific place; we just wanted to go somewhere. We wanted to be useful and busy with a goal in mind. We also preferred to be invisible. Many of our missions were classified. Even family could not be told where we were going.

The main reason a mission would become well known was usually due to someone leaking information or something going wrong. When we succeeded, with no outside leaks, nobody knew what we had done.

We were perfectly happy with that scenario.

Pre-deployment training was of paramount importance to Special Forces. The training was accomplished as a team, not as individuals. It covered everything from history of the country or area, to the spoken language. As much as possible, it was conducted by indigenous personnel from the location or experts in the field.

The subjects covered varied widely. Anything that could or would affect us was included in the training. That included the weather we were to expect during our deployment, the terrain, and the wild animals we would be dealing with. Nothing was left out. We would be living in our area of operation in a foreign environment. Knowledge and self-discipline were keys to our success, and our safety.

You rarely saw a Green Beret outwardly angry. We held our anger in, and became completely focused, planning our next move. Special Forces might not have physically been the toughest commandos in the United States military; Navy SEALS and Army Rangers were the trained door kickers and brute force units.

Special Forces was better at adapting to changing situations and could more effectively deal with indigenous forces consisting of far different cultures. That took patience, maturity, understanding, and being able to act as a diplomat. The diplomatic aspect was especially useful when dealing with indigenous personnel in a foreign country.

Because we were also teachers and advisers, we had to be able to gain the respect and trust of our students. Respect and trust couldn't be stressed any more than it was. Without popular support, all is lost. Especially in an insurgent environment, the good guys had to win over the locals.

Historically, and to this day, you can find Special Forces teams in every corner of the world, training and advising indigenous personnel in hundreds of countries, and winning over the hearts and minds of the locals.

Those teams were experts in helping the local indigenous personnel, whether they were soldiers or civilians, in all the little things that the common American soldier never cared about. That included well digging to obtain more water for the locals, and simple bridges to make accessibility better. We lived with those same indigenous people, paying attention to their needs, eating the same food, drinking the same drinks, and conversing with them in their own language. That was why the ability to learn languages was such an important part of the selection process for Special Forces.

In almost all cases, Special Forces units went through language training prior to deployment to a foreign nation. It was amazing how much respect could be gained from indigenous personnel and the local populace if they realized that you understand their language. LTG William P. Yarborough, U.S. Army (Retired) stated, "In the United States Army, the Green Berets were the first to be taught that concern for indigenous civilians is paramount for winning the war," and put it into practice as a principle of war. Our medics played a huge part in that scenario, treating those same indigenous people, soldiers, and civilians.

During a guerrilla warfare scenario, the medics were the people who kept the guerrillas in good health, treating illnesses and wounds, and keeping them in the fight. There were no hospitals to send guerrillas to, behind enemy lines, so the medics were their medical clinic physicians.

The Communist powers of the time (China, Cuba, and the USSR) had become experts in the field of guerrilla warfare and were trying to spread their system throughout the globe. Ripe for those insurgencies were Central America, Africa, and Southeast Asia. Special Forces was to see record deployment to those continents, attempting to stem the tide. Security of the missions was of prime importance. Even our wives didn't know where we were some of the time.

There were instances where we wore military clothing with no unit patch, nametag, or rank insignia. There were also times during which we wore only civilian clothing, sometimes without any form of ID, and with our names being dropped from the military roles. We didn't exist. In addition, there were occasions in which we were "assigned" to a fictitious unit. Some operations and missions were so secret, they weren't declassified for decades.

The intelligence required to be accepted into Special Forces was as high as to be an officer. We enlisted members always enjoyed kidding the officers about that. Special Forces units had a completely different makeup than did other military units.

To begin with, the men in Special Forces were highly specialized (while also being very well qualified in other than their own specialties) and extremely qualified (as well as experienced). Every man on a Special Forces A-team was a leader (no matter his rank) and had to use those leadership qualities on a regular basis. When training, the enlisted men instructed the officers, and vice versa.

Experience and expertise defined Special Forces. No other similarly sized military combat unit on the ground could claim the experience and military knowledge of an A-team. The lowest denominator in Special Forces was the A Detachment (also known as an A-team, now designated as an operational Detachment A, or ODA). The A-team was, and still is, the action unit of Special Forces.

The TO&E (Table of Organization & Equipment) of the A-team called for twelve men, consisting of (with recommended rank of individual) a Commanding Officer aka Team Leader (Captain), Executive Officer (First Lieutenant, in modern day a Warrant Officer), Operations Sergeant aka Team Sergeant (Master Sergeant), Intelligence Sergeant (Sergeant First Class), Heavy Weapons Leader (Sergeant First Class), Light Weapons Leader (Sergeant First Class), Radio Operator Supervisor (Staff Sergeant), Radio Operator (Sergeant), Demolition Sergeant (Staff Sergeant), Combat Demolition Specialist (Sergeant), Medical Specialist (Sergeant First Class) and Assistant Medical Specialist (Staff Sergeant).

A-teams could have more (or fewer) men and could operate as two separate mini teams. That, in fact, was the main reason for the duplication of job specializations and heavy reliance on cross-trained team personnel. Numerous were the occasions half A-teams were assigned to a location and job responsibility.

Some teams in Vietnam also operated with civil affairs and/or psychological operations specialists as team members. There were also teams that operated with two intelligence specialists on the team.

Officers often moved to other units to further their careers, while enlisted men of all ranks (including NCOs) usually remained in SF, gathering more experience. Because the team sergeant almost always had more experience and expertise than the officers, he was usually considered to be the real leader of the team. If the teams had been religions, the team sergeant would have been the god of that religion.

Among the varied techniques taught to Special Forces men in special courses were HALO and HAHO parachute operations and SCUBA operations. Both techniques were prime methods to be used by Special Forces when infiltrating into enemy territory. SCUBA was also taught with offensive missions, underwater reconnaissance, rescue, and recovery operations in mind. The SCUBA course was taught by the Special Warfare Center at Key West, Florida.

A-teams almost always had one or two men at a time undergoing specialized training. This included, but was not limited to, SCUBA, HALO, seaborne infiltration, Jungle Warfare School, mountain warfare, cold weather training, rappelling, Ranger School, jumpmaster school, atomic demolition training, Engineer NCO School, Operations and Intelligence School, espionage training, and Defense Language Institute (language training). There were, in addition, specialized training cycles that would include the entire team training together as a cohesive unit. Training was an ongoing ritual in Special Forces. Between deployments overseas (and within the continental United States) and training, we were gone from "home" a lot.

On top of having to learn their own jobs, Special Forces personnel had to learn how to teach these skills to others, usually foreign speaking personnel, as well as the jobs of their teammates. Special Forces personnel were not only operators, they were teachers as well, many times having to instruct while in a combat situation, under fire. For that reason alone, Special Forces soldiers had to be experts in their fields.

Special Forces was broken down into various units and sub-units. The main unit was known as 1st Special Forces and came under the command of the U.S. Army. The mission of Special Forces in 1962 was simple and direct; to develop, organize, equip, train, and direct indigenous forces in the conduct of guerrilla warfare. It was also tasked to advise, train, and assist indigenous forces in counterinsurgency operations.

Various Special Forces Groups were, and have been, formed to operate under the leadership of 1st Special Forces. The Group designations, as well as number of groups, has varied over the year, depending upon need. Although the basic premise of Special Forces was the Special Forces A Detachment, there was, and is, much more to Special Forces than just 12-man A-teams.

Each Group had its own assigned Area of Operation (AO), usually specified by continent. Each Special Forces Group was capable of (1) deploying their operational detachments (teams) by air, sea, or land when provided with transportation; (2) organizing, training, and directing guerrilla units; (3) controlling, by long-range communications, the operations of unconventional warfare (UW) forces in enemy or enemy controlled territory to reduce his combat effectiveness, industrial capacity, and morale; (4) perform intelligence missions; (5) provide training and assistance to friendly foreign armies or guerrilla and counter guerrilla operations; (6) and establish a Special Forces Operational Base (SFOB) when augmented by support and service units.

The makeup of a Special Forces Group was usually a Headquarters & Headquarters (Hq & Hq) Company, a Signal Company, and four companies, and was commanded by a Colonel. The headquarters company contained the staff sections (S-1, S-2, etc.) for command and control, parachute rigging and air delivery elements, as well as most of the group medical capabilities. The signal company was similar to a battalion, in terms of capabilities, supporting the group it was attached to. An SF Group was usually manned by about 1,200 troops, only about 2/3 of whom were Special Forces qualified.

Some Groups also had Military Intelligence (MI), Psychological Operations (PsyOps), Civil Affairs (CA), Signal (Communications) and Combat Engineer units attached, none being denoted as Special Forces qualified, although some individuals were SF qualified, especially Signal personnel. In 1962 the Department of the Army (DOA) decided that those attached units would make Special Forces a better fighting unit.

Each Special Forces company consisted of approximately 250 men, broken down into a company headquarters. This included: one operational C Detachment (usually 24 personnel, also known as a C-team, manned by 6 officers and 12 NCOs), three operational B Detachments (or B-teams, each led by a major and manned by 6 officers and 17 NCOs — this varied widely in Vietnam), and 12 operational A Detachments (or A-teams, four per B-team, manned by 2 officers and 10 NCOs — this also varied in Vietnam).

Each company TO&E called for a lieutenant colonel to fill the commander position, acting as both the company and C Detachment commander. The lead NCO of a group was a command sergeant major, while B- and C-teams had sergeants major as their head NCO. The administrative detachment (consisting of 2 officers and 13 support personnel — cooks, clerks, supply, etc.) basically performed administrative and personnel functions, acting as the company headquarters.

The operational detachment C was the senior operational unit of the company. When the C Detachment deployed on operational status, the administrative detachment reverted to Group control. Each C Detachment was responsible for (1) conducting operations with guerrilla forces; (2) exercising operational control over its subordinate detachments; and (3) liaising in the event the detachments came under the control of conventional tactical unit commanders.

B Detachments, like C Detachments, conducted operations with guerrilla forces. They usually numbered 23 personnel, and also were tasked with controlling the operations of subordinate A Detachments, and acting as liaison between subordinate A Detachments and tactical unit headquarters. The norm was four A Detachments under the command of a B Detachment. B Detachments were, in turn, under the command of a C Detachment. B Detachments exercised operational control over its subordinate A Detachments (usually 4).

The basic operational unit of Special Forces was the A Detachment. A Detachments were tasked with conducting operations with guerrilla forces. Almost every Special Forces-qualified man wanted to be on an A-team.

A single Special Forces Group was designed to be able to deploy its detachments via air, sea, or land, to be used to organize, train, and direct any number of guerrilla warfare units. It was also capable of participating in intelligence gathering operations. A Special Forces Group usually operated from a Special Forces Operational Base (SFOB), augmented by support and service units.

In Vietnam there were many special overt (openly known) and covert (classified, usually top secret, many times not even known to fellow Special Forces personnel) units within the 5th SFG. Some of the overt units were special training units run by SF, CIDG units and Mike Forces (quick reaction forces, one in each corps area); covert units were Delta Project, projects Omega & Sigma, SOG (Studies and Observations Group, sometimes referred to as Special Operations Group), CCN (Command & Control North), CCC (C&C Central), CCS (C&C South) and Mobile Guerilla Forces. Some even came under the watchful eye of the CIA.

Besides missions in South Vietnam, SOG units also participated in numerous operations in North Vietnam, Laos and Cambodia, mostly of an intelligence gathering nature. SOG members KIA in those other countries were not admitted to having been KIA in those countries. In fact, SOG members on patrols never carried identification of any type, many times dressing in the manner of the enemy. The life expectancy of SOG members was very short, and the number of medals earned for valor was very high. SOG members were wounded constantly (often with casualty rates of over 100%), being awarded multiple Purple Hearts per person, yet getting right back into the fight.

Most conventional Army officers believed that the Viet Cong and North Vietnamese could be defeated by numbers alone, not by stealth or psychological operations. Most conventional officers and units also showed very little concern for the local civilian populace, believing that military strength and tactics alone would win the battle, not popularity.

Special Forces always worked on the premise of winning the hearts and minds of the civilian population, then combating the enemy by surprise, beating them at their own game. The welfare of the local populace was always on the minds of Special Forces personnel. In many cases our teams even lived with the local population, placing security beneath friendship and mingling.

Every A Camp I was assigned to, but one, sent out MEDCAPs (MEDical Civilian Assistance Programs), as well as combat patrols. MEDCAPs were patrols sent out with a Special Forces Medic as one of the patrol members. The medic had a specially packed case, with which to set up clinics in the villages as we entered them. The villagers lined up for anything from a toothache to an injury or disease. Our medic cared for them on the spot, with instructions to come to the camp if further work was needed.

Unlike the preponderance of military medics, our medics went through 38 weeks of intense medical training (even though they were only enlisted men), which included emergency room procedures and operations. They received a lot of practice in amputations in Vietnam, due to the numerous mines dug in by the Viet Cong. I trusted our medics with any medical problem. They were among the best in the world. In fact, many went on to become doctors after serving their military time. One even became the Surgeon General of the United States.

While the medic treated the villagers, the other patrol members handed out packets of individual care items and/or government T-shirts for the children. The children always loved to see us arrive, as did most of the adult villagers. Our Vietnamese soldiers formed a protective perimeter around the village while we were occupied with the MEDCAP. Make no mistake, our medics were medical marvels working with very limited equipment, but they were also Special Forces trained combatants, just like the rest of us. They also cross-trained in our combat fields..

In parts of Vietnam, especially the Central Highlands, team members were admitted into the villages as equals, partaking in ritual ceremonies, dressing like the villagers, eating the same food as the villagers and living as one with the population. Special Forces always tried to fit in with, and look like, the indigenous personnel. That was another sticking point with the Pentagon and Army leadership. They hated the fact that we grew beards, let our hair grow long, or were out of uniform. They felt that showed lack of leadership and discipline.

If the locals had beards, we grew beards. If they wore black pajamas, we wore black pajamas. Why try to pretend you are better than the personnel you are tasked to work with, or to look better than those same personnel? Dressing and looking different accomplished one major drawback in a combat situation—TARGET! In Vietnam we already had one strike against us when trying to blend in with the locals. In almost all instances, we physically stood head and shoulders above our Vietnamese counterparts. We were tall, and they were short.

"The purpose of all war is peace." — *Saint Augustine, 354-430*

Special Forces acted like an armed Peace Corps, in a way. Special Forces teams worked with local villagers to make their life better through all manner of projects and training. We helped the locals with everything from agriculture to engineering (including building bridges for villages). We learned their language before departing for our destination. We also studied their way of life and (very important) learned what pleased the indigenous personnel, and what was taboo in their eyes. We might not have had the expertise in some areas, but we had methods of finding the information and putting it to use. We always did our best to win the favor of the locals, and usually departed with the locals feeling much better about us than upon our arrival.

Much of the success of Special Forces missions relied upon the team's relationship with the locals. Our work was usually done side-by-side with the indigenous personnel. That way, the locals could be proud of their accomplishments since they had helped. Remember, in most cases our missions were predicated upon the team being advisers, not merely doers. That is why a large part of our training dealt with instructing us how to teach. And, because much of our work was in Third World Countries, that meant teaching individuals who were not as intelligent or educated as we were and did not have the equipment we had. Sometimes the people we taught and advised could not even read or write their own language.

It was a shame that the conventional U.S. military units didn't have the pre-mission training we had. It would have been terrifically helpful for those units, especially Army Engineer and Navy Seabee units, to have understood the Vietnamese situation and language. There were so many construction projects that could have been done by those units, resulting in much needed civilian support for our military. Instead, Special Forces units, especially team demolition (engineer) members, who weren't nearly as qualified in engineering expertise as their Army and Navy equivalents, did their best to complete the projects.

Special Forces medics much of the time made it their responsibility to keep the local civilian population healthy, whereas military medical personnel could have taken much of that load off SF, had they been so trained. That type of aid could have had a very positive effect on the outcome of the war. One of the major assets obtained by those type of projects could have been a civilian population that was much more willing to give intelligence information about the enemy to our personnel.

"Generals think war should be waged like the tourneys of the Middle Ages. I have no use for knights; I need revolutionaries." — Adolf Hitler

One thing I learned very early in Special Forces was the immense dislike of our unit in the Pentagon and among commanders in combat arms units. There were some commanders who believed in our mission, but not enough to help us. We were the bastards of the Army. A person who would have been a perfect conventional soldier, probably could not have been a good Special Forces soldier, and vice versa.

Most of the Pentagon leadership and high-ranking Army career officers disliked us due to our unique and unorthodox ways, especially our unorthodox guerrilla warfare methods. They felt there was no need for such a unit in the United States military. They firmly believed that all future conflicts would be conducted using large unit warfare, as well as atomic bombs and intercontinental rockets. They also believed that the country with the strongest military might would be the least apt to be involved in warfare of any kind.

Regular Army officers did not understand guerilla warfare, or the methods used to combat it. Their idea of counter-guerilla warfare was to fight the guerillas (Viet Cong) as they would any other regular army, using "proven" land warfare tactics, much the same as the British tried to fight the revolutionaries in the Revolutionary War, and getting their asses kicked because of it.

Getting supplies and promotions to Special Forces was next to impossible. You would have thought that Special Forces was an enemy unit, out to destroy the U.S. military. That U.S. military anti-Special Forces sentiment was also very strong in Vietnam, resulting in some failed Special Forces operations and, worse yet, the resulting death of some Special Forces personnel, attributable to U.S. Army officers who screwed us, sometimes on purpose. That was not the case with all Army officers in other than SF units but was still common.

Most low-grade promotions (i.e. Private First Class, Specialist 4th Class [basically the same as Corporal] and Sergeant) came from other units on post who didn't have enough men qualified for the promotion, thereby letting us have the promotions. Commanders of combat arms units didn't like us because so many of their best men volunteered for Special Forces. Good enlisted men (including NCOs) who had planned a military career tended to remain with Special Forces once they were accepted and trained. Commissioned officers were a different story.

"Battles are sometimes won by generals; wars are nearly always won by sergeants and privates." — F.E. Adcock, British classical scholar

Commanders of conventional combat units believed that the historic method of warfare, slugging it out on the battlefield, toe-to-toe, with tanks and artillery supporting, was the only way to do battle. It mattered not that men were killed. After all, they were only soldiers, pawns in war, trained to go forward, and die if need be. I compare it to a general playing a board game, in which individual units were cardboard tiles being sent forth to be possibly annihilated, as if no human bodies were involved.

Those generals didn't dare be sentimental. They needed their share, and then some, of the military budget. They were seeing Special Forces getting some of THEIR share of the money, as well as some of THEIR best men, and it didn't sit well with them.

We loved getting even. Any time we could screw with conventional troops in the field, we did with a vengeance. After all, we were trained to harass and make enemy conventional units ineffective. Doing the same to friendly conventional units was fun, good payback, and good training.

In the field we could almost always be differentiated from conventional units. We didn't usually wear the beret in the field, but we also didn't wear, or even take, a helmet. We usually wore "boonie" hats—unofficial headwear and against regulations. We delighted in flaunting authority, and looking different, as well as distinctive.

The typical Special Forces soldier loved being in the boondocks, away from the boring repetition and close supervision of garrison duty. We hated strict discipline. Those of us who had spent time in conventional military units usually did not handle the nit-pickiness of those units well.

Officers were "commissioned." In other words, they held a commission, signed by the President of the United States, authorizing them to command. Noncommissioned officers (NCOs) held no such commission, and therefore were not "authorized" to command. Warrant officers possessed a warrant, which did not authorize them to command, although they were deemed worthy of being saluted by enlisted personnel (just like officers), as well as being called "sir" by enlisted personnel (also like officers). Warrant officers were usually experts in a specialty field.

A large portion of regular Army commissioned officers came from service academies, mainly the United States Military Academy (USMA) at West Point, Virginia Military Academy (VMI), Norwich, The Citadel, Texas A&M, and a small number of smaller academies. In addition, many officers went the route of Officer Candidate School (OCS), a military school designed to make officers out of enlisted members of the Army. Other locations from which officers could join the ranks of the regular Army included the Army Reserves and the Army National Guard.

We had some good officers, but they didn't generally stay in SF very long or their career would suffer greatly with promotion difficult, if not impossible, because of the higher echelon hatred of SF. Because of the constant turnarounds of officers in SF, it was difficult to find officers with any experience or ongoing training in SF. Some officers volunteered for short stints in Special Forces, so they could act macho and live the "wild life." Those were transferred out quickly, although some were able to linger longer than acceptable, only because there weren't any acceptable officers to replace them.

Because the highest officer rank on an A-team was Captain, there was no way an officer could stay on a team and go through his promotions. Therefore, most of the time the NCOs were more informed about the SF mission and tactics than their team commanders were. NCOs, in general, firmly believed that it was up to them to train the A-team officers.

Sometimes officers were assigned to A-teams without any Special Forces training or assessment at all. That was a recipe for team problems, especially if the officer believed he knew all he had to know about running a team. A lot of the problems stemmed from the fact that officers learned from lectures and books, while NCOs gained most of their knowledge from hands-on experience, including combat experience.

In general, I found the West Point officers to be the worst Special Forces commanders, especially at the A-team level. Their training was just geared too much toward conventional warfare, with very little or no training in unconventional warfare. West Point officers were also generally not the least bit comfortable with the team interaction concept of Special Forces, one in which the officers conversed with, and interacted with, their enlisted teammates. Also difficult with a West Pointer was the thought of his enlisted team members being capable of making important decisions about team actions and being capable of making command decisions on their own. That's not to say, however, that we didn't have any good West Point officers.

After returning from Vietnam, I was in the company area and overheard a Lieutenant tell a Sergeant Major that the Sergeant Major didn't know what he was talking about. That kind of an attitude was the kind that could cause the death of an entire team. It was also the kind of attitude that bolstered my decision to get out after my second enlistment was over.

When I first entered SF, there were no 2nd Lieutenants (lowest grade officer) in SF. The lowest officer rank permitted was that of 1st Lieutenant. In later years 2nd Lieutenants were permitted if they had spent prior enlisted time in SF. Even later, due to a shortage of officers, any 2nd Lieutenant who could qualify was permitted in SF. The fact is that almost all (myself included) NCOs considered most 2nd Lieutenants to be as worthless as tits on a boar hog. PFCs were considered by most of us to be better soldiers than 2nd Lieutenants.

Now Special Forces A Detachment executive officers are warrant officers, which are kind of a cross between an enlisted man and an officer. One of the major problems keeping good officers was the Pentagon's reluctance to promote officers while they were in SF. To make a career in the military, and be promoted to the higher ranks, officers had to spend only a short term in SF, the overwhelming balance of time having to be in conventional line units.

Finally, in the 80s or 90s, the Pentagon okayed an officer (and enlisted) career field in SF. Finally, officers could remain in Special Forces and be promoted through the ranks at a normal pace if they deserved it. Because of that, Special Forces now has some great officers who don't have to worry about a stigma due to SF service.

There are some high-ranking officers who are still old school and don't like Special Forces, mostly West Pointers (U.S. Army Military Academy). General Creighton Abrams was one of them. When General Westmoreland departed South Vietnam (thankfully after my tour there), Abrams was appointed to replace him.

Abrams was an idiot and a jerk. He was so anti-Special Forces, he appointed non-Special Forces trained officers to positions of command in Special Forces units. One of the appointments was even responsible for the death of several good Special Forces men, as well, of course, as a very low morale in that unit.

Norman Schwartzkopf was another anti-Special Forces commander. He had to be forced to include Special Forces in the Iraqi invasion, after which he complemented the Special Forces participants for a job well done, having been won over by the Special Forces units under his command. Thankfully, anti-Special Forces high-ranking officers are finally in the minority.

When stateside, one of our favorite activities was screwing over conventional U.S. units; we did it often and with great glee. A good example was mentioned in COL Simpson's book, from when Special Forces had been invited to participate in a major field exercise in 1956.

The SF men did their job extremely well, causing major disruptions. "Convoys were misrouted, false orders were issued on the radio, fuel and chow trucks were commandeered, and, in general, hell was raised." General Paul Adams' tactical field headquarters was even penetrated. "The degree of chaos and confusion reached such a point that everything had to be stopped. Special Forces were summarily ordered out of the maneuver." General Adams was livid. That same year he prohibited the wearing of the beret at Ft. Bragg. The ban remained in effect until 1961.

When I graduated from Training Group there were five Special Forces Groups within Special Forces. They were the 1st Special Forces Group (stationed on Okinawa and responsible for the Far East sector), 5th and 7th Special Forces Groups (stationed at Ft. Bragg, North Carolina), 8th Special Forces Group (stationed in Panama and responsible for Central and South America), and 10th Special Forces Group (stationed at Bad Tolz, Germany and responsible for Europe). Other Special Forces units included Special Forces Reserve units with teams scattered throughout the United States.

It is important to realize that SEALs, Rangers, Air Commandos, etc., ARE NOT Special Forces. They are Special Operations forces, not to be confused with Special Forces (Green Berets). On the other hand, Special Forces is a Special Operations unit. Green Berets also ARE NOT Special Services. Special Services are military bands, boxing teams, libraries, etc. DON'T EVER CALL A GREEN BERET A MEMBER OF SPECIAL SERVICES! That happened a lot to me in later years. I was quick to explain the differences.

The types of missions assigned to Special Forces grew as new methods of deploying the specialized troops were envisioned. The most visible of those missions were direct action (DA). Direct action missions entailed raids, ambushes, enemy leader snatches or assassinations, etc. Most of them were actions of short duration.

Special reconnaissance (SR) was another mission, often limited to intelligence gathering. It took a special man to participate in those missions. Stealth was of utmost importance. When on missions to gather intelligence, units had to do everything possible to avoid detection, including combat. Those were clandestine, covert missions in which the presence of any United States personnel must not be detected.

Foreign internal defense (FID) missions were ones in which SF teams were sent to countries that were in danger of having their governments toppled by external forces. SF teams were sent to such countries with the mission of teaching the government and their troops how to protect themselves. It often entailed participating in counterguerrilla and/or counterinsurgency operations.

Last, but not least, was unconventional warfare (UW), the original mission for which Special Forces was formed. UW missions usually entailed a form of guerrilla warfare. They were usually offensive actions conducted by units that were not regular (conventional) forces. Often those actions were clandestine, and sometimes they were covert. They usually consisted of indigenous personnel, advised by SF, fighting either a hostile government or an invading army.

Organized as specialists in unconventional warfare, SF was the only U.S. military unit designed to also conduct counter-insurgency operations. Name the terrain, Special Forces was and is, capable of fighting in or on it, whether it be waterborne, arctic, desert, jungle, or mountain environment.

"Special: Distinguished by some uncommon quality, designed or selected for some particular purpose, having an individual character, noteworthy, unique." — As defined by the Miriam Webster Dictionary

Although I had absolutely no idea what was ahead of me when I signed on for Special Forces, I sure was glad I had. We knew what we were doing. We made friendships with the indigenous people, who we needed on our side. "Going native" helped us to form that important bond. Our teaching abilities helped us to make those indigenous personnel better fighters, thus making our combat group a stronger unit, capable of destroying the enemy.

"I don't know what effect these men will have on the enemy, but, by God, they frighten me." — Arthur Wellesley, Duke of Wellington

Yes, we had egos. Pretty much everybody in Special Forces had a somewhat sizable ego. We were authorized those egos for what we had finished and what lay ahead of us. All in all, Special Forces personnel were, and are, professional soldiers with expertise in the business of helping others during peacetime and war. A Special Forces 12-man A-team was a force to be reckoned with. Because of the training and expertise of each man on the team, it was much stronger and deadlier than any similar sized unit.

The indigenous personnel fighting by our side added to that expertise and deadliness, mainly because of their familiarization with the area and terrain. Each team had their own attitude, their own culture, and their own way of accomplishing tasks. While they had standard operating procedures (SOPs) in place, teams remained flexible and versatile, able to adapt to new situations and missions that emerged. The expertise of the Special Forces teams was maintained through rigorous ongoing training programs.

Just because a man had graduated from Special Forces Training Group and had been assigned to a unit didn't mean his training days were finally over. Far from it! Indeed, they had just begun. The future for each graduate meant more in-depth training and specialty training not covered in Training Group to really hone his expertise.

When a Special Forces man was asked to differentiate between Special Forces (Green Berets) and the Marines and Rangers, invariably the pat answer was:

"You tell the Marines to take a hill, they'll salute, and head straight for the hill, fighting through anything in their way. They'll kill and die going up that hill, and if a Marine is left standing, he'll take the hill.

"If you tell a Ranger unit to take that same hill, they'll salute, then make plans to attack the hill. The planning will take a couple of days, with orders and battle plans being formulated. They will then find the most difficult route, preferably through a swamp or up vertical cliffs, and wait for the worst possible weather. They will then attack, losing half of their men to exhaustion. If a Ranger remains, he'll take the hill.

When you tell Special Forces to take that identical hill, they will stare at you and ask why. Once the reason is explained they will disappear. They might take the hill. They might also take another hill explaining, rightly so, that the other hill was obviously the right one to take, and it was so obvious that you couldn't dispute their argument. The third possibility was that they would convince another outfit that it was to their benefit to take the hill. There was also a fourth possibility: They went to the club, ignoring orders. If you dared to question their intentions, they would convince you that taking the hill would have been so costly that you could have been court-martialed. They saved your ass."

Again, Special Forces believed in accomplishing objectives with a minimum of loss. After all, each Special Forces soldier was too important to a team to be lost in battle. Mass battles were for the conventional units, not for small SF teams.

Specialized Training

Specialty training had almost no bounds in Special Forces. If it affected the conduct of warfare, especially of an unconventional nature, Special Forces considered it to be of an appropriate nature. Foremost among the specialized training schools popular in Special Forces were the Jungle Warfare School (aka Jungle Expert School), SCUBA diving, HALO parachuting, Jumpmaster School (for paratroopers), SADM (Special Atomic Demolition Munitions), Engineer NCO School, Ranger School, and DLI (Defense Language Institute).

The Jungle Warfare School was at the Jungle Operations Training Center in Ft. Sherman, Panama Canal Zone. The jungle warfare training was great for Special Forces, since so many of our missions involved time in the jungle. The course began, of course, with jungle living, which included surviving in the jungle.

After learning how to live and survive in the jungle, the students were taught how find their way in the jungle (land navigation). The land navigation course included methods to ease movement, such as how to make rafts out of ponchos and construct rope bridges, in addition to the operation of small boats in a jungle environment. After mastering those subjects, the students learned combat operations in the jungle.

Operating in dense jungles was much more difficult than in open terrain. Surprise, however, was generally much easier, hence a lot of training was provided on quick reaction drills (ambush survival). Because of the denseness of jungles, combat movement and techniques were considerably different than the norm.

The Special Forces SCUBA School was in Florida. Military SCUBA divers had a long, diverse, history, known previously as frogmen — a fitting name as SCUBA divers usually swam underwater utilizing swim fins as propelling devices. SCUBA fit right into the Special Forces scheme of operating, as a method of infiltration, mining operations, and underwater demolition. It could also be utilized in many other combat roles.

HALO began in the early 1960s in Special Forces. In fact, during the time that I was in training, rumor had it that it was going to be part of required training, although it never was. HALO was, and still is, a great way to infiltrate. Its first use in combat was during the Vietnam War.

HALO operations were called for when small units were to be infiltrated, especially if there was a fear of being spotted or being shot down by antiaircraft fire or a SAM (surface-to-air) missile. Typically, the parachutist wore special breathing apparatus and clothing when jumping from a high altitude.

When jumping from altitudes higher than 22,000 feet, oxygen was required. Jumping from very high altitude could also require the wearing of a pressurized suit. When making a HALO jump, the parachutist exited the aircraft, free-falling at terminal velocity for a distance, then deploying his parachute at a low altitude. The reason HALO was so stealthy was the combination of the lack of metal, and the fast downward speed, which fooled radar. The short period of time in the air also served to make ground observation difficult. Keep in mind that it was military HALO, not civilian skydiving. The men were jumping with full combat equipment.

SADM training will be described later in the next book. DLI (Defense Language Institute) training usually applied to pre-mission or pre-deployment training.

Special Forces teams were deployed across the globe, in countries that did not speak run-of-the-mill languages. We had teams in far-flung locations in Central and South America, the Caribbean, Pacific islands, Africa, Europe, Middle East, and Asia. To aid SF teams in communicating with the indigenous personnel, language training was part of the training given prior to deployment. Sometimes the training was given at Ft. Bragg, while other times it was given at the Defense Language Institute in the Presidio of Monterey in Monterey CA. The language training at DLI was normally much more intense than any other language instruction.

A Special Forces Soldier
(Author Unknown)

As seen by the Department of the Army
An overpaid, over-ranked tax burden who is indispensable because he has volunteered to go anywhere, do anything, at any time, so long as he can booze it up, brawl, steal Jeeps, corrupt women, lie, wear a star sapphire ring, a Rolex watch and carry a demo knife.

As seen by his Post Headquarters
A drunken, brawling, Jeep stealing, woman corrupting liar, with a star sapphire ring, Rolex watch and demo knife.

As seen by his Commander
A fine specimen of a drunken, brawling, Jeep stealing, woman corrupting liar, with a star sapphire ring, Rolex watch and demo knife.

As seen by his Wife
A stinking member of the family who comes home once a year in the back door with a rucksack full of dirty laundry, a hard-on, and three

months later goes out the front door for another year.

As seen by Himself

A tall, handsome, highly trained professional killer, female idol, star sapphire ring wearing, demo knife carrying gentleman who is always on time due to the reliability of his Rolex watch.

As seen by the Enemy

The meanest mother in the valley.

ENDNOTES

1   The word semi-automatic signified a weapon that, when fired, would automatically eject the spent cartridge out of the weapon; in the case of the Garand, out the right side.

2   There were five DEFCON levels, 1 through 5. DEFCON was an acronym for "DEFense readiness CONdition." DEFCON5 was the lowest state of readiness, also known as normal readiness. DEFCON4 increased the level of readiness, requiring strengthened security. DEFCON3 increased readiness even further, with the added stipulation that the Air Force be able to mobilize in 15 minutes. DEFCON2 was the last step before nuclear warfare was to begin, with all our armed forces to be ready to deploy and engage the enemy within 6 hours. DEFCON1 meant that nuclear war was imminent, and all our armed forces were at maximum readiness.

3   When I played baseball as a high school junior, I was unrecognizable much of the time anyway. I was the team catcher. I wore a catcher's mask and a chest protector, camouflaging me very well. On the track team, my senior year, I ran the 880-yard run. I was only running on the track for a little over two minutes, and half of that was in the other side of the oval track, much of it among a pack of other runners, therefore hard to recognize by half the audience. As a freshman at San Jose State College, I was on the freshman basketball team. There was no junior varsity team in college. The freshman team was the stepping-stone to varsity ball. During our games, I spent almost all my time warming the bench as a last string guard. I was on the court for all of about five total minutes during the season. I continued to be shy.

4   The 8th Special Forces Group (Airborne) was deactivated in 1972, during the large drawdown of Special Forces units.

5   The Operations Center generally consisted of the S-2 (intelligence), S-3 (operations), assistant S-4 (supply and logistics), plans element (assistant S-2 and S-3), signal officer (communications), communication center, Area Specialist Teams (AST), and liaison of-

ficers (from other units, services, and allied countries involved in the operations).

6   C-46s were used a lot during World War II, especially for parachute personnel and cargo drops. They were also used in the China sector to fly the "Hump" cargo route supplying the Chinese in their war against the Japanese. The C-46 was a twin-engine propeller driven airplane.

ABOUT THE AUTHOR

Dick James was born on 7 October 1942, in Flushing, Long Island NY, but only spent the first year of his life there. Being an airline employee, his father worked on seaplane bases in South America and eastern Africa during World War II. When he departed for overseas, Dick and his mother moved in with his grandmother in her Bedford PA boarding house.

When the war ended, Mr. James was transferred to Limerick, Ireland, to work at nearby Shannon Airport. Dick and his mother soon followed. The James family remained there until his father was transferred to the Stockholm, Sweden airport two years later, and the family moved there Three years later the family moved back to the Bedford rooming house, where they remained until Mr. James found a job in the East San Francisco Bay Area, and they moved to Castro Valley CA. Dick began working at a young age, beginning as an Oakland Tribune newspaper boy at 12 years old. He has continued with that work ethic ever since.

In 1958 Mr. James was transferred to the Monterey CA Airport, so it meant another family move, this time to Carmel-by-the-Sea. Dick graduated from Carmel High School in June 1960, after having gone to ten different schools during his twelve years of education.

Dick was accepted into San Jose State College in San Jose CA, majoring in Aeronautical Operations. In late 1961, after his third semester of college, Dick went to the Army recruiter, saying that he wanted to enlist, and become a paratrooper, figuring that would be the toughest unit to be a part of. He also requested a Valentine's Day enlistment, to get even with his girlfriend who had left him, LOL.

While in training at Fort Ord, his class was visited to two Green Beret recruiters. What they described was a unit that Dick decided he would dearly love to be a part of, so he volunteered for Special Forces. The rest is history. He graduated from Special Forces Training Group in April 1963, as a "Green Beret" explosives expert, after undergoing 14 months of Army training.

He underwent much more training while assigned to Special Forces A-teams, as well as spending 7 months in Ethiopia and 18 months in South Vietnam during their wars. Upon returning to the U.S. from Vietnam, Dick had two more Special Forces MOSs (Military Occupational Specialty) in his personnel folder. The MOSs of 05B4S (Radio Operator) and 11F4S (Intelligence Sergeant) were added to his already 11C4S (Heavy Weapons Leader) and 12B4S (Engineer/Demolition Sergeant) MOSs. He was also awarded the Bronze Star Medal for his service in Vietnam.

After reenlisting once, Dick decided, as a Staff Sergeant, to separate from the Army and use his GI Bill to become a civilian commercial pilot. After three years as a commercial pilot, his world came crashing down upon him, when he was put on a blood-thinning medication for a service-related ailment. That resulted in him no longer being able to fly as a pilot.

Dick spent a little over a year as a security company officer, computer services salesman, director of data communications for a new helicopter ambulance service that went bankrupt, and bartender. Seeing an advertisement that the U.S. Postal Service was hiring mail carriers, Dick took the test, and was hired as a mail carrier within two weeks.

After retiring on disability (due to the same service-connected disability that caused him not to be able to be an aircraft pilot), Dick became a commercial freelance stock photographer of landscapes and scenic images, being published thousands of times in publications and wall calendars world-wide, and winning several prestigious awards. He was also published several times as a magazine feature article writer. He finally retired from photography in 2016, and began writing.

Since the late 1970s Dick has been a member of the Special Forces Association, serving in several positions, including President, of the central California Chapter XXIII. In the early '80s, while producing the monthly chapter newsletter, he was presented the SFA Golden Quill Award, for writing and producing the best newsletter in the worldwide SFA. He was later named by Radix Press owner Steve Sherman as the "official historian" for two of the Vietnam Special Forces camps he served in, Cai Cai and Vinh Gia.

In mid-2019, Dick was asked to participate in the Special Forces Oral History Project of the University of South Carolina Veterans Oral History Project. He gave a 3 ½-hour videotaped oral history presentation of his life as a "Green Beret," including describing his time in Ethiopia and South Vietnam. Parts of his military history have also been published in several books and magazines/newsletters.

Made in the USA
Monee, IL
04 April 2022

94058777R00225